Mainstreaming politics:
Gendering practices and feminist theory

by
CAROL BACCHI & JOAN EVELINE

Mainstreaming politics:

Gendering practices and feminist theory

by
CAROL BACCHI & JOAN EVELINE

UNIVERSITY OF
ADELAIDE PRESS

THE UNIVERSITY
OF ADELAIDE
AUSTRALIA

Published in Adelaide by

University of Adelaide Press
Barr Smith Library
The University of Adelaide
South Australia
5005
press@adelaide.edu.au
www.adelaide.edu.au/press

The University of Adelaide Press publishes externally refereed scholarly books by staff of the University of Adelaide. It aims to maximise the accessibility to its best research by publishing works through the internet as free downloads and as high quality printed volumes on demand.

Electronic Index: this book is available from the website as a down-loadable PDF with fully searchable text. Please use the electronic version to complement the index.

Subject Keywords
Gender mainstreaming - organizational sociology - sex discrimination against women - women's rights - Women:social conditions - Feminist theory

For the full Cataloguing-in-Publication data please contact National Library of Australia: cip@nla.gov.au

ISBN 978-0-9806723-8-1 (electronic)
ISBN 978-0-9806723-9-8 (paperback)

Book design: Céline Lawrence
Cover design: Fiona Cameron
Cover photo: Carol Bacchi

To Joan

Contents

Preface

We decided to produce this compilation of articles, in the main published elsewhere, because we thought it worthwhile to reflect on developments in our thinking in connection with a large research project on gender analysis of policy. Over four years, as laid out in more detail in the Introduction, we were the Chief Investigators for an ARC-funded Linkage grant project to assist in the design of gender analysis procedures for the South Australian and Western Australian public sectors. In the lead-up to and over the course of the project (referred to as the Gender Analysis Project or GAP) we collaborated closely in the production of papers which became articles that traced the 'learnings' generated by the project. We are grateful to the various journal publishers for the opportunity to reprint these articles. Previously published articles are listed at the end of this preface.

Because the published articles necessarily include essential background information, there will inevitably be some repetition. Some themes also reappear in several chapters. We hope that this repetition does not prove onerous to readers. All articles were approved for publication by the relevant industry partners.

Reviewing the published material, and again in close collaboration, we decided that there was something to be learned from examining the themes developed in these articles and from considering how our specific theoretical backgrounds shaped these themes. In the process of undertaking this task we realised that some of the underlying theoretical premises that grounded these analyses might well be less visible to readers than to us. Hence we took the opportunity, through this book, to lay out more clearly the precepts undergirding our joint reflections on gender analysis procedures.

We accomplish this objective in two ways. Each previously published article has a new, co-authored introduction, explaining its place in the overall project and the thinking that informed its production – obviating the need for chapter summaries in the Introduction. In addition, some new chapters have been added to ensure that underlying theoretical premises are spelt out in an accessible manner. In Chapter 5 we explain more fully the notion of policies as *productive* practices, while in Chapter 6 we outline the premises of poststructural organisation studies. A new chapter – Chapter 11 – was added to address the contours and possibilities of university-public sector collaborations, such as the one in which we were engaged.

The book then is a compilation of a different sort. It provides a mapping of premises and concepts in an effort to make the analysis it offers more meaningful and more useful. It is also an exploration of theory generation. As the Introduction explains in more detail, we come from different disciplinary backgrounds – Carol Bacchi from public policy and Joan Eveline from organisational studies – while both share a poststructural theoretical orientation. Our collaborative interactions are reflected both in the shape of the project and in the analyses which emerged. Collaborative research is not unusual. However, it is unusual for those involved in such research to reflect upon the nature and outcomes of that collaboration. The book is innovative in undertaking this task.

Carol Bacchi and Joan Eveline

Personal reflection

Due to Joan's illness and subsequent death in July 2009 I performed the final revisions on the new sections of the manuscript. This was necessary but difficult. Our method of writing always involved checking by the other person, but this was no longer possible. It is important to mention this situation because, as mentioned above, Joan and I came from different fields and had different emphases in our work. At times we did not always exactly agree on some point of the argument or, perhaps more precisely, we could not always quite see how the other person's perspective produced different emphases.

At this level the book can be seen as a kind of dialogue, which is perhaps the nature of collaboration. This dialogue is clearest in Chapters 5 and 6. Joan drafted Chapter 6 as a 'response' to Chapter 5, highlighting both the power effects of the WPR approach, introduced in that chapter, and a tendency she saw in the approach to portray subjects as (solely) produced in discourse. Subsequently I returned to Chapter 5 to clarify certain points in response to Joan's reflections. Joan saw the changes and approved. Nevertheless, we both agreed that the exchange in these chapters on the 'power effects' of our work remained useful. Indeed, as becomes clear in the book, the project left Joan and I concerned about those effects and humbled by our recognition of them. I explain all this because it doesn't feel quite right for me to have 'the last word'. I hope any final changes I made to the text – usually at the prompting of invited readers – are in tune with Joan's vision. At any rate I take heart in the fact that the whole message of the book is that 'last' words, while necessary, still remain provisional. I write in this spirit.

Carol Bacchi

Publisher's note

The publisher and authors are grateful for permission to reproduce the following articles:

Bacchi, C. 2004. 'Gender/ing impact assessment: Can it be made to work?' *Journal of Interdisciplinary Gender Studies* 9 (2): 93-111.

Bacchi, C. and Eveline, J. 2003. 'Mainstreaming and neoliberalism: A contested relationship', *Policy & Society: Journal of Public, Foreign and Global Policy* 22 (2): 119-143.

Bacchi, C. and Eveline, J. 2009. 'Gender mainstreaming or diversity mainstreaming? The politics of "doing"', *NORA – Nordic Journal of Feminist and Gender Research* 17(1): 3-18. See http://www.informaworld.com

Bacchi, C., Eveline, J., Binns, J., Mackenzie, C. and Harwood, S. 2005. 'Gender analysis and social change: Testing the water', *Policy and Society. Special issue: Reinventing gender equality and the political*, Bacchi, C. and Schofield, T. (eds) 24 (4): 45-68.

Eveline, J. and Bacchi, C. 2005. 'What are we mainstreaming when we mainstream gender?' *International Feminist Journal of Politics* 7 (4): 496-512.

Eveline, J. and Bacchi, C. 2009. 'Obeying organizational "rules of relevance": Gender analysis of policy', *Journal of Management and Organization* 15 (5): 566-581.

Eveline, J., Bacchi, C. and Binns, J. 2009. 'Gender mainstreaming versus diversity mainstreaming: Methodology and emancipatory politics', *Gender, Work and Organization* 16 (2): 198-216.

Eveline, J. and Todd, P. 2009. 'Gender mainstreaming: The answer to the gender pay gap', *Gender, Work and Organization* 16 (5): 536-558.

Osborne, K., Bacchi, C. and Mackenzie, C. 2008. 'Gender analysis and community consultation: The role of women's policy units', *The Australian Journal of Public Administration* 67 (2): 149-160.

Vincent, K. and Eveline, J. 2008. 'The invisibility of gendered power relations in domestic violence policy', *Journal of Family Studies* 14: 322-333.

List of authors and project personnel

Carol Bacchi is Professor of Politics in the School of History and Politics, University of Adelaide. She researches and writes in the following theoretical fields: policy, feminism, citizenship and embodiment. Recent publications include: (2007, with Chris Beasley) 'Envisaging a new politics for an ethical future', *Feminist Theory* 8 (3), and *Analysing policy: What's the problem represented to be?* (Pearson Education, 2009).

Jennifer Binns is an independent scholar and Labour Relations Adviser in the Department of Commerce, Western Australian Government. She has drawn on extensive experience at senior management levels in the public sector to develop her understanding of leadership, government employment policy, gender mainstreaming and work-life balance. She was a Research Associate for the Gender Analysis Project from 2005 to 2007.

Joan Eveline (recently deceased) was Associate Professor in the Business School, University of Western Australia (UWA), and Co-Director of the Consortium for Diversity at Work, UWA. She researched and taught in the sociology of work, critical management, leadership, and industrial relations. Recent publications include: (2007, with Patricia Todd) 'The gender pay gap in Western Australia: Gross inequity, women still "counting for nothing"?' *Labour and Industry: Special issue: The way forward in the gender pay gap challenge* 17 (4); and *Ivory basement leadership: Power and invisibility in the changing university* (UWA Press, 2004).

Zoe Gordon is a PhD student in the Politics Discipline, University of Adelaide. She acted as a Research Associate for the Gender Analysis Project in 2007. In that role she was the primary author of an unpublished report entitled 'Gender analysis and social change: Comprehensive comparisons', which provided valuable background material for subsequent publications.

Susan Harwood was a Research Associate on the GAP project between 2005 and 2006, while she was undertaking her PhD, 'Gendering change'. She is now an independent scholar who applies her research on gender equity and masculinist organisations to her work as a management consultant. Forthcoming chapter: 'The critical [and subversive] act of [in]visibility: A strategic reframing of "disappeared and devalued" women in a densely masculinist workplace', in Lewis, P. and Simpson, R. (eds) *Revealing and concealing gender: Visibility in gender and organization research* (London, Palgrave Macmillan, 2010).

Catherine Mackenzie is a PhD student in the Southgate Institute for Health, Society and Equity, Flinders University of South Australia. She acted as a Research Associate for the Gender Analysis Project from 2005 to 2008. In that role she conducted a policy analysis which provided material for a social policy seminar and subsequent publication: Bacchi, C., Eveline, J., Binns, J., Mackenzie, C. and Harwood, S. 2005. 'Gender analysis and social change: Testing the water', *Policy and Society* 24 (4): 42-68.

Katy Osborne is a Research Fellow in the Southgate Institute for Health, Society and Equity, Flinders University of South Australia. Her research interests include community participation, gender, and health inequities. She acted as a Research Associate for the Gender Analysis Project in 2006. In that role she conducted qualitative research relating to how gender analysis can incorporate community consultation. This research led to a publication: Osborne, K., Bacchi, C. and Mackenzie, C. 2008. 'Gender analysis and community consultation: The role of women's policy units', *Australian Journal of Public Administration* 67 (2): 149-160.

Patricia Todd is Associate Professor in the Business School and Co-Director of the Consortium for Diversity at Work at the University of Western Australia. Her most recent research has focused on the implementation of work-life balance practices and the gender pay gap; she teaches in Employment Relations. Recent publications include (with Joan Eveline) 'The gender pay gap in Western Australia: Gross inequity, women still "counting for nothing?"', *Labour and Industry* 2007, 18 (2): 105-120, and (with Joan Eveline) 'Gender pay equity: It's time (or is it?)', in Davis, E.M. and Pratt, V. (eds), *Making the Link* no. 17, Affirmative Action and Employment Relations, Sydney Commercial Clearing House.

Karen Vincent is a PhD candidate with the University of Western Australia and was involved with the Gender Analysis Project through an APAI (Australian Postgraduate Award Industry) Scholarship. Karen's research project relates to Indigenous issues in gender mainstreaming of Australian public policy, focusing on the fields of family and domestic violence.

Anne Wilson was a Research Assistant for the Gender Analysis Project for the full three-and-a-half years. She also prepared the manuscript for publication.

Acknowledgements

These acknowledgements were drafted by the two authors separately. Just weeks prior to her death, I asked Joan what she would like to appear in the way of acknowledgements. She wrote:

> When I was told I had breast cancer twelve years ago I was given a minor oncologist, whom I called Dr Death. He told me (Mrs Eveline he used, despite protests) that, if I didn't take his chemotherapy, I had at the most three years to live. I didn't take his chemo and I am thankful that he was wrong. I thank Carol Bacchi who came to Western Australia almost immediately, with her small son, Stephen, and helped move me along. Since before then, Carol and I have worked together several times. Since we began collaborating on this study, Carol and I keep moving each other along. I thank her for all of that.
>
> There are many people I wish to thank for joining in the project that became this book. Most of you know who you are. Special mention to Maria Osman, Helen Creed, Mary Gurgone, Jasmina Brankovich, Denise Griffin and Vanessa Elliott, all of OWP (Office for Women's Policy, Western Australia), Lynnley McGrath of the Health Department, WA, as well as research associates Jennifer Binns and Susan Harwood, PhD student Karen Vincent, and Research Assistant Elyane Palmer.

I am indebted to Joan Eveline for her patience and her wisdom. Working with her over the years has been a huge privilege, and I will miss her sorely. I thank Joan for the commitment and support under (unbelievable) duress that made this book possible.

Among other acknowledgements I include: the many women over the years from OFW (Office for Women, South Australia), notably: Carmel O'Loughlin, Lindy McAdam, Anna Lewkowicz, Sandy Pitcher, Fiona Mort and Margaret Cameron; Research Associates Catherine Mackenzie, Katy Osborne and Zoe Gordon, who made huge contributions to the project through their written work and at Reference

Group meetings (Catherine deservers a special mention for shepherding the project over three-and-a-half years); and Anne Wilson, for always being on call to assist with reference queries, for typing the manuscript and for assisting with the Index; John Emerson and Fiona Cameron of the University of Adelaide Press, editor Penelope Curtin, and Céline Lawrence for prompt and professional guidance; the anonymous reader for helpful suggestions; and finally the Australian Research Council for supporting the Gender Analysis Project financially. As always sincere thanks to Stephen for his patience and support.

Carol Bacchi

Introduction

This book is about change and how it happens. It draws upon the research and experiences of its contributors to provide glimpses into the challenges facing those who care to produce more egalitarian relationships between and among women and men, and into the 'spaces' found within constraints to advance such an agenda. Its specific topic is gender analysis, a form of policy analysis associated with the equality policy initiative called gender mainstreaming.

The setting for the production of the book involved a large Linkage Grant project funded by the Australian Research Council (ARC), entitled 'Gendering impact assessment: A new framework for producing gender-inclusive policy'. The authors of this volume, Carol Bacchi and Joan Eveline, located in South Australia and Western Australia respectively, were the Chief Investigators for the project. Our Linkage partners included, in South Australia, the Office for Women (OFW) and, in Western Australia, the Office for Women's Policy (OWP) and the Health Department. A number of other public sector agencies in both states were participants (for details see Chapter 3). The project involved a PhD student, Karen Vincent, and several Research Associates (Jennifer Binns and Susan Harwood in Western Australia; Katy Osborne, Zoe Gordon and Catherine Mackenzie in South Australia), who became co-authors of some papers and reports, some of which are published here.

The goal of the project was to design gender analysis procedures appropriate to the respective contexts of the public service in the two states. It involved nine interrelated tasks (see Chart at the end of this Introduction), the performance of which collectively contributed to the production of the reflections which ensue. Although the chapters do not follow a strict chronology they allow readers to track how understandings developed over the three and a half years of the project (from December 2004 to June 2008), providing highly novel insights into collaborative research practices.

Gender analysis procedures, as mentioned, are commonly associated with a relatively recent policy development, called gender mainstreaming. The idea behind 'mainstreaming' is that *every* policy should address the needs of so-called disadvantaged

1

or marginalised groups (such as women, the 'disabled' and 'Indigenous' peoples[1]). *Gender* mainstreaming, perhaps the best publicised of these initiatives, appears in many industrialised states (for example, Canada, New Zealand, the Netherlands), in some 'developing' states (for example, South Africa, India, Indonesia), and in the protocols of international organisations such as the ILO (International Labour Organization) and the World Bank. The expressed objective of gender mainstreaming programs is to promote 'gender equality'.

Gender mainstreaming is often compared with earlier equality initiatives, such as equal opportunity and positive/affirmative action. Put briefly, organisations that *mainstream* 'gender' putatively move beyond these forms of policy because they ensure that *every part of that organisation* becomes gender-inclusive and gender-sensitive. Reflecting on government policy as an example, the declared goal is to ensure that *each* policy produced by a government is examined to see that it treats both women and men fairly. This kind of approach is described as being more comprehensive than equal opportunity policies, which focus on increasing women's access to *existing* organisations, and as more transformative than positive action policies, which aim (simply) to increase the numbers of women in certain jobs or positions of influence (Rees 1998). As becomes clear in Chapter 2, these claims about the transformative potential of gender mainstreaming are hotly contested.

A range of procedures, variously called 'handbooks', 'guides' or 'tool kits', are commonly put in place to 'vet' policies for their gender-inclusiveness. These guidelines have different names in different sites, for example, 'gender proofing', 'gender impact assessment', 'gender analysis'. We have selected the term 'gender analysis' to refer collectively to these forms of policy analysis. *Gender analysis of policy* is therefore our primary focus, although it should be made clear that there is no assumption that such scrutiny of policies for gender biases constitutes, on its own, a full and effective mainstreaming program (Chapter 1).

Not only do gender analysis procedures come with different names, they also reflect different premises and involve varied practices, which affect how they are applied and what they can accomplish. As March, Smyth and Mukhopadhyay (1999: 15) propose, models of gender analysis are not purely technocratic tools, but highly political and politicised interventions. As a result, although 'gender equality' is commonly put forward as the taken-for-granted goal of such policies, it does not necessarily follow that the same social vision accompanies the invocation of this term

(Magnusson, Rönnblom and Silius 2008). Rather, politics features largely in shaping how a gender analysis policy is imagined and configured. This perspective – that politics is central to the meaning of gender analysis – provides the starting point for this study, as is reflected in the title, *Mainstreaming politics*.

The title can be read in two ways. Most obviously, it refers to the *expressed* goal of gender (and other, for example, disability) mainstreaming initiatives to transform (or mainstream) *politics*. In this meaning politics is understood, therefore, in conventional terms as governmental institutions, and the goal becomes shifting issues that are frequently sidelined, such as those to do with 'gender equality', into the 'mainstream' business of politicians, bureaucrats and policymakers more generally.

In its second meaning the title refers to *the politics involved* in gender mainstreaming (that is, the politics of mainstreaming, or *mainstreaming's* politics) – how politics affects every level of the production, development, implementation and research surrounding mainstreaming initiatives. Our experience with this politics, as related in this book, puts in question the tendency to treat mainstreaming and gender analysis as generic reform initiatives that automatically, through their introduction, signal some sort of great leap forward in advancing 'gender equality'. Rather, through specific practices in selected sites, we find 'spaces' where shifts towards a more egalitarian politics emerge and 'spaces' where such moves are effectively blocked. In the course of the project we developed the language of 'somewhere in the middle' to capture this sense that change takes place through paths that do not start or end at fixed points, but which are often circuitous and unexpected. Such a perspective means that the project of achieving something called 'gender equality' ought to be understood to be a long-term and ongoing project, always involving 'unfinished business'.

To understand our more questioning and piecemeal approach to the anticipated transformative potential of gender mainstreaming, it is necessary to reflect further on the meaning of politics, as we understand it in the second reading of the title. Politics here includes but extends far beyond governmental institutions to encompass the *full range of interpersonal and inter/intra-organisational practices*, including the discursive practices, that produce gender mainstreaming as a particular sort of event. Importantly, this second, less conventional understanding of politics highlights the centrality of *meaning-making* to these practices – how specific meanings or characterisations are imparted to 'things', people and concepts, including 'gender

3

mainstreaming' and 'gender analysis', in specific locations at particular times. Our perspective emphasises the contestation that takes place over the meanings imparted to reforms like gender mainstreaming, showing how some meanings have more transformative potential than others (Chapters 2 and 4).

The phenomenon we are describing here needs to be generalised. The tendency to 'fix' certain meanings to 'things', people and concepts (such as gender analysis and gender mainstreaming) leaves the impression that these 'things', people and concepts can be understood only in one way, that they are readily understood, and that their content and value are clear and indisputable. The process of 'fixing' meanings in this way, however, detracts attention from (and hence denies) the 'effort' that goes into meaning-making activities, producing each item as one thing rather than another. Because fixed characterisations direct attention to some aspects of an event or person while closing off consideration of other aspects, they can have beneficial effects for some groups and deleterious effects for others. Recognising the 'effort' or activity that goes into producing these meanings and their effects destabilises meaning and highlights meaning-making as a highly politicised activity, necessarily involving competition among, or contestation over, the various meanings that are produced and supported.

This shift in emphasis from the fixed meaning of things to the political dimension of meaning-making activities is a hallmark of poststructural analysis. As Dumont (1998: 229) describes, the primary focus in poststructural approaches is on 'the textually-unstable and always contestable nature of social reality'. In this view language gives a *version of meaning* to things and events retrospectively, rather than reflecting a meaning which is 'given' and indisputable (Chapter 6). For those involved in policymaking at all levels, such an approach represents a challenge to the view that policy design is a rational process performed by disinterested actors intent on the common good. In the place of rational design we find multiple layers of meaning-creation that are the products of intense contestation.

Based on this argument the book develops two central propositions, elaborated below, each of which has important practical implications:

- Policies are gender*ing* practices (as per the book's sub-title), and hence it is essential that fundamental precepts in policy proposals be scrutinised for their gendering effects.

- The practice of gender analysis enables a politics of movement – a non-linear and unpredictable shifting of hearts and minds (see Conclusion) – and hence all public servants, especially those in positions of influence, need to 'do' gender analysis.

To understand these propositions, a brief introduction to some key concepts is needed.

Discourse

The contestation or struggle over meaning, mentioned above, takes place in discourse, a key term in poststructuralist analysis. Discourse, as understood here, refers to relatively bounded, socially produced forms of knowledge that set limits upon what it is possible to think, write or speak about a 'given social object or practice' (McHoul and Grace 1993: 31). For example, the ways in which 'gender mainstreaming', 'gender analysis' and 'gender equality' are 'spoken' about creates them as forms of social knowledge that make it difficult – but not impossible – to think or to speak outside the terms of reference they establish for conceptualising people and social relations. As Barad (2003:821) explains, 'Discourse is not what is said; it is that which constrains and enables what can be said'. Some other examples of powerful discourses in current political debate include: 'climate change', 'environmental sustainability', 'lifelong learning', 'human capital', and 'globalisation' (see Bacchi 2009: 35).

The point to remember is that these 'knowledges' do not exist apart from the statements and signs that constitute them. In this sense they are fictions. However, due to their commonly accepted status as truth, they are powerful fictions. Calling something a 'discourse' means putting its truth status into question.

Importantly, some discourses have greater status than other discourses. These tend to be discourses that are institutionally sanctioned and which reinforce established economic, legal, familial, religious and educational norms. Foucault (1991a: 6; McHoul and Grace 1993: 54) directs attention to the institutional mechanisms that allow some knowledges to become dominant in the 'struggle for control of discourses'. For example, gender analysis policies have an uphill battle in gaining credibility because they confront the 'rules of relevance' in conventional policy practices that render gender an extraneous consideration in most policies (Chapters 6 and 12). Put in other words, there exist hierarchical networks of discursive relations which affect one's discursive positioning, the discursive power one has in particular contexts, and which fix specific meanings of, say, 'gender analysis'.

There are, however, a finite number of discourses and these are often in competition. This lack of discursive unity opens up spaces for contestation. In Foucault's (1972: 120) words, discourse is an 'asset', 'by nature, the object of a struggle, a political struggle'. Discourses of status may sideline but can never eliminate (what Foucault calls) 'subjugated knowledges' – 'erudite' and local knowledges that create the space for challenge (Foucault 1980: 83). A related point, clarified shortly, is that practices 'from below' are themselves constitutive (Peterson 2003: 198).

Drawing attention to discourses, as we do in this book, does not involve collapsing everything into language, as some might infer. Rather, discourses 'form a practice which is articulated upon the other practices' (Foucault 1991b: 70). Discourses accomplish things. They make things happen, most often through their truth status. Discursive practices then can be understood – not as 'linguistic performances' nor as 'human based practices' – but as the multiple, ongoing and contested means through which some statements, but not others, are rendered credible and consequential (Barad 2003: 818-821).

All of this means that there can be no assumption that we can know, outside the specifics of particular, historically situated times and places, how gender analysis will be interpreted and what it can accomplish. Instead we need to inquire into the on-the-ground political deliberations and practices that give the reform a specific meaning in selected sites. This is the task undertaken in this book, both through examining some gender analysis initiatives in other places, including Canada, New Zealand, Ireland and the Netherlands (Chapters 1, 4 and 5), but, more specifically, through reflecting on the dynamics involved in attempting, through the Gender Analysis Project, to develop gender analysis procedures for the South Australian and Western Australian public services.

Subjectification

A poststructural politics also creates a particular understanding of political subjectivity, one tied to the notion of discourse. In tune with the emphasis on the discursive shaping of meaning, political subjects are understood to be constituted temporarily within the discourses available to them. That is, individuals do not pre-exist discourse and use it to their purposes; rather, they are effects of discourse – a perspective captured in the term 'subjectification'.

While this proposal may appear to portray subjects as determined by discourse, the relationship here is more volatile than this first impression suggests. Policies, as discursive practices, create certain possibilities for being – 'subject-positions and subject-functions' (Foucault 1991b: 58; Gottweis 2003: 253) – which political subjects (are impelled to) take up. However, subjectification – taking up subject positions – is an incomplete process. Policies *elicit* certain subject positions; they do not impose or determine them (Dean 1999: 32). In addition, the plurality of discourses ensures a plurality of subject positions. Subjectivity, then, is open to constant redefinition.

To illustrate what this means, consider how, in the current intellectual and political climate, a good deal of emphasis is placed on individuals as freely choosing beings who are responsible for the exigencies of their life. A powerful 'choice' discourse lies behind the political precept that individuals are responsible for any difficulties, including ill health or unemployment, they experience (Bacchi 2009: 17, 268). The 'choice' discourse is ambiguous, however. For example, it facilitates campaigns for 'consumer choice' and hence for consumer protection. Political subjects thus are constrained and yet enabled by a 'choice' discourse, creating room for manoeuvrability.

The idea here is that political subjects are not fixed essences, as is assumed in post-Enlightenment humanist thought, but emergent 'types', shaped in interaction with discourse and other practices. For example, a major argument in the book is that policies, like other institutional practices, ought to be seen as gender*ing* in their effects, producing and reinforcing specific categories of political subject, such as 'women' and 'men'. This idea of subjects as emergent rather than fixed is captured in the phrase 'ontology of becoming', which is set against the humanist 'ontology of being' (Chia 1996; Eveline 2005).

The proposal that policies are gender*ing* in their effects directs attention to the practices that influence the shape and nature of human existence. This proposal stands in opposition to some idealised version of human beings outside practice. The book uses the language of 'doing' to describe this practice-based interpretation. For gender therefore we want to see which practices 'do' gender or, in other words, which practices 'make' gender happen as a relation of inequality. As just described, the book emphasises the ways in which policies 'do' gender. Clearly this position is a direct challenge to the traditional view that policies sit outside people and either work with them to solve 'problems' or *impact upon* them, as if they exist as forms of being separate from and outside policy practices.

This proposal that policies produce or constitute political subjects is a major argument in the book and one of its most innovative contributions. To bring this insight to policy analysis is no easy feat, however, since most policies assume and work with categories of people as if these are fixed and readily identifiable. Consider, for example, 'youth' policy, or policies targeting 'the elderly'. The same is the case for 'women' and 'men'.

The counter view that, rather than being natural categories, 'men' and 'women' are produced through policies and other discursive practices, is doubtless confronting. However, it is possible to trace how the designation of 'women' as 'carers' (and of men as 'non-carers') is accomplished through a range of practices expressed through child-rearing manuals, advertising protocols and religious texts (for example, the Bible), among others (Bacchi 1996). As seen in several chapters (5, 6 and 12), the book is also concerned with 'heteronorming', 'classing', 'racialising' and 'disabling' policy practices, a theme revisited in the Conclusion.

It needs to be remembered, however, that these practices are ongoing and incomplete processes, with political subjects always more than the products of government regulation, explicit or implicit. In addition, policies and other mainstream institutional practices are not the only practices that involve people, and hence they are not the only factors that shape them. Practices 'from below', such as participation in advocacy or community activities, are also constitutive, creating new subject positions and the potential to challenge dominant discursive constructions. For example, the 'doing', or performing, of gender analysis by those involved in the Gender Analysis Project created political subjects who understood the need for gender analysis, illustrating how new practices enable change 'somewhere in the middle' (Chapter 4 and Chapter 12).

Power and practice

Poststructural politics relies upon a distinctive understanding of power as productive, an idea elaborated in Chapter 6. Put briefly, power is conceived of, not as a possession – not as something people *have* – but as a dynamic within relationships. Therefore, instead of asking *who has power*, the focus shifts to *how power operates and what it produces* (Gunn 2006: 709). The idea here is that power and resistance both take place through actions (Eveline 2004: 29-30), explaining our focus on 'doings'. Power relations (power) are the generative effects of particular practices. We do things, practise certain forms of thinking and doing, which bring power into effect.

The productive capacity of policies – how policies exercise productive power – is a central concern in the book. This dynamic is observed in two areas: firstly, how policies produce understandings of the 'problems' they purport to address (in opposition to the common view that they react to social 'problems'); and secondly, how, through this process, certain kinds of political subjects are constituted (Chapter 5).

Brought to the topics of gender analysis and gender mainstreaming, these ideas raise a range of novel questions, such as:

- What kinds of meanings are attached to gender mainstreaming programs, including gender analysis procedures, in specific contexts?

- How do diverse gender analysis frameworks constitute the 'problem' of 'gender inequality'?

- How do specific gender analysis procedures shape the social categories of 'men' and 'women'?

- How do organisational practices within specific public sector sites influence the ways in which gender analysis is understood and implemented?

- Which 'knowledges' are taken for granted in specific gender analysis procedures?

- At which sites can we recognise competition over the meanings attached to these procedures?

In addressing these questions the authors draw upon and engage with an extensive body of feminist theory and poststructural theory, with obvious overlaps between these categories. The book also engages with several important feminist debates, specifically on the status of bodies in feminist theory (Chapter 4), on the place of gender in organisation theory (Chapters 10 and 12), and on identity politics and democratic practice (Chapter 13). Specific authors who influenced the thinking behind the project include Joan Acker (2000), Dorothy Smith (2005) and

Judith Butler (1990). The numerous references to Foucault, Deleuze and Guattari throughout the book indicate our engagement with their ideas.

The authors have had a long association with the women's movement and with feminism. At different times they have been involved in campaigns for pay equity, for increasing the representation of women in leadership positions, for the decriminalising of prostitution, and against sexual harassment and violence towards women. Joan Eveline (1994) completed a PhD in women's studies, comparing 'work' and 'care' practices in Sweden and Australia. Carol Bacchi (1976) wrote her PhD thesis on the history of the enfranchisement of women in English-speaking Canada.

Against this background the authors have developed academic careers in different disciplines, different both from each other and from their fields of doctoral study. Bacchi works in a politics discipline at the University of Adelaide and focuses in her writing on policy theory. Eveline has been based in a business school at the University of Western Australia, teaching and researching in organisation theory. These distinct disciplinary backgrounds influenced their particular research emphases within the project, with Bacchi primarily interested in the constitutive dimension of public policies and Eveline focused on the organisational practices involved in producing policies. These divergent emphases are clear in the stated objectives of the Linkage Grant proposal:

- first, to trial competing models (or frameworks) of gender analysis that were based on sharply differentiated theoretical stances (Bacchi's primary interest)

- second, to contribute to organisation theory on the importance of involving policy actors directly in the development of reform initiatives in order to create a sense of ownership (Eveline's primary interest).

Beyond these different foci the authors share the poststructural perspectives developed above.

The book brings together papers written before and during the project, with three new chapters added, together with newly produced introductions for each chapter, and a new general introduction and conclusion. None of the papers started out as chapters but as papers that were worked on at various times. The chronology of the published papers is at times misleading, due to the fact that the authors were often working on more than one paper at the same time and to the exigencies of publication processes. The new chapters (Chapters 5, 6 and 11) were inserted where they appeared to make most sense. Bacchi and Eveline (1996: 79-100) had collaborated previously and had discussed their research on numerous occasions. The material in the book feeds off this long history of collaboration, as well as on research conducted outside the Gender Analysis Project.

The authors adopted the following procedure for writing all the papers that include *both* their names (Chapter 8 on community consultation was written solely by the research team in South Australia, while Eveline's contributions with Todd (Chapter 7) and Vincent (Chapter 9) were produced without direct input from the SA team). Following emails, telephone discussions and research meetings, where the bare bones of a paper were laid out, either Bacchi or Eveline wrote the first draft of a paper, sending it through to the co-author for queries, comments and elaborations. The paper travelled back and forth until both authors declared it 'done'. The same methodology was used for the newly produced sections of this book.

Not surprisingly, given this procedure, the papers reflect the divergent disciplinary interests of the primary authors. Where Eveline is listed as the first author, the chapter directs attention very specifically to the organisational contexts in which policy is developed and to the roles played by policy workers in those processes. When Bacchi is the first author, there is more concern with the implicit understandings within specific gender analysis programs. Alongside and overriding these different emphases lies the authors' shared poststructural understanding of power and politics as immanent, diffused and ongoing practices.

The collaboration generated a growing understanding of the ways in which a focus on policy actors' practices (Eveline) and a focus on policy as constitutive practice (Bacchi) complemented each other. Because the project has as a goal generating gender analysis procedures for public servants, the organisational practices shaping their work contexts featured significantly in the study. It became increasingly clear that gender analysis became meaningful for those who had the opportunity to practise it and that those policy workers tended in the main to be women who lacked institutional authority (Chapter 12). It became equally apparent that the deadline-driven nature of bureaucratic work practices (Chapter 3) meant that policy workers often lacked the space and time to reflect on the constitutive dimension of policies – how policies are gender*ing*, for example. It was concluded that this lack of opportunity to probe the constitutive effects of deep-seated policy premises undermined the transformative potential of gender analysis practices (Chapter 5). For this reason the project recommended *new* work practices, either a form of 'deep evaluation' that incorporates Bacchi's WPR (**W**hat's the **P**roblem **R**epresented to be?) methodology (Chapters 2, 3 and 5) as part of gender analysis, or a form of gender*ing*-awareness 'training' (Chapter 4). Other methodological suggestions include the introduction of institutional ethnography, as developed by Dorothy Smith (2005; Chapter 9).

As noted several times in the text, in the current political climate, where public servants are continually asked to do more with less, it seems unlikely that gender analysis procedures which include these recommended relatively time-consuming work practices will develop any time soon. Indeed, it seems much more likely that gender analysis will end up involving simple procedural checklists and brief 'training' sessions. What this means in terms of the future of gender analysis is considered in the concluding chapter.

The authors' poststructural orientation led to numerous exchanges about the authors' place as research 'experts' within the project. As the project developed, both Bacchi and Eveline found themselves confronting an uncomfortable 'truth' — that the project presumed a prior discursive positioning of 'gender' which partially displaced the perspectives of the Aboriginal communities of Western Australia and South Australia. Chapters 10 and 13 address this conundrum. To confront the power exercised through the 'truths' we produce — a particular concern given the current funding-driven nature of much academic research — we turn our attention to ways to build reflexivity, or critical self-scrutiny, into research practices (Chapters 6 and 13; Conclusion) and to elaborate a theory responsive to these insights. We give these ideas a brief airing here.

As academics we recognise our need to fix meaning in order to have our work read as useful by others. At the same time we are all too aware of the (at times) unquestioned presuppositions that inform our work, presuppositions that might well have deleterious effects for some social groups. The priority placed on 'gender' in gender analysis, which diverts attention from racialising practices, is one example. However, it is clear that in many instances categories of analysis such as 'gender', and indeed 'women' and 'men', will need to be used. How are we to proceed in this situation? The argument developed in this book is that the 'fixed' meanings we necessarily impart must be regarded as temporary and subject to continuous critical scrutiny in order to elaborate new, more inclusive meanings (Chapters 5 and 13). We capture this dialectic between fixing and unfixing meaning in the phrase 'a politics of movement', a phrase that evokes discontinuous and unpredictable change. The key to generating this movement, as explored in the book, is active participation in reform efforts (Chapters 7 and 12) and collaborative engagement that emphasises contingency (Chapters 8 and 13).

Recognising that 'knowledge' is always political, a 'politics of movement' relies upon willingness to self-identify as *critical* researchers, with the decisions about when to fix and when to unfix meanings dependent upon reflexive judgment about the political exigencies of the particular situation. The question, in our view, is not *whether* to fix meaning – since for a range of reasons fixing must occur – but *when* to fix meaning and *who* to involve in the 'fixing' exercise. The task, as we see it, is to formulate guiding principles for this inevitably political practice, a task begun in Chapter 13. With Foucault, the perspective affirmed is 'that of those who resist' (Simons 1995: 91).

Reflecting this perspective, readers will notice 'movement' in the text between fixing and unfixing the categories of 'women' and 'men'. That is, at times inverted commas are inserted around 'women' and 'men', raising questions about their status as natural or essential categories; at other times the inverted commas disappear and the terms are treated as unproblematic. Some chapters are also more 'fixed' than others in their propositions (for example, Chapter 12) and some are determinately unfixed (Chapter 6). The hope is that this introduction prepares readers to expect this unevenness and to understand, through demonstration, how movement between fixing and unfixing meaning works as a form of politics committed to egalitarian political objectives.

Note

1   For political reasons the term 'Indigenous' is currently unacceptable to Aboriginal communities in South Australia but is considered appropriate to those communities in Western Australia. Hence, there is some unevenness in the use of these terms in the book.

References

Acker, J. 2000. 'Gendered contradictions in organizational equity projects', *Organization* 7 (4): 625-632.

Bacchi, C. 1976. 'Liberation deferred: The ideas of the English-Canadian suffragists, 1877-1918'. PhD thesis, McGill University, Montreal.

Bacchi, C. 1996. *The politics of affirmative action: 'Women', equality and category politics*. London: Sage.

Bacchi, C. 2009. *Analysing policy: What's the problem represented to be?* Frenchs Forest, NSW: Pearson Education.

Bacchi, C. and Eveline, J. 1996. 'The politics of incorporation', in Bacchi, C., *The politics of affirmative action: 'Women', equality and category politics*. London: Sage.

Barad, K. 2003. 'Posthumanist performativity: Toward an understanding of how matter comes to matter', *Signs: Journal of Women in Culture and Society* 28 (3): 801-831.

Butler, J. 1990. *Gender trouble: Feminism and the subversion of identity*. New York: Routledge.

Chia, R. 1996. 'The problem of reflexivity in organisational research', *Organization* 3 (1): 31-59.

Dean, M. 1999. *Governmentality: Power and rule in modern society*. London: Sage.

Dumont, C. 1998. 'The analytical and political utility of poststructuralism: Considering affirmative action', *Canadian Journal of Sociology/Cahiers canadiens de sociologie* 23 (2/3): 217-237.

Eveline, J. 1994. 'The politics of advantage: Managing "work" and "care" in Australia and Sweden'. PhD thesis, Murdoch University, Perth.

Eveline, J. 2004. *Ivory basement leadership: Power and invisibility in the changing university*. Perth: University of Western Australia Press.

Eveline, J. 2005. 'Women in the ivory tower: Gender*ing* feminised and masculinised identities', *Journal of Organizational Change Management* 18 (6): 641-658.

Foucault, M. 1972. *The archaeology of knowledge*. Trans. A.M. Sheridan. New York: Pantheon.

Foucault, M. 1980 [1976]. 'Two lectures', in C. Gordon (ed.) *Power/knowledge: Selected interviews and other writings 1972-1977/Michel Foucault*. Trans. C. Gordon & others. Sussex: Harvester Press.

Foucault, M. 1991a [1980]. 'Questions of method', in Burchell, G., Gordon, C. and Miller, P. (eds) *The Foucault effect: Studies in governmentality*. Chicago: University of Chicago Press.

Foucault, M. 1991b [1968]. 'Politics and the study of discourse', in Burchell, G., Gordon, C. and Miller, P. (eds) *The Foucault effect: Studies in governmentality*. Chicago: University of Chicago Press.

Gordon, Z., Binns, J., Palmer, E., Bacchi, C. and Eveline, J. 2008. 'Gender analysis and social change. Task 1. Comprehensive comparisons'. Adelaide, unpublished manuscript.

Gottweis, H. 2003. 'Theoretical strategies of poststructuralist policy analysis: Towards an analytics of government' in Hajer, M. and Wagenaar, H. (eds) *Deliberative policy analysis: Understanding governance in a network society*. Cambridge, UK: Cambridge University Press.

Gunn, S. 2006. 'From hegemony to governmentality: Changing perceptions of power in social history', *Journal of Social History* 39 (3): 705-721.

March, C., Smyth, I. and Mukhopadhyay, M. 1999. *A guide to gender-analysis frameworks*. Oxford: Oxfam.

Magnusson, E., Rönnblom, M. and Silius, H. (eds) 2008. *Critical studies of gender equalities: Nordic dislocations, dilemmas and contradictions*. Göteborg: Makadam Publishers.

McHoul, A. and Grace, W. 1993. *A Foucault primer: Discourse, power and the subject.* Melbourne: Melbourne University Press.

Petersen, A. 2003. 'Governmentality, critical scholarship, and the medical humanities', *Journal of Medical Humanities* 24 (3/4): 187-201.

Rees, T. 1998. *Mainstreaming equality in the European Union: Education, training and labour market policies.* London: Routledge.

Simons, J. 1995. *Foucault and the political.* New York: Routledge.

Smith, D.E. 2005. *Institutional ethnography: A sociology for people.* New York: AltaMira Press.

Gendering Impact Assessment: Project Tasks

Task 1: Comprehensive Comparisons	Produce a report comparing gender analysis practices in selected industrial and industrialising countries (see Gordon et al. 2008 and Chapter 11).
Task 2: The Gendering of Policy Formation	Conduct a benchmarking (audit) process to examine to what extent selected previous policies of participating agencies intended to be gender-inclusive, to what extent they were perceived to have fulfilled that goal, and how gender analysis would have affected the development and implementation of those policies.
Task 3: Deep Evaluation: *ex ante* policy analysis	Develop a form of policy evaluation that encourages critical scrutiny of conceptual premises, models of implementation and conventional forms of evaluation within a proposed or existing policy.
Task 4: Testing and evaluating a rational policy model	Introduce participating agencies to a gender analysis framework that uses salient features of the rational policy model (Canadian Gender Based Analysis).
Task 5: Testing and evaluating a gender relations model	Introduce participating agencies to a gender analysis framework that starts with an analysis of existing gender relations (Dutch Gender Impact Assessment).
Task 6: Incorporating a Regional Focus	Work with regional and local government bodies to identify and analyse the constraints and opportunities offered by policy and programs for rural and regional communities, with a particular emphasis on Indigenous women (see especially Chapter 9).
Task 7: Progressive Evolution of New Model of Gendering Impact Assessment	Shape, test, evaluate and refine gender analysis frameworks appropriate to the specific contexts of Western Australia and South Australia.
Task 8: Community, Diversity and Collaboration	Explore how best to include community consultation within gender analysis processes (see especially Chapter 8).
Task 9: Addressing Training and Education Needs	Explore the role and efficacy of training in each of the models tested.

16

1

Gender/*ing* impact assessment: Can it be made to work?

CAROL BACCHI

Introduction: Carol Bacchi and Joan Eveline

This article was written prior to the commencement of the Gender Analysis Project, discussed in the Introduction. Reflecting Bacchi's policy background, it focuses primarily on connections between how policy is theorised and divergent models of gender analysis. This focus remains a theme throughout the chapters to follow, especially in Chapter 5. Eveline's influence is apparent towards the end of the article, where reference is made to ways of engaging policy workers in the organisational change process (see Eveline and Booth 2002; Eveline and Harwood 2002). Her breakthrough contribution to rethinking asymmetrical power relations between women and men as 'the politics of advantage' is also introduced (see Eveline 1994). The authors' shared commitment to recognising power as a generative force is captured in the term 'gender*ing*' (Eveline 2005).

Bacchi's primary purpose in the article is to alert readers to the existence of different frameworks for gender analysis and to suggest that, in terms of prospects for progressive change, the framework adopted matters. She identifies conceptual limitations in the dominant mode of gender analysis, which she calls a 'differences approach'. She also explores the potential for change in the Netherlands 'gender relations' approach, which starts from the premise that there are inequitable power relations between women and men.

Bacchi's major concern with both these models is the continuing tendency to consider policy as a *reaction* to the 'problem' of gender inequality. Here she brings to bear her rethinking of public policy as creative or productive, rather than as reactive (Bacchi 1999b, 2009). In this understanding it becomes appropriate to think about policy as a gender*ing* process, as *producing* 'gender' as a relation of inequality, rather than as reacting to gender 'differences' or to 'gender relations'. A key point accompanying this perspective is the role of policy in constituting subjects and subjectivities, in producing us as embodied 'men' and 'women' (see Chapter 4).

Bacchi's hope is that thinking about policy in this new way creates the space to reflect on underlying premises in proposed policies rather than to attempt to estimate whether these policies will *impact* differently on women and men, or on gender relations (as if these sit outside the policy process). In her view this kind of analysis is necessary in order to be able to expose the ways in which underlying gendering premises in neoliberal policies often serve to undermine gender equality agendas, a theme pursued in Chapter 2. One recommended way to open up policy proposals to this kind of conceptual interrogation is to involve community participants in the policy discussion, a topic developed in more depth in Chapter 8. As another intervention Bacchi suggests finding ways to create space and time in the everyday practices of policy workers for 'deep evaluation', incorporating her WPR methodology (Chapter 5) to interrogate the meaning of concepts such as 'gender' and 'equality'.

Some of the premises in this chapter continue to inform succeeding chapters, highlighting the need to:

- rethink policy as a creative rather than as a reactive process (see Chapter 5)

- consider policy as a gendering process

- consider the ways in which policies and policy proposals shape our subjectivities and our embodied existence

- find ways to scrutinise fundamental presuppositions within policy proposals rather than attempting to assess the 'impact' of those policies.

The Gender Analysis Project created circumstances in which to test these premises and to raise questions left unaddressed at this stage of the analysis, including:

- Do conceptual models (that is, 'differences' versus 'gender relations') matter when gender analysis is 'performed' 'on the ground', in actual sites?

- How can the ideas behind 'deep evaluation' be made meaningful to policy workers?

- Is it realistic to suggest that deep conceptual scrutiny of policy proposals can become part of the policy process?

- How are men configured in this analysis?

- Where are differences among women considered?

References

Bacchi, C. 2009. *Analysing policy: What's the problem represented to be?* Frenchs Forest, NSW: Pearson Education.

Eveline, J. 1994. 'The politics of advantage'. *Australian Feminist Studies.* Special issue: *Women and Citizenship*, 19 (Autumn): 129-154.

Eveline, J. 2005. 'Woman in the ivory tower: Gendering feminised and masculinised identities', *Journal of Organizational Change Management* 18 (6): 641-658.

Eveline, J. and Booth, M. 2002. 'Gender and sexuality in discourses of managerial control', *Gender, Work and Organization* 9 (5): 556-578.

Eveline, J. and Harwood, S. 2002. 'Policing the margins of collaborative leadership: Gender and culture change in the WA Police Service', *11th International Women in Leadership Conference,* Churchlands Campus, ECU, November.

Abstract

Forms of gender analysis are being introduced worldwide as new methods for achieving gender equality. This paper identifies limitations in dominant frameworks and puts forward suggestions to improve the process. It advances a form of deep evaluation to institutionalise conceptual analysis as a part of policy design. It also proposes the development of a Gendering Impact Assessment model that attends to the ways in which policy produces gender, and that has the potential to put in question the strategic norms of broad policy objectives.

Gender analysis is a tool associated with gender mainstreaming, the most recent innovation in equality policy. Broadly, mainstreaming is a commitment to guarantee that every part of an organisation assumes responsibility to ensure that policies impact evenly on women and men. Gender analysis, in its most common form, describes a methodology for assessing if policy is, or is not, attentive to the 'differences' between women and men.

I specify 'its most common form' because gender analysis has several incarnations. The approach has its genesis in the development field where there currently exists a plethora of frameworks (see March et al. 1999). Most of the major international organisations, including the United Nations, the World Bank and the ILO, employ forms of gender analysis. It is also being used in many western democracies, including Canada, New Zealand, parts of Europe and the European Commission itself.

In Australia the Women's Budget Program (1984-1996) is often identified as a precursor of gender analysis models (Sharp and Broomhill 2002; Rankin and Vickers 2001). AusAID (1998) referred to gender analysis as a part of social analysis as early as 1998.[1] More recently, the Howard Government has signalled an interest in gender mainstreaming and gender analysis. The Office of the Status of Women has been shifted from the Prime Minister's Department to the Department of Family and Community Services, moving 'so-called women's issues into the mainstream' (Goward 2004). Federal Sex Discrimination Commissioner, Pru Goward (2004), announced that this move creates the opportunity for 'the entire public service to adopt gender analysis'. Given this development, it seems more important than ever to reflect upon just what 'gender analysis' entails.

For the sake of simplicity I identify two contrasting models. The first, associated with a rational policy development model (see Edwards 2001), appears in Canada, New Zealand and in international organisations. The second, a 'gender relations' approach, is most comprehensively developed in the Netherlands. Below I outline the two approaches and indicate the reasons the Netherlands model offers more potential for change. I also suggest limitations in existing models, and directions that need to be explored to improve the process. Crucially, I argue that, in order to be effective, gender analysis processes need to provide scope for putting in question strategic policy goals and for attending to the ways in which policy *produces* gender.

Background: Mainstreaming and gender analysis

The move to mainstreaming has been driven, at least in part, by a frustration with the fact that efforts on behalf of women have tended to be located in separate institutional units, cut adrift from the seats of power. Hence, the directives of those units, it is argued, could easily be ignored. The insistence that all parts of an organisation have a responsibility to attend to gender is an attempt, according to its supporters, to move away from this 'ghettoisation'.

While it is important to recognise 'the role of the global feminist movement in the rapid take-up of gender mainstreaming' (True and Mintrom 2001), the reform is suspect in many quarters. In some cases those very units dedicated to pursuing women's interests have been disbanded on the grounds that they are no longer needed, since gender is now 'mainstreamed'. This same rationale has been used in some places to attack women-specific measures, including positive/affirmative action. When this is put together with the frequent under-resourcing of the mainstreaming agenda and its low profile in many organisations, it is unsurprising that some commentators conclude, with Eleanor Ramsay, that '[t]he compelling logic of the mainstreaming argument, that equity matters should become everyone's responsibility in the organisation has distracted attention from the result, whether intended or not, that there is a danger that it will become nobody's' (Ramsay 1995 in Bacchi 2001a).[2]

Given this experience, feminists have attempted to find ways to ensure that gender mainstreaming improves upon, rather than weakens, efforts to institutionalise gender equality. To this end, the literature now tends to state explicitly that mainstreaming procedures need to *accompany*, not replace, dedicated women's units and women-specific measures, including positive/affirmative action:

> Gender mainstreaming cannot fully develop, cannot thrive in a climate that dies not allow the articulation of feminist organization, be it inside institutions or autonomous. Gender equality units are a valuable asset for gender mainstreaming. They do not become redundant. Their position should be strengthened, not weakened. (Verloo 2002: 4)

For the same reason, to try to make gender mainstreaming work for women, it is described as a wide and complex process, including but not synonymous with gender analysis. For example, the Council of Europe (1998: 21-23) states explicitly that mainstreaming is 'more than a gender-based approach'. It lists the following as 'necessary prerequisites or facilitating conditions for gender mainstreaming': political will, specific gender equality policy, statistics, comprehensive knowledge of gender relations, knowledge of the administration, necessary funds and human resources, and participation of women in political and public life and in decision-making processes (see also Mackay and Bilton 2000: 1). The implication here is that, as a stand-alone initiative, the potential of gender analysis is clearly limited. I return to this point at the end of the paper.

Non-governmental organisations led the way in the 1980s in implementing a shift in approach from a focus on 'women' to attention to 'gender' and mainstreaming. In policy terms this shift is commonly described as a move from Women in Development (WID) to Gender and Development (GAD) (Chant and Gutmann 2000). The goal of those committed to WID was to erase women's invisibility in development programs (White 1994: 99). The postulated reasons for the shift to GAD include the point raised above, to put an end to the 'ghettoisation' of women's issues. In addition, the use of the term 'gender' is invoked to challenge assumptions that women are destined by their biology to fill certain roles. Much of the literature draws a distinction between 'sex' as biology and 'gender' as socially constructed roles and characteristics. The turn to 'gender' is also intended to be a means of drawing attention to the need for men to change. Practical examples to illustrate the importance of including an analysis of men's behaviours include the transmission of sexually communicated diseases, especially HIV/AIDS, and domestic violence. Finally, GAD highlights the gendered character of development bureaucracies and other related organisations, 'in terms of their culture, rules and outcomes' (March et al. 1999: 9).

There is considerable disagreement in the development field about whether or not the turn to 'gender' and mainstreaming has been useful. The closure of dedicated women's units and the removal of women-specific reforms is one concern. In addition, in some places it seems that the introduction of the term 'gender' has not changed much. As Ann Oakley (1998: 135) says, 'A somewhat insidious synonymy between "women" and "gender" developed; men remained the sex, while women became the gender'. Moreover, in places where men have been considered a necessary part of the equation, 'gender' is used at times to divert attention to a new high priority category, 'men at risk' (Staudt 2003: 49).

The key distinction between gender analysis approaches, according to March et al. (1999: 9), is whether or not they remain 'narrowly applicable to programmes and projects', or whether they are able 'to broaden out and apply to the social organisational contexts'. This is not a new problem. Feminists have consistently faced the difficulty of fitting proposals for change into existing institutional frameworks. According to March et al. (1999) only the DPU framework[3] and Kabeer's (1994) Social Relations Approach provide the possibility for the kind of institutional analysis required to promote meaningful change. Below I compare the idealised rational framework developed in Canada and New Zealand, and the Netherlands 'gender relations' approach, suggesting that the latter, which has distinct similarities with Kabeer's framework, offers a more sophisticated analysis of the relationship between gender and policy. However, even the Netherlands model has difficulty raising fundamental questions about social organisational contexts. The challenge here, I suggest, is to introduce a process able to put in question the assumed strategic norms of proposed or existing policies. Suggestions about ways to move in this direction are offered later in the paper.

Rational gender analysis versus a gender relations approach

In Canada and New Zealand gender analysis flows from the idealised rational development model found in many standard policy texts.[4] This conventional policy development framework conceives of policy as a sequence of stages: identifying the issue; defining desired/anticipated outcomes; information gathering; development and analysis of options; communication; evaluation (Women's Bureau 1997). The expressed goal is to ensure that the differential impact of policy on women and men is considered at each stage. To this end sex-disaggregated statistics, focused primarily on women and men's differential location in the labour market, are collected. There is an assumption that, since the goal of policy development is effective and efficient policy, policymakers will recognise the importance of addressing the 'differences' in their target groups, women and men. The intention is to prevent 'policy failure', as the New Zealand Ministry of Women's Affairs (MWA 2001) explains: '[g]ender analysis provides a basis for robust analysis of the differences between women's and men's lives, and this removes the possibility of analysis based on incorrect assumptions and stereotypes'.

In contrast, the Dutch framework takes environmental impact assessment as a guide. The methodology is called EER, translated as Emancipation Impact Assessment, which highlights the connection. EERs follow the five steps of an Environmental Impact Assessment:

1. Description of current gender relations;

2. Description of probable developments without new policy;

3. Description and analysis of the new policy plan;

4. Description of potential effects on gender relations;

5. Evaluating the positive and negative effects on gender relations (Verloo and Roggeband 1996).

A theoretical framework designed to answer three questions underpins the approach: Where are the structurally unequal power relations between women and men to be found? How do they function? And, how are they to be evaluated? The theoretical framework contains three elements: structures, processes and criteria. 'Structures' refers to the core of gender power relations, and which institutions and organisations are most important. Two structures are identified: the gendered division of labour, and the organisation of intimacy. 'Processes' refers to the mechanisms that produce and reproduce the unequal power relations. Two are selected as pivotal: the distribution of resources, and the operation of rules (interpretations or norms) about or connected to gender. 'Criteria' provide the normative ground for assessing whether a situation is to be positively or negatively judged. Three criteria are identified: equality, autonomy and pluriformity/diversity. Equality is interpreted to mean equality before the law, or equal treatment in similar circumstances. Autonomy is defined as the possibility for women to decide for themselves what is a good life.

Taking autonomy into account ensures that equality means more than sameness or adaptation to a male norm. Pluriformity/diversity indicates a commitment to a society in which differences are not hierarchical (Verloo 2000).[5]

Points of contrast

- The Canadian/New Zealand rational development model focuses consistently on women and men as separate categories of people, indicated in the primary focus on gender-disaggregated statistics, whereas the starting place for analysis in the Netherlands is 'gender relations'. The latter focus, I maintain, is more useful because gender needs to be thought of as 'a principle of social organization' (Ferree et al. 1999; see also Bacchi 2004) rather than as a characteristic of a person.

- The Netherlands model usefully identifies *unequal power relations* between women and men as a necessary component of the analysis. In contrast, the Canadian approach endeavours to present itself as a neutral examination of 'socioeconomic data broken down by gender' (Women's Bureau 1997: 22).

- The focus in the Netherlands on the gendered division of labour and on the organisation of intimacy promises a more comprehensive analysis than the rational development model, which concentrates almost exclusively on the relationship between paid employment and family responsibilities. There is also more space in the Netherlands model to raise questions about the ways in which sexuality creates and reproduces 'systemic differences in the positioning of different groups of people' (March et al. 1999: 103).

Limits of dominant models

Dominant models of gender analysis tend to conceptualise the nature of the dynamic between policy and gender in limited ways. The rational development approach, for example, makes a case for policy to *respond* to 'gender *difference*'. As Fiona Wilson (1996 in Benschop and Dooreward 1998: 789) argues, '[i]nstead of looking at gender as a difference perhaps we need to look … at how this is done'. To see how gender is 'done', we need to analyse the ways in which gender is 'constructed as a relationship of inequality by the rules and practices of different institutions' (Kabeer 1994: 84).

Four institutions are critical to this process: household/family, state, market and community. Identifying the state as one institution involved in the production of unequal gender relations constitutes public policy as a *gendering process* rather than a 'response' to assumed static 'differences' between women and men. Policy does not just 'act upon' people; it is itself active in 'creating' people (Bacchi 2005).

Doubtless, the Dutch model is more sensitive to this dynamic, but it still tends to focus on the 'potential effects' of policy on 'gender relations', as if these relations are fixed and/or stand outside the policy process. Despite the awareness among Dutch analysts of the ways in which '[p]olicies and structures ... often institutionalize the maintenance and reproduction of the social construction of gender' (Council of Europe 1998: 7), the gender impact assessment framework inadequately captures the role of policy in constituting subjects and subjectivities (Nettleton 1997: 208; Bacchi 1999: 45). As an example of this process, the lack of good, publicly funded child care will be one reason why many women decide to work part-time or to forego paid labor. Along related lines, lack of pay equity encourages men to continue in full-time paid labor, instead of taking time to care for their children.

The distinction drawn in many versions of gender analysis between *practical gender needs* and *strategic gender needs* is an attempt to capture the role of policy as a gender*ing* process. The distinction is intended to make a deceptively simple point – that, if a policy attends only to the immediate *practical* needs of a woman, it will very likely reinforce the conditions that put her in that situation in the first place. Mark Lansky (2001: 499) states perceptively that addressing practical needs 'makes gender roles easier to perform'. Awareness of this limitation has led to the insistence that, alongside attempts to respond to practical needs, other reforms which have more transformative potential are required. These reforms, we are told, will attend to women's 'strategic needs'. Making a related point, Jahan (1995) draws a distinction between 'integrationist' mainstreaming and 'agenda-setting' mainstreaming. However, the focus on practical and strategic *needs* encourages a top-down analysis, where women are constituted as 'needy' (Chant and Gutmann 2000: 51, fn. 6; Beveridge et al. 2000). The distinction is also difficult to operationalise since every practical intervention has an effect on power relations, whether this is intended or not (Longwe 1995 in March et al. 1999: 20).

Maxine Molyneux's (1985) original distinction between practical and strategic *interests* is more promising theoretically. Molyneux introduced the concept of gender interests to distinguish 'the interests that women, or men, have because of their gender from those which are due to their class, ethnicity, or other factors' (White 1994: 99). She had two goals: to deal with the increasing awareness that women are not a homogenous group, and to highlight the ways in which men's gender interests either accelerate or impede change. Both these issues – how to deal with 'diversity' among women, and how to deal with men – are at the forefront of discussions about gender analysis.

Regarding the former, some models (see March et al. 1999) mention the importance of recognising the impact of class or ethnicity on women's experiences. Very few directly address the position of lesbians. In fact, the central focus in most gender analysis on the relationship between family responsibilities and paid labour almost always assumes heterosexual family units as the target group. Katherine Teghtsoonian (1999) recommends that separate instruments be developed and elaborated for other groups, including Aboriginal women and lesbians, before there are attempts to blend the analyses.

Gender-Based Analysis (GBA) in Canada makes a token nod to address the differences among women. We are told that '[a]ll women and all men in Canadian society are not the same. Research shows that their life opportunities are affected by race, ability, geographic location, sexual orientation, and individual characteristics' (Women's Bureau 1997: 9).[6] However, there is no explanation of how to integrate this insight into the analysis. By way of contrast New Zealand's program makes a genuine attempt to keep the distinctive position of Maori women in view (Teghtsoonian 2003a).

In so far as men are concerned, the focus in Canadian GBA on sex-disaggregated statistics tends to 'a static and reductionist definition of gender (as woman/man)', failing to address the 'relational aspects of gender, or power and ideology, and of how patterns of subordination are reproduced' (Baden and Goetz 1997: 3). By contrast, both the Netherlands model and Kabeer's Social Relations approach attend to men as 'gendered beings'. This means making 'male gender-identities themselves an issue in development' (White 1994: 99). The argument here is that, for real change to take place in women's lives, men will also need to change. This focus is potentially transformative because it puts in question the male norms which characterise most of our institutions and organisations. Women are no longer the only ones under scrutiny, the only ones 'done to', or the only ones who need to change.

On this point Molyneux's (1985) insistence that men have 'gender interests' is a useful theoretical move, making it possible to reflect upon which of these interests work against change and which provide the basis for potential collaboration. Taking her lead from Molyneux, Sarah White (1994) uses Connell (1987) to address the ways in which gender forms the basis of hierarchies, not only between men and women, but also among men. Her examples are gay men, and young men in some contexts. It is also clear that, when men lose authority due to unemployment or de-skilling, this will have effects on their relationships with women. Mark Lansky (2001: 94) makes this point: 'lacking access to the breadwinner role, these men often define masculinity more in terms of sexual performance and displays of toughness' (see also White 1994; Chant 2000). Here, the concept 'masculinism' has more explanatory power than 'masculinity' which, as an assumed descriptor of socialised traits, tends to sit outside the real advantages that accrue to some men in current social relations (Duerst-Lahti 1998; Eveline 1994). The turn to men therefore potentially provides a path to a demand for institutional change. It is inadequate, however, to *describe* men's and women's 'actual lives' or 'lived realities' as 'similar' or 'different'; rather we need to reflect upon the contexts that produce those experiences.

The chief obstacle blocking this breadth of analysis is the *ex post* or reactive character of gender analysis. That is, existing models offer ways to vet or 'proof' *existing* or *proposed* policies. The analyses remain *ex post* despite attempts in Canada to insist that input is necessary early in the policy cycle, and despite the commitment in the Netherlands to create a 'virtuous circle' whereby the results of EER are fed back into the policymaking system to create better (and *ex ante*) policy proposals (Mackay and Bilton 2000: 31). This is because the problem is more than a matter of timing. *Ex post* analysis tends to ask how a proposal or policy can be introduced with fewer negative effects for women, instead of examining how the policy or policy proposal is itself implicated in constituting the problem (Bacchi 1999b). That is, there is a lack of questioning of overall strategic norms. This leaves gender analysis subservient to other policy goals. Worse still, it adds a 'veneer of legitimacy' to objectives that remain unexamined (Teghtsoonian 2003a).

I use the following examples to illustrate how the *ex post* character of gender analysis has meant an inability to put in question neoliberal premises in specific policy proposals, severely limiting the possibilities for progressive change:

- The World Bank's (2002: 5, fn. 3) 'Case for Mainstreaming Gender' has as a goal a 'less rigid or extreme gender-based division of labour' in order to increase 'female productive capital, which has important pro-growth effects'. The responsibilities of caring are difficult to address given this objective, as are the potential negative effects of a pro-growth ethic.

- New Zealand's Ministry of Women's Affairs (MWA 2001: 1) offers a gender analysis on retirement income which accepts as a 'Defined Desired Outcome' the government's aim to 'encourage greater financial self-reliance for retired people'. With this as a goal closed to interrogation, there is automatic acceptance of individual autonomy as a model for social relations, making it difficult to acknowledge the interdependence of people in many contexts.

- The European Commission's (1998: 17) Guide to gender impact assessment takes as axiomatic the goal of 'eliminating labour market rigidities'. To this end the Guide endorses 'positive action in favour of men to a careful selection of professions related to child care', ignoring the ways in which this policy entrenches groups of women in low-paying jobs or out of work altogether (Bacchi 1996: 113).

- In the Netherlands the *New General Social Assistance Act* (1996) places an emphasis on what is called the 'activating effect'. The obligation to work, or at least to apply for work, has been extended to lone mothers with children five years old or over. A GIA (Gender Impact Assessment) concluded that for most women the new Act means an improvement. As Plantenga (2000: 9) states, this ignores the absence of a 'national framework for care' to accompany the 'national framework of a general obligation to work'.

Rosalind Petchesky (1995: 156) notes the 'large silences' in the 1994 Programme of Action of the International Conference on Population and Development:

> The practical implementation of this reproductive health and rights agenda will be impossible without the allocation of resources globally and nationally to assure the full funding of social programmes, especially health – in other words, without radically new development alternatives.

Petchesky's analysis makes explicit 'the concrete links between macro-economic policies and the materialisation of reproductive and sexual rights for all the world's women'. Her point is that, unless macro-economic frameworks are identified as crucial to people's lives, commitments to women's health needs will accomplish little. It follows that, to be effective, gender analysis needs to be able to put in question neoliberal economic frameworks (Teghtsoonian 2003b; Bacchi and Eveline 2003).

New directions

Both Kathleen Staudt (2003) and Mieke Verloo (2002) insist that the only way to ensure that gender analysis has the ability to move outside of and critique the broad premises of policy proposals, which ultimately limit the transformative potential of the analysis, is to put specific equality objectives onto the agenda. Staudt calls them 'outcomes'. In Verloo's (2002: 8) words, 'the absence of precise objectives on reduced gender inequalities' means that the treatment of gender 'can be easily located within, and then be subject to, other policy goals, such as employment creation, economic growth or poverty reduction'. Both also emphasise the importance of community participation and consultation as a way of freeing analysts from the limitations imposed by their 'inside government' positioning (see also Sharp and Broomhill 2002). Naila Kabeer (in March et al. 1999: 14) agrees that community consultation and participation is one way to avoid the 'project trap' – the tendency to see the goal in terms of effective *implementation* of a designated policy, leaving the broad goals of the policy outside scrutiny.

These are important directions to pursue. Another way forward, I suggest, is to formalise the need for conceptual analysis in policy design. To this end, I am developing a procedure I call 'deep evaluation', which incorporates an ability to put in question the grounding premises of any proposed or existing policy. This framework is not a conventional form of evaluation, applied *ex post* to see if objectives have been achieved. Rather, as a form of *ex ante* policy analysis, it offers a way to scrutinise critically conceptual premises, modes of implementation, *and* conventional forms of evaluation.

Deep evaluation consists of a series of questions, with rationales provided for each, under two headings: Conceptual Premises and Operational Practices. Under Conceptual Premises I identify three foci for critical analysis in policy development: i) the meanings attached to key concepts; ii) how the problem is represented (Bacchi 1999b); iii) the ways in which context is represented. Under Operational Practices, I propose to examine five issues: i) location of responsibility for implementation; ii) methods of analysis; iii) resource allocation; iv) forms of evaluation and v) training.

Deep evaluation is an intervention that can be deployed in any policy field, not just in the area of gender policy. Needless to say, therefore, it would need to be tailored to the goals of the analysts. These may be to examine a policy for its gendering effects, or to consider underlying premises about law enforcement, or to reveal premises about the goals of economic development. In each case the procedure is intended to open up political discussions about policy options, empowering policy activists (Yeatman 1998). It rests on the assumption that many involved in policy formulation want to do more than participate in a technocratic exercise, but need ways to insist that other forms of analysis are a legitimate part of their mandate. The hope is that deep evaluation will assist them in this task, in the specific case examined in this paper, facilitating the development of new, more effective gender analysis processes.

Because the goal is to make gender analysis more democratic and less technocratic, any new framework, including deep evaluation itself, needs to be developed and refined in concert with policy staff in specific departmental contexts. It is crucially important to avoid the trap of developing a 'one size fits all' approach, which has proven to be the downfall of many previous policy initiatives (Eveline 1994; Bacchi 1999a; Eveline 2001). The success of the project depends on select staff with knowledge and expertise in the functions and culture of those government departments taking a high degree of ownership in the refining and testing of the process.[7] For this reason Joan Eveline and I are currently engaged in a Linkage-funded [Australian Government-funded] project to test and evaluate Canadian and Dutch approaches to gender analysis in Western Australia and South Australia. The project is designed as an iterative process so that the experiences and views of policy workers can be fed back into proposals for modification of aspects of the gender analysis framework, used as the starting point for the process. The method I call deep evaluation will be tested for its potential to identify: i) the ways in which gender is a process, rather than a characteristic of a person; ii) the ways in which policy *produces* gender; iii) the masculine norms of seeing and doing, which sustain a gendered 'politics of advantage' (Eveline 1994); iv) the broad contextual factors that impinge on transformative visions. Other issues to be addressed include: the extent to which community involvement is necessary; how to develop sound and realistic training programs; how to attend to the diversity among women. The long-term goal is to develop a uniquely Australian gender analysis method, which I call Gender*ing* Impact Assessment, to be applied across the public sector in both states.

Conclusion

Turning to the question in the title – can gender analysis be made to work? – a first step towards development of an effective process, I suggest, is confronting and discussing the political implications of different gender analysis frameworks. One of the goals of this paper has been to initiate this process. It is important , I argue, to reflect upon the contrasting effects of a model which sees gender analysis as a matter of 'evening up' 'differences' between women and men, and a method which confronts issues to do with power and gender relations.

A second goal has been to insist upon the need to empower those committed to gender analysis to put in question the strategic goals of the policies they are asked to 'vet' for their different impacts. Establishing deep evaluation as a necessary step in policy formulation is recommended as a means to achieve this goal. The focus in deep evaluation on representations of 'problems' and representations of contexts, for example, encourages scrutiny of important international developments in trade and commerce, raising questions about the dangers of accepting these developments as given. This kind of conceptual interrogation, I suggest, provides the starting place for development of an innovative and reflexive gender analysis process, with the potential to broaden the gender equality agenda in important ways. Specifically, it creates the opportunity to draw attention to the role of policy in producing gender, and to make it clear that gender equality requires attending to general policy objectives.

Needless to say, there is no suggestion that any stand-alone method of gender analysis can achieve real and meaningful change. Clearly, the introduction of a Gendering Impact Assessment process should form part of a wider agenda that includes women-specific reforms and affirmative action to increase women's representation in positions of influence (Bacchi 1996). Indeed, these reforms must be pursued alongside campaigns for the introduction of deep evaluation and Gendering Impact Assessment in order to increase the likelihood that these initiatives will be accepted and applied. Finally, to those who suggest that turning to the state is unwise in a period when states are being 'hollowed out', I insist, with Rankin and Vickers (2001: 21), that engagement remains critical since states are being internationalised, not eliminated.

Notes

1. Some more interesting developments are taking place in several states. In addition, the Women's Electoral Lobby demanded a 'gender impact analysis of proposed budgetary measures' in their 2003 pre-budget submission (WEL 2003). A group of policymakers and academics also produced a gender analysis of the questions posed for the recent Constitutional Convention in South Australia (Donaghey 2003). AusAID (1998) referred to gender analysis as a part of social analysis as early as 1998.

2. The concept is viewed with suspicion by women's organisations in Australia, 'where it has been seen to have provided the rationale for abolishing or down-grading women's units, services and policies at various government levels, by different administrations, at different times'(Mackay and Bilton 2000: 62; see also Bacchi 2000, 2001a, 2001b). Referring to the development arena, where mainstreaming originated, Caren Levy et al. (2000: 94) note that 'GAD [Gender and Development] can jeopardize decades of work when it is used as a rationale for dispensing with the organizational structures created for WID [Women in Development], without proper thought to its replacement'. On the European front, Alison Woodward (2001: 4) identifies a similar concern that 'states actually use the policy as an excuse to reduce woman-focused programming'.

3. The DPU (Development Planning Unit), University College, London, usefully breaks down WID and GAD into subcategories that reflect the climate of prevalent economic and political thought in particular periods. So, for example, we get 'the WID equity approach', followed by 'the WID anti-poverty approach (1970s)', followed by 'the WID efficiency approach (1980s/90s) under structural adjustment and economic efficiency measures', and 'the GAD efficiency approach', 'the GAD equity approach' and 'the GAD anti-poverty approach'. The DPU employs these subcategories to highlight the crucial impact of macro-economic climates on equality policy.

4. In this paper I concentrate on the model of gender analysis employed at the federal level in Canada. It is important to note that, because of decentralising of decision-making, there are important differences in design and implementation in some Canadian provinces. British Columbia, for example, actually anticipated the development of a federal model by introducing *The Gender Lens* in 1993. While this framework had challenging components to it, since a neoliberal government has come to power it has been replaced with a much less comprehensive framework. See British Columbia 2003; Teghtsoonian 2003b.

5. It is important to note that Dutch theorists continue to explore and develop the conceptual framework of an EER. In 1998, Mieke Verloo, the person responsible for the Netherlands approach, suggested adding one more structure, the organisation of citizenship, one more mechanism, violence, and one more criterion, care/social responsibility. To date these suggestions have not been taken up (Verloo 2001: 18, fn. 14).

6. This mention of 'individual characteristics' suggests links with the equity approach, diversity management, which preceded gender-based analysis in Canada and which tends to individualise the problem of inequality. See Bacchi 1999a. On this point Woodward (2001: 2, fn. 2) notes the ease with which mainstreaming, with its focus on 'building equality into the culture of the organisation and treating the employee as a whole person with respect and dignity', can become part of human resource management rather than a specific policy approach.

7. An example here is the model developed in a current Linkage project with the Western Australian Police Service (Eveline and Harwood 2002). That model, called 'companionate leadership' (Booth and Eveline 2001), is proving successful in building a team who 'own' the organisational responsibility for designing and implementing their collaboratively chosen projects.

References

(*Websites valid at time of publication*)

AusAid. 1998. *A guide to gender and development.* <ausaid.gov.au> accessed 22 October 2009.

Bacchi, C. 1996. *The politics of affirmative action: 'Women', equality and category politics.* London: Sage.

Bacchi, C. 1999a. 'Managing diversity: A contested concept', *International Review of Women and Leadership* 5 (2): 1-9.

Bacchi, C. 1999b. *Women, policy and politics: The construction of policy problems.* London: Sage.

Bacchi, C. 2000. 'The seesaw effect: Down goes affirmative action, up comes workplace diversity', *Journal of Interdisciplinary Gender Studies* 5 (2): 64-83. Special issue: *Gender and Workplace Relations.*

Bacchi, C. 2001a. 'Managing equity: Mainstreaming and "diversity" in Australian universities', in Brooks, A. and Mackinnon, A. (eds) *Gender and the restructured university: Changing management and culture in higher education.* Buckingham: Open University Press.

Bacchi, C. 2001b. 'Gender mainstreaming: A new vision, more of the same, or backlash?' *Dialogue: Academy of the Social Sciences* 20: 16-20.

Bacchi, C. 2005. 'Policy', in Essed, P., Kobayashi, A. and Goldberg, D.T. (eds) *Blackwell companion to gender studies.* London: Blackwell.

Bacchi, C. and Eveline, J. 2003. 'Mainstreaming and neoliberalism: A contested relationship', *Policy and Society: Journal of Public, Foreign & Global Policy* 22 (2): 98-118.

Baden, S. and Goetz, A. M. 1997. 'Who needs [sex] when you can have [gender]? Conflicting discourses on gender at Beijing', *Feminist Review* 56: 3-25.

Benschop, Y. and Dooreward, H. 1998. 'Covered by equality: The gender subtext of organizations', *Organization Studies* 19 (5): 787-805.

Beveridge, F., Nott, S., and Stephen, K. 2000. 'Moving forward with mainstreaming', in Beveridge, F., Nott. S. and Stephen, K. (eds) *Making women count: Integrating women into law and policy-making.* Aldershot: Ashgate.

British Columbia. 1993. *Gender lens: A guide to gender-inclusive policy and program development.* Vancouver: Ministry of Women's Equality.

British Columbia. 2003. *Guide to best practices in gender analysis.* Vancouver: Ministry of Community, Aboriginal and Women's Services.

Chant, S. 2000. 'From "woman-blind" to "man-kind": Should men have more space in gender and development?'. *IDS Bulletin* 31 (2): 7-17.

Chant, S. and Gutmann, M. 2000. *Mainstreaming men into gender and development: Debates, reflections, and experiences.* GB: Oxfam.

Connell. R. 1987. *Gender and power.* Oxford: Polity Press.

Council of Europe. 1998. *Conceptual framework, methodology and presentation of good practices: Final report of activities of the group of specialists on mainstreaming* [EG-S-MS (98) 2]. Strasbourg.<coe.int/t/e/human_rights/equality/02._gender_mainstreaming/100_EG-S-MS%281998%292rev.asp#TopOfPage>accessed 22 October 2009.

Donaghey, T. 2003. *Women and the South Australian Convention: Submission to the Constitutional Convention*. Adelaide: University of South Australia.

Duerst-Lahti, G. 1998. 'Masculinism as governing ideology: Epistemological consequences'. Paper delivered at the Annual Meeting of the Western Political Science Association, Los Angeles, 20-22 March.

Edwards, M. 2001. *Social policy, public policy: From problem to practice*. Crows Nest, NSW: Allen & Unwin.

European Commission. 1998. *A guide to gender impact assessment. Employment & social affairs, equality between women and men*. Luxembourg: Office for Official Publications of the European Commission.

Eveline, J. 1994. 'The politics of advantage'. *Australian Feminist Studies*. Special issue: *Women and Citizenship*, 19 (Autumn): 129-154.

Eveline, J. 2001. 'Feminism, racism and citizenship in twentieth century Australia', in Crawford, P. and Maddern, P. (eds) *Women as Australian citizens: Underlying histories*. Melbourne: Melbourne University Press.

Eveline, J. and Booth, M. 2002. 'Gender and sexuality in discourses of managerial control', *Gender, Work and Organization* 9 (5): 556-578.

Eveline, J. and Harwood, S. 2002. 'Policing the margins of collaborative leadership: Gender and culture change in the WA Police Service', 11th International Women in Leadership Conference, Churchlands Campus, ECU, 26-28 November.

Ferree, M., Lorber, J. and Hess, B.B. (eds) 1998. *Revisioning gender*. London: Sage

Goward, P. 2004. 'Now everyone can focus on women', *The Age*, 30 October.

Haas, L. 1992. *Equal parenthood and social policy. A study of parenting in Sweden*. New York: State University of New York Press.

Jahan, R. 1995. *The elusive agenda: Mainstreaming women in development*. London: Zed Books.

Kabeer, N. 1994. 'Gender-aware policy and planning: A social-relations perspective', in Macdonald, M. (ed.) *Gender planning in development agencies: Meeting the challenge*. UK: Oxfam: 80-97.

Lansky, M. 2001. 'Gender, women and all the rest (Part II)', *International Labour Review*, 140 (1): 85-115.

Levy, C., Taher, N. and Vouhe, C. 2000. 'Addressing men and masculinities in GAD', *IDS Bulletin* 31 (2): 86-96.

Longwe, S. 1995. 'Supporting women's development in the Third World: Distinguishing between intervention and interference', *Gender and Development* 3 (1): 47-50.

Mackay, F. and Bilton, K. 2000. *Learning from experience: Lessons in mainstreaming equal opportunities*. University of Edinburgh: Governance of Scotland Forum.

March, C., Smyth, I., and Mukhopadhyay, M. 1999. *A guide to gender-analysis frameworks*. Oxford: Oxfam.

Molyneux, M. 1985. 'Mobilization without emancipation? Women's interests, the state, and revolution in Nicaragua', *Feminist Studies* 11 (2): 227-254.

MWA (Ministry of Women's Affairs) New Zealand. 2001. *Gender-based policy analysis: A resource for policy analysts*. Auckland: MWA.

Nettleton, S. 1997. 'Governing the risky self: How to become healthy, wealthy and wise', in Petersen, A. and Bunton, R. (eds) *Foucault, health and medicine*. New York: Routledge.

Oakley, A. 1998. 'Science, gender, and women's liberation: An argument against postmodernism', *Women's Studies International Forum* 21 (2): 133-146.

Petchesky, R.P. 1995. 'From population control to reproductive rights: Feminist fault lines', *Reproductive Health Matters* 6: 152-161.

Plantenga, J. 2000. 'Gender impact assessment and the employment strategy: The case of the Netherlands'. External Report commissioned and presented to the European Commission. <mbs.ac.uk/research/europeanemployment/projects/gendersocial/documents/GIA_NL.pdf> accessed 22 October 2009.

Ramsay, E. 1995. 'The National Framework for Institutional Equity in Australian Higher Education – current achievements and future possibilities'. Paper presented to the Second National Conference on Equity and Access in Tertiary Education, Melbourne, 3-7 July.

Rankin, L.P. and Vickers, J. 2001. *Women's movements and state feminism: Integrating diversity into public policy*. Ottawa: Status of Women Canada. <rwmc.uoguelph.ca/cms/documents/88/Rankin_1-68.pdf> accessed 21 October 2009.

Sharp, R. and Broomhill, R. 2002. 'Budgeting for equality: The Australian experience', *Feminist Economics* 8 (1): 25-47.

Staudt, K. 2003. Gender mainstreaming: Conceptual links to institutional machineries', in Rai, S.M. (ed.) *Mainstreaming gender, democratizing the state? Institutional mechanisms for the advancement of women*. Manchester: Manchester University Press.

Teghtsoonian, K. 1999. 'Centring women's diverse interests in health policy and practice: A comparative discussion of gender analysis'. Paper prepared for *Made to measure: Accessing approaches to eliminate gender inequity*, hosted by the Maritime Centre of Excellence for Women's Health, Halifax, Nova Scotia. <.acewh.dal.ca/eng/reports/teghtsoonian.pdf> accessed 21 October 2009.

Teghtsoonian, K. 2000. 'Gendering policy analysis in the Government of British Columbia: Strategies, possibilities and constraints', *Studies in Political Economy* 61: 105-127.

Teghtsoonian, K. 2003a. 'Gender analysis mainstreaming in Aotearoa/New Zealand'. Paper presented at the ECPR Joint Sessions, Edinburgh.

Teghtsoonian, K. 2003b. 'W(h)ither women's equality? Neoliberalism, institutional change and public policy in British Columbia', *Policy, Organisation & Society* 22 (1): 26-47. Special Issue: *The Politics of Women's Interests*, Chappell, L. and Hill, L., Guest Editors.

True, J. and Mintrom, M. 2001. 'Transnational networks and policy diffusion: The case of gender mainstreaming', *International Studies Quarterly* 45: 27-57.

Verloo, M. 2000. 'Making women count in the Netherlands', in Beveridge, F., Nott, S. and Stephen, K. (eds) *Making women count: Integrating gender into law and policy-making*. Dartmouth: Ashgate.

Verloo, M. 2001. 'Another velvet revolution? Gender mainstreaming and the politics of implementation'. IWM working paper no. 5. Vienna: IWM.

Verloo, M. 2002. 'The development of gender mainstreaming as a political concept for Europe'. Paper presented at the Conference on Gender Learning, Leipzig, 6-8 September.

Verloo, M and Roggeband, C. 1996. 'Gender impact assessment: The development of a new instrument in the Netherlands', *Impact Assessment* 14 (1): 3-21.

WEL (Women's Electoral Lobby). 2003-2004 *Pre-Budget submission*. Canberra: WEL.

White, S. 1994. 'Making men an issue: Gender planning for "the other half"', in Macdonald, M. (ed.) *Gender planning in development agencies: Meeting the challenge.* Oxford: Oxfam.

Wilson, F. 1996. 'Research note: Organizational theory: Blind and deaf to gender?' *Organizational Studies* 17 (5): 825-842.

Women's Bureau, Strategic Policy Branch. 1997. *Gender-based analysis backgrounder.* Ottawa: Women's Bureau.

Woodward, A. 2001. 'Gender mainstreaming in European policy: Innovation or deception?' Discussion paper FS 101-103. Wissenschafftszentrum Berlin Fur Sozialforschung.

World Bank. 2002. *Integrating gender into the World Bank's work: A strategy for action.* <siteresources. worldbank.org/INTGENDER/Resources/strategypaper.pdf> accessed 21 October 2009.

Yeatman, A. (ed.) *Activism and the policy process.* Sydney: Allen & Unwin.

2

Mainstreaming and neoliberalism: A contested relationship

CAROL BACCHI AND JOAN EVELINE

Introduction: Carol Bacchi and Joan Eveline

As with the previous chapter this article was written in the lead-up to the commencement of the Gender Analysis Project. It pursues the increasing controversy about whether or not gender mainstreaming ought to be considered a victory for feminist reformers. This debate was generated in part due to the proliferation of gender mainstreaming initiatives in organisations and states with free market agendas and the associated removal of women's policy units and positive action initiatives. Those who believed that mainstreaming was in fact resistant to free market liberalism tended to argue that the expansion of state activities associated with the reform challenged the neoliberal focus on small government.

Our contribution to this debate emphasises the need to recognise that neoliberalism is not anti-state but that it encourages a particular kind of state, one that steers from a distance. Hence there is no necessary tension between neoliberalism and forms of gender mainstreaming that focus on strengthening the political arm of government.

We also develop the hypothesis that the degree of resistance or complicity between gender mainstreaming and neoliberalism is related to the form of gender mainstreaming (or gender analysis) introduced. Following from Chapter 1 the case is made that a 'differences' model of gender analysis rests on individualist premises that provide some congruence with neoliberalism, while a 'gender relations' approach is more likely to be resistant. The relationship between gender mainstreaming (and gender analysis) and neoliberalism is therefore described as 'contested'. The theoretical concept of contestation is central to this and to subsequent chapters. It highlights the politics – that is, the processes and practices – involved in the competition over meaning that generates social relations and social subjects.

As an intervention in this politics we suggest designing gender analysis guidelines that scrutinise the broad political objectives and strategic norms of policy proposals in an *ex ante* fashion ('deep evaluation') rather than directing attention to the *impact* of policies on women and men, and/or on gender relations *ex post*, as if these exist separately from the policies that shape gendered beings and gendered lives. The theoretical focus on policy as *productive* (creative) of social relations, bodies and subjectivities rather than as *reactive* to 'problems', introduced in Chapter 1, is employed here. With this understanding the goal becomes identifying and scrutinising gender*ing* effects within policy proposals, highlighting how specific policies reproduce 'gender' as a relation of inequality. The challenge we faced was whether or not it might be possible to alter conventional forms of implementation and evaluation within the public sector in the manner suggested. Since, as with Chapter 1, this article preceded the onset of the Gender Analysis Project, the feasibility of this proposal had yet to be tested. Chapter 3 initiates this process.

Abstract

The paper offers a comparative analysis of dominant mainstreaming and gender analysis frameworks to consider the nature of the relationship between these equality initiatives and neoliberalism. We challenge the portrayal of mainstreaming as necessarily resistant to neoliberalism, and show how dominant forms of mainstreaming illustrate characteristics congruent with neoliberal premises and policy agendas. Our particular concern is the extent to which some forms of mainstreaming and gender analysis are unable to put in question neoliberal premises because of their ex post *character. For this reason we describe the relationship as contested. Our goal is to identify ways to strengthen the potential of mainstreaming initiatives to step outside of and critique neoliberalism's strategic norms. To advance this objective we offer some first steps towards producing gender analysis as an* ex ante *intervention. Significantly, we suggest that effective implementation requires a focus on policy's creative (active) role in constructing 'problems' and in shaping gender relations.*

Mainstreaming is the most recent innovation in equality policy, with gender analysis its most common method of intervention. Broadly, mainstreaming is a commitment to guarantee that every part of an organisation assumes responsibility to ensure that policies impact evenly on women and men. Gender analysis is a tool for vetting policies to ensure that they pay due heed to the differential location and experiences of women and men. With origins in the development field, mainstreaming and gender analysis have been introduced in key international organisations, including the World Bank, the United Nations and the International Labour Organization (ILO). Versions also appear in many western democracies, including Canada, New Zealand, parts of Europe and the European Commission itself. There is some debate, as we will see, about whether mainstreaming ought to be considered a victory for feminist reformers, or whether it actually undermines important equality initiatives.

Our contribution to this discussion is twofold. Firstly, we argue that there are certain continuities between dominant mainstreaming approaches and neoliberalism, both in understandings of the roles of states and markets, and in underlying individualist premises. These continuities help to explain the rapid diffusion of the reform in organisations and states strongly associated with neoliberal agendas. This is not to deny the progressive and often feminist intentions motivating those who support the reform. Secondly, we suggest that the best intentions of feminist reformers will be thwarted so long as gender analysis is positioned as an *ex post* commentary on proposed or existing policies. In our view, to reconstitute mainstreaming as able to put neoliberal agendas into question requires a form of *ex ante* gender analysis which includes scrutiny of broad policy objectives. In the second half of the paper we outline a proposal for producing such an instrument. By way of providing the background to that proposal we show how dominant forms of gender mainstreaming are formed to fit neoliberal agendas.

The mainstreaming debate: How do we know when we are winning?

The move to mainstreaming has been driven, at least in part, by a frustration with the fact that efforts on behalf of women have tended to be located in separate institutional units, cut adrift from the seats of power. Hence, the directives of those units, it is argued, could easily be ignored. The insistence that all parts of an organisation have a responsibility to attend to gender is an attempt, according to its supporters, to move away from this 'ghettoisation'. Non-governmental organisations led the way in the 1980s in implementing a shift from Women in Development (WID) to Gender and Development (GAD), which had as an explicit goal gaining organisation-wide commitment to gender equality (Chant and Gutmann 2000).

There is, however, considerable disagreement in the development field and elsewhere about whether or not mainstreaming has been effectively implemented. Indeed, there are debates world-wide about whether mainstreaming has improved the chances of advancing women's cause, or whether it has worked against women's equality. In a study of European Union mainstreaming policies, for example, Guerrina (2003: 104) concludes that 'far from creating the necessary conditions for substantive equality, mainstreaming can serve to silence women and remove gender from the political agenda'. An important concern is that units dedicated to pursuing women's interests have been disbanded on the grounds that they are no longer needed, since gender is now 'mainstreamed'. Teghtsoonian (2003b) shows how this has occurred in British Columbia, Canada, with a neoliberal government demolishing the free-standing Ministry of Women's Equality, which for a decade had provided a voice for women in high-level decision making. In the development field, Caren Levy et al. (2000: 94) note that 'GAD can jeopardize decades of work when it is used as a rationale for dispensing with the organizational structures created for WID, without proper thought to its replacement'. This same rationale has been used to attack women-specific measures in the developed world, including positive/affirmative action. On the European front, Alison Woodward (2001: 4) notes that states actually use the policy as an 'excuse to reduce woman-focused programming'. In Australia, mainstreaming is widely considered to have provided the 'rationale for abolishing or downgrading women's units, services and policies at various government levels, by different administrations, at different times' (Mackay and Bilton 2000: 62; see also Bacchi, 2000, 2001a, 2001b). When this is put together with the under-resourcing of the mainstreaming agenda and its low profile in organisations, it is unsurprising that some commentators conclude, with Eleanor Ramsay, that '[t]he compelling logic of the mainstreaming argument, that equity matters should become everyone's responsibility in the organisation has distracted attention from the result, whether intended or not, that there is a danger that it will become nobody's' (Ramsay 1995 in Bacchi 2001a).

On the other side many scholars and activists see great promise in mainstreaming. According to Teresa Rees (1998: 27), for example, mainstreaming moves beyond earlier equality initiatives by seeking 'to transform organizations and create a culture of diversity in which people of a much broader range of characteristics and backgrounds may contribute and flourish'. Rees identifies and characterises three developments in equality policy: the 'early days' of equal treatment, which she describes as 'tinkering'; the more recent 'positive action' initiatives, which she calls 'tailoring'; and mainstreaming, characterised as 'transforming'. The argument here is that other reforms sought only to slot women into existing organisations, while mainstreaming sets out to change the character of those organisations. This is so, says Rees, because mainstreaming is informed by a 'politics of difference' that 'recognises the androcentricity of organisations and seeks to change it, thus facilitating women's full participation on equal terms'. True and Mintrom (2001: 34) are similarly impressed by mainstreaming, which they describe as 'an exemplary case of the expansion of the role of the state'.

How are these contrasting views on mainstreaming to be reconciled? To an extent the problem stems from the contested terrain surrounding the use of mainstreaming, which sees the reform being recast to fit a variety of purposes. Rees (1998: 192) herself describes the method of gender analysis or 'gender proofing' of policies as '*post hoc*' and 'reactive'. True and Mintrom, by contrast, are content to identify the diffusion of mainstreaming machineries as an unquestioned victory for the women's cause. They claim that mainstreaming is impelled by 'a desire to resist arguments and pressure faced by nation-states to accept uncritically economic reforms inspired by the neoliberal global governance agenda' (True and Mintrom 2001: 34). Without denying the role of the global feminist movement in the rapid take-up of gender mainstreaming, we intend to show that, in their current manifestation, mainstreaming initiatives are in several ways congruent with neoliberalism. We argue that the proliferation of state machineries to implement mainstreaming and gender analysis is more complicated and less one-sidedly a story of progressive change than True and Mintrom suggest.

Specifically, the new equality regimes follow the neoliberal insistence that governments only manage, rather than get involved in the direct delivery of services. They can also result in reduction of forms of oversight of private enterprise, another neoliberal project, and often evince individualist premises, despite declared commitments to a form of group equity. Our argument is not that mainstreaming necessarily suits neoliberal agendas. Rather we argue that, to the extent that mainstreaming and gender analysis remain subservient to wider policy objectives, the possibility of contesting neoliberal economic agendas is seriously compromised. While not wishing to paint a picture of inevitable co-option of reform activists, we believe it is necessary to recognise that one reason mainstreaming has become popular and spread so quickly is that dominant models pose no real threat to neoliberal projects. From that position we move on to outline some first steps towards creating an instrument capable of putting in question neoliberal strategic norms.

Mainstreaming, states and markets

As mentioned above, True and Mintrom (2001: 34) consider mainstreaming a challenge to neoliberalism. The grounds for their argument is that mainstreaming is an 'exemplary case of the expansion of the role of the state'. Their claim rests upon a common assumption that neoliberalism involves a reduction in the size and regulatory mechanisms of the state. Indeed, neoliberal advocates encourage this representation of their agenda (Teicher and Barton 2002; Hughes 1998; McEachern 1995). However, other authors have pointed out that neoliberalism is about re-regulation rather than de-regulation, with no subsequent decrease in state mechanisms of control. Shields and Evans (1998: 85), for example, argue that 'neoliberalism is not necessarily or generally anti-state. It is, more accurately, a project to construct a particular kind of state'. This means that, in order to understand the relationship between mainstreaming and neoliberalism, it is necessary to reflect upon the ways in which mainstreaming can be congruent with developments in the new public sector management.

New Public Management (NPM) is driven by governments of a neoliberal persuasion, with key principles of user-pays and small government providing the rationale (for an example, see Reith 1996). In administering NPM, public servants are instructed to operate more as private sector managers than as administrators delivering the 'public good' (Pusey 1991; Osborne and Gaebler 1992). Self-surveillance and self-management characterise and monitor the performance of public officials (Blackmore and Sachs 2001). For example, Australia's new *Public Service Act* (1999) follows neoliberal principles in its 'market-based reconceptualisation' of the roles of public servants (Shields and Evans 1998: 86). Its declared goal is that the APS (Australian Public Service) 'should operate on the same basis as applies to the private sector'. To this end, responsibility for employment decisions has been devolved to Agency Heads, 'vesting in them greater flexibility and authority to manage their own workplaces'. This, it is claimed, will produce 'a more flexible, less regulated workplace', involve the 'removal of unnecessary prescription and red tape', and translate a desire by staff for 'security in employment' to 'a greater focus on maintaining and upgrading their employability' (Kemp 1999 in Bacchi 2000). Employability in this system, however, means the removal of employee rights. Leslie Riggs (1999: 128), Group Manager, Workplace Reform Group, notes that one of the key impacts of reform has been 'limitations on an employee's right to strike'. Under the new Act, employees are subject to the government's *Workplace Relations Act*, which gives high priority to individual contracts between employer and employee (Teicher 1998).

According to Shields and Evans (1998: 8), what is involved in neoliberal public sector reform is a paradigmatic shift to a conception of government as a 'steering' institution from a conception of government as a 'rowing' institution, 'in other words, to withdraw from the direct production and delivery of public goods and services, and to focus on the policy-setting and the management aspects of providing public programs'. This is accomplished by downsizing the public sector and by bringing the market principle into government-supported sectors of government.

This model of governance introduces a level of self-managed surveillance within a discourse of 'devolved' responsibility. Higher education in Australia provides a clear illustration of how this 'steering from a distance' (Marginson 2001) operates. Distribution of responsibility for providing the means to mass education and a key place in the new knowledge economy is left to increasingly self-managed universities, but this distribution of responsibility is *not* accompanied by an appropriate distribution of resources. Instead, government funding levels have moved to an all-time low, leaving universities and TAFEs under-funded and vulnerable therefore to 'special funding' incentives which allow governments to control political and education agendas (Blackmore and Sachs 2003; Currie et al. 2002; Eveline 2004). According to Tom Buhrs (2002 in Teghtsoonian 2003a: 1), the result of neoliberal reforms in the public sector generally is that 'the strong emphasis on vertical accountability … makes policy coordination and integration even more problematic than before'.

Dominant forms of mainstreaming are clearly congruent with this self-managed model of governance. They put in place processes of accountability and self-surveillance over the performance of public officials. Despite the rhetoric of devolution and self-management they strengthen the political arm of government through under-funded expectations that public servants will do more for less, and through subsequent controls over competitive and ad hoc distribution of resources. At the same time they remain cut-off from the specific delivery of services. In line with these developments the UK Commonwealth Secretariat (in Mackay and Bilton 2000: 26) report that their Gender Management System is 'aimed primarily at governments' and is based on a 'stakeholder approach', encouraging 'partnerships between the government, the private sector, and civil society'.

Mainstreaming efforts try to capitalise on the self-surveillance aspects of public sector reform by insisting that gender issues be treated seriously by every part of an organisation. For example, the UK Commonwealth Secretariat (in Mackay and Bilton 2000: 26) believes that it is possible to exploit new management systems which emphasise performance appraisal to monitor gender mainstreaming: 'performance targets will explicitly include gender equality goals. This ensures accountability is the basis of decisions on what incentives and sanctions can be applied in each case'. Kathy Teghtsoonian (2004) identifies this approach as a form of the 'feminist judo' described by Hester Eisenstein (1996: 82), 'that is, mobilizing the full weight of the "capitalist patriarchal state" against itself in pursuing feminist goals'.

On the other side, however, this model of governance has characteristics that limit the opportunities for mainstreaming to impact significantly on political developments. For example, in Canada, where gender-based analysis has been institutionalised since 1995, the 'paradoxical and simultaneous' tendencies toward centralisation and decentralisation have created 'special challenges'. Status of Women Canada (SWC 2001: 77), the agency charged with oversight and implementation, notes that the insistence that 'gender concerns need to be inserted horizontally' (Woodward and Meier 1998: 95) means that 'responsibility for policies that affect women is shared by a large number of federal departments'. While SWC can and does influence other departments, it seldom possesses the direct authority to lead policy development. In addition, as Marian Sawer (2003: 250) points out in relation to the Australian situation, accountability measures focus on 'performance agreements between chief executive officers and ministers', without external scrutiny.

With its internal processes of self-management and self-surveillance, the model produces mainstreaming as an issue of human resource management, seriously reducing the potential for oversight by women's units within government. Equal opportunity personnel in Australia have qualms about moves to integrate equal opportunity into human resource management, which is happening in many Australian universities. As one woman puts it, '[w]e are here to monitor what goes on in human resources as well as elsewhere. If equal opportunity were not a separate unit, I would not be able to get my concerns heard' (Bacchi 2001a). Margitta Edgren (1999: 41) former chair of an advisory group for the Swedish Ministry of Education, offers similar words of warning: 'please note you must have watchdogs. Without them, equality drowns in the stream'. However, as noted earlier, mainstreaming often means the removal of these 'watchdogs'!

Neoliberal regimes are above all committed to facilitating business activities, in the name of producing unfettered markets. To this end, as part of a commitment to reduce 'red tape', Australia's *Public Service Act* removes specific commitments to tackle discrimination, bringing 'the APS under the same anti-discrimination regime that applies to other sections of the industry' (PSMPC 1999). The Howard Federal Government has also introduced a new *Equal Opportunity for Women in the Workplace Act* (1999), reducing the reporting requirements for industry, which existed under the previous *Affirmative Action [Equal Employment Opportunity for Women] Act* (1986). The Explanatory Memorandum (Reith 1999a: 9) described the Bill as 'more business friendly' and as 'moving towards a more business-regulated [i.e. regulated by business] approach'. A Ministerial press release on 16 December 1999 stated that: '[t]here will be a new emphasis on a facilitative rather than a punitive approach to compliance' (Reith 1999b). It is difficult to see how mainstreaming can operate effectively given this reduction in oversight of potentially discriminatory behaviours, pursued in the name of self-managed accountability.

In fact, mainstreaming is at times defended and legitimised as a means of *facilitating* market activities. For example, the Ministry for Women's Affairs (MWA 2001) encourages private sector employers to take up gender analysis because it 'enables the private sector to tap into women's markets'. Hence, it reflects 'good business sense': 'Gender analysis improves opportunities for increased sales, innovation, niche marketing and extra productivity'. The emphasis here is explicitly on 'women as customers', a common neoliberal mantra (Shields and Evans 1998: 79-80), rather than on women as a 'protected' equity group. Further, the 'The full picture' (MWA 1996), New Zealand's mainstreaming framework, argues that 'an improved information base and expertise in gender analysis will enhance the business sector's ability to influence government policy'. This marks an explicit shift in the role of government as overseer of fair business practices to facilitator of business enterprise. Mainstreaming's object of analysis is government, not industry. Beveridge et al. (2000: 282) confirm that mainstreaming is not expected to resolve questions regarding relationships between governments and markets. Perhaps this helps explain its ready acceptance in the current political climate.

Mainstreaming, individualism and 'difference'

There is some disagreement as to whether mainstreaming conforms to or contests neoliberalism's individualist premises. There are countervailing factors to consider. Teghtsoonian (2000: 110) notes that the focus on 'identity-based politics' in mainstreaming is at odds with neoliberalism's emphasis on individuals and 'suspicion of identity-based politics'. On the other hand Grace (1997) insists that the focus on women as workers in British Columbia's *Gender lens* , a gender analysis framework introduced in 1993, means precisely a production of women as individuals. The production of women as consumers, as seen in New Zealand's gender analysis framework, strengthens Grace's argument. The models of equality endorsed in different mainstreaming approaches helps to clarify this issue.

Some mainstreaming models, including the New Zealand example, are still working within a narrow understanding of equal opportunity as equal treatment (Verloo 2002: 4). Equal treatment produces members of equity groups as individuals. The argument in this model of equality is that individuals should be judged, not by unsubstantiated generalisations, dubbed 'stereotypes', but by their personal abilities. Within this tradition the American Equal Rights Amendment, which has yet to be ratified, calls for the elimination of 'rigid sex role determinism' and the recognition of 'individual potential' and 'individual self-fulfillment' (Bacchi 1990: 163). There is no tension between this understanding of equal opportunity and a neoliberal emphasis on individual performance. People are to be treated in the same way, regardless of 'difference' produced by group location. 'Different treatment' is deemed to be, by its nature, discrimination. Rees (1998: 34) identifies the limitations of the equal treatment approach, which 'suggests that people should be treated simply as individuals without recognizing the impact of group membership in the allocation of positions and the implications of this for cultural reproduction'.

In Canada, by contrast, equality is given a more comprehensive meaning. There, it has been accepted that the problem of discrimination is *harmful* treatment, not 'different' treatment. This has made it possible to argue that groups designated 'different' might indeed need 'different' and sometimes 'favourable' treatment.[1] In 1985 Judge Rosalie Abella, who headed the 1984 Royal Commission into Equality in Employment, identified the limitations of a formal equal treatment approach:

> There is a difference between treating people equally as we do in civil rights
> and treating people as equals as we do in human rights. For purposes of
> the former, we treat everyone the same; for purposes of the latter, we treat
> them according to their differences. (Abella 1987: 2)

While recognising the progressiveness of this shift from equal treatment, Teresa Rees insists that deciding that groups designated 'different' require 'special treatment' does little to challenge organisational norms, which should be the goal. In her view, mainstreaming builds on and moves beyond the recognition of the relevance of 'difference' to opportunity because it insists that workplace culture must change to accommodate those who are 'different': 'From this perspective, the transformation of institutions becomes the agenda, rather than the continuing attempt to improve women's access and performance within organisations and their hierarchies as they are' (Rees 1998: 41).

We contest this assessment. Despite the declared commitment to culture change, in our view most versions of mainstreaming are shaped by the neoliberal agendas driving globalised economies. In this context, the turn to 'difference' continues to produce women as individuals and, hence, to undermine attempts to deliver substantive gender equality (Guerrina 2003). We develop this argument in the next section.

Gender analysis, difference and advantage

There are many frameworks for gender analysis (March et al. 1999); however, the dominant model used in western democracies and in international organisations is an idealised rational mode based upon a conventional policy development framework. It conceives of policy as a sequence of stages: identifying the issue; defining desired/anticipated outcomes; information gathering; development and analysis of options; communication; evaluation (Women's Bureau 1997). The expressed goal is to ensure that the differential impact of policy on women and men is considered at each stage. To this end sex-disaggregated statistics, focused primarily on women and men's differential location in the labour market, are collected. There is an assumption that, since the goal of policy development is effective and efficient policy, policymakers will recognise the importance of addressing the 'differences' in their target groups, women and men. The goal is to prevent 'policy failure', as the New Zealand Ministry of Women's Affairs (MWA 2001) explains: 'Gender analysis provides a basis for robust analysis of the differences between women's and men's lives, and this removes the possibility of an analysis based on incorrect assumptions and stereotypes'.

The turn to 'gender' is meant to challenge an individualistic focus on biological characteristics. 'Gender' is most often referred to as a social and cultural product. However, the emphasis on sex-disaggregated statistics means that gender tends to get produced as a part of a person rather than as a 'principle of social organization' (see Ferree et al. 1998). As Baden and Goetz (1997: 7) insist,

> 'the gender-disaggregation approach' … tends to a static and reductionist definition of gender (as woman/man) … Bureaucratic requirements for information tend to strip away the political content of information on women's interests and reduce it to a set of needs or gaps, amenable to administrative decisions about the allocation of resources.

Most defenders of mainstreaming locate 'difference' *in* women. For example, there is a tendency to insist that women's ability to procreate be acknowledged as a 'difference' that should be recognised. This position continues to support an ontological view that attaches biological characteristics to human beings, instead of focusing on the politics that privilege some and de-privilege other characteristics. With this ontological position, women continue to be identified as the central problematic in designing policy. This 'distillation of information about women's experiences' is unable to accommodate or validate issues of gender, power and discourses advantaging men (Eveline 1998).

The production of women as 'different' therefore fails to challenge individualist premises. As Bacchi (2001c: 115-116) argues, locating difference in a group or individual fails to recognise the activity involved in allocating or claiming difference. Women are 'different' only if someone says they are, or if they claim to be. A person is 'different' only in relation to someone else. Hence, in order to change the unremarkable norms that advantage men, it is necessary to focus attention on the practices that render women 'different' and 'disadvantaged' (Eveline 1994).

The point here is that mainstreaming models generally remain caught within an epistemological framework which asks only that some attention be paid to women's 'difference'. To this extent the claim to challenge organisational norms is overstated. So long as the focus remains on presumed biological characteristics, a neoliberal argument for freeing up economic arrangements to encourage individual success is uncontested. By contrast, insisting that 'difference' emerges from relationships of power rather than inhering in individuals or in members of particular groups puts those relationships and the factors sustaining them under critical scrutiny.

Significantly, the Netherlands has developed a gender analysis model that focuses on *gender relations* rather than on individual women and men (Verloo and Roggeband 1996). The Dutch model also explicitly addresses the 'structurally unequal power relations between women and men'. This marks a significant advance on models that focus on women's and men's 'differences'. However, as we argue below, even the Dutch model has difficulty putting neoliberal norms in question, due largely to the location of gender analysis as *ex post* and reactive.

According to March et al. (1999: 9), the key distinction between gender analysis frameworks is whether or not they remain 'narrowly applicable to programmes and projects', or whether they are able 'to broaden out and apply to the social organisational contexts'. Dominant frameworks, such as those adopted in Canada, New Zealand and in international organisations, remain within what Naila Kabeer (1994) calls the 'project trap'. This is because they are located as *ex post* forms of analysis which vet or proof existing or proposed policies, to test their impact on women and men. Even in the Netherlands, the Emancipation Impact Assessments (in Dutch EERs) identify the 'potential *effects*' of proposed policies on gender relations (Verloo and Roggeband 1996; emphasis added). The goal in these frameworks is to ask how a proposal or policy can be introduced with fewer negative effects for women. This makes it extremely difficult to put in question the framing principles and objectives of the policy under examination, be these neoliberal or otherwise.

Towards a model of gendering based assessment

In order to challenge this locating of gender analysis as *ex post*, it is necessary to rethink the understanding of policy at work here. In dominant models of gender analysis mainstreaming policy is understood as a 'response' to a 'problem', and as having an 'impact' on people. Two things are missed here. Firstly, the way/s in which policies or policy proposals constitute or give shape to problems is not considered (Bacchi 1999). Secondly, this understanding of policy fails to identify or address the ways in which policies encourage and hence produce particular social relations, including gender relations. Policies do not simply 'impact' on people; they 'create' people. Again, this explains the lack of attention in dominant gender analysis frameworks to the ways in which policies produce women as consumers or as 'individual workers' with goals similar to men, subject positions that fit neoliberal agendas.

The language in several examples of mainstreaming analysis reveals some of these unquestioned neoliberal presumptions. In each case we have highlighted the terms which presage a neoliberal agenda. For example, the World Bank's (2002: 5: fn. 3, emphasis added) 'Case for Mainstreaming Gender' has as a goal a 'less rigid or extreme gender-based division of labour' in order to increase 'female *productive capital*, which has important *pro-growth effects*'. New Zealand's Ministry of Women's Affairs (MWA 2001: 1, emphasis added) offers a gender analysis on retirement income, which accepts as a 'Defined Desired Outcome' the government's aim to 'encourage greater *financial self-reliance* for retired people'. The European Commission's (1998:

17, emphasis added*) Guide to gender impact assessment* takes as axiomatic the goal of 'eliminating *labour market rigidities*'. In the Netherlands the *New General Social Assistance Act* (1996) places an emphasis on what is called the '*activating effect*'. The obligation to work, or at least to apply for work, has been extended to lone mothers with children five years old or over. A GIA (Gender Impact Assessment) concluded that for most women the new Act means an improvement. As Plantenga (2000: 9) states, this ignores the absence of a 'national framework for care' to accompany the 'national framework of a general obligation to work'.

In order to create a form of gender analysis mainstreaming which can break out of the 'project trap', we need to be able to critique the frameworks of meaning that underpin policies and to identify how policies produce particular kinds of subjects. To this end, in collaboration with selected government departments in South Australia and Western Australia, we are in the first stages of developing an early intervention strategy we call 'Deep Evaluation', which incorporates an ability to put in question the grounding premises of any proposed or existing policies. The idea behind Deep Evaluation is the need to create a space at the beginning of a policy development process to allow policy analysts to reflect upon the full implications of pursuing a particular policy objective. A Deep Evaluation would include: examining the way/s in which the 'problem' under consideration is represented and with what effects (Bacchi 1999); noting how particular assumptions about contexts underpin the policy; and paying heed to the particular interpretations of key concepts and how these impose certain understandings of the issue/s. A guiding premise is that policy is a 'creative' rather that a 'reactive' process; hence the need to examine how issues are shaped. Operational practices would also be scrutinised, on the assumption that these are intimately related to ways of thinking about the issues under consideration. Under Operational Practices, we identify five issues which require scrutiny: i) location of responsibility for implementation; ii) methods of analysis; iii) resource allocation; iv) terms of evaluation; and v) training.

Deep Evaluation can be applied in any policy area. It has as its goal widening the space to consider policy alternatives, in the process empowering policy activists and equity practitioners. It rests on the assumption that many involved in policy formulation and implementation want to do more than participate in a technocratic exercise, but need ways to insist that other forms of analysis are a legitimate part of their mandate.

The insights generated through Deep Evaluation would lead to the development of a different form of gender analysis. This form of analysis would encourage reflection on the ways in which 'problems' and 'contexts' are represented in specific policy projects, encouraging scrutiny of important developments in trade and commerce, instead of accepting these as given or inevitable. It would incorporate an understanding of policy as 'creative', and of policy as *producing* gender. Hence, while sex-disaggregated statistics would remain useful, there would need to be a much closer focus on the terms of a policy to discern any gender*ing* effects it might have. The ultimate goal of our collaboration with select agencies in WA and SA is the production of a gender analysis framework, which we intend to call Gender*ing* Based Assessment, capable of capturing this dynamic. Importantly, we believe that it should not be assumed that 'one size fits all' in the development of such a gender analysis framework. Rather, we believe it is crucial to the success of the project that select staff with knowledge and expertise in the functions and culture of particular government departments take a high degree of ownership in the refining and testing of the model.[2]

We locate our initiatives – Deep Evaluation and Gendering Based Assessment – alongside those of other feminists who wish to overcome the limitations of current gender analysis frameworks and to make mainstreaming more effective. Usefully, the Council of Europe (1998: 21-23) suggests that gender analysis be considered only a part of mainstreaming, and that certain prerequisites are needed to make mainstreaming work. These include: political will, specific gender equality policy, statistics, comprehensive knowledge of gender relations, knowledge of the administration , necessary funds and human resources, and participation of women in political and public life and in decision-making processes (see also Mackay and Bilton 2000: 1). As a way forward, Kathleen Staudt (2003) and Verloo (2002: 8) recommend that specific equality objectives be identified in mainstreaming proposals. According to Verloo, it is this 'absence of precise objectives on reduced gender inequalities' which allows the treatment of gender to be 'easily located within, and then be subject to, other policy goals, such as employment creation, economic growth or poverty reduction'. Staudt and Verloo also emphasise the importance of community participation as a way of freeing policy analysts from the limitations imposed by their 'inside government' positioning (see also Sharp and Broomhill 2002). These are important directions to pursue. Yet taking those directions, we suggest, will be more successful if policymakers formalise the need for conceptual analysis in policy design, accomplished through Deep Evaluation and Gender*ing* Based Assessment.

Conclusion

According to True and Mintrom (2001) the proliferation of state bureaucracies for gender mainstreaming offers an example of 'policy diffusion', driven mainly by transnational networks composed largely of non-state actors (notably women's international nongovernmental organisations and the United Nations). There is no doubt that women, who are often feminist policy activists, have played key roles in disseminating mainstreaming. It is naïve, however, to celebrate these efforts if they lead us to ignore the contested terrain on which gender mainstreaming is played out. As outlined in this paper, we believe that it is important to consider the reasons particular versions and certain parts of feminist mainstreaming agendas have been taken up, while others are ignored. In our view this politics of appropriation occurs because existing versions of mainstreaming are crafted to fit neoliberal administrative models. They strengthen the political arm of the state and facilitate business activities. Furthermore, they rest on understandings of equality which minimise structural change. Finally, because gender analysis remains an *ex post* exercise in these models, neoliberal policy parameters remain hegemonic.

Debates about relationships between feminists and the state – to what extent they have influence, or are co-opted – are long-standing (Franzway 1989). With Pringle and Watson (1992) our analysis conceptualises the state as plural sites of contestation. Feminists work with, through and against dominant normative agendas. Hence, their successes and the limitations on their successes cannot be understood without looking beyond the formal installation of policy machineries. Along related lines, proposals to increase the effectiveness and responsiveness of these machineries need to focus on altering conventional forms of implementation and evaluation. We offer Deep Evaluation and Gendering Based Assessment as measures to encourage scrutiny of broad policy objectives and to draw attention to the ways in which policy shapes subjects/subjectivities and social relations. These forms of *ex ante* policy analysis are necessary, in our view, to contest the neoliberal premises that currently infiltrate and constrain gender analysis and mainstreaming.

Notes

1. Bacchi (2004) usefully contests the construction of positive/affirmative action as 'favourable' or 'preferential treatment'.

2. An example here is the model developed by Eveline and Harwood (2002) in a current Linkage project with the Western Australian Police Service. That model, called 'companionate leadership' (Booth and Eveline 2002), is proving successful in building a team who 'owns' the organisational responsibility for designing and implementing their collaboratively chosen projects.

References

(Websites valid as of publication date)

Abella, R. 1987. *Employment equity – implications for industrial relations*. Industrial Relations Centre reprint series no. 73. Kingston: Queen's University.

Bacchi, C. 1990. *Same difference: Feminism and sexual difference*. Sydney: Allen & Unwin.

Bacchi, C. 1999. *Women, policy and politics: The construction of policy problems*. London: Sage.

Bacchi, C. 2000. 'The seesaw effect: Down goes affirmative action, up comes workplace diversity', *Journal of Interdisciplinary Gender Studies* 5 (2): 64-83. Special issue: *Gender and Workplace Relations*.

Bacchi, C. 2001a. 'Managing equity: Mainstreaming and "diversity" in Australian universities', in Brooks, A. and Mackinnon, A. (eds) *Gender and the restructured university: Changing management and culture in higher education*. Buckingham: Open University Press.

Bacchi, C. 2001b. 'Gender mainstreaming: A new vision, more of the same, or backlash?' *Dialogue: Academy of the Social Sciences* 20: 16-20.

Bacchi, C. 2001c. 'Dealing with "difference": Beyond "multiple subjectivities"', in Nursey-Bray, P. and Bacchi, C. (eds) *Left directions: Is there a third way?* Perth: University of Western Australia Press.

Bacchi, C. 2004. 'Policy and discourse: Challenging the construction of affirmative action as preferential treatment', *Journal of European Public Policy* 11 (1): 128-146.

Baden, S. and Goetz, A.M. 1997. 'Who needs [sex] when you can have [gender]? Conflicting discourse on gender at Beijing', *Feminist Review* 56: 3-25.

Beveridge, F., Nott, S., and Stephen, K. 2000. 'Moving forward with mainstreaming', in Beveridge, F., Nott, S., and Stephen, K. (eds) *Making women count: Integrating women into law and policy-making*. Aldershot: Ashgate.

Blackmore, J. and Sachs, J. 2001. 'Women leaders in the restructured university', in Brooks, A. and Mackinnon, A. (eds) *Gender and the restructured university*. Buckingham: Society for Research into Higher Education and Open University Press.

Blackmore, J. and Sachs, J. 2003. '"Zealotry or nostalgic regret"? Women leaders in technical and further education in Australia: Agents of change, entrepreneurial educators or corporate citizens?', *Gender, Work and Organization* 10 (4): 478-503.

Booth, M. and Eveline, J. 2002. 'Gender and sexuality in discourses of managerial control', *Gender, Work and Organization* 9 (5): 556-578.

Buhrs, T. 2002. 'New Zealand's capacity for green planning: A political-institutional assessment and analysis', *Political Science* 54 (1): 27-46.

Chant, S. and Gutmann, M. 2000. *Mainstreaming men into gender and development: Debates, reflections, and experiences.* GB: Oxfam.

Council of Europe. 1998. *Conceptual framework, methodology and presentation of good practices: Final report of activities of the group of specialists on mainstreaming* [EG-S-MS (98) 2]. Strasbourg. <coe.int/t/e/human_rights/equality/02._gender_mainstreaming/100_EG-S-MS%281998%292rev.asp#TopOfPage>accessed 22 October 2009.

Currie, J., Thiele, B., and Harris, P. 2002. *Gendered universities in globalized economies.* Lanham, MD: Lexington Books.

Edgren, M. 1999. 'Parliament and government actions to promote gender equality in higher education in Sweden', in Fogelberg, P., Hearn, J., Husu, L. and Mankkined, T. (eds) *Hard work in the academy: Research and interventions on gender inequalities in higher education.* Yliopistopaino, Helsinki: Helsinki University Press.

Eisenstein, H. 1996. *Inside agitators: Australian femocrats and the state.* Philadelphia: Temple University Press.

European Commission. 1998. *A guide to gender impact assessment. Employment & social affairs, equality between women and men.* Luxembourg: Office for Official Publications of the European Commission.

Eveline, J. 1994. 'The politics of advantage'. *Australian Feminist Studies.* Special issue: *Women and citizenship*, 19 (Autumn): 129-154.

Eveline, J. 1998. 'Heavy, dirty and limp stories: Male advantage at work', in Gatens, M. and Mackinnon, A. (eds) *Gender and institutions: Welfare, work and citizenship.* Cambridge: Cambridge University Press.

Eveline, J. 2004. *Ivory basement leadership: Power and invisibility in the changing university.* Nedlands, WA: UWA Press.

Eveline, J. and Harwood, S. 2002. 'Policing the margins of collaborative leadership: Gender and culture change in the WA Police Service', 11th International Women in Leadership Conference, Churchlands Campus, ECU, 26-28 November.

Ferree, M., Lorber, J. and Hess, B.B. 1998. *Revisioning gender.* London: Sage.

Franzway, S., Court, D. and Connell, R.W. 1989. *Staking a claim: Feminism, bureaucracy and the state.* Cambridge: Polity Press.

Grace, J. 1997. 'Sending mixed messages: Gender-based analysis and the "status of women", *Canadian Public Administration* 40 (4): 582-598.

Guerrina, R. 2003. 'Gender, mainstreaming and the EU Charter of Fundamental Rights', *Policy, Organisation and Society* 22 (1): 97-115.

Hughes, O. 1998. *Public management and administration: An introduction.* Macmillan Education: South Melbourne.

Kabeer, N. 1994. 'Gender-aware policy and planning: A social-relations perspective', in Macdonald, M. (ed.) *Gender planning in development agencies: Meeting the challenge*. Oxford: Oxfam.

Kemp, D. 1999. 'A new act for a new century: Address to mark the commencement of the *Public Service Act 1999*'. <apsc.gov.au/minister/kemp21299.htm> accessed 1 November 2009.

Levy, C., Taher, N. and Vouhe, C. 2000. 'Addressing men and masculinities in GAD', *IDS Bulletin* 31 (2): 86-98.

McEachern, D. 1995. 'Business power and the politics of industrial relations reform', in Hunt, I. and Provis, C. (eds) *The new industrial relations in Australia*. Sydney: Federation Press.

Mackay, F. and Bilton, K. 2000. *Learning from experience: Lessons in mainstreaming equal opportunities*. University of Edinburgh: Governance of Scotland Forum.

March, C., Smyth, I. and Mukhopadhyay, M. 1999. *A guide to gender-analysis frameworks*. Oxford: Oxfam.

Marginson, S. 2001. 'Research as a managed economy: The costs', in Coady, T. (ed.) *Why universities matter*. Sydney: Allen & Unwin.

MWA (Ministry of Women's Affairs) New Zealand. 1996. 'The full picture: Guidelines for gender analysis. Te Tirohanga Whanui: Nga aratohu mo nga rereketanga ira tangata'. Wellington: The Ministry of Women's Affairs.

MWA (Ministry of Women's Affairs) New Zealand. 2001. *Using gender analysis to improve the quality of policy advice*. Auckland: MWA.

Osborne, D. and Gaebler, T. 1992. *Reinventing government: How the entrepreneurial spirit is transforming the public sector*. New York: Plume.

Plantenga, J. 2000. *Gender impact assessment and the employment strategy: The case of the Netherlands*. External report commissioned and presented to the European Commission. <mbs.ac.uk/research/europeanemployment/projects/gendersocial/documents/GIA_NL.pdf> accessed 22 October 2009.

Pringle, R., and Watson, S. 1992. '"Women's interests" and the post-structuralist state', in Barrett, M. and Phillips, A. (eds) *Destabilising theory: Contemporary feminist debates*. Cambridge: Polity Press.

PSMPC (Public Service and Merit Protection Commission). 1999. Advice no. 22: Discrimination in APS Employment'. Canberra: PSMPC.

Pusey, M. 1991. *Economic rationalism in Canberra: A nation-building state changes its mind*. New York: Cambridge University Press.

Ramsay, E. 1995. 'The National Framework for Institutional Equity in Australian Higher Education – current achievements and future possibilities'. Paper presented to the Second National Conference on Equity and Access in Tertiary Education. Melbourne, 3-7 July.

Rees, T. 1998. *Mainstreaming equality in the European Union: Education, training and labour market policies*. London: Routledge.

Reith, P. 1996. 'Towards a best practice Australian Public Service'. Discussion Paper. Canberra: Commonwealth Government Printer.

Reith, P. 1999a. 'Equal Opportunity for Women in the Workplace Amendment Bill 1999: Explanatory memorandum'. Canberra: Commonwealth Government Printer.

Reith, P. 1999b. Media release. December 16, 1999. < dewrsb.gov.au/ministers/reith/speeches/1999/december16.htm> Website valid in 2003. For alternative reference see Australian Government 2001. *1998 Review of the Affirmative Action (Equal Employment Opportunity for Women) Act 1986.* Canberra: Equal Opportunity for Women in the Workplace Agency. <eowa.gov.au/About_EOWA/Overview_of_the_Act/Review_of_the_Act.asp> accessed 9 November 2009.

Riggs, L. 1999. 'Establishing a cooperative workplace relations culture based on consultation and communication', in *Building the foundation: APS values at work.* Conference proceedings. Canberra: Public Service and Merit Protection Commission.

Sawer, M. 2003. 'The life and times of women's policy machinery in Australia', in Rai, S.M. (ed.) *Mainstreaming gender, democratizing the state? Institutional mechanisms for the advancement of women.* Manchester: Manchester University Press.

Sharp, R. and Broomhill, R. 2002. 'Budgeting for equality: The Australian experience', *Feminist Economics* 8 (1): 25-47.

Shields, J. and Evans, B.M. 1998. *Shrinking the state: Globalization and public administration 'reform'.* Halifax: Fernwood Publishing.

Staudt, Kathleen. 2003. 'Gender mainstreaming: Conceptual links to institutional machineries', in Rai, S.M. (ed.) *Mainstreaming gender, democratizing the state: Institutional mechanisms for the advancement of women.* Manchester: Manchester University Press.

SWC (Status of Women Canada). 2001. *Canadian experience in gender mainstreaming 2001.* Ottawa: Gender-Based Analysis Directorate (GBA), Status of Women Canada.

Teicher, J. and Barton, R. 2002. 'The vanishing public sector', in Teicher, J., Holland, P. and Gough, R. (eds) *Employee relations management: Australia in a global context.* Frenchs Forest, NSW: Prentice Hall.

Teghtsoonian, K. 2000. 'Gendering policy analysis in the Government of British Columbia: Strategies, possibilities, and constraints', *Studies in Political Economy* 61: 105-127.

Teghtsoonian, K. 2003a. Gender analysis mainstreaming in Aotearoa/ New Zealand. Paper presented at the ECPR Joint Sessions, Edinburgh.

Teghtsoonian, K. 2003b. 'W(h)ither women's equality? Neoliberalism, institutional change and public policy in British Columbia', *Policy, Organisation and Society* 22 (1): 26-47.

Teghtsoonian, K. 2004. 'Neoliberalism and gender analysis mainstreaming in Aotearoa/ New Zealand', *Australian Journal of Political Science* 39 (2): 267-84.

True, J. and Mintrom, M. 2001. 'Transnational networks and policy diffusion: The case of gender mainstreaming', *International Studies Quarterly* 45: 27-57.

Verloo, M. 2002. 'The development of gender mainstreaming as a political concept for Europe'. Paper presented at the Conference on Gender Learning, Leipzig, 6-8 September.

Verloo, M. and Roggeband, C. 1996. 'Gender impact assessment: The development of a new instrument in the Netherlands', *Impact Assessment* 14 (1): 3-21.

Women's Bureau, Strategic Policy Branch. 1997. *Gender-based analysis backgrounder*. Ottawa: Women's Bureau.

Woodward, A. 2001. 'Gender mainstreaming in European policy: Innovation or deception?' Discussion paper FS 101-103. Wissenschafftszentrum Berlin Fur Sozialforschung.

Woodward, A.E. and Meier. P. 1998. 'Gender impact assessment: A new approach to changing policies and contents of citizenship?', in Ferreira, V., Tavares, T. and Portugal, S. (eds.) *Shifting bonds, shifting bounds: Women, mobility and citizenship in Europe*. Oeiras: Celta Editoria.

World Bank. 2002. 'Integrating gender into the World Bank's Work: A strategy for action'. <siteresources. worldbank.org/INTGENDER/Resources/strategypaper.pdf> accessed 21 October 2009.

3

Gender analysis and social change: Testing the water

CAROL BACCHI, JOAN EVELINE, JENNIFER BINNS,
CATHERINE MACKENZIE AND SUSAN HARWOOD

Introduction: Carol Bacchi and Joan Eveline

The title to this chapter indicates the major goal of the Gender Analysis Project: to identify the factors that could create gender analysis as a long-term process of emergent changes to the asymmetrical power relations between women and men. The sub-title, 'testing the water', indicates that it was written in the early stages of the project. However, it is important to note that the papers are not strictly chronological in their production. The Chief Investigators (Bacchi and Eveline) took turns as 'lead authors' and Chapter 4, with Eveline the lead author, was actually completed before this chapter, with Bacchi the chief author. Insights from Chapter 4 are therefore incorporated in this chapter. The resultant analysis represents a cross-fertilisation of ideas, as is the nature of collaboration.

The chapter emphasises the importance of involving policy workers actively in practising gender analysis (that is, in applying gender analysis guidelines), a significant learning outcome for the project (Chapter 12). We also suggest that it is useful to conceptualise and to talk about social change in a different way, as the unpredictable effect of complex and continuous processes, occurring 'somewhere in the middle' and therefore always involving 'unfinished business' (see Introduction; see also the discussion of the 'rhizomatic' in Chapter 6). This approach directs attention to the everyday work practices that reproduce gendering as an always-incomplete relation of inequality. In this understanding gender is not an attribute of a person; rather, a wide range of social and institutional practices, including policy practices, produce gendered people, 'women' and 'men', and also usually conceal heteronormative, racist, class and 'ablest' assumptions.

The specific contexts in Western Australia and South Australia affected the ways in which the Gender Analysis Project proceeded. At the time of commencement (late 2004) several of the agencies in Western Australia were already exploring a form of gender analysis, based on joint work done by the research partners. This prior work meant that a body of policy actors was available to participate readily in working groups. In South Australia, by contrast, the first stage of the project involved introductory presentations to representatives from select agencies, which had indicated a desire to participate in the project. In both states, representatives were asked to test and evaluate guidelines (in booklet form) based on either the Canadian ('differences') or Netherlands ('gender relations') model (Chapter 1).

The testing of selected gender analysis frameworks 'on the ground' revealed that such frameworks are not static; rather, they are malleable and subject to continual political pressures, reflecting the changing contexts in which they operate. Importantly, in Western Australia, the space and time to discuss and debate the meaning and usefulness of the project and the concepts upon which it relied (for example, 'gender') proved to be more important in changing hearts and minds than the form or framework of gender analysis introduced (that is, 'differences' approach or 'gender relations' framework). Through these discussions, the need to challenge the fundamental precepts in policy proposals that were already gendering in their effects became clear to those who used the gender analysis, as did the difficulty of attempting this form of intervention, given the pervasive influence of established bureaucratic conventions in shaping those proposals. For example, time constraints imposed by neoliberal management practices (New Public Management) placed a significant obstacle in the path of proposals to engage further staff and more senior staff in the actual development and implementation of gender analysis procedures, engagement that we consider necessary to recognising the need for gender analysis. Gendered hierarchies in the public sector also determined that the staff most likely to *undertake* the gender analysis procedures (as opposed to *sponsoring them from above*), and who usually gain a more concrete understanding of the need for them, would be women with less institutional influence (Chapter 12).

The chapter notes difficulties surrounding the meaning and usefulness of 'gender' as a concept, a topic highlighted in Chapter 4. It also begins to explore the learning experienced by researchers in their encounter with Aboriginal approaches to gender (Chapters 9, 10 and 13).

Abstract

This paper uses preliminary findings from an ARC-funded Linkage grant to speculate on the requirements for producing gender analysis as a change process. Gender analysis, commonly associated with gender mainstreaming, is a methodology aimed at ensuring that all projects, programs and policies are gender-inclusive and gender-sensitive. In the Linkage study existing models of gender analysis taken from Canada and the Netherlands are being tested for their usefulness in selected agencies in South Australia and Western Australia. The goal is to design gender analysis processes appropriate to specific Australian contexts. This paper reflects on the challenges and obstacles encountered in the project to date. It focuses in particular on the importance of creating space for extended debate and discussion of the concepts and issues relevant to gender equality and social change. The authors describe this space as 'somewhere in the middle'.

Introduction

In many countries and in many international organisations forms of gender analysis are being introduced as part of a new approach to gender equality, commonly described as gender mainstreaming. Gender analysis is the generic term describing a process or a set of processes for analysing policies, existing or in a formative stage, to encourage the development of gender inclusivity and gender sensitivity.

There are several gender analysis frameworks, which according to March, Smyth and Mukhopadhyay (1999), differ in their potential to produce meaningful social change. As part of a Linkage Project funded by the Australian Research Council in December 2004, the authors have selected two frameworks, which we label the Canadian model and the Netherlands model, for trial in selected public sector agencies in South Australia and Western Australia. The overall goal is to develop processes of gender analysis appropriate to specific Australian contexts.

In this paper we elaborate the shape of the project and offer, on the basis of preliminary observations, some general comments on the possibilities and limitations of gender analysis as a change process. We will focus on some of the blockages we have encountered and speculate about ways to intervene to reduce the impact of these blockages. In the process we will introduce some innovative ideas about the necessarily partial, messy and unfinished character of change processes (Eveline 2005) and how they circumscribe policy processes (Ailwood 2003).

Background

Gender mainstreaming is the term used increasingly in Europe, in some other countries and in major international organisations, such as the ILO and the World Bank, to describe a new approach to achieving gender equality. Its appearance in Australia is more recent. We refer here to the identification of mainstreaming by Pru Goward (2004), Australia's Federal Sex Discriminations Commissioner, as the Howard Liberal Government's preferred approach to gender equity.[1] Forms of gender analysis, systematic procedures to detect gender bias in policies, are offered as methods to achieve mainstreaming.

Theoretically gender mainstreaming and gender analysis reflect a commitment to institutionalise gender equality concerns throughout the whole organisation, instead of leaving these matters to specialist equal opportunity units, which tend to be marginalised from decision-making. The argument here is that isolating gender equity from the mainstream business of an organisation has meant that women have been encouraged to adopt existing organisational norms and practices, instead of making organisations women-friendly.

The rationale for gender mainstreaming and gender analysis therefore differs from that for equal opportunity. Equal opportunity is a human resources strategy to ensure non-discriminatory employment practices, aimed at guaranteeing women equal access to existing job opportunities. Gender analysis is not about anti-discrimination in the legal sense. That is, it is carried out, not by courts, but by every component of the legal machinery of government. It requires that gender equality becomes a guiding principle in the development of any policy, program or project.

In this understanding, gender analysis is an intervention aimed at identifying policies and laws that can contribute to the elimination of discrimination in the substantive sense. Where equal opportunity is about access, gender analysis is about reshaping organisational structures to ensure that women and men benefit equally. According to Rees (1998: 41) a shift to mainstreaming means that 'the transformation of institutions becomes the agenda, rather than the continuing attempt to improve women's access and performance within organisations and their hierarchies as they are'.

However, there is increasing concern in a number of quarters that mainstreaming does not necessarily deliver on its promise. In some cases those very units dedicated to pursuing equal opportunity have been disbanded on the grounds that they are no longer needed, since gender is now mainstreamed. This same rationale has been used in some cases to attack women-specific measures, including positive/affirmative action. When this is put together with the under-resourcing of the mainstreaming agenda and its low profile in organisations, it is unsurprising that some commentators conclude, with Eleanor Ramsay (1995 in Bacchi 2004: 94) that 'the compelling logic of the mainstreaming argument, that equity matters should become everyone's responsibility in the organisation has distracted attention from the result, whether intended or not, that there is a danger that it will become nobody's'.

The uncertainty surrounding the outcomes of mainstreaming and gender analysis has led to a debate about the reasons for their rapid adoption in many states and organisations. On the one side True and Mintrom (2001) see the proliferation of mainstreaming initiatives as due to intense feminist lobbying, while on the other side some authors, like Young (2000), consider mainstreaming popular in part due to the fit between neoliberal objectives and the way in which mainstreaming understands equality. The authors tend to inhabit a middle ground in this debate, describing the meaning of mainstreaming as contested (Bacchi and Eveline 2003). This position, that in some contexts mainstreaming can be useful in advancing a change agenda while in others it can serve as a rationale for undermining equity, means that it becomes crucial to identify the factors that create gender analysis as part of a meaningful change process. This rationale lies behind the Linkage Project introduced in the next section.

The Linkage Project

This project, won in July 2004 and operative from December 2004, is based on a partnership between: University of Adelaide, Office for Women (SA) and three additional participating agencies (Department of Correctional Services, Department of Health, and the Department of Further Education, Employment, Science and Technology), University of Western Australia, Office for Women's Policy (WA), the Health Department WA and four other participating agencies (Department of Community Development, Department of Local Government and Regional Development, Department of Consumer and Employment Protection, WA Police). The project, funded by an ARC Linkage grant and partner contributions, is at the time of writing (July 2005) mid-way through the first of three years. The first two authors are the Chief Investigators.

The goal of the project is to test two existing models of gender analysis from overseas and, through an iterative methodology of adaptation and modification, to develop gender analysis processes that suit the specific contexts of Western Australia and South Australia. The project is underpinned by a commitment to working with policymakers and implementers to find out what works for them. It involves close engagement with members of participating agencies over the period of the project to produce gender analysis processes that can then be applied across the public sector.

To date we have been involved in two tasks, operating simultaneously:

- an audit of selected policies from the previous five years in each participating agency to test (i) the extent to which they were intended to be gender-inclusive; (ii) the extent to which they are perceived to have fulfilled that goal; and (iii) how gender analysis would have affected the development and implementation of these policies.

- introducing participating agencies to selected gender analysis frameworks (the Canadian and Netherlands models) and working with them to assess the usefulness or limitations of these frameworks when applied to new policy developments or reviews of existing policies.

We selected the Canadian and the Netherlands models for testing because of distinct differences in the forms of gender analysis they espouse. The Canadian model, called Gender Based Analysis, offers a step-by-step approach to policy development, along the lines of the commonly identified rational development model of policymaking. It emphasises the identification of sex-differentiated statistical differences between women and men, and declares as its goal evening out those differences. The model is described as gender-neutral, identifying the ways in which policies can discriminate against either sex.

In the Dutch approach, called EER (translated as Emancipation Impact Assessment), the problem is identified, not as differences between men and women, but as 'unequal power relations between women and men' (Bacchi 2004). Three structures are identified as central to the operation of those unequal relations – the gendered division of labour, the organisation of intimacy and the organisation of citizenship – and two processes are described as pivotal to their reproduction – the distribution of resources and the operation of rules (interpretations or norms) about or connected to gender (Verloo and Roggeband 1996; Verloo 2001). The Dutch approach also includes criteria as the normative grounds for assessing whether a policy development is to be judged positively or negatively: equality, autonomy and pluriformity/diversity.

It is important to note that models of gender analysis are not static and that they reflect the changing contexts within which they operate. For example, Gender Based Analysis in Canada now incorporates what Canadians call *gender* disaggregated data (Status of Women Canada 2001: 59), in addition to *sex* disaggregated data, to draw attention to the need to incorporate qualitative, as well as quantitative, information. In a further change, Canadian implementation tools now recognise that gender-neutrality can mean gender-blindness, with a consequent shift to the terminology of 'gender-integrated' (Eveline and Bacchi 2005). In addition, gender analysis guides in Canada refer increasingly to gender relations alongside mention of specific differences between women and men. A 2001 *Policy training handbook* (Status of Women Canada 2001: 149) specifies that gender means more than biological sex and is a 'relational term referring to the relationship that exists between women and men and also includes the expectations held about characteristics, aptitudes and likely behaviours of women and men'. At the same time the prescribed aim of gender neutrality often produces analyses that are blind to the unequal power relations highlighted in the Dutch model, reflecting a tension between attempts to increase the critical potential of gender analysis while finding ways to encourage its adoption.

On the other side, attempts have been made in the Netherlands to incorporate new dimensions in EER, such as recognising violence as a process and care/community as an additional criterion in assessing degrees of gender justice associated with specific policies. However, to date, these attempts to broaden the analysis have been unsuccessful, due to the current Dutch government's right-of-centre ideology (Roggeband and Verloo 2005). Nor are the guidelines always applied as they read. For example, in the Netherlands the structure called 'the organisation of intimacy' is seldom included in gender impact assessments because it is considered to be too confrontational. Roggeband and Verloo (2005: 330) report that to date assessment reports focus mainly on the relationship between family responsibilities and paid employment, avoiding the more contentious discussion around sexuality, personal relationships and reproduction.

These examples illustrate that gender analysis strategies are open-ended, malleable and subject to continual political pressures. Rather than static frameworks it is appropriate to envisage them as fields of contestation in a continuing quest for gender justice. This theme is pursued later in the discussion of social change as 'unfinished business'.

Responsiveness to context has meant that the tools imported from Canada and the Netherlands for trial in SA and WA have already been modified in significant ways. In South Australia, for example, eight to ten page toolkits for both the Canadian and the Dutch approaches have been designed and distributed as guides to implementation. However, the guidelines have been modified to reflect the views and suggestions of groups of Indigenous women. In South Australia two agencies are trialling the Canadian model and one, the Netherlands model. In Western Australia, by contrast, the two models have been introduced simultaneously to participating agencies and in place of toolkits, training modules have been produced, coupled with intensive training development sessions. In the WA method of implementation the researchers work closely with the participating agencies, assessing and developing specified projects in both inter-agency development sessions and intra-agency advisory meetings, reflecting the emphasis in the WA Office for Women's Policy on the need for organisational reflexivity as well as new whole-of-government criteria for policy developments. These developments indicate the necessarily fluid character of the Linkage Project and of gender analysis itself.

The following section reflects our experiences to date based on ongoing interactions with participating agencies in both the audit of previous policies and in the trial of gender analysis processes. Three themes have been selected to organise the material: 1) perceptions of influence and the power to make change; 2) perceptions of gender equality and the possibility or need for change; 3) structural impediments to change. In the last section we build upon these themes to theorise the complex and unfinished nature of the change agenda and to offer suggestions for interventions aimed at expanding the potential of gender analysis to improve the lives of diverse groups of women and men.

Insights from the coalface

Preamble

It is important to identify the participants in the interactions described below. On the one side are the Chief Investigators, their teams of Research Associates and some public sector equality personnel (see lists of names in Appendix). On the other side are selected members of specific public sector agencies. In the analysis that follows, the names of these members and the agencies to which they belong have not been used in order to preserve anonymity.

Theme 1: Perceptions of influence and the power to make change

In early discussions about the possibility of introducing gender analysis many participants expressed the view that the important decisions took place elsewhere, above them. When an attempt was made to reflect upon the usefulness of applying gender analysis to a specific policy it was made clear that specific policies already had a shape, one determined at a higher level of government. The Research Teams were advised to direct their attention to where the decision-making really takes place. At one session in South Australia, for example, it was suggested that members of business groups needed to be educated about gender analysis. In Western Australia, three of the agency project teams initially felt it would be difficult to make progress unless their senior management was given some intensive training. Another WA team saw the key need as finding ways to influence the political agenda through the current minister.

Two issues are raised by these comments. First, there is the impression that attempts to introduce gender analysis 'down the track' will be unable to reshape policies that inherently already have a gendered character. Second, there is the impression that real influence in policymaking lodges elsewhere, outside and above the level of implementation.

The benchmarking/audit exercise confirmed that policies already had a gendered shape by the time policy workers in specific areas had a chance to intervene. For example, the experience in one South Australian agency was that policies and programs were designed for a prototypical man, since men constituted the majority of the group targeted by this department. Women were expected to fit in. In another case 'women' were identified as a target group, but only in an ad hoc fashion. There was no real attempt to consider why women clustered in particular places or were under-represented in some activities. The possibility of shaping a policy to include sensitivity to women's lives *from the outset* appeared to lie outside the field of action of public servants assigned the task of applying gender analysis to policies shaped elsewhere.

March, Smyth and Mukhopadhyay (1999: 49) describe this particular dilemma as the 'project trap'. As they (1999: 9) explain, the key distinction between gender analysis frameworks is whether or not they remain 'narrowly applicable to programmes and projects', or whether they are able 'to broaden out and apply to the social organisational contexts'. The problem here is that gender analysis becomes simply a method designed 'to increase the efficiency of the project or programme' rather than an attempt 'to create more balanced gender relations'. That is, so long as gender analysis is conceived of as a procedure to vet or 'proof' designated policies for uneven impacts on women and men, it becomes difficult to analyse the gender biases inherent in proposals themselves, in the way in which they construct the problem.

This situation confronts proponents of gender analysis who work within neoliberal contexts. Under the cloak of assumed equality, neoliberalism perpetuates a kind of gender blindness that 'disappears' the different (and often unequal) experiences of men and women. Because of this assumed gender-blindness, members of some participating agencies made it clear that it is not quite acceptable to talk the gender talk. The mission, vision, strategic plan and policies – the official texts which, Dorothy Smith (2005) argues, organise people's 'doings' – are couched in gender-neutral terms. The basic premise of gender analysis, that no policy can have neutral effects when the players do not start out as equals, thus flies in the face of neoliberal orthodoxy. The further claim that such policies actually shape gender relations and reinforce gender inequality is even more difficult to mount.

Here we offer an example from the international field to illustrate how neoliberal policies can survive the scrutiny of gender analysis procedures that fail to put basic terms of reference into question (that is, the 'project trap'). The World Bank's (2002: 5, fn. 3) 'Business Case for Mainstreaming Gender' has as a goal a 'less rigid or extreme gender-based division of labor' in order to increase 'female productive capital, which has important pro-growth effects'. Given this objective and an understanding of gender analysis as *vetting* policy proposals for uneven effects, it is difficult to point to the underlying privileging of paid labour in this proposal.

Hence, while women are encouraged to join the labour force alongside men and to accept existing working conditions, the tasks of caring, traditionally assumed by women, are not factored into the equation. As a result women will continue to fill these tasks and, as a consequence, become tied to paid labour as auxiliaries, temporary, part-time and underpaid.

Within this environment, however, it is clear that individual members of public sector agencies find spaces to intervene and reshape, to an extent, the interpretation and implementation of specific policies. We found a good deal of evidence of what Lipsky (1980) calls 'street level bureaucracy'. Public policy, according to Lipsky, is best understood as being made 'in the crowded offices and daily encounters of street level workers' (MacDougall 2000: 125) rather than in the legislature or senior administrations. Discretionary powers and the dual role of welfare support and social control leads Lipsky (1980) to describe mid-level and front-line staff – his 'street-level bureaucrats' – as having such an impact on people's lives that they hold the keys to a 'dimension of citizenship'.

The evidence also fits Ball's (1993) distinction between 'policy as discourse' and 'policy as text'. On one level the parameters for change were established discursively by the dominant paradigm, but, on the ground, individual policy actors found room to manoeuvre, to read and interpret policy texts. As one of the project teams expressed it, within a broad policy framework community agencies have the flexibility to develop services and programs attuned to local patterns of disadvantage. And, the argument goes, because women are the most 'disadvantaged' they are the main beneficiaries of these interventions. In particular, women working in policy areas servicing a predominance of female clientele were thus inclined at times to suggest that they were well tuned to the practices of gender analysis – which they saw as a form of affirmative action for women. Consequently, they felt they had long been applying those practices, although in most cases they admitted they needed to couch those practices in gender-neutral terms. As trust began to build up in the project teams, however, several team members grew more likely to admit the failure and problems of such 'street-level' procedures. The emphasis on training and the intensive time put into this in the Western Australian context produced a consequent growth in awareness, enthusiasm and trust, though this rarely applied to all members of the teams and is vulnerable to being over-run by time demands for other duties and projects (see Theme 3: Structural impediments to change).

Space also exists to exploit neoliberal themes and to attempt to make them work for women, as was made clear in one audit exercise. The current popularity of the need to balance work and family demands, in order to produce a more productive workforce, for example, creates space to draw attention to women's inordinate contribution to care and maintenance of the working population.

There are of course dangers when gender sensitivity 'sneaks in' by the back door in this way, where it operates silently and invisibly under the surface and against the grain of the dominant discourse. For example, the policy officers involved in the policy development around work and family spoke of the surveillance by men's organisations and conservative politicians who were ever ready to condemn what they saw as examples of pro-women/anti-men bias. Aligned to this was the need for constant vigilance to ensure that scarce resources were not diverted into minority programs for men (for example, single fathers) based on a simplistic notion of gender balance. This theme – the 'what about the men?' question – is pursued in the next section.

It is clear from these early exchanges with members of participating agencies that at least some public servants are willing and indeed eager to debate the shape of the policies they are directed to implement. Moreover, it is clear that this degree of openness can increase as the level of trust begins to build in project teams. In this view policy development and implementation need to be conceived as woven together somehow, not as separate exercises. It is certainly clear that gender analysis can produce significant social change only in such an environment; otherwise interventions will remain piecemeal and ad hoc.

It is also clear that, as Larner (2000: 19-20) reminds us, neoliberalism is not of a piece, without fractures. Rather, for Larner, 'contemporary forms of rule are inevitably composite, plural and multi-form'. It follows that the transformation of a policy involves the 'complex linking of various domains of practice, is ongoingly contested, and the result is not a foregone conclusion'. Our experiences with frontline policy workers confirm this insight.

Theme 2: Perceptions of gender and the possibility or need for change

Members from agencies participating in the Linkage Project reflected a variety of views on the *gender question*. Some were whole-heartedly in favour of exploring new ways to achieve gender equality. Others were convinced equality already existed. This distinction did not necessarily break down according to sex. That is, some women and some men could be found on either side of this divide.

The term 'gender' caused a good deal of understandable confusion. Given the tendency, in popular culture, to talk about one's gender as a synonym for biological sex, the meaning of gender (or gendering) as a social process was difficult to establish. At times the Research Teams invoked the 1970s distinction between sex as biology and gender as cultural roles simply to establish gender as an analytical category. The Canadian model, in common with the vast majority of gender analysis frameworks, makes exactly this distinction in a list of definitions in early guides to application (Women's Bureau 1997). Perhaps for this reason, the Canadian model proved more popular among participating agencies as a tool for our testing of gender mainstreaming techniques.

Dissatisfaction with the sex/gender distinction appears in talk about gender relations as a way of bringing men under analysis, alongside women. As noted above, the language of gender relations now appears regularly in Canadian GBA documents. However, it sits alongside the sex as biology versus gender as culture distinction. The Netherlands model is more consistent in its usage of gender relations, explicitly characterising these relations as demonstrating unequal power between women and men.

A good deal is involved in the conception of gender employed in gender analysis frameworks. Elsewhere (Eveline and Bacchi 2005) the authors explore the implications of deploying specific meanings of gender. We argue that using gender as a descriptive rather than as an active and activating concept restricts gender analysis to a balancing exercise and precludes deeper analysis of the factors producing gender inequality. It also encourages a gender-neutral understanding of the problem, in which gendered power relations are ignored, with men at times identified as the 'losers'. To counter that misreading we have suggested viewing gender as a verb. With a focus on gender*ing*, we argue, as 'the always partial, fragmentary and unfinished business of gendering women and men', policy workers can make conceptual links with the premises of gender mainstreaming as an always incomplete *process* since 'it must necessarily be sustained for as long as policy-making endures' (Eveline and Bacchi 2005: 10).

In our early sessions with members of participating agencies, gendered power relations provided a hidden sub-text driving concerns about men onto centre stage.

The subject of men – what about the men? – came up often. Sometimes the question was raised for strategic reasons (Verloo 2001). That is, it was stated that we would never be able to 'sell' gender analysis unless we could show that there was something in it for men. At other times there were suggestions that gender analysis had to be designed to identify when the 'differences' weighed against men.

The solid focus on differences between women and men as a foundational plank for policy analysis and development in Canadian gender analysis allows men to be identified as potential beneficiaries of the approach. There are explicit references to the fact that men can be a disadvantaged group and that gender analysis can help identify this fact (Women's Bureau 1997; Status of Women Canada 1998). The training manual for GBA (Status of Women Canada 2001) outlines how men's needs should be addressed in an even-handed analysis.

By contrast the Netherlands framework does not pretend to be gender-neutral in its application. Gender is understood as a social principle, not as a statistical difference, and men are described as having power over women. At the same time, however, men are explicitly a part of the analysis. That is, the Dutch make it clear that gender analysis does not aim to achieve a women-only perspective in policy; nor is it solely concerned with examining the implications of policy for women. Rather, men are described as an important part of a gender analysis approach for the reason Lansky (2001: 86, emphasis in original) identifies: we need a focus not only on women (or on men) but on 'what really goes on when women *and* men live together in families and communities'.

Here it is interesting to observe that a focus on sex-disaggregated statistics, characteristic of the Canadian approach, could and often did lead to an awareness of asymmetrical power relations between women and men. In the Western Australian context, for example, both the Canadian and Netherlands models led to discussions of unequal power. It all depended on the questions asked. Discussion and group work proved more important in achieving awareness of the asymmetrical power relations between women and men than the particular framework adopted (i.e. Canadian or Dutch). This outcome points to the importance, once again, of bridging the existing chasm between policy development and policy implementation, and creating the space for debate and discussion of key concepts among policy workers. The emphasis on training in the WA groups has allowed a concentration on this aspect of the Project.

Competing understandings of equality were enmeshed in discussions of gender. For many, indicators that more women were gaining access to paid labour confirmed that equality had already been achieved. Others agreed that access to paid labour could be taken as a marker of equality, but believed that women still had a way to go. It is fairly common to represent the 'problem' of women's inequality in terms of their labour force participation. Indeed, this is the dominant understanding of gender inequality in western industrialised countries and has been so since the 1960s. The argument here is that equality means equal access to existing institutions and work structures. This understanding of the problem lies behind existing anti-discrimination law and equal employment policies. The problem representation (Bacchi 1999) associated with gender analysis and gender mainstreaming – that organisations, rather than women, need to change – challenges this equal treatment model of equality.

In the early discussions of gender analysis with members of participating agencies, there was recognition by some participants of the limitations of an equal treatment model. Women were identified as one among a number of disadvantaged groups, and where disadvantage was identified, the need for different treatment was accepted. The idea that treating unequals in the same way perpetuates inequality seemed well entrenched. However, the continuing focus on outgroups as 'different' and 'needy' made it difficult to reflect on the advantages that flowed to ingroups from current social relations (Eveline 1994).

Moreover, the need to alter gender roles was raised but only occasionally. More often the focus remained on finding ways to make women's lives easier, to address their needs. For example, on the issue of work/family 'balance', the emphasis remained on 'freeing' more women (and men) to work rather than on getting men to change their behaviours and take up family care responsibilities. The current economic climate affected the ways in which these issues were addressed. It was very difficult to move discussion beyond a focus on women's practical needs to reflect on a more transformative agenda, creating different lives for women (Bacchi 2004: 99).

Diversity issues formed a part of every interaction. For some the whole focus on gender seemed to indicate an inability to incorporate diversity issues. It looked like a 'women only' approach, yet again. This issue is clearly critical for feminists elsewhere. Canadian Gender Based Analysis pays an increasing amount of attention to 'the interconnection between gender and other patterns of social division such as race, ethnic origin, disability' (Status of Women Canada 2001: 20) and is particularly sensitive to the position of Native women. The New Zealand model consistently pays heed to the specific needs of Maori women (Cabinet Office Circular 2002: 5; Teghtsoonian 2004). The challenge becomes finding ways to theorise multiple subjectivities under the rubric 'gender'. Hill Collins' (1999: 263) 'logic of intersectionality', which redefines gender as 'a constellation of ideas and social practices that are historically situated within and that mutually construct multiple systems of oppression', provides a language to negotiate this challenging terrain.

Practical outcomes of these negotiations are indicated in some additions to the South Australian toolkits. For example the term 'cultural analysis' has been added to broaden the gender-based framework. The revised toolkits also specified that Aboriginal women are not one homogeneous group and that 'Aboriginal women's concerns regarding equity are most often driven, not by the desire for equality with men, but by community based issues and fundamental human rights' (Office for Women and The University of Adelaide 2005: 6-8).

In Western Australia a policy audit of the Local Government Electoral Strategy, designed to encourage more eligible voters to enrol, vote and stand for local government, showed some intriguing developments when an Indigenous team was employed to design and implement the component intended for Aboriginal communities.

In developing their Indigenous policy, the Indigenous Development Officers saw as a primary task the redesign of the original 'high English' document that was used by local government authorities to generate community interest. They intended to develop an approach that would be both culturally sensitive and culturally inclusive. The stated purpose was twofold: to counter stereotypes of white men and women as voters and councillors in local government, and to place such stereotyping within the context of a history of Indigenous oppression. In mainstreaming Aboriginality the Project team positions gender quite differently to the usual form of gender analysis. Rather than a representation of gender as a product of unequal power relations, the emphasis is on how gender might be 'done' as a relation of unremarkable equity within a portrait of Indigenous democracy.

To this end, the project team insisted that the Strategy demonstrate a positive vision of democratic Indigenous participation, in which gender equality was to be taken for granted rather than portrayed as absent. In pictorial representations of the Strategy: participants would be in a circle with no one person shown playing a central role; there would be equal numbers of men and women shown in discussions and making decisions, with children included in discussions; Aboriginality was to be visible, as well as there being some visual uncertainty about the ethnicity of some people. In implementing the Strategy, the Development Officers insisted that an Indigenous woman and a man went together when taking the case for local government involvement into Indigenous communities.

The Development Officers highlight three outcomes of this six-month Strategy: i) a significant rise in Indigenous councillors, almost half of them women; ii) the document developed for Indigenous communities was found to be more user-friendly than 'high English' versions for the general public and has become a template for all subsequent 'marketing' documents in the department; and iii) the department has resolved to mainstream Indigenous issues into all further policy developments.

While the white, western approach to gender analysis tends to highlight inequalities of gender and 'race' in order to rectify them, this Indigenous strategy erased them at the level of textual representation, while insisting on modelling them as relations of fluid equality when presenting policy in action. In this context it became clear to us that we were asking the wrong questions in our policy audit process. For example, our Question 3, 'In what ways *could* a gender perspective have been applied?', was not helpful in this case. Instead we have learned that we may need to ask: 'what is your strategy of doing gender in your community, and how does that relate to policy directions?' Understanding how learning and doing inter-relate is critical to what Dorothy Smith (2005: 5) calls the 'stance of the learner'. As Smith readily acknowledges, when both researcher and participants take up that stance they can gain a view of how their own practices enable power to circulate as a specific form of knowledge.

As the examples above illustrate, a process of give and take, of challenge and compromise, characterised the interchanges between the Research Teams and members of the participating agencies. New ideas emerged and some people shifted position, at least ostensibly. It is this messy, partial and unpredictable exchange we characterise as a change process that does not begin or end in chronological time but operates spatially – 'somewhere in the middle'. Before we pursue this theme it is necessary to confront the very real structural obstacles that block the kinds of interchanges we see as necessary to make gender analysis transformative in its impact.

Theme 3: Structural impediments to change

There is a great deal of good will for the Project among the members who participated in the audit and initial testing of gender analysis frameworks. However, a number of structural factors made it difficult to mobilise that good will.

Resources and time are constant constraints affecting the progress of the Project. Public sector participants seem always to have too much to do and too little time in which to do it. The Research Teams were asked to spell out clearly 'time commitments' for the Project. The words we keep hearing are 'snowed under'.

The pressures of high expectations and demands on human services personnel are experienced internationally, judging by the literature (Deverteuil 2003; Nittoli 2003). There are global influences on institutions and individuals alike that arise from social and economic changes sweeping from western nations into the fourth world (O'Brien and Fairbrother 2000). The growth of managerialism characterised as 'New Public Management' has transformed the public service, bringing marketisation, privatisation, increased competition and casualised workforces for service delivery (Teicher and Barton 2002). This culture of 'busyness' blocks the potential for the kind of change agenda heralded by gender analysis. In addition, organisational restructuring has, for some policymakers, brought about a form of policy paralysis where they feel they cannot begin to look at any policy until the restructuring process is complete and the organisational strategic directions are clear.

For example, it is clear that any model of gender analysis requires a good deal of training and debate, focusing on the conceptual issues raised in the preceding section – meanings of gender, equality, diversity. Training, however, is expensive and time-consuming. It is as yet unclear if this issue will be addressed adequately across the research project as a whole, given the unevenness of funds distribution within the public sector. The tendency to under-fund and hence to marginalise gender-related initiatives highlights the importance of gender responsive budgets. As Rhonda Sharp (2003: 1) points out, 'Many gender equality initiatives are never implemented because they do not form part of the budgetary decision making processes of government'.

In addition there was keen recognition of the importance of community consultation in policymaking. However, yet again it was made clear that short-cuts would always be found, for example, by using the same groups time and again, by consulting only with high-level 'stakeholders' or by having the consultation process at a late stage of policy development in order to meet deadlines.

The fact that governance at the coalface is time-poor and resource-poor created conditions that favour technocratic over democratic approaches to gender analysis. There is a tendency to cling to numbers, things that can be measured, since these are easier to identify and to use in argument. The more complex and sophisticated categories of analysis, associated with the Netherlands model, seem just too hard to deal with under these conditions. The task becomes identifying and introducing organisational features that create the possibility of democratic political practices.

Top-down, bottom-up or somewhere in the middle: Ways forward

In methods of reform a contrast is often drawn between top-down and bottom-up models. In terms of gender analysis some authors believe that the reform needs to be imposed upon those lower down in the chain of command for meaningful change to occur (Roggeband and Verloo 2005). Others focus on the need to cultivate a sense of ownership of reform processes among those asked to implement them (Bacchi and Eveline 2003). Our experience to date identifies a different space, where change is slow, messy and marked by unpredictable connections. Building on a Deleuzian notion of 'rhizomatic assemblage', Eveline (2005: 22) describes this process as 'both paradox and disjunction; disjunctive syntheses can enfold, sprout from or fuse with each other in unpredictable molecular connections'. We call this process 'sprouting from somewhere in the middle'.

Our debt here is not simply to Deleuze but to Spinozist ethology. For Deleuze and Guattari (1987 cited in Eveline 2005: 21), Spinoza offers 'an ethics of the molecular', a rhizomatic form of becoming with 'neither beginning nor end but always a middle ... from which it grows and which it overspills'.

We use these ideas of non-linear, unexpected processes to talk about change among those actively involved in applying gender analysis to specific policies. The interaction and sharing of views in sessions where this has occurred changed hearts and minds. Some of those who had earlier expressed the view that this was all 'old hat' came to appreciate the usefulness of the approach. Some who tentatively questioned the need for equality for women expressed more sympathetic views by the end of the session. These kinds of subtle changes in perceptions express a kind of Deleuzian becoming. In this view, '[a]cts of speaking, writing and thinking are events within life, producing the sense of the world, allowing life to change and become' (Colebrook 2002: 51).

In order to reflect further on the possibility of change through these partial and at times unpredictable interactions it is necessary to reflect on the nature of subjectivity within change processes. We need to pay heed to the shaping impact on subjects of cultural narratives, and the role of policies and forms of work organisation in producing us as particular kinds of subjects. As Colebrook (2002: 47) describes: 'We no longer look at relations among already formed subjects within the law; we need to see the way in which the becoming of law produces a political terrain and the subjects who occupy it'.

Legal, medical and linguistic assemblages shape a rule-based and transcendental subject by attempting to block the mobility and dynamism of thinking and becoming otherwise (Eveline 2005). Yet such blocking is always incomplete. As described above and experienced in our interactions with frontline policy workers, people do not stand outside these forces that then act as constraints. Just as problems are not simply there to be found but are actively assembled through particular assumptions and responses (Bacchi 1999), there is no pre-determined subject of policymaking but rather people engaged in acts of incomplete becoming. Focusing on how images and practices produce subjects assembled through effort, creativity and effect 'allows us to move beyond dupes and false consciousness' (Colebrook 2002: 99). Hence, in the case of gender analysis, calling for new practices in policy formulation, overcoming the divide between development and implementation, stands to create new types of policy workers, with the opportunity for more dynamic and more democratic interactions and interventions.[2]

Policy itself is described as a process of 'uneasy, messy settlements, requiring strategic compromises, resistances and defences' (Ailwood 2003: 29). Moving policy into nuanced discussion at the contested policy site can challenge simplistic understandings of gender and strengthen our analyses of how gender intersects with a range of other factors.

Currently the public sector is driven by deadlines and 'hard' figures. Yet the Project Teams have discovered a keen desire to reshape these working arrangements. And this reworking, we suggest, will open the space to reshape the ways in which policy actors think about what they do and the kinds of policy they produce. The argument here is that, in order to challenge the 'counting culture' that reinforces neoliberal premises about the way the world works, it is necessary to challenge the 'anti-intellectualism' that currently characterises the policy realm (Gilroy 1994: 189).

New tools and frameworks are required to accomplish this task. In other work we have produced interventions with exactly this goal in mind: an approach to policy called 'What's the Problem represented of be?' (Bacchi 1999), and the 'politics of advantage' (Eveline 1994). In this article we use the interactions in the early stages of a demanding change process, introducing gender analysis, to capture the idea of social change as unfinished business, as slow or unpredictably swift, as messy and full of pitfalls, as open and immanent (in the sense of grounded in tacit, ever-flowing experiences which can never be captured in the simplifying practices of language and documentation). We argue further that describing change in exactly this way, as 'unfinished business', creates a culture that empowers policy actors to see themselves as part of the process of policy development and not simply as passive implementers of directives from above. Theoretical interventions of this sort need to be appreciated for the role they play in change processes.

Acknowledgements

We wish to thank the members of participating agencies for their time and assistance with this project. We also wish to acknowledge the Australian Research Council, which funded the project.

Notes

1. The reform approach in Australia doubtless has a longer heritage that this. Australia's Women's Budget Program (1984-1996) is often identified as a precursor to gender analysis. The language of mainstreaming appeared in some Australian universities in the 1990s (Bacchi 2001), while AusAid (1998) referred to gender analysis as part of social analysis as early as 1998. Significantly, the Liberal Government's new direction in Indigenous policy is also being called 'mainstreaming'. This has involved the abolition of ATSIC (Aboriginal and Torres Strait Islander Commission), a national democratically elected body of Indigenous leaders, and handing over funding programs to mainstream departments (Kemp 2005: 29). This example illustrates a central theme in this paper – the contentious nature of mainstreaming initiatives and terminology.

2. Zoe Gill, in the Politics Discipline, University of Adelaide, is currently completing a PhD that examines the subjectivities of policy workers in the field of gender equity and education (see Gill 2006).

References

(Websites valid as of publication date)

Ailwood, J. 2003. 'A national approach to gender equity policy in Australia: Another ending, another opening?' *International Journal of Inclusive Education* 7 (1): 19-32.

AusAid. 1998. *A guide to gender and development.* AusAid. <ausaid.gov.au/publications/pdf/guidetogenderanddevelopment.pdf> accessed 28 October 2009.

Bacchi, C. 1999. *Women, policy and politics: The construction of policy problems.* London: Sage.

Bacchi, C. 2001. 'Managing equity: Mainstreaming and "diversity" in Australian universities', in Brooks, A. and Mackinnon, A. (eds.) *Gender and the restructured university: Changing management and culture in higher education.* Buckingham: Open University Press.

Bacchi, C. 2004. 'Gender/ing impact assessment: Can it be made to work?' *Journal of Interdisciplinary Gender Studies* 9 (2): 93-111.

Bacchi, C. and Eveline, J. 2003. 'Mainstreaming and neoliberalism: A contested relationship', *Policy and Society: Journal of Public, Foreign and Global Policy* 22 (2): 98-111.

Ball, S. 1993. 'What is policy? Texts, trajectories and toolboxes', *Discourse* 13 (2): 9-17.

Cabinet Office Circular. 2002. *Gender analysis: Inclusion of gender implications statement in all submissions to the Cabinet Social Equity Committee.* Ministry of Women's Affairs, New Zealand: CO(02)2.

Colebrook, C. 2002. *Understanding Deleuze.* Sydney, NSW: Allen and Unwin.

Deleuze, G., and Guattari, F. 1987. *A thousand plateaus: Capitalism and schizophrenia.* Trans. B. Massumi. Minneapolis, MN: University of Minnesota Press.

Deverteuil, G. 2003. 'Welfare reform, institutional practices, and service-delivery settings', *Urban Geography* 24 (6): 529-550.

Eveline, J. 1994. 'The politics of advantage', *Australian Feminist Studies.* Special issue: *Women and citizenship* 19 (Autumn): 129-154.

Eveline, J. 2005. 'Woman in the ivory tower: Gendering feminised and masculinised identities', *Journal of Organizational Change Management* 18 (6): 641-658.

Eveline, J. and Bacchi, C. 2005. 'What are we mainstreaming when we mainstream gender?' *International Feminist Journal of Politics* 7 (4): 496-512.

Gill, Z. 2006. 'Discourse, subjectivity and the policy realm: Reconceptualising policy workers as located subjects'. PhD thesis, Politics Discipline, School of History and Politics, University of Adelaide.

Gilroy, P. 1994. 'Foreword', in Gaber, I. and Aldridge, J. (eds.) *In the best interest of the child: Culture, identity and transracial adoption.* London: Free Association Books.

Goward, P. 2004. 'Now everyone can focus on women'. *The Age,* 30 October.

Hill Collins, P. 1999. 'Moving beyond gender: Intersectionality and scientific knowledge', in Ferree, M.M., Lorber, J. and Hess, B.B. (eds.) *Revisioning gender.* Sage: London.

Kemp, M. 2005. 'Struggle for control of Aboriginal revolution'. *The Advertiser,* 5 February.

Lansky, M. 2001. 'Gender, women and all the rest (Part II)', *International Labour Review* 140 (1): 85-115.

Larner, W. 2000. 'Neo-liberalism: Policy, ideology, governmentality', *Studies in Political Economy* 63: 5-25.

Law, I. 1997. 'Modernity, anti-racism and ethnic managerialism', *Policy Studies* 18 (3/4): 189-205.

Lipsky, M. 1980. *Street-level bureaucracy: Dilemmas of the individual in public services.* New York, NY: Russell Sage Foundation.

MacDougall, C. 2000. 'Public policy and physical activity: A South Australian study'. PhD thesis, Department of Public Health, University of Adelaide.

March, C., Smyth, I. and Mukhopadhyay, M. (eds) 1999. A *guide to gender-analysis frameworks.* Oxford: Oxfam.

Nittoli, J. 2003. *The unsolved challenge of system reform: The Condition of the frontline human services workforce.* Baltimore, MD: The Annie E. Casey Foundation.

O'Brien, J. and Fairbrother, P. 2000. 'A changing public sector: Developments at the Commonwealth level', *Australian Journal of Public Administration* 59 (4): 59-66.

Office for Women and University of Adelaide. 2005. *Gender analysis: Implementing the Canadian model.* Adelaide, SA: Office for Women.

Ramsay, E. 1995. 'The National Framework for Institutional Equity in Australian Higher Education – current achievements and future possibilities'. Paper presented to the Second National Conference on Equity and Access in Tertiary Education, Melbourne, 3-7 July.

Rees, T. 1998. *Mainstreaming equality in the European Union: Education, training and labour market policies.* London: Routledge.

Roggeband, C. and Verloo, M. 2005. 'Evaluating gender impact assessment in the Netherlands: A political process approach' ('De emancipatie-effe-crapportage [EER in Nederland geevalueerd 1999-2004] een poltiek-pro-cesbenadering']), *Beledsweterschap* 18 (4): 320-346.

Sharp, R. 2003. *Budgeting for equity: Gender budget initiatives within a framework of performance oriented budgeting.* New York, NY: UNIFEM.

Smith, D. 2005. *Institutional ethnography.* Toronto, ON: AltaMira Press.

Status of Women Canada. 1998. *Gender-based analysis: A guide for policy-making.* Ottawa, ON: Status of Women Canada.

Status of Women Canada. 2001. *Gender-based analysis (GBA) policy training: Participant handbook.* Ottawa, ON: Status of Women Canada.

Teghtsoonian, K. 2004. 'Neoliberalism and gender analysis mainstreaming in Aotearoa/ New Zealand', *Australian Journal of Political Science* 39 (2): 267-284.

Teicher, J., and Barton, R. 2002. 'The vanishing public sector', in Teicher, J., Holland P. and Gough, R. (eds.) *Employee relations management: Australia in a global context.* Frenchs Forest, NSW: Pearson Education Australia.

True, J., and Mintrom, M. 2001. 'Transnational networks and policy diffusion: The case of gender mainstreaming', *International Studies Quarterly* 45: 27-57.

Verloo, M. 2001. 'Another velvet revolution? Gender mainstreaming and the politics of implementation', IWM working paper no. 5/2001. Vienna: IWM.

Verloo, M. and Roggeband, C. 1996. 'Gender impact assessment: The development of a new instrument in the Netherlands', *Impact Assessment* 14 (1): 3-20.

Women's Bureau, Strategic Policy Branch. 1997. *Gender-based analysis backgrounder.* Ottawa, ON: Women's Bureau.

World Bank. 2002. *Integrating gender into the World Bank's work: A strategy for action.* <siteresources. worldbank.org/INTGENDER/Resources/strategypaper.pdf> accessed 21 October 2009.

Young, B. 2000. 'Disciplinary neoliberalism in the European Union and gender politics', *New Political Economy* 5 (1): 77-98.

4

What are we mainstreaming when we mainstream gender?

JOAN EVELINE AND CAROL BACCHI

Introduction: Carol Bacchi and Joan Eveline

This chapter explores the proposition that how gender is conceptualised has implications for the efficacy of gender mainstreaming and gender analysis as change processes. It makes the case that gender is a contested concept, that it can be defined in ways that reproduce male, white, able-bodied privilege, or in other ways that reduce certain inequalities. In particular it develops in some depth our suggestion that both gender analysis and gender mainstreaming be conceptualised as always incomplete, thus 'unfinished business', rather than as fixed categories of analysis. The goal here is to shift attention from the idea that we may 'have' either a gender or a gender mainstreaming policy/program to the continual effort involved in fixing or 'doing' the gendered subject or in giving 'content' (meaning) to gender mainstreaming.

The chapter begins with a brief history of 'gender' as a political concept within feminist theory. It explains how the theorising of masculinities and the growing attention to differences among women put the utility of the concept in dispute, and how the 1970s idea of a sex/gender distinction was found wanting. We make the case that part of the problem with the category 'gender' is the common way in which it is conceptualised as a part of a person rather than as a process that is ongoing, contested and incomplete. Thinking about gender as a verb, or as a gerund (gender*ing*), we suggest, is more likely to capture how gender differentiation is continually 'done' through discursively-mediated institutional and organisational processes, including policymaking. The question we proceed to take up is whether or not gender analysis procedures can be designed to incorporate this understanding of gendering as an unfinished, embodied effect of discourse or whether they are likely to remain trapped by 'categoricalism'.

In this regard, the experience of gender mainstreaming in Canada is salutary. There, we suggest, the frameworks and toolkits used represent gender as something people have (a 'difference'), rather than as a gendering process. Gender analysis therefore is put forward as an attempt to make policies gender-neutral, to 'even up' measurable 'differences' between women and men. As a result it becomes difficult to draw attention to the unequal power relations between women and men. The focus on measurable outcomes in this 'differences' approach, moreover, ignores the ways in which policies are gender*ing* processes, shaping gender relations and embodied subjects.

In the Netherlands model, by contrast, gender is considered to be an attributional process, always involving politics and power, rather than an attribute of a person. As a result there is explicit attention to the inequitable power relations between women and men. There is no pretence to be gender-neutral. Rather, the message is that women's lives will not change unless men's lives change. As in the Canadian model, however, an important lacuna in the Netherlands model is lack of attention to the ways in which policies themselves are gender*ing* processes, a theme explored more fully in Chapter 5.

We conclude that how gender is conceptualised matters politically. It follows that feminists and policymakers ought to be encouraged to engage collaboratively in theoretical conversations about how 'gender', and other concepts (for example, equality, gender equality), are understood (Chapters 9, 10 and 11). Clearly, context will affect what is feasible, both in terms of creating the conditions for these conversations and in determining which meaning of 'gender' will be deemed to be appropriate to specific political circumstances. Nonetheless, the need for ongoing deliberation about the concepts we use and the effects they produce means that, alongside gender mainstreaming, we need to mainstream 'gendering awareness' as a new kind of policy practice, creating the conditions for policy workers to reflect upon and debate contested meanings of gender. We argue that involvement in such practices in turn produces new types of policy workers who recognise policy proposals as constitutive practices that represent 'problems' in particular and possibly limited ways, with effects that need to be carefully considered (Chapters 5 and 11; Gill 2006).

Reference

Gill, Z. 2006. 'Discourse, subjectivity and the policy realm: Reconceptualising policy workers as located subjects'. PhD thesis, Politics Discipline, School of History and Politics, University of Adelaide.

Abstract

In the policies and practices of gender mainstreaming, gender itself is a contested concept. This article examines versions of gender mainstreaming in two countries, focusing on approaches we term the Canadian and Netherlands models. We show how different understandings of gender are attached to different reform approaches, and intimate how particular ways of conceptualising gender inhibit the efficacy of the mainstreaming strategy. In order to increase that effectiveness we suggest that gender mainstreaming models incorporate a view of gender as a verb rather than as a noun, so that the focus is on the processes of gendering rather than on the static category of 'gender'. We make the argument that such a shift could: a) incorporate a feminist ontology of the body; b) align an understanding of gender as an unfinished process with the ways in which those who make and implement policy experience gender mainstreaming as always partial and incomplete.

Introduction

Through the policies and practices of 'gender mainstreaming', the concept of gender is appearing in policy documents in many nations of the developed and developing worlds. Yet the usefulness of gender for feminist theory is currently in dispute, with some theorists suggesting we should abandon it altogether (Moi 2001). Others problematise its over-use. Kasic (2004), for example, coins the term 'over-genderization' for the widespread tendency in academic, policy and activist contexts to ignore women and their needs while naming, and purportedly mainstreaming, gender. Indeed, in both lay and professional contexts, the diversity of gender concepts proliferates to the point where it has come to include even biology (Mitchell 2004: 420). It is also clear that different understandings of gender are attached to different reform approaches. In some cases these understandings reproduce and increase the male, white and able-bodied privilege they seemingly challenge; in others certain inequalities are remedied. In short the meaning of gender is 'contested', along with the utility of the mainstreaming strategy (Bacchi and Eveline 2004). Hence the importance of our question – what are you mainstreaming when you mainstream 'gender'?

The article explores that question in two stages: 1) we review recent debates over gender as a feminist construct to make our case for representing gender as a verb; 2) we examine two quite different models of gender mainstreaming based on developments in two countries (Canada and the Netherlands), drawing some conclusions about the concepts of gender they deploy and what those concepts might mean for translating gender analysis into effective policy practice. Throughout, we suggest it is crucial to recognise the power relations through which problem-formation takes effect.

Given the rapid diffusion of gender mainstreaming approaches we suggest it is particularly important to reflect on how gender itself is being understood. There is a conversation here that needs to occur. Although we propose that feminists and policymakers develop a view of gender as a verb, our goal is to initiate this conversation, not to suggest that every feminist policy network will be able or willing to incorporate the understandings of gender we recommend.

In examining how gender is used in two mainstreaming approaches we highlight the importance of context – what works in one situation may not be possible or may not have the same effects elsewhere. Any tendency to generalise about the appropriateness of a particular approach, therefore, can come unstuck when complex institutional and political factors are taken into account. For example, as Eveline (1994) showed with regard to equal opportunity policy, the ubiquitous phrase 'women's disadvantage' normalises the taboo on speaking of 'men's advantage'. In short, meanings can congeal in ways that perpetuate established forms of seeing, or of representing problems in ways that instantiate the social status quo (Bacchi 1999).

The 'slippery terms of gender'

As a political concept the history of 'gender' can be tracked to the distinction that second wave Anglophone feminism made between biological 'sex' and socially constructed 'gender'. Whereas sex was biological destiny, gender could be changed. The term 'gender' came from grammar, in which words had either a masculine or feminine association. Feminists incorporated gender into political analysis to identify the ways in which masculinity and femininity influenced women's lives. Since then gender has been a wellspring for feminist debate. Referring to that continuing debate Essed et al. (2004: 2) highlight the 'slippery terms of gender'.

By distinguishing sex (as biology) from gender (as social attributes, norms and behaviours) feminists were able to argue that there was no natural basis to the 'caring' expected of women, and to affirm that while women and men may generally be different in physique and reproductive function those differences had no relevance for the opportunities they should be offered and the activities in which they could engage (Mitchell 2004).

The use of gender in the 1960s/70s was attached to notions of stereotypes, socialisation and conditioning. Sex role theory explained any systematic differences in men's and women's behaviours in terms of different social expectations rather than biological factors. While Parsons and Bales (1995) saw a perfect partnership between social pressures for women's 'expressiveness' and men's 'instrumentalism', later theorists saw the socialisation of men and women into sex roles as a deeply damaging process from which both women and men needed liberating (Nichols 1975). Later critiques of sex role theory pointed out how closely it relied on biological premises, with Connell (1987) and Brittan (1989) arguing that it simply adds roles to biology to give us gender.

The goal became offering women more 'challenging' alternatives (for example, non-traditional jobs in mining, building or welding, educational opportunities in engineering, 'hard' sciences or agriculture, or pathways into management). Subsequent programs focused on giving women the trade or managerial qualifications and experiential capabilities to succeed in male fields (Eveline 1995), although it was always women who had to be made to fit the male model (Eveline 1998).

At the same time feminists challenged the feasibility and desirability of women trying to be 'like men' (Ferguson 1984). There were many versions of this critique but they all hinged on some view of women as 'different' (Chodorow 1978; Gilligan 1982) or as 'other' (Irigaray 1985). Later theorists argued that such claims of women's 'difference' sustained a male norm (MacKinnon 1989; Bacchi 1990) and naturalised the power relations by which men and masculinity were treated as the unremarkable standard (Eveline 1994). Others showed how the institutional and organisational arrangements within which women were being asked to compete were left untouched (Cockburn 1991). The 'add women and stir' perspective positioned women as the problem that must be fixed, while relying on an idea of gender as an overlay of social attributes in which bodies did not matter (see critiques in O'Brien 1981; Gatens 1983).

For most of that early theorising, 'gender' was considered a problem only for 'women', with 'the feminine' something they should endeavour to shed, deny or celebrate. That strong association between 'gender' and 'women' was attacked on two fronts: by those who wished to theorise men and masculinity (Collinson and Hearn 1994) and by those who wished to highlight the tendency to essentialise or universalise the category 'woman' (Spelman 1988; Scott 1990).

While some theorists of masculinity were only concerned with what was happening to men (Weeks 1977), or with how feminists were oppressing men (Bly 1990), others focused on how contemporary gender relations were a problem for men and for women (Hearn 1992; Kerfoot and Knights 1996). The most useful of the critiques incorporated the notion of 'hegemonic masculinity' (Carrigan et al. 1985) to show how some men benefited much more than others from the 'gender regime' (Connell 1987) and subsequently placed the emphasis on 'masculinities' in the plural (Connell 1995), in part to avoid the charge of an essentialist view of masculinity.

Also labelled as essentialist was the 'commonality of differences' view of women and their interests, based in the main on women's experiences or potentialities as mothers. The most significant of these critiques focused on the lack of attention to how race, class and sexual preference could constitute very different experiences among women (Spelman 1988). Critics asked what it meant to be a woman, a mother and a worker if, for example, one was Black, Chicano, lesbian or Vietnamese in a white, heterosexist society (Hull et al. 1982; Mohanty 1991; Sandoval 1991; Wishik and Pearce 1991; Bulbeck 1998). Such charges of universalism and ethnocentrism moved the concept of gender from its woman-centric foundations, prompting theoretical and political tensions that remain largely unresolved.

Before long those who used the concept of gender were charged not only with universalising 'women' but also with essentialising 'sex' (Butler 1990). Butler maintained that the sex/gender distinction was unsustainable – it is not that sex shapes gender, but that gender constructs sex. Thus the relation between sex and gender is a purely political one – all that we know about the body occurs at the level of representation. Butler conceptualises gender as 'performative', that is, as the effect of routine, repeated acts that are themselves discursively regulated. Colebrook (2001: 78) agrees with Butler that 'the body is only *thought* after the event of discourse', but argues that Butler's deconstruction technique leaves her on one side only of the presupposed sex/gender division: seeing sex merely as 'the effect of an entirely arbitrary and disembodied representation'. Indeed, based on Colebrook's critique we might argue that Butler's deconstructive method ultimately 'fixes' the very dualism she ostensibly sets out to (dis)solve.

Like Colebrook, Toril Moi (1999) intimates that Butler's theorising has become too abstracted from the body, and indeed that Butler herself remains too tied to the terms of the sex/gender distinction. Yet rather than looking for better ways to challenge that distinction Moi decides that gender theory has no defence against Butler's critique. Consequently, she recommends that feminist and queer theorists should abandon the concept of gender in favour of an account of the 'lived body', drawing on the existential phenomenology of Simone de Beauvoir. Because each person is viewed as a specific body, with distinctive features, capacities and desires, the problem of categoricalism (Connell 1987), in which group identities such as 'gender', 'race', and 'sexual orientation' vie for supremacy in positioning any one individual, is claimed to be overcome.

Iris Marion Young (2002) agrees that Moi's account of the lived body provides a way through the problems of the sex/gender distinction – but only with regard to subjectivity. Young is prepared, therefore, to follow Moi in deleting 'gender' from theories of subjectivity, but she argues for gender as a category of analysis when dealing with women's needs at the level of politics and policy. Because feminist and queer theories are efforts to identify and challenge wrongful harms and injustices, the theorist, in Young's view (2002: 419), cannot do without an account of gender as 'social structures'.

In making her argument about social structures, Young sets up an either/or relation between 'structure' and the 'lived body' and thus falls into the trap that Moi seeks to avoid. In effect, her dualism reinforces the tradition of western philosophy that feminists have rightly critiqued: that the body politic cannot accommodate an account of the body. In her response to Moi, therefore, Young throws the body out with the bathwater. In making her argument for the need to retain a concept of gender as (only) a structure of inequality, she opts for an objectivist and abstract (rather than an embodied) account of gender. The problem, therefore, is that her disembodied account of structure reinforces the subject/object, mind/body dualism of Cartesian philosophy, which suffuses our economic and political systems. While Young may well respond that her framework is designed to overcome the assumed gender-neutrality of those systems, it lacks the insight that Acker (1990) brought to feminist organisational theory – that unless we bring an account of the body into our analysis of how inequalities are structured we can lose sight of the specificities of gender and sexuality that both perpetuate and challenge male dominance.

Young sees Moi's concept of the lived body as lacking the capacity to politicise gendered structures. We take a different view. As we see it, the problem is that Moi's theory suffers most from the idea that feminism *should abandon the concept of gender*. In agreeing with Butler's representationalism Young is led to believe feminist theory can and should separate the body from an account of how those institutions 'do' gender by reproducing gendered bodies. The trouble with both Moi's and Young's accounts is that in one way or another they sustain a notion of both sex and gender as fixed, oppositional categories rather than living, unfinished and uncertain processes.

Hoagland (1988: 224) describes that wish to affix certainty to fluid processes as a tendency among users of the English language, who 'focus more on categories and classifications which define a thing and fix its nature for all time, and are less concerned with processes, movement and change'. Despite Moi's attempt to avoid the fixedness of gender as a category, her terminology of 'lived body' rather than 'living body' evokes finality across an inevitably unending process. Young admits to wanting an account of the objective 'structures' of inequality as a secure basis for a feminist politic. Yet the concept of structure invokes metaphors of solidity and containment that fail to encapsulate the partial and incomplete character of asymmetrical power relations. Perhaps it is not so much a theory of objective 'gender structures' that we need as an account of how gender differentiation is continually 'done' through the implication of bodies in institutional and organisational *processes*, constituting power effects of asymmetries and inequalities.

We would argue that gender, like theory, is not a fixed structure, but a contingent and located social process, with specific effects of power and advantage. Some years ago Kirstie McClure (1992: 365) argued for a rethinking of theory as a verb rather than as a noun, so that theorising could be seen as 'a political practice always and inescapably implicated with power'. We suggest a similar conceptualising of gender – as a verb rather than a noun. As one example, consider the way in which 'gender' as a noun creates problems for diversity issues. As a noun gender assumes fixity, and is 'attached to people', much in the way we do with 'race' and 'disability'. So we focus on 'disabled people', for example, instead of paying heed to the impact of disabling institutions (Fulcher 1989). Viewed as a verb, gender could be seen as an inescapably unfinished gender-*ing* process in which the body both informs and resonates with relations of power and privilege. The question is then: to what extent do we find that *process* understanding of gender in contemporary feminist theory?

The idea of gender as an effortful social and political process is certainly not new. West and Zimmerman (2003), for example, use ethnomethodology in an attempt to highlight how gender is 'done'. Their aim is to demonstrate empirically how gender is accomplished through the disciplining of bodies, actions and language, effecting organisational and institutional arrangements primed to reproduce identifiable categories of 'women' and 'men'. Yet their ethnomethodology, while it encapsulates the processes of gender differentiation, gives no account of why gender should reproduce inequalities except to hint that the asymmetrical outcomes of 'doing gender' permeate all cultures. Moreover, although their idea of 'doing gender' is useful as a way of intimating an ongoing and effortful process, their own process of doing gender promulgates a dualistic view by situating categories of masculine/feminine as universally oppositional and unchangeable in their asymmetry.

For Moira Gatens (1983, 1996), interrogating the body offers possibilities for a non-dualistic interpretation, one which could emphasise the incompleteness of both embodied and political processes and has important implications for a feminist concept of gender. In Gatens' framework a dualistic understanding of sex/gender is problematic on at least two counts: a) it is epistemologically flawed, in that it leaves women's alignment with nature and men's with culture undisturbed; and b) it perpetuates an inadequate ontology of corporeality. While Gatens makes no case for breaking away from an account of gender, she nonetheless wants to rework sex and gender in non-oppositional terms. There is a connection here between male/female bodies and masculinity/femininity, but it is not one that can be explained away with a theory of representation. In other words, the 'representational side is no less problematic than the putative brute givenness of sex' (Colebrook 2001: 83). For example, the biological fact of menstruation becomes in some societies a signifier of femininity as weak, earthy and irrational, but how is that discourse articulated in and through the body given that some women undoubtedly suffer menstrual cramps (Gatens 1983)?

In Gatens' thought the expression or style of gender is always a stylisation of some specific body. The project, then, is to locate intelligence and the emergence of meaning at the level of embodied being, and Gatens draws on theories of immanence and power in Spinoza and Foucault to argue her case. An immanent view of power moves away from the idea that power is something we have or accumulate to the idea of power as a multiplicity of effects through which being and identity is situated and known. Gatens (1996: 149) sees power as expressive of sexual difference through the becoming of a particular quality, developed through regulation and cultivation but always in relation to others. Yet the expressive effects of power are not simply representational, because 'the body is both the locus of thought and that which remains (necessarily) unthought' (Colebrook 2001: 82) – what is said about the body, identity and power is always incomplete, despite continual striving within organised language and cultural formations to 'fix' the truth of any privileged utterance. As Gatens (1996: 183) notes: 'Any plane of organization selects possibles from the plane of immanence and attempts to pass these possibles off as actual – the *only* possible actual'. Thus feminists need to address both the fixed political realities that organise our social possibilities while simultaneously experimenting with the incomplete and scarcely understood micropolitical possibilities that our lived experiences create (Gatens 1996: 178).

Gatens' feminist project is designed to show the inescapable symbiosis between living bodies and the always incomplete meanings they produce. Her theorising demonstrates why our attempts to place 'women' and 'men' in fixed categories will inevitably be inadequate, yet invariably when policy addresses the question of gender that is the prevailing approach. If gender mainstreaming is to avoid categoricalism a feminist analysis of policy needs to find ways of translating feminist theories of bodies-and-politics-in-process into terms that make sense to policymakers.

Our contribution to that project of recognising process is to suggest that feminists and policymakers view gender as a verb rather than as a noun. Such an analysis would focus on the gender*ing* of policy, institutions and organisations, and view gendering as an incomplete and partial process in which bodies and politics are always becoming meaningful. We would argue that theorising gender as an embodied process offers a way of linking the body of feminist writing to the living bodies of women and men.

There are important ramifications here for how an understanding of gender as a verb could inhabit a politic of gender mainstreaming. As we note above, an acknowledged premise of gender mainstreaming is that no policy is gender-neutral. Less openly acknowledged but nonetheless encapsulated in the notion of mainstreaming is the idea that the process of gender analysis of policy has no foreseeable end point – it must necessarily be sustained for as long as policymaking endures. Can we link those premises of gender mainstreaming with the always partial, fragmentary and unfinished business of gendering women and men? Can gender mainstreaming accommodate an understanding of gender as an unfinished and embodied process?

Real world politics

The theoretical developments and contestations over how gender is represented take place in a parallel universe to policy development. Feminists 'at the coal face' encounter a number of challenges: taking on board new and difficult attempts to theorise 'women's condition', and translating these new understandings to policy communities with very different histories.

In this section we use the experiences with gender mainstreaming in Canada and the Netherlands to examine the complexities of these interactions. Our goal is not to suggest that there is a single meaning of gender, which ought to be applied everywhere, but to indicate how specific understandings of gender are tied to particular political agendas which in turn become part of the embodied experiences of women and men.

The Canadian experiment with mainstreaming goes back to the early 1990s. Initial mainstreaming documents (British Columbia 1993; Status of Women Canada, 1997)[1] elaborated the sex/gender distinction commonly accepted in 1960s/70s feminism. However, Canada's experience with sex discrimination law had driven home the limitations of the equal treatment approach that dominated that era. By the mid-1980s Justice Rosalie Abella, who headed the Canadian Commission on Equality in Employment, explained that treating unequals equally simply reinforced inequality (Abella 1984). The initial focus in Canadian gender-based analysis, therefore, is on men's and women's 'differences' and the need to accommodate these to accomplish 'real equality'.

The goal in this approach is to identify 'gender' 'differences' as a base-line for policy development. Hence we see the emphasis on 'gender-disaggregated statistics', presented as a neutral examination of 'socio-economic data broken down by statistics' (Women's Bureau 1997: 22). The emphasis on statistical differences allows policies to focus on the fact that more women are sole parents, for example, or that more women than men are the victims of sexual violence. However, both statistics and the representation of 'differences' also foster an understanding of gender as simply something people *have*, rather than drawing attention to the unequal power relations between women and men. Proposing a policy difference for women and men based on existing differences, then, may simply entrench inequalities.

An example would be a program to improve employment opportunities for those seeking jobs. In one Canadian province, sole supporting mothers were given funds to attend higher education on the grounds that they could couple education with child care and eventually obtain jobs. Men seeking work (whether supporting parents or not) were located in wage-supported enterprises, where they not only obtained a trade training, but gained immediate access to superannuation and sick-leave benefits. The policy of drawing on statistical differences thus exacerbated the existing advantages of financial independence that men statistically hold over women (Status of Women Canada 2001: 32).

The example emphasises a frequently identified dilemma for feminist reformers – addressing women's immediate needs through a differences approach can and often does simply entrench the status quo, by categorising women as 'needy' (Beveridge et al. 2000), or by allowing the asymmetrical relation of power and advantage between women and men to disappear from the analysis (Eveline 1994). This approach can lead to proposals that women's different needs have to be met to allow them to participate in a 'man's' world, as in the case above. At other times it can reinforce the current sexual division of labour – women, it is argued, care for the young and the elderly, and this 'fact' of their 'difference' needs some recognition – again often with consequences similar to the case above. The Canadian response to such inadequacies in the differences approach has been to incorporate into their gender-based analysis a further step that supposedly goes beyond 'gender-specificity', moving the focus away from 'women' to a 'gender-integrated' approach, an analysis 'based on the relational nature of gender differences' (Status of Women Canada 2001: 49). With this approach the represented problem is not that women's difference demands they be treated differently from men but that both women and men are different from each other. Yet the 'relational nature of gender differences' deletes power relations from the analysis, and relies on notions of 'fixed' differences that cannot accommodate an account of gendering processes.

Although Canadian approaches to training policymakers in gender mainstreaming show some understanding that policy itself is an incomplete process (Status of Women Canada 2001), their gender-based assessment (GBA) approach shows no evidence that a process account of *gender* is built into the analysis. The GBA model begins by showing that a gender-neutral framework can be gender-blind (Status of Women Canada 2001: 18), yet because it lacks an account of gendering processes, the model ultimately reinforces what it sets out to challenge.

Revealingly, some of those implementing GBA have been forced to incorporate new materials and frameworks to address the constraints stemming from their lack of process analysis. They do this in two ways. Firstly, GBA makes a distinction between 'practical' and 'strategic' 'needs' (Status of Women Canada 2001: 50). This distinction is an attempt to translate a more sophisticated understanding of 'gender' into policy terms (White 1994: 99). The goal with this intervention is that identified by Jahan (1995), to distinguish between an 'integrationist' and a 'transformative' mainstreaming agenda. In this view it is recognised that both equal treatment – allowing individual women to be 'like men' – and different treatment– compensating women for the consequences of being women – are integrationist. They both leave the status quo with its privileging of masculine norms, and consequently of the men who most closely match those norms, in place. In the Canadian model, however, distinguishing between practical and strategic needs is insufficient to overcome the conceptual problems of their 'differences' approach.

Secondly, and in order to deal with those conceptual problems, Canadian exponents of GBA have developed training which sets policymakers on a course of moving through three successive frameworks. The first framework is what they term 'gender-neutral' – 'assumes that policies affect all people in the same way' (Status of women Canada 2001: 18) and this is critiqued in training sessions for its inability to deal with issues of gender, 'race', cultural difference, ethnicity and disability. The second is 'gender-specific' – 'proactive measures necessary to overcome system bias' (Status of Women Canada 2001: 49) proposed as the way to ensure attention towards women. The third is 'gender-integrated' – 'based on the relational nature of gender differences' (Status of Women Canada 2001: 49), developed as a response to the inequalities that arise or are reinforced through the 'gender-specific' approach. These additional measures create blinkers of their own, however, linked again to their inability to represent the gendering process.

The solid focus on 'differences' as foundational planks for policy analysis and development allows Canadians to include men as potential beneficiaries of the approach. There are explicit references to the fact that men can be a disadvantaged group and that gender analysis can help identify this fact (Women's Bureau 1997; Status of Women Canada, 1997). The training manual for GBA (Status of Women Canada 2001) outlines how men's needs should be addressed in an even-handed gender analysis. One case focuses on secondary school student dropout rates, showing that the dropout rate for boys is twice that of girls, and leading to a policy suggestion that the resources put into supporting young men should be double that set aside for young women. Further gender analysis, however, based not only on sex-disaggregated statistics but also on what the Canadians now call 'gender-disaggregated data'[2] (Citizenship and Immigration Canada 2002: 1) brought to light how young women actually faced a higher degree of 'disadvantage'. Twice as many women as men who drop out end up in the low-waged service economy, three times as many men as women gain jobs in the higher paid primary sector, and wages of the men in the service sector are twice that of women who dropped out at a similar time (Status of Women Canada 2001: 60).

It is clear that the concern for masculinity and men provokes a considerable tension in gender mainstreaming of policy. On the one hand focusing on men's behaviour provides a useful corrective to the entrenched practice of associating 'women' and 'gender'. Similarly, the idea that gender mainstreaming will benefit both women and men proves useful in winning over some men and women who might well oppose an approach that problematises the behaviours and advantages of (some) men. On the other hand, including 'men' in 'gender' occurs in a depoliticised way in many cases, suggesting merely that men too will benefit from gender mainstreaming. Feminists note that this framing often diverts attention to a new high-priority target group, 'men at risk' (Staudt 2003: 49), who represent a very small minority of the population. Levy et al. (2000: 88) attempt to steer a middle way through these troubled waters. They insist that men and masculinity be treated as a core element of a gender mainstreaming methodology, as a way of indicating the power relations of any given context.

Yet an immanent view of power and bodies would caution against seeing power relations as gendering inequalities in ways which invariably favour only men. A further policy example from the Canadian training kit can flesh out this point. The example, a decision about whether to save health insurance funds by making

101

men pay for vasectomies, is useful here since it raises questions of how bodies are themselves implicated in gendering change. In 1986 the Quebec government amended its *Health Act* to include free vasectomies. Women already had free tubal ligations and it was argued that men should have the same benefit. In the ten years after the Act was amended vasectomies rose to 20,000 a year, far exceeding the 12,600 tubal ligations. The GBA training module points out, quite rightly, that there are decided benefits for women and society as a whole in this policy: tubal ligations are a much more serious and expensive procedure and they place the responsibility for family planning on women alone. But because the GBA model sees success purely in terms of fixed and measurable outcomes, there is no mention of the shifting gender relations involved in this higher take-up rate of vasectomies, nor of what that shift might forecast in reshaping corporeal masculinities and the gender identities of both present and future generations of women and men.

Recognising that gender is something that people-as-bodies 'do' through their practices, legislation and relationships with others may help policy people who undertake a gender analysis to see how the policy process has gender effects. Those effects need to be taken into account *before* they reproduce existing inequalities, since the cost of rectifying mistakes can be expensive. A recognition of how gendering is being done could also lead to a better mapping of policies that generate transformative change. A transformative agenda means challenging the norms and practices that produce gender inequalities, by highlighting and intervening in the gender*ing* process of policymaking.

Here the Netherlands model (Verloo and Roggeband 1996; Plantenga 2000) makes an important contribution. It makes the key point that women's lives will not change until men's lives change. The starting place for gender analysis in the Netherlands is 'gender relations', defined as 'structurally unequal power relations between women and men' (Verloo 2000: 61). That framework takes environmental impact assessment (EIA) as its basic guide. The gender mainstreaming methodology is referred to as EER, translated as Emancipation Impact Assessment.

The theoretical framework for Gender Impact Assessment comprises three elements: a) locating the structurally unequal power relations between women and men; b) highlighting the processes or mechanisms that produce and reproduce those unequal power relations; and c) providing criteria for evaluating the data which allow for the inclusion of 'unequal power' – namely equality, autonomy, and diversity/

pluriformity. 'Equality' is defined as equality before the law, or equal treatment in similar circumstances; 'autonomy' means women can decide for themselves what is a good life; and 'diversity/pluriformity' signals a commitment to a society in which differences are not hierarchical.

Men are introduced in this analysis not as a way of softening the blow of a demand for change but to insist that men themselves need to change. This key emancipatory demand reveals a very different political vision from the one we find outlined in the Canadian model. The Netherlands refuses to see the objective as the inclusion of women in the status quo, by demanding that conditions of work change to accommodate women's 'differences'. The goal explicitly is challenging the 'male norm' and the 'masculine ideal' in organisations.

Importantly, the Netherlands model does not use a sex/gender distinction. Along with the social relations approach outlined by Kabeer (1994),[3] it offers instead an understanding of gender as a *political process*. The inclusion of power in the analysis is crucial here. As Verloo (2000: 61-2) notes this was possible because of an established statement in Dutch policies that there were 'unequal power relations between the sexes', stemming in turn from a relatively long engagement between Dutch feminism and the state.[4] Dutch change agents attempt to consolidate that modicum of political support by stressing the need for a policy plan to include a very precise and detailed analysis not only of 'the solutions proposed but also the problem-definition itself for its gender impact' (Verloo 2000: 63). They also warn policymakers against harbouring any 'secret wish for a simple idiot-proof instrument', citing its elevated level of conceptual sophistication as an aid to avoiding simplified check-lists which foster 'sex without gender' evaluations, categorising women as 'vulnerable victims,' (Verloo 2000: 63) and perpetuating the myth of gender-neutral policy.

The Netherlands approach offers a useful emphasis on the unequal power relations between women and men, while the focus on gender as a political process contests the tendency to deploy gender as a euphemism for sex – as an attribute of bodies rather than attributional processes. It also offers a high level of conceptual sophistication, which in turn could foster a necessary process of gender-sensitivity training among policymakers, evaluators and implementers. Moreover, the suggestion, noted above, that policy plans interrogate problem definitions goes some way to raising awareness of how policy is itself implicated in constituting the problem (Bacchi 1999). There is also considerable insight in those who developed this framework that gender mainstreaming is always incomplete (Verloo and Roggeband 1996; Verloo 2000).

Yet these insights into the 'doing' of policy are not so advanced when it comes to the 'doing' of gender. For example, the model still tends to emphasise the 'potential effects' of policy on 'gender relations' rather than simultaneously evaluating how 'doing gender' is part of the policy process. The result is that gender relations are treated as fixed within a binary opposition, and as existing beyond the process of policymaking. Despite its claim to be *ex ante* (proactive), therefore, the model is restricted to assessing the *impact* of proposed/existing policies. One problem is that the impact assessment framework is itself ill suited to capturing the role of policy in gendering subjects and subjectivities (Bacchi 2004). Another is that it leaves out the embodied experiences of policymakers themselves. Indeed, it relies on 'experts' outside the policy realm to conduct its impact assessments, thus deleting a crucial component of bringing about the organisational change to which it aspires (Verloo 2000). Despite an ability to move towards an account of gender as an unfinished process, therefore, the Netherlands approach would require careful modification if it is to translate deeper insights about gendering into effective policy practice.

Conclusion

For strategic and explanatory reasons some feminist theorists want to stop using gender as a category of analysis. We disagree. We have suggested here that, as theorists and change agents, feminists need to reinstate a political dimension to the term, while including an account of the body. A first step is to use gender as a verb – gender*ing* – which we suggest is even more useful than as an adjective – gendered. When applied to gender mainstreaming, using gender as a noun fixes the categories and denies the effortful 'do-ing' of asymmetrical power relations and the gendering of policy itself. Using the term as a verb, by contrast, has the potential to build on the insights that a feminist ontology of representation can provide for our understanding of the embodied effects of power and advantage which are always partial and incomplete.

To capture this understanding of gender-as-becoming we recommend a reframing of 'gender mainstreaming' as 'gendering-awareness mainstreaming'. That reframing would emphasise the need to analyse how gender is being conceptualised at an early stage of the mainstreaming process. The problems of explanatory inadequacy that the Canadian model faces, and the difficulty of effecting a realisable *ex ante* approach in the Netherlands model might thus be overcome.

As this article has shown, different understandings of gender are attached to different reform approaches. In arguing that feminists begin to treat gender as a verb, therefore, we are sensitive to those contexts. It is no simple matter to suggest that those engaged in 'gender' mainstreaming ought to use one understanding of gender over another. To say it is not a simple matter does not mean that it should not be said. But it needs to be said with due regard for political and cultural context. Feminist change agents are working within a specific political environment that necessitates at some level the conception of gendering they invoke. A clear example here is the way in which the Netherlands model was seen as too complex and advanced for use in Flanders (Woodward and Meier 1997).

Our theoretical concepts bear a necessary relation to the 'real world'. They grow from it and feed into it. Theoretical conversations are therefore conversations about what needs to change and what can change. These conversations are valuable at precisely this level – elaborating new visions for new 'real worlds'. Mainstreaming gender by emphasising gender-awareness mainstreaming may well create more than visions.

Notes

1. Although Canada has had gender-based analysis programs in place since 1995, it did not start using the language of 'gender mainstreaming' until 2001. See Status of Women Canada, Gender-Based Analysis Directorate (GBA)(2001).

2. The term 'gender-disaggregated data' refers to qualitative studies. In this case they were focused on the reasons why young men and women leave school and the results in terms of job prospects.

3. Kabeer (1994: 84) notes that gender is 'constructed as a relationship of inequality by the rules and practices of different institutions'. Her social relations framework is seen by March et al. (1999) as having transformative potential.

4. This could mean that this model is not easily transportable to other contexts (see Woodward and Meier 1997).

References

(Websites valid as of publication date)

Abella, R. 1984. *Report of the Commission on Equality in Employment.* Ottawa: Supply and Services Canada.

Acker, J. 1990. 'Hierarchies, jobs, bodies: A theory of gendered organizations', *Gender and Society* 4: 139-58.

Bacchi, C. 1990. *Same difference: Feminism and sexual difference.* Sydney: Allen and Unwin.

Bacchi, C. 1999. *Women, policy and politics: The construction of policy problems.* London: Sage.

Bacchi, C. 2004. 'Gender/ing impact assessment: Can it be made to work?' *Journal of Interdisciplinary Gender Studies* 9 (2): 93-111.

Bacchi, C. and Eveline, J. 2004. 'Mainstreaming and neoliberalism: A contested relationship', *Policy and Society: Journal of Public, Foreign and Global Policy* 22 (2): 98-118.

Beveridge, F., Nott, S. and Stephen, K. 2000. 'Moving forward with mainstreaming', in Beveridge, F., Nott, S. and Stephen K (eds) *Making women count: Integrating women into law and policy-making.* Aldershot: Ashgate.

Bly, R. 1990. *Iron John.* Shaftesbury: Element Books Limited.

British Columbia. 1993. *Gender lens: A guide to gender-inclusive policy and program development.* Vancouver: Ministry of Women's Equality.

Brittan, A. 1989. *Masculinity and power.* New York: Blackwell.

Bulbeck, C. 1998. *Re-orienting Western feminisms.* Melbourne: Cambridge University Press.

Butler, J. 1990. *Gender trouble: Feminism and the subversion of identity.* New York: Routledge.

Carrigan, T., Connell, R. and Lee, J. 1985. 'Toward a new sociology of masculinity', *Theory and Society* 14 (5): 551-604.

Chodorow, N. 1978. *The reproduction of mothering.* Berkeley, CA: University of California Press.

Citizenship and Immigration Canada. 2002. *Gender-based analysis at CIC: Training handout.* Ottawa: Status of Women Canada.

Cockburn, C. 1991. *In the way of women: Men's resistance to women in organizations.* London: Macmillan Education.

Colebrook, C. 2001. 'From radical representations to corporeal becomings: The feminist philosophy of Lloyd, Grosz and Gatens', *Hypatia* 15 (2): 76-93.

Collinson, D., and Hearn, J. 1994. 'Naming men as men: Implications for work, organisation and management', *Gender, Work and Organization* 1 (1): 2-22.

Connell, R. 1987. *Gender and power: Society, the person and sexual politics.* Sydney: Allen and Unwin.

Connell, R. 1995. *Masculinities.* Cambridge: Polity Press.

Essed, P., Goldberg, D. and Kobayashi, A. (eds) 2004. *A companion to gender studies.* Malden, MA: Blackwell.

Eveline, J. 1994. 'The politics of advantage', *Australian Feminist Studies* 19: 129-54.

Eveline, J. 1995. 'Surviving the belt shop blues: Women miners and critical acts', *Australian Journal of Political Science* 30: 91-107.

Eveline, J. 1998. 'Heavy, dirty and limp stories: Male advantage at work', in Gatens, M. & Mackinnon, A. (eds) *Gender and institutions: Welfare, work and citizenship*. Cambridge: Cambridge University Press.

Ferguson, K. 1984. *The feminist case against bureaucracy*. Philadelphia: Temple University Press.

Fulcher, G. 1989. *Disabling policies? A comparative approach to education policy and disability*. East Sussex: The Falmer Press.

Gatens, M. 1983. 'A critique of the sex/gender distinction', in Allen, J. and Patton, P. (eds) *Beyond Marxism? Interventions after Marx*. Sydney: Intervention Publications.

Gatens, M. 1996. 'Through a Spinozist lens: Ethology, difference, power', in Patton, P. (ed) *Deleuze: A critical reader*. Oxford: Blackwell.

Gilligan, C. 1982. *In a different voice*. Cambridge, MA: Harvard University Press.

Hearn, J. 1992. *Men in the public eye*. London: Routledge.

Hoagland, S. 1988. *Lesbian ethics: Toward new value*. Palo Alto, CA: Institute of Lesbian Studies.

Hull, G.T., Scott, P.B. and Smith, B. (eds) 1982. *All the women are white, all the blacks are men, but some of us are brave*. New York: The Feminist Press.

Irigaray, L. 1985. *This sex which is not one*. Trans. Porter, C. and Burke, C. Ithaca, NY: Cornell University Press.

Jahan, R. 1995. *The elusive agenda: Mainstreaming women in development*. London: Zed Books.

Kabeer, N. 1994. 'Gender aware policy and planning: A social relations perspective', in MacDonald, M. (ed.) *Gender planning in developing agencies: Meeting the challenge*. Oxford: Oxfam.

Kasic, B. 2004. 'Feminist cross mainstreaming within "East-West" mapping', *European Journal of Women's Studies* 11 (4): 473-85.

Kerfoot, D. and Knights, D. 1996. 'The best is yet to come', in Collinson, D. and Hearn, J. (eds) *Men as managers, managers as men*. London: Sage.

Levy, C., Taher, N. and Vouhe, C. 2000. 'Addressing men and masculinities in GAD', *IDS Bulletin* 31 (2): 86-96.

MacKinnon, C.A. 1989. *Toward a feminist theory of the state*. Harvard, MA: Harvard University Press.

McClure, K. 1992. 'The issue of foundations: Scientized politics, politicized science and feminist critical practice', in Butler, J. and Scott, J. (eds) *Feminists theorize the political*. New York: Routledge.

March, C., Smyth, I. and Mukhodpadhyay, M. 1999. *A guide to gender analysis frameworks*. Oxford: Oxfam.

Mitchell, J. 2004. 'Procreative mothers (sexual difference) and child-free sisters (gender)', *European Journal of Women's Studies* 11 (4): 415-26.

Mohanty, C.T. 1991. 'Cartographies of struggle: Third World women and the politics of feminism', in Mohanty, C.T., Russo, A. and Torres, L. (eds) *Third World women and the politics of feminism.* Bloomington, IN: Indiana University Press.

Moi, T. 1999. 'What is a woman?: Appropriating Bourdieu: feminist theory and Pierre Bourdieu's sociology of culture', in Moi, T. *What is a woman and other essays.* New York: Oxford University Press.

Nichols, J. 1975. *Men's liberation.* New York: Penguin.

O'Brien, M. 1981. *The politics of reproduction.* London: Routledge and Kegan Paul.

Parsons, T. and Bales, R. 1995. *Family, socialisation and the interaction process.* New York: Free Press.

Plantenga, J. 2000. 'Gender impact assessment and employment strategy: The case of the Netherlands'. External Report commissioned and presented to the European Commission. <mbs.ac.uk/research/europeanemployment/projects/gendersocial/documents/GIA_NL.pdf> accessed 22 October 2009.

Sandoval, C. 1991. 'U.S. Third World feminism: The theory and method of oppositional consciousness in the postmodern world', *Genders* 10: 1-24.

Scott, J.W. 1990. 'Deconstructing equality-versus-difference, or, the uses of poststructuralist theory for feminism', in Hirsch, M. and Fox Keller, E. (eds) *Conflicts in feminism.* New York: Routledge.

Spelman, E. V. 1988. *Inessential woman: Problems of exclusion in feminist thought.* Boston, MA: Beacon Press.

Status of Women Canada. 1997. *Gender-based analysis backgrounder.* Ottawa: Status of Women Canada.

Status of Women Canada. 2001. *Gender-based analysis* (GBA): *Policy training: Participant handbook.* Ottawa: Status of Women Canada.

Staudt, K. 2003. 'Gender mainstreaming: Conceptual links to institutional machineries', in Rai, S.M. (ed.) *Mainstreaming gender, democratizing the state: Institutional mechanisms in the advancement of women.* Manchester: Manchester University Press.

Verloo, M. 2000. 'Making women count in the Netherlands', in Beveridge, F., Nott, S. and Stephen, K. (eds) *Making women count: Integrating gender into law and policy-making.* Dartmouth: Ashgate.

Verloo, M. and Roggeband, C. 1996. 'Gender impact assessment: The development of a new instrument in the Netherlands', *Impact Assessment* 14 (1): 3-21.

Weeks, J. 1977. *Coming out: Homosexual politics in Britain, from the nineteenth century to the present.* London: Quartet.

West, C. and Zimmerman, D. 2003. 'Doing gender', in Ely, R., Foldy, E. and Scully, M. (eds) *Reader in gender, work and organization.* Malden, MA: Blackwell Publishing.

White, S. 1994. 'Making men an issue: Gender planning for "the other half"', in Macdonald, M. (ed.) *Gender planning in development agencies: Meeting the challenge.* Oxford: Oxfam.

Wishik, H. and Pearce, C. 1991. *Sexual orientation and identity: Heterosexual, lesbian, gay and bisexual journeys.* Laconics, NH: New Dynamics Publications.

Women's Bureau, Strategic Policy Branch. 1997. *Gender-based analysis backgrounder*. Ottawa: Women's Bureau.

Woodward, A. and Meier, P. 1997. 'Gender impact assessment: Tool in mainstreaming or tool to begin mainstreaming? A comparison of Dutch and Flemish approaches'. Paper for the ECPR Joint Sessions, Bern.

Young, I.M. 2002. 'Lived body vs. gender: Reflections on social structure and subjectivity', *Ratio* XV (December): 410-428.

5

Approaches to gender mainstreaming: What's the problem represented to be?

CAROL BACCHI AND JOAN EVELINE

Introduction: Carol Bacchi and Joan Eveline

Previous chapters have made reference to the need to rethink policy as a creative (productive or constitutive) process. The major purpose of this chapter is to clarify what this means and to illustrate the usefulness of this way of thinking about policy for studying gender mainstreaming and gender analysis. The specific focus is 'gender proofing' in Ireland and 'gender impact assessment' in the Netherlands.

The underlying proposition in thinking about policies as productive, or as constitutive, is that policies and policy proposals *give shape and meaning* to the 'problems' they purport to 'address'. That is, policy 'problems' do not exist 'out there' in society, waiting to be 'solved' through timely and perspicacious policy interventions. Rather, specific policy proposals 'imagine' 'problems' in particular ways that have real and meaningful effects. Hence, to understand how policies operate requires that we ask of policy proposals 'What's the **P**roblem **R**epresented to be?'. This question forms the starting place for Bacchi's (1999; 2009a) novel method of policy analysis (elaborated below), captured in the acronym WPR.

The proposition that 'problems' do not 'exist' 'out there' in society does not ignore or downplay the full range of troubling conditions, including the subordination of women, that characterise social relations. Instead, it insists that how 'problems' are represented in policies – how they are discursively produced – affects the particular

111

understanding given to those conditions at points in time and space, and that these understandings matter. That is, how 'problems' are represented has important effects for what can be seen as problematic, for what is silenced, and for how people think about these issues and about their place in the world. Problem representations (the ways in which 'problems' are represented) therefore are political interventions that constitute policy 'problems' *in the real* (Bacchi 2009a: 35).

It follows that policies do not simply 'deal with' the 'problem' of 'gender inequality'. Rather, policies *create* different impressions of what the 'problem' of 'gender equality' entails, as this chapter illustrates. When policies are described as *gender equality* initiatives, therefore, it is necessary to see just what meanings are attached to this term 'gender equality' (Magnusson et al. 2008). A WPR approach to policy analysis assists in this task.

The idea that policies are productive or constitutive also means attending to the ways in which policies, through their representations of 'problems', produce and reinforce categories of people, including 'women' and 'men'. The notion, developed in previous chapters (Chapters 1, 3 and 4), that policies are gender*ing*, reflects this proposition. That is, policies as discursive practices open up certain 'subject positions' that individuals either adopt or resist, affecting interpersonal interactions and the meanings attached to those interactions. In this way they are constitutive of gender relations and of particular kinds of social being, such as 'women' and 'men'.

For example, many policies (including many gender analysis guidelines) – think of tax regimes that offer rebates for dependent spouses – encourage heteronormative coupling and penalise homosexual pairing. Hence, they reinforce a two-sex model of social relations (Honkanen 2008: 206), an effect that can be described as heteronorm*ing*. Along this line of thinking, it is useful to think of policies as racial*ising*, as class*ing* and as (dis)abl*ing* (Fulcher 1989), always recognising the incomplete nature of these processes. This way of thinking about policies as discursive practices that produce and reinforce specific categories of social being and specific patterns of social organisation assists in working through some of the blockages in theorising (and in policy design) caused by focusing on fixed identity categories (see for example the issue of 'commatisation' in the introduction to Chapter 9). At the same time, this position recognises the need to acknowledge and work through identity categories when the people who inhabit those categories deem such a stance to be politically necessary (Chapter 13).

In this chapter we trace how two gender analysis frameworks – 'gender proofing' in Ireland and 'gender impact assessment' in the Netherlands – produce two quite different understandings of the 'problem' of 'gender inequality'. As we shall see, Ireland's 'gender proofing' framework represents 'gender equality' to be a matter of extending 'equal opportunities' to women. It produces 'women' as individuals who have fewer 'opportunities' than men to access existing occupations and positions of influence, and who need additional 'opportunities'. It therefore rests upon an assumption that 'gender equality' means integrating women into the social and political status quo. By contrast gender impact assessment in the Netherlands pursues a broader agenda of reshaping gender relations to make them more equitable. It therefore involves more substantive alterations to the political and social status quo than the Irish model. Applying the WPR approach to the specific policy proposals in these contrasting gender analysis frameworks assists in identifying their possibilities and their limitations, including how they are at times gender*ing*, class*ing*, racialis*ing* and heteronorm*ing* in their effects. As a result, a WPR approach to policy analysis provides a powerful methodology for discerning the ways in which specific policies enshrine inequitable social relations.

As discussed in the Introduction, *Mainstreaming politics* presumes the always-incomplete and political nature of claims to 'knowledge'. In this spirit the WPR approach builds a level of reflexive self-scrutiny into the analysis by incorporating a directive to apply its six questions (see below) to *one's own* policy proposals. This directive is aimed at both policy workers and researchers. Put more broadly, accepting ourselves as always located social subjects (whether as researchers, policymakers or teachers) requires us to be reflexively vigilant in thinking through the forms of social explanation we produce, including the inevitably provisional meanings we attach to the concepts and categories we adopt and their constitutive effects (Chapters 6, 10 and 13).

The chapter opens with an elaboration of Bacchi's WPR approach to policy analysis and of what it means to talk about policy as productive. The second section introduces the theoretical traditions informing a WPR approach. Section three applies the approach to two contrasting models (or frameworks) of gender analysis, 'gender proofing' in Ireland and 'gender impact assessment' in the Netherlands. The fourth section illustrates how the approach assists in identifying the gender*ing* effects in a selection of economic and social policies, potentially extending the scope and political purchase of gender analysis policy processes.

A new way to think about policy

The idea that policies are developed to 'solve' social and policy problems is a common-sense proposition in most thinking about public policy. It is this very proposition that a WPR approach to policy analysis seeks to overturn. Challenging the view that policies are designed in *reaction* to pre-existing problems, it makes the case that policies and policy proposals *create* or produce policy 'problems' as *particular kinds* of problems, with important 'shaping' effects for social subjects and social relations.

A few examples will illustrate how this rethinking works. In many countries leadership training programs for women are offered as a means of increasing women's representation in positions of influence or in higher-paying jobs. So, training programs, it is implied, will help to 'solve' the 'problem' of women's under-representation. A WPR approach directs attention to the proposal of leadership training programs, asks how this proposal represents (or 'creates' or 'imagines') the 'problem' of women's representation and raises questions about what this *problem representation* (how the 'problem' is represented) leaves unaddressed. Pursuing our example, representing the 'problem' to be women's lack of training presumes that women need training because they are behind or out of touch in certain ways. Women, in other words, are constituted *as the 'problem'*, silencing consideration of the social rules that determine the meaning of 'success' and of 'successful' (Eveline 2004).

As another example, in Australia in 2007 the Howard-led Coalition Government introduced a swathe of policies, dubbed 'the intervention', in 'response' to a report on child sexual abuse in outback Aboriginal communities. Initially the decision was made to send in troops and to increase the police presence in those communities. Such a policy produces the 'problem' of child sexual abuse as a law and order 'problem', leaving unaddressed (silenced) the history of Aboriginal dispossession and its myriad effects in the lives of Aboriginal peoples (Altman and Hinkson 2007; Bacchi 2009a: 116-120; Chapter 6).

These examples illustrate the bare bones in a WPR approach to policy analysis. The methodology involves starting with a policy or policy proposal, ensuring understanding of its context, and 'working backwards' to see how the 'problem' is represented – the meaning it is given or how it is discursively constituted – within the policy or proposal. The next proposition is that how policy proposals represent 'problems' *matters*. That is, identified *problem representations* (how the 'problem' is represented) become the starting place for thinking about a wide range of implications and repercussions that accompany specific representations. For example, we probe problem representations for their underlying and taken-for-granted assumptions and presuppositions, and raise questions about the origins and relevance of these presuppositions. We also ask what fails to be problematised in particular ways of representing an issue and how the 'problem' could be thought about differently, creating space for inventive thinking around the issue. Further, we inquire into the effects that follow from identified representations of a 'problem'.

In terms of effects a WPR approach draws attention to three overlapping kinds of implications or repercussions as a way of assessing the usefulness or, alternatively, the limitations or even dangers of a particular policy or policy proposal:

- discursive effects (limiting what can be said)

- subjectification effects (the kinds of political subjects produced in and through discourse)

- lived effects (the material impact on people's lives).

Notably, the form of policy evaluation offered here is highly unconventional. We are not attempting to measure 'outcomes', such as how many more women gain seats in parliament or how many fewer women receive welfare benefits. Rather, the kinds of effects of interest in a WPR approach are *those that accompany the way in which the 'problem' is represented*. It is important to note that 'representations', in this understanding, are not opposed to the 'real'. As Shapiro (1988: xi) says, 'representations do not imitate reality but are the practices through which things take on meaning and value'. Hence, we ask: What will be done, given this representation of the 'problem'? To whom? What will stay the same? Who will benefit from this representation of the 'problem'? Who will be harmed? Who is 'blamed' in this representation of the 'problem'? How does this attribution of blame affect the ways in which those targeted as responsible for the 'problem' think about themselves and their place in the world?

In short, a WPR approach to policy analysis directs attention to the ways in which problem representations sustain or challenge hierarchical power relations, *countering* a relativist presumption that any one 'truth' is as good as any other. By inquiring into the history and struggle through which specific problem representations come to prominence (their genealogy; Bacchi 2009a: 36-37), how they are disseminated or popularised, and if they were/are contested, it also provides insights into the power relations that affect the success of some problem representations and the defeat of others.

In this account, policy is not the government's best attempt to 'solve' a 'problem'. Rather, policies characterise 'problems' in ways that affect what gets done or not done, who gets harmed and who benefits. While policy 'problems' may at times be characterised intentionally in particular ways, a WPR approach is not concerned with deliberate or strategic framing of 'problems'. The suggestion is not that politicians, bureaucrats, or other members of the policy community *devise* specific ways of representing policy 'problems'. Rather, the approach operates at a different level of analysis. It starts from the premise that, since all policies make proposals for change, by their very nature they contain *implicit* representations of 'problems'. The task therefore becomes interrogating unexamined assumptions and deep-seated conceptual logics within implicit problem representations, and considering what follows from these representations of the 'problem' (see Bacchi 2009a for elaboration of a WPR approach to policy analysis).

To facilitate application of a WPR approach to policy analysis, the chart below lists six questions and an injunction, at the bottom of the list, to apply the questions to one's own policy proposals. There is no suggestion in this simple listing of questions that a WPR approach is to be applied as a sort of formula; rather, the objective is to encourage a form of critical thinking by questioning the oft-presumed empirical status accorded social and policy 'problems', and by imagining how 'problems' could be thought about differently.

The directive to apply the six questions to one's own policy proposals builds a level of reflexivity – critical self-scrutiny or 'self-problematization' (Connolly 1995: 92) – into the approach (Chapters 6, 10, 12 and 13). It stands as a reminder that any policy proposal we might advance constitutes a 'fixing' of meaning that may well rely on unexamined presuppositions and may well, therefore, require rethinking and modification. This proposition extends to analyses produced through applying the WPR approach, including those in this chapter, and to the theoretical presuppositions that underpin those analyses (Bacchi 2009a: 101, 270). As described in the Introduction to the book, the intention is to move between the necessary 'fixing' of 'knowledge' claims and the equally necessary bracketing or querying of those claims.

What's the problem represented to be?
An approach to policy analysis

1. What's the 'problem' (for example, of 'problem gamblers', 'drug use/abuse', 'gender inequality', 'domestic violence', 'global warming', 'child sexual abuse' etc.) represented to be in a specific policy?

2. What presuppositions or assumptions underlie this representation of the 'problem'?

3. How has this representation of the 'problem' come about?

4. What is left unproblematic in this problem representation? Where are the silences? Can the 'problem' be thought about differently?

5. What effects are produced by this representation of the 'problem'?

6. How/where has this representation of the 'problem' been produced, disseminated and defended? How could it be questioned, disrupted and replaced?

Apply this list of questions to your own problem representations (Bacchi 2009a: 2).

Theoretical resources

A WPR approach to policy analysis draws upon four theoretical traditions: social construction theory, poststructuralism, including poststructural discourse psychology, feminist body theory and governmentality studies. Key precepts of these traditions are introduced briefly below, indicating how these ideas provide useful resources for thinking about gender, gender mainstreaming, gender analysis and gender*ing* practices.

Social constructionism – or perhaps more accurately, social 'productivism' (Massumi 2002: 12) – emphasises the extent to which our understandings of the world are the *products* of social forces (Burr 2003: 19-20). 'Knowledge' in this understanding is a social construction. 'Knowledges' do not exist apart from the statements and/or signs that constitute them (see Introduction to the book). This perspective highlights the need to scrutinise taken-for-granted ways, including our own ways, of representing 'problems' since they are constituted in discourse. In this chapter we interrogate competing representations of the 'problem' of 'gender inequality'.

Poststructuralism brings an awareness of politics, understood broadly (see Introduction to the book), to bear on this social understanding of knowledge. With Foucault (1980), there is recognition of a power-knowledge nexus in which power is involved in producing forms of knowledge, such as the authority accorded to 'expert' 'knowledges', and in which knowledges exercise power or influence in shaping people's lives. The idea of contested concepts, a central theoretical premise in the book, derives from this perspective. In this view concepts and categories have no essential or trans-historical meaning but are parts of discourse or discursive formations (Bacchi 2009a: 35). 'Equality' for example cannot be defined finally and forever; it is not descriptive of anything. Rather, 'equality' is an open signifier that can be defined for certain purposes and redefined for other purposes, with disputes over its meaning related to competing political visions. As Tanesini (1994: 207) contends, in effect, concepts and categories are 'proposals about how we are to proceed from here' whose purpose is 'to influence the evolution of ongoing practices' (Tanesini 1994: 207). A central focus in a WPR analysis is to track and assess the contested meanings attached to key terms including 'gender', 'gender mainstreaming' and 'gender equality' (Chapters 2 and 4).

As with 'knowledge', the political subject in poststructuralist thinking is considered to be emergent rather than a fixed essence, in stark contrast to humanist conceptions of the individual. This means that who we are and who we assume ourselves to be are, at least in part, reflections of the discourses and social practices, including policy practices, in which we are embedded. Accepting this view, as developed in the work of poststructuralist discourse psychologists (for example, Davies 1994), a WPR approach works from the premise that the discursive constitution of problem representations produces political subjects of particular types (gendered, sexed, (dis)abled, racialised etc.) through eliciting certain 'subject positions'. As examples Marston and McDonald (2006: 3) identify the subject position of 'worker-citizens' in workfare programs, 'parent-citizens' in child and family services, and 'consumer-citizens' in a 'managerial and marketised mixed economy of welfare'.

Further and crucially, how this *subjectification* (see Introduction to the book) occurs has political ramifications – stigmatising some, exonerating others, and keeping alterations in the asymmetrical status of social groups within limits. For example, in some gender mainstreaming and gender analysis programs, as we shall see later, women are discursively constituted as 'different' and as needing forms of 'special' treatment. In and through these programs, women are positioned as supplicants and as exceptions to accepted standards, leaving those standards and those who benefit from them undisturbed (see Bacchi 2004, 2005, 2009b). As elaborated below, none of this assumes that political subjectivity is *determined* through these processes.

Feminist body theory (Beasley and Bacchi 2007; Gatens 1995) ensures that we keep an eye to the ways in which problem representations have real and meaningful effects for lived/living bodies (see Chapter 4). Repeating a point raised earlier, representations are not opposed to 'the real'. Rather, through the meanings they introduce, they are political interventions in 'the real', affecting how people are treated and how they live their lives. Chapter 4 for example raises a question about how the free availability of vasectomies in Quebec post-1986 might reshape corporeal masculinities. Policy representations therefore affect socially embedded bodily possibilities, often with life and death effects (Dean 2006). For example, constituting welfare benefits as a form of handout rather than a right influences the level of support accorded to welfare recipients, with clear embodied effects for those struggling to survive on meagre incomes.

Governmentality studies, associated with Foucault, broaden our understanding of government to include the full array of institutions, agencies and 'knowledges', including but also beyond the state, that shape and regulate social behaviours. While a WPR approach takes policies, most often public policies, as the entry points for analysis, it understands government (or governance) in this broader sense. So, professionals and researchers, including gender mainstreaming 'experts', are recognised as involved in the task of societal administration. Attention therefore comes to bear on the political significance of the concepts and categories they (and we) adopt and deploy, and the need to scrutinise reflexively the nature and effects of those categorical creations (Chapter 13).

Clearly in a WPR approach the study of policy looks very different from conventional forms of policy analysis. The ambit of governing 'agents', including professionals and 'experts', for example, is wider, and the kinds of questions addressed are highly unusual. For example, we ask: How do public policies, through their problem representations, *constitute* the targets of policy, the general population and policymakers as particular kinds of political subjects? How do they influence people's conceptions of themselves and of others? How do they influence and shape people's embodied existence? How would different forms of problematisation – other ways of representing the 'problem' – create other kinds of political subjects and other futures?

In this understanding, instead of thinking about 'women' and 'men' as existing separate from and outside policies *addressed* to their needs, policies are perceived to have activating effects at the level of subjectivity and of embodiment. In effect they play a significant role in producing and reinforcing the categories 'women' and 'men' in ways that have significant impacts on people and their lives. To capture this way of understanding policies (as creative, as productive, as constitutive), we need new languages that move away from assumed fixed categories of people (the humanist subject who just 'is') and which are able to identify processes of subjectification. To achieve these goals we suggest talking about policy practices as gender*ing*, heteronorm*ing* (Annfelt 2008), class*ing*, (dis)abl*ing* and racialis*ing* in their effects.

Importantly, these practices are described as continuous, contested and uncertain so that outcomes are considered to be neither determined nor predictable. That is, policies *elicit* forms of subjectivity; they do not impose them (Dean 1999: 32). The concept of gender*ing*, therefore, describes an ongoing and always incomplete process, explaining why gender analysis must necessarily be considered as part of a long-term and continuing change agenda rather than as a policy with a planned end date (Chapter 4). The next section brings this perspective to two existing gender analysis frameworks, 'gender proofing' in Ireland and 'gender impact assessment' in the Netherlands, asking in each case 'what's the problem represented to be?'.

Applying a WPR approach to gender mainstreaming and gender analysis

Chapter 2 explores current debates among espoused feminists as to whether gender mainstreaming challenges or is congruent with neoliberal premises (Rönnblom 2008). The assumption, as explained in that chapter, is that 'gender equality' in a neoliberal frame belies the *promise* of gender mainstreaming which, according to Rees (1998: 41), involves 'the transformation of institutions … rather than the continuing attempt to improve women's access and performance within organizations and their hierarchies as they are'. This chapter applies the set of questions in a WPR approach (see chart above) to two contrasting frameworks for gender analysis to consider the extent to which they fit within or contest neoliberal precepts. Parenthetical references indicate when a specific question from the WPR approach (for example, Question 2, Question 4) has been applied.

We compare 'gender proofing' in Ireland, characterised as a 'differences' approach that focuses on (what are described as) empirical differences in the 'real' lives of men and women, and 'gender impact assessment' in the Netherlands, characterised as a 'gender relations' approach. By asking 'what's the problem represented to be?' we attempt to identify more precisely significant distinctions in the political visions associated with these two frameworks. The analysis reveals important contrasts in the meanings of key concepts such as 'gender' and 'equality' (Chapters 2 and 4), and indeed in the whole way in which 'gender inequality' is understood as a 'problem'. It also encourages reflection on other possible representations of the 'problem' (Question 4).

For Ireland the primary sources include the *Irish gender proofing handbook* (Crawley and O'Meara 2002), two additional documents on 'mainstreaming equality between women and men' produced by the NDP (National Development Plan) Gender Equality Unit (Polverari and Fitzgerald 2002a, 2002b), and a later *Gender impact assessment handbook* (Crawley and O'Meara 2004). For the Netherlands we base our comments on the EER (translated as *Emancipation Impact Assessment*) approach developed by Verloo and Roggeband (1996).

Before commencing it is worthwhile repeating the point made in the introduction to Chapter 3 that gender analysis frameworks are not static; rather, they are malleable and subject to continual political pressures, reflecting the changing contexts in which they operate. Hence the kind of analysis offered here, which focuses on the content of documents fixed in time, should be read with this in mind. It is also worthwhile noting that documents such as the ones analysed here tend to be complex and nuanced, capturing different voices and perspectives. There is not always a single message nor, for that matter, a single problem representation. Still, we suggest, a good deal can be learned from examining how, in general terms, the 'problem' of 'gender inequality' is conceptualised in specific proposals, at particular times.

'Gender proofing' in Ireland

Ireland's 'gender proofing' initiative has to be seen within the context of obligations under the Treaty of Amsterdam (1997), which established 'equality between men and women as a specific tool of the European Union' (Crawley and O'Meara 2002: 12). European regulations on the Structural Funds made available to EU members also require 'that all measures supported by the Funds be gender mainstreamed' (Crawley and O'Meara 2002: 12). In accordance with these provisions Ireland introduced anti-discrimination legislation, the *Employment Equality Act (1998)* and the *Equal Status Act (2000)*.

The Irish gender proofing process involves five steps. First, establish 'the *different* experiences and roles of men and women which might have an effect on how they benefit from/get involved' in some specific objective or action. Next, consider the 'implications of the *differences* (outlined above) for this objective'. Third, given these implications, decide what needs to be done 'to ensure equality of outcome for men and women'. Fourth, decide who will assume responsibility for ensuring these actions are carried out. Lastly, set indicators and targets to measure success in the area (Crawley and O'Meara 2002: 18-20; emphasis added).

The focus in this form of gender analysis is on the 'differences' in the lives of women and men, as is clear in the quotes above. To establish the nature of these 'differences', prior to Step 1, there are instructions to 'Gather any available gender disaggregated statistics, facts and information being addressed by the action/objective' in order to 'give an accurate response to Step 1 and to set realistic targets in Step 5' (Crawley and O'Meara 2002: 19). Those applying the approach are instructed to: 'Keep it simple! The differences in the lives of women and men, in particular those which contribute to inequalities, are part and parcel of everyday experiences' (Crawley and O'Meara 2002: 20).

This form of gender analysis, which we characterise as a 'differences' framework, for obvious reasons, is the dominant form of gender analysis in western industrialised states and in international organisations such as the World Bank and the International Labour Organization (ILO). To speculate on the possibilities and limitations in the ways in which this form of gender analysis understands the 'problem' of 'gender inequality' requires a close examination of specific proposals and how these proposals represent the 'problems' they purport to address, as we now proceed to do.

In a sample from a training session on how to 'develop geographically spread affordable workspace, in a range of sizes (and areas)', the following 'different experiences and roles of men and women' are identified under Step 1 of the approach:

a) Women work in the home, managing people, finance, resources. They may lack confidence or self-belief in relation to enterprise. Women may have little experience of structured employment or of managing adults. Men have greater experience of structured employment and experience of risk taking with a work situation outside the home.

b) Women assume primary responsibility for child rearing.

c) Women are less likely to have transport available to them.

d) Women are seen to be more vulnerable to physical attack.

e) Women's prior experience of sourcing finance may have been negative (Crawley and O'Meara 2002: 24).

Step 2 details accompanying 'implications':

a) Women may not have the confidence to set up in business. Unless proactive measures are taken to address the lack of previous experience and/or confidence for women, they are unlikely to be in a position to avail of the workspace. Men are more likely, on the basis of previous experience, to avail of workspace.

b) There is a need for child care in the centre or immediate area to make it accessible to women.

c) Without transport women are less likely to avail of the workspace.

d) Issues of safety, in particular for women (as workspaces tend to be located in quiet locations on the outskirts of towns), may put women off using such spaces.

e) Women may not have the confidence/skills to seek business loans.

Finally in Step 3, proposals for change are put forward:

a) Run 'start your own business' courses designed for, and targeted at, women.

b) Provide on-site crèches for both workers and clients.

c) Provide transport or ensure location is served by public transport.

d) Ensure design is safety conscious (i.e. lighting, personal security system).

e) Work with financial institutions such as Credit Unions and banks, with regard to interest rates, long term loans etc. and encourage them to adopt a gender sensitive approach in their work (Crawley and O'Meara 2002: 25).

Each proposal reveals a particular representation of the 'problem', underpinned by specific presuppositions. For example proposals addressed to women's 'lack of confidence' represent the 'problem' to be character deficiencies within women (Question 1), assuming a particular understanding of psychological development (Question 2). The suggestion that women lack 'skills' (Question 1) relies upon a western discourse that imagines human beings as 'skill-*acquiring*' and 'skill-*possessing*' creatures (Question 2; Bastalich 2001). The proposal to provide child care facilities on site, to 'make it accessible to women' (see above), represents the 'problem' to be caring responsibilities (Question 1), here designated as *women's* responsibilities (Question 2). The focus on a 'safety conscious' work site, including better lighting, represents violence against women to be a matter of situational opportunity (Question 1), assuming that violent crime is a rational decision of self-interested actors (Question 2; Bacchi 2009a: 103).

Questions 4 and 5 in a WPR approach raise questions about the adequacy and effects of these problem representations, such as:

- Is it adequate to portray women's lack of access to workspaces as due to women's lack of confidence or experience?

- Does characterising women as lacking confidence and/or skills position them as deficient in ways that may affect how they think about themselves, and/or how others think about them, and their place in society?

- How will social relations alter if caring responsibilities continue to be designated women's responsibilities? What will stay the same?

- To what extent does this characterising of caring responsibilities as women's responsibilities presume and reinforce the social categories of 'women' and of 'men', and hence a two-sex model of social relations (Honkanen 2008)?

- Is violence against women a matter only of situational opportunity? What else needs to be considered?

Taking a broader perspective, the proposals regarding transport, safety and finance all produce the 'problem' as women's lack of access to *existing* work structures, and address what must be done to facilitate access (Question 1). What we have identified here, despite the claim that the goal is 'to ensure equality of outcome for men and women' (Crawley and O'Meara 2002: 18-20), is a fairly common representation of the 'problem' of women's inequality as a matter of women lacking opportunities to participate in society on the same terms as men. Indeed the idea that women require opportunities to access existing organisational contexts is the dominant understanding of gender equality in western industrialised countries and has been so since the 1960s. The argument, that equality means equal access to existing institutions and work structures, lies behind anti-discrimination laws and equal opportunity policies (Bacchi 1990). The surprise perhaps is that this rather conventional representation of the 'problem' goes under the name of 'gender mainstreaming', which is supposed to be a *new* approach to equality issues that 'necessarily produces institutional transformation' (Rees 1998: 4; Question 4). Asking 'what's the problem represented to be?' assists in this instance in identifying that gender mainstreaming initiatives in Ireland remain largely a matter of 'mainstreaming of equal opportunities' (Polverari and Fitzgerald 2002a: 4).

The specific social, economic and political conditions in Ireland help to explain how this particular representation of gender inequality came to prominence (Question 3). The widely accepted conviction that Ireland must develop industrially underlies the assumption that 'female involvement in the workplace should continue to grow' (Polverari and Fitzgerald 2002a: 38). This dominant focus on increasing productivity makes gender mainstreaming, in this incarnation, congruent with free market neoliberal agendas (Question 5). Nowhere is this clearer than in the production of gender analysis as a marketing tool for private enterprise. Gender impact assessment, we are told, 'can result in better information about customers and their needs':

> For example, a 1994 study showed that even though men mostly controlled the family finances, it is usually women who manage the household money on behalf of the family – buying groceries, paying bills, booking holidays, et cetera. This is important information in the effective targeting of goods and services. (Crawley and O'Meara 2004: 24)

Admittedly, recognising 'gender differences' can be considered an important step forward in understandings of equality, since it marks an advance on the dominant model of 'equal treatment' enshrined in anti-discrimination law (Bacchi

2009a: 181-183). Certainly, the relevance of providing more child care and better transport should not be discounted. At the same time, however, it is important to draw attention to the limitations of a 'differences' approach as a prompt to imagining different understandings of the 'problem' of 'gender inequality'.

Basically Irish gender proofing offers an integrationist representation of the 'problem' of gender inequality (Jahan 1995) – assimilating women into the economic and social status quo. This perspective is reflected in the way in which the concept of gender is understood (Question 2). The definitional section of the Irish *Gender proofing handbook* (Crawley and O'Meara 2002: 6) offers a fairly conventional distinction between 'biological' sex and 'cultural' gender differences. 'Sex' as biology is distinguished from 'gender' as social attributes, norms and behaviours (Chapter 4). This understanding of gender is linked to the premise of equal opportunity – that women's abilities have been judged falsely because of stereotypes and that these 'cultural' stereotypes need to be overthrown because *some* women (it is argued) can be *like* men. Without diminishing the significance of this challenge to the assumption that women are destined by biology to confine their activities to the 'domestic sphere', it is relevant to ask what does not get problematised in this representation of the 'problem' (Question 4). In this explanation, for example, it becomes difficult to put in question the masculine norms of the workplaces to which women are demanding access, norms which reinforce the marginalisation of women and which hence are gender*ing* in their effects – producing gender as a relation of inequality.

Illustrating this point, the Irish mainstreaming agenda is described as gender-neutral. The *Gender proofing handbook* (Crawley and O'Meara 2002: 8-9) states explicitly that 'gender proofing' is 'premised on recognition that inequalities exist which can and do discriminate against either sex' (see also Polverari and Fitzgerald 2002a: 1). As exemplars the *Handbook* highlights the need for 'more emphasis' on men's health and men's right to paternity leave entitlements. Social services are criticised for being 'geared towards women' with 'no alternative or complementary supports for men'. Because this supposedly 'even-handed' approach includes men in 'gender' in a depoliticised way, it silences the unequal power relations between women and men and ignores the normative status ascribed to masculine characteristics (Question 4). In keeping with this perspective the Irish *Gender impact assessment handbook* insists that 'Increased representation of women in decision-making positions will of course be based on merit' (Crawley and O'Meara 2004: 63). Merit here is assumed to be an objective method of evaluation, precluding consideration of the gendered biases within the criteria by which abilities are assessed (Burton 1987; Questions 4 and 5).

It is possible, of course, that representing the 'problem' in gender-neutral terms, in the ways we have just seen, might be part of a strategic framing exercise by Irish feminist campaigners to win over men supporters (Verloo 2005; Chapter 3). The point we are making here, however, is that gender neutrality follows logically the understanding of the 'problem' as *identifiable statistical differences in the experiences of women and men*, 'differences' that must be 'evened out'. That is, gender neutrality follows the conceptual logic informing a 'differences' approach (Question 2); it is a discursive effect of a 'differences' discourse (Question 5). 'Gender' comes to be understood as a characteristic of a person, an attribute, much in the way eye colour is conceived, so that it *makes sense* to try to 'even up' the numbers of women and men in different sites of employment, for example, in an 'even-handed' or 'gender'-neutral way.

As explained in the Introduction to the book there is an alternative way to look at one's position in the category 'man' or 'woman'. The focus in this alternative approach is on the practices, including policy practices, that encourage the production of these categories and that impel people to see themselves in those categories. The term 'gendering' was introduced there to direct attention to the 'doing' that is necessary for gender categories to emerge. Gendering, then, is an *attributional process or practice* rather than a personal characteristic. Hence the task becomes identifying the political factors involved in *producing* some 'differences' as disadvantages and others as advantages (Eveline 1994) rather than 'evening out' 'differences'. For example, with this focus on 'doing', it becomes possible to ask how primary responsibility for nurture of the young becomes a 'difference' about women that serves specific advantages for those who are most like men are meant to be.

Going further it is possible to argue that certain of the proposals in the *Gender proofing handbook* (see above) are themselves gendering. For example, a proposal that represents the 'problem' to be deficiencies in women's character or experience constitutes women as the ones who need to change, reinforcing the cultural location of women as outsiders whose different-from-the-norm 'needs' might be accommodated. As another example, a proposal that represents the 'problem' to be caring responsibilities and *women's* lack of access to child care reinforces the assumption that the domestic division of labour and the heterosexual nuclear family are unchangeable facets of life, rather than the constraints of a particular form of economic organisation.

Recalling that gender analysis frameworks are subject to continuous political pressures, the 2004 updated version of 'gender proofing', now called 'gender impact assessment' (Crawley and O'Meara 2004), suggests ongoing contestation in Ireland about how to make gender analysis effective. While the approach remains basically the same as that outlined above, starting from the 'identification' of 'real differences' in the lives of men and women, the number of steps is reduced from five to four and a new question (3b) is included: 'If any of the implications identified above are "macro issues", what can you do within the scope of your job to progress action in this area?' (Crawley and O'Meara 2004: 35).

Under this question, a completed gender impact assessment, which addressed 'the under representation of women in decision making positions', endorsed the following proposal: 'Advocate for a firm requirement on public bodies to achieve a 60:40 (of either sex) gender balance'. Significantly, this intervention recognises the potential inadequacy of addressing women's 'different' 'needs', and the possibility that 'firm requirements' may be necessary when confronting entrenched inequality. At the same time the gender neutrality ('of either sex') of the proposal reveals a continuing reluctance or inability to push the matter further. The Netherlands model below provides a useful contrast here.

'Gender impact assessment' in the Netherlands

In the Dutch approach, called EER (Emancipation Impact Assessment), the 'problem' is explicitly identified, not as 'differences' between men and women, but as 'unequal power relations between men and women' (Question 1). In contrast to Irish 'gender proofing', therefore, the Dutch 'gender relations' approach understands 'gender', not as a characteristic of people nor as a cultural cloak to be removed, but as a political process, necessarily involving power (Question 2; see Introduction to the book). Three structures are identified as central to the operation of gender relations: the gendered division of labour, the organisation of intimacy and the organisation of citizenship. Two processes are described as pivotal to the reproduction of those structures: the distribution of resources, and the operation of rules (interpretations or norms) about or connected to gender (Verloo and Roggeband 1996; Verloo 2001). The Dutch approach also includes criteria as normative grounds for assessing whether a situation is to be judged positively or negatively: equality, autonomy and pluriformity/diversity (Chapter 4).

These shifts in representations of the 'problem' have important implications (Question 5). For example:

- Identifying the 'gendered division of labour' as a structure of inequality means that, rather than inserting women into existing or slightly modified work structures as in Ireland, it becomes possible to put men's contribution to domestic labour on the agenda.

- Highlighting the 'organization of intimacy' as central to gender inequality puts aspects of people's so-called private lives, including violence, on the agenda. Violence in this case is represented to be a 'problem' of unequal gendered power relations, rather than a matter of situational opportunity, as in Irish 'gender proofing' (see discussion above).

- The explicit targeting of the 'organization of citizenship' as a structure of inequality puts any presumed gender-neutral understanding of citizenship in question.

Men therefore enter the analysis in the Netherlands, not as a statistical category to be set in comparison with 'women', but as 'gendered beings', whose behaviours need to change when those behaviours reinforce asymmetrical power relations (Question 2). This understanding of the 'problem' is potentially transformative since it challenges the masculine norms that characterise mainstream institutional practices. Shifting the focus from 'gender' as a part of people to gender as political process also creates the opportunity to examine the impact of gendered assumptions on the maintenance of hierarchical social relations *beyond those between 'women' and 'men'* (that is, including social relations around 'race'/ethnicity, class, sexuality and disability), a project of pressing concern for contemporary feminism. This form of analysis therefore facilitates what Patricia Hill Collins (1999: 263) describes as a 'logic of intersectionality' (Question 5; Chapters 10 and 13).

It is important to reflect on the specific conditions in the Netherlands that allowed this more confrontational form of gender analysis (or gender impact assessment) to emerge (Question 3). As Verloo (2000: 61-62) notes, this was possible because of an established statement in Dutch policies that there were 'unequal power relations between the sexes', stemming in turn from a relatively long engagement between Dutch feminism and the state. This history could well mean that the Dutch model is not easily transportable to other contexts (see Woodward and Meier 1997).

Moreover, as in Ireland there are signs of continuing political contestation about the meaning of gender impact assessment (Question 6), indicating the always-incomplete and unpredictable character of such interventions (Chapter 6). For example, the Guidelines are not always applied as they read. Specifically, the structure called 'the organization of intimacy' is seldom included in gender impact assessments because it is considered to be too intrusive into 'private' lives. Roggeband and Verloo (2006) report that to date assessment reports focus mainly on the relationship between family responsibilities and paid employment, avoiding the more contentious discussion around sexuality, personal relationships and reproduction. In addition, attempts to incorporate 'care/community' as a new criterion (to sit alongside equality, autonomy and pluriformity/diversity; see above) have been unsuccessful due to the current Dutch Government's right-of-centre ideology (Roggeband and Verloo 2006).

A further constraint on the transformational possibilities of Dutch gender impact assessment is clear in the very language of 'impact assessment', which suggests examining the *impact* of policies *on* gender relations, as if such relations are exogenous to (outside) policy processes. Such a stance, in our view, limits the ability to identify how policies are themselves gendering practices. For example, the *New General Social Assistance Act* (1996 in Plantenga 2000) placed an emphasis on what was called the 'activating effect' in the labour market, the imperative to engage as many people as possible in paid labour. The obligation to work, or at least to apply for work, was extended to lone mothers with children five years old or over. A 'gender impact assessment' (GIA) concluded that for most women the new Act meant an improvement.

Asking 'what's the problem represented to be?' produces a very different assessment. This question draws attention to the way in which constituting the 'problem' to be people's (in this instance single mothers') absence from paid labour (Question 1) ignores the care needs of the population (Question 4). And, as Plantenga (2000: 9) concludes, so long as there is no 'national framework for care' to accompany the 'national framework of a general obligation to work', women will continue to be expected to provide such care. Hence policies that aim simply to increase women's labour force participation effectively have a gendering effect, (re) producing women as carers.

To increase the critical potential of gender analysis processes, therefore, it is insufficient to 'vet' or to 'proof' designated policies for uneven *impacts* on 'women' and 'men' (as in Ireland), or even on 'gender relations' (as in the Netherlands). Rather, we need to be able to detect how policies generate or constitute specific social conditions, social subjects and social relations as effects of power. The next section illustrates how a WPR approach assists in this task.

Policies as gender*ing* practices: Avoiding the 'project trap'

Currently, as several authors (Armstrong 2002; March et al. 1999) have identified, an important constraint on the transformative potential of gender analysis processes is their subservience to wider policy objectives (which they call the 'project trap'). As March et al. (1999: 9) describe, the key distinction among gender analysis frameworks is whether or not they remain 'narrowly applicable to programmes and projects', or whether they are able 'to broaden out and apply to the social organisational contexts'. In their view (and we concur), unfortunately, most gender analysis procedures (handbooks, guides or tool kits) fall victim to the 'project trap', explaining the odd confluence between market activating policies, often called neoliberal, and gender mainstreaming in some sites (Chapter 2).

This outcome is unexpected given that gender analysis is often described as a form of *ex ante* analysis, examining the possible *impact* of policies, *prior to their implementation*, on women and men. However, if there is no questioning of the ways in which policies actually *shape* 'women' and 'men', and the relations among them, the analysis is severely constrained in what it can accomplish. To identify the sorts of policy changes that might redress the asymmetrical power relations between and among 'women' and 'men', gender analysis processes need to be able to examine and question the underlying presuppositions in policies that generate gendered beings, that is, their gender*ing* effects. The following examples, which apply the WPR approach (Bacchi 2009a), illustrate how this form of analysis works.[1]

- The World Bank's (2002: 5 fn. 3) 'Case for Mainstreaming Gender' has as a goal 'a less rigid or extreme gender-based division of labour' in order

131

to increase 'female productive capital, which has important pro-growth effects'. We can see similarities here with the Irish concern that 'female involvement in the workplace should continue to grow' (Polverari and Fitzgerald 2002a: 38) and with the focus on the 'activating effect' in the Dutch Social Assistance Act. As in those cases, the 'problem' is represented to be the limits imposed on productivity by caring responsibilities (Question 1). Such a position envisages 'freeing' women from such responsibilities to allow them to engage in paid labour. As we have already seen, it says nothing, however, about how caring responsibilities will then be carried out (Question 4). This implicit devaluing of caring activities (Question 2) has gender*ing* effects, leaving in place the assumption that these activities are 'private' and less important than paid work, and that women in the main will do them (Question 5).

- New Zealand's Ministry of Women's Affairs (MWA 2001: 1) offers a gender analysis on retirement income, which accepts as a 'Defined Desired Outcome' the government's aim to 'encourage greater financial self-reliance for retired people'. Along similar lines Australia's *Intergenerational report* (Australian Government 2002 in Lee 2004: 54) endorses the principle that neither the overall tax burden nor the nation's debt should increase to deal with the 'problem' of Australia's ageing population. Rather, the declared goal is long-term strategies to reduce per capita expenditure in health and aged care, and in individual welfare payments. In both cases older people's dependence on state benefits is represented to be the 'problem' (Question 1).

Drawing on Ireland's 'gender proofing' framework it could be pointed out, usefully, that these proposals may well have adverse effects *on* women (compared with men) due to women's *different* relationship to paid labour. However, it is another exercise altogether to point out that the grounding premise of reduced budget deficits has gender*ing* effects (Question 5). That is, so long as women are the ones held primarily responsible for caring responsibilities, reduced welfare budgets reinforce this presumption and women's subordinate status.

Along similar lines Pat Armstrong (2002) insists that the role of gender analysis is not simply to 'vet' single policies for their *impact* on women and men but to subject the whole direction of government policy (her example is health policy) to scrutiny. In this vein she shows how privatisation of health care shifts responsibility out of hospitals to the household, and thus to women – a gender*ing* effect since it increases the caring work that those marked as 'women' will have to perform.

- As another example, the removal of the operational subsidy from community-based child care by the Howard Government in 1997 forced some centres to increase fees and others to close, affecting women's access to the labour force. A 2001 report (Smith and Ewer 2001) found that, due to the change in funding arrangements, an estimated 1547 women in two socio-economically disadvantaged suburbs of Sydney had been forced to leave their jobs or were prevented from seeking full-time work due to rising child care costs. This policy practice produces a gender*ing* effect by putting in place circumstances in which those marked as 'women' will continue to perform nurturing activities.

- Finally, the European Commission's (1998: 17) *Guide to gender impact assessment* takes as axiomatic the goal of 'eliminating labour market rigidities'. To this end the *Guide* endorses 'positive action in favour of men to a careful selection of professions related to child care'. Unless the grounding premise – that labour market rigidities are the 'problem' (Question 1) – is put into question, it becomes difficult to draw attention to the ways in which creating child care jobs for men entrenches groups of women in low-paying jobs or out of work altogether, reinforcing many women's marginal economic position (Bacchi 1996: 113) – a gender*ing* effect (Questions 4 and 5).

These examples illustrate that policies do not simply *impact* on women and men, or on gender relations; instead, in many cases they *produce* gendered lives and gender as a relation of inequality. As poststructuralist theory explains (see Theoretical resources section above), who we are and how we live are, to an extent, an effect of social and institutional practices, including state policies. Asking 'what's the problem represented to be?' alerts us to this productive or constitutive dimension of public policies. Why is this important? And where does it lead?

Conclusion

As argued earlier, gender analysis strategies ought to be considered as open-ended, malleable and subject to continual political pressures. Rather than static frameworks it is appropriate to envisage them as fields of contestation in a continuing quest for gender justice. As part of this contestation, a WPR analysis, which describes policy as *productive* of social meanings and social relations, helps to identify aspects of mainstreaming agendas that may need to be debated and even rethought. Specifically, as this chapter shows, applying a WPR lens to Irish and Dutch gender analysis processes assists in identifying limitations in focusing on apparently real and empirical 'differences' in the lives of men and women, or in thinking about policies as simply *impacting* on presumably already existing gender relations.

While we are acutely aware of the contextual factors that influence what is possible in terms of gender mainstreaming programs (Chapter 4) we believe that the kind of questioning of proposals offered in this chapter would be useful to those involved in designing gender analysis instruments. There is no assumption that these policy workers will be able to overturn policies whose underlying precepts they identify as problematic. However, the exercise of asking of specific proposals 'what's the problem represented to be?' enables a different level of scrutiny of government practices. It also encourages a kind of analysis that helps practitioners to identify aspects of a policy that may benefit from the kind of rethinking encouraged here.

To this end, Chapters 1 and 2 recommend introducing a WPR approach as a reflexive practice, called 'deep evaluation', within mainstreaming processes. The argument here is that *doing* a WPR analysis increases the ability to detect the constitutive dimension of policy practices, an instance of 'sudden seeing' as described in Chapter 12. In Chapter 4 we encourage what we call 'gendering-awareness mainstreaming' as a related practice with this same objective. The further implication is that a WPR approach could provide significant stimulus to critical self-scrutiny in all policy development processes.

Clearly, in the current economic and political climate, when public servants are asked consistently to do more with less (Chapter 3), these proposals face significant challenges. Nonetheless, as subsequent chapters (Chapters 10, 12 and 13) argue, we remain convinced that substantive alterations to the asymmetrical power relations among social groups require the opening-up of spaces among a diversity of policy workers, and between policy workers and the wider community (see Chapter

8), to discuss and debate the contested meanings of gender and of gender equality. We see our task as offering ways of thinking differently to facilitate and encourage that discussion, in terms that make sense to policy workers, as well as to researchers. To this end this chapter recommends the usefulness of reflecting on how specific policies represent the 'problem' of 'gender inequality', and with what effects.

Notes

1. The issue of the 'project trap' and some of these examples are addressed briefly in Chapters 1 and 2. Greater detail is provided here to illustrate how the WPR approach assists in revealing deep-seated conceptual premises that can undermine espoused political objectives.

References

(Websites valid as of publication date)

Altman, J. and Hinkson, M. (eds) 2007. *Coercive reconciliation: Stabilise, normalise, exit Aboriginal Australia*. North Carlton, Melbourne: Arena Publications.

Annfelt, T. 2008. 'From soft fathers to the rights of the sperm? Biologism as a heteronorming resource', in Magnusson, E., Rönnblom, M. and Silius, H. (eds) *Critical studies of gender equalities: Nordic dislocations, dilemmas and contradictions*. Göteborg: Makadam Publishers.

Armstrong, P. 2002. 'Speaking notes', Public consultations of the Commission on the Future of Health Care, 30 May, Toronto, Ontario. <cewh-cesf.ca/PDF/health_reform/speaking-notes.pdf> accessed 1 November 2009.

Australian Government. 2002. *Intergenerational report 2002-2003*, Budget paper no. 5. Canberra: Commonwealth of Australia.

Bacchi, C. 1990. *Same difference: Feminism and sexual difference*. Sydney: Allen & Unwin.

Bacchi, C. 1996. *The politics of affirmative action: 'Women', equality and category politics*. London: Sage.

Bacchi, C. 1999. *Women, policy and politics: The construction of policy problems*. London: Sage.

Bacchi, C. 2004. 'Policy and discourse: Challenging the construction of affirmative action as preferential treatment', *Journal of European Public Policy* 11 (1): 128-46.

Bacchi, C. 2005. 'Affirmative action for men: A test of common sense?', *Just Policy* 36 (June): 5-12.

Bacchi, C. 2009a. *Analysing policy: What's the problem represented to be?* French's Forest, NSW: Pearson Education.

Bacchi, C. 2009b. 'Challenging the displacement of affirmative action by gender mainstreaming', *Asian Journal of Women's Studies* 15 (4): 7-29.

Bastalich, W. 'Politicizing the Productive: Subjectivity, Feminist Labour Thought and Foucault'. PhD thesis, Departments of Politics and Social Inquiry, University of Adelaide.

Beasley, C. and Bacchi, C. 2007. 'Envisaging a new politics for an ethical future: Beyond trust, care and generosity – towards an ethic of "social flesh"', *Feminist Theory* 8 (3): 279-98.

Burr, V. 2003. *Social constructionism*, 2nd edition. London: Routledge.

Burton, C. 1987. 'Merit and gender: Organisations and the mobilisation of masculine bias', *Australian Journal of Social Issues* 22 (2): 424-435.

Connolly, W.E. 1995. *The Ethos of Pluralization*. Minneapolis: University of Minnesota Press.

Crawley, M. and O'Meara, L. 2002. *Gender proofing handbook*. Dublin: NDP Gender Equality Unit.

Crawley, M. and O'Meara, L. 2004. *Gender impact assessment handbook*. Belfast: Gender Equality Unit.

Davies, B. 1994. *Poststructuralist theory and classroom practice*. Geelong: Deakin University.

Dean, M. 1999. *Governmentality: Power and rule in modern society*. London: Sage.

Dean, M. 2006. 'Governmentality and powers of life and death', in Marston, G. & McDonald, C. (eds) *Analysing social policy: A governmental approach*. Cheltenham, UK: Edward Elgar.

European Commission 1998. *A guide to gender impact assessment. Employment & social affairs, Equality between women and men*. Luxembourg: Office for Official Publications for the European Communities.

Eveline, J. 1994. 'The politics of advantage', *Australian Feminist Studies*. Special issue: *Women and citizenship* 19: 129-54.

Eveline, J. 2004. *Ivory basement leadership: Power and invisibility in the changing university*. Nedlands: University of Western Australia Press.

Foucault, M. 1980 [1977]. 'Truth and power', in Gordon, C. (ed.) *Power/knowledge: Selected interviews and other writings 1972-1977/Michel Foucault*. Trans. C. Gordon & others. Sussex: Harvester Press.

Fulcher, G. 1989. *Disabling policies? A comparative approach to education policy and disability*. East Sussex: The Falmer Press.

Gatens, M. 1995. *Imaginary bodies: Ethics, power and corporeality*. London: Routledge.

Hill Collins, P. 1999. 'Moving beyond gender: intersectionality and scientific knowledge', in Ferree, M.M., Lorber, J. and Hess, B.B. (eds) *Revisioning gender*. London: Sage.

Honkanen, K. 2008. 'Equality politics out of the subaltern', in Magnusson, E., Rönnblom, M. and Silius, H. (eds) *Critical studies of gender equalities: Nordic dislocations, dilemmas and contradictions*. Göteborg: Makadam Publishers.

Jahan, R. 1995. *The elusive agenda: Mainstreaming women in development*. London: Zed Books.

Lee, C. 2004. 'Australian women facing the future: Is the *Intergenerational Report* gender-neutral?' *Dialogue* 23 (3): 53-56.

Magnusson, E., Rönnblom, M. and Silius, H. (eds) 2008. *Critical studies of gender equalities: Nordic dislocations, dilemmas and contradictions*. Göteborg: Makadam Publishers.

March, C., Smyth, I. and Mukhopadhyay, M. (eds) 1999. *A guide to gender-analysis frameworks*. Oxford: Oxfam.

Marston, G. and McDonald, C. 2006. 'Introduction: Reframing social policy analysis', in Marston, G. and McDonald, C. (eds) *Analysing social policy: A governmental approach*. Cheltenham, UK: Edward Elgar.

Massumi, B. 2002. *From parables to the virtual: Movement, affect, sensation*. Durham: Duke University Press.

MWA (Ministry of Women's Affairs). 2001. *Gender-based policy analysis: A resource for policy analysts*. Auckland: MWA.

Plantenga, J. 2000. 'Gender impact assessment and the employment strategy: The case of the Netherlands'. External report commissioned and presented to the European Commission. <mbs.ac.uk/research/europeanemployment/projects/gendersocial/documents/GIA_NL.pdf> accessed 22 October 2009.

Polverari, L. and Fitzgerald, R. 2002a. *Integrating gender equality in the evaluation of the Irish 2000-06 National Development Plan, vol. I: Background concepts and methods*. Glasgow: NDP Gender Equality Unit, European Policies Research Centre, University of Strathclyde.

Polverari, L. and Fitzgerald, R. 2002b. *Integrating gender equality in the evaluation of the Irish 2000-06 National Development Plan, vol. II: Tool kit for gender evaluation*. Glasgow: NDP Gender Equality Unit, European Policies Research Centre, University of Strathclyde.

Rees, T. 1998. *Mainstreaming equality in the European Union: Education, training and labour market policies*. London: Routledge.

Roggeband, C. and Verloo, M. 2006. 'Evaluating gender impact assessment in the Netherlands (1994-2004): A political process approach', *Policy & Politics* 34 (4): 615-32.

Rönnblom, M. 2008. 'De-politicizing gender? Constructions of gender equality in Swedish regional policy', in Magnusson, E., Rönnblom, M. and Silius, H. (eds) *Critical studies of gender equalities: Nordic dislocations, dilemmas and contradictions*. Göteborg: Makadam Publishers.

Shapiro, M. J. 1988. *The politics of representation: Writing practices, photography and policy analysis*. Madison: University of Wisconsin Press.

Smith, M. and Ewer, P. 2001. *Changes to childcare funding and women's labour force participation in Western Sydney*, WSROC (Western Sydney Regional Organisation of Councils), Blacktown, NSW. <wsroc.com.au/page.aspx?pid=58&vid=1&fid=34&ftype=True> accessed 1 November 2009.

Tanesini, A. 1994. 'Whose language?', in Lennon, K. & Whitford, M. (eds) *Knowing the difference: Feminist perspectives in epistemology*. New York: Routledge.

Verloo, M. 2000. 'Making women count in the Netherlands', in Beveridge, F., Nott, S. and Stephen, K. (eds) *Making women count: Integrating gender into law and policy-making*. Dartmouth: Ashgate.

Verloo, M. 2001. 'Another velvet revolution? Gender mainstreaming and the politics of implementation', *IWM working paper no. 5/2001*. Vienna: Institute of Human Sciences (IWM).

Verloo, M. 2005. 'Mainstreaming gender equality in Europe: A critical frame analysis approach', *The Greek Journal of Social Research* 117, B': 11-34.

Verloo, M. and Roggeband, C. 1996. 'Gender impact assessment: The development of a new instrument in the Netherlands', *Impact Assessment* 14 (1): 3-31.

Woodward, A. and Meier, P. 1997. 'Gender impact assessment: Tool in mainstreaming or tool to begin mainstreaming? A comparison of Dutch and Flemish approaches'. Paper for the ECPR Joint Sessions, Bern, 27 February - 3 March.

World Bank. 2002. *Integrating Gender into the World Bank's work: A strategy for action.* <siteresources. worldbank.org/INTGENDER/Resources/strategypaper.pdf> accessed 21 October 2009.

6

Power, resistance and reflexive practice[1]

JOAN EVELINE AND CAROL BACCHI

Introduction: Joan Eveline and Carol Bacchi

This chapter examines the primary organising processes which produce the meanings of policy statements. It outlines and inspects the social power circumscribing these policy statements, the relations of power and resistance involved in such statements, and their effects on those subject to the policy.

The previous chapter outlined how the WPR approach concentrates on the constitutive effects of existing or proposed policies, showing how the characterising of policy 'problems' within those policies or proposals (what the 'problem' is represented to be) 'shapes' (or constitutes) people as particular kinds of subjects. This chapter pursues the point that policies *elicit* subjectivities, rather than *determine* them (Dean 1999: 32). It highlights the always-incomplete nature of subjectification processes, emphasising that the subjects of policy are always more than the products of policy regulation, whether explicit or implicit, as is the case in problem representations. In this view political subjects, both those who 'do' policy and those to whom it is 'done', are both *subjected* and *resistant* to policy discourses. A particular focus of this chapter and of the book is how 'doing' policy both produces and enables the subjectivities of those who analyse and develop it, including ourselves as researchers.

The influences of feminist poststructuralism and recent organisational theory shape the propositions in this chapter. It was prompted by our wish as authors to fill a gap in our earlier and later chapters. A reader will find little explicit discussion of power, resistance, and subjectivity, and how these relate to knowledge production, in other chapters. Although there is much in the book's other chapters which assumes (and indeed in many cases takes further) the concepts we deal with here, we wanted a feminist account of policy analysis to address more directly the *ubiquity of power relations*. In tune with poststructuralist thinking one specific goal is to show that any shaping of knowledge, including our own, is a social production, formed through *productive* power relations, with unpredictable effects.

The chapter begins with two brief sections, the first on poststructuralist developments in organisational theory, followed by a section on how meaning is produced in language and discourse. It then turns to examining the relationship between power, knowledge, and resistance, using gender mainstreaming as its exemplar. Section four asks two important questions: a) how can such feminist poststructuralist concepts locate the unstable and shifting subjectivities of those engaged in policy work? and b) how might we understand change, given these propositions for how meaning is both fixed and enabled? The chapter concludes by arguing for a policy practice which permits a 'temporary fixing' of meaning, plus a *reflexive practice* for challenging those meanings and elaborating new ones.

Studies of organisation

For our purposes organisational studies can be divided into two groups or paradigms of thinking. By far the best established in contemporary academic disciplines is the first of these 'thinking' paradigms. Studies in this canon of literature generally privilege organisational behaviour, using organisational psychology and to a far less extent organisational sociology. Most conventional studies of leadership and management are linked to this extensive canon of conventional literature. This way of thinking is inclined to investigate how people, and the things they produce, fit within 'the organisation', or different organisations. 'The organisation' is generally understood as a noun, with organisations as relatively stable 'things' engaged in finding predictable mechanisms for growth and development. There is also the belief that such necessary development can be perfected by increasing 'expert' knowledges about organisational management, strategies and competitors. This notion that an organisation is a 'thing' that makes certain other things happen tends to reify 'the organisation' itself as an agentic, rational actor. Our chapter is not concerned with this paradigm for studying organisations or organisational behaviour.

We are much more interested in a second set of propositions for studying organisation, one which comes from relatively recent configurations of organisational studies researchers. These 'organisation' theorists are informed by critical, poststructural and sometimes postmodern thinking, which seeks to move the subject of study away from 'things' such as 'organisations' onto the *processes and practices* that bring those 'things', and the people who work in such contexts, into order as fixed 'properties' and essences that we take for granted as 'things' (see Chapter 12). Such researchers ask: how do we organise our knowledges and understand the work we do? how do we 'fix' those knowledges and understandings into taken-for-granted 'truths' of the world (establish them, privilege them, prioritise them), particularly if, as people informed by poststructuralism, we understand that the knowledges we produce are always provisional social constructions?

The wider concerns most of these researchers study are likely to be discourses, or discursive fields and their effects, including their effects on people and how they do their jobs and think things through. As with the WPR approach outlined in the previous chapter, these studies draw on poststructuralist premises to reject humanist concepts of the individual as a pre-discursive agentic subject. The argument, as outlined in the Introduction to the book, is that to see human beings as fixed essences ignores how practices, including policy practices, shape emergent individuals and relations. This chapter elaborates some of the theory underpinning this argument and its relevance for policy actors and researchers in the gender equity field.

Language structures and discursive positioning

The notion of 'structuralism' that post-structuralism attempts to move beyond stems from the structural elements of language (Saussure 1974). People must use language (sign language included) to formulate thoughts and meanings about their lives and interests. For Saussurean linguistics, meaning does not pre-exist language but is formed within its linguistic confines. Meaning is not *reflected* by language but is *produced* by it. Language is not a natural phenomenon which just happens to groups of people, but follows a fixed ordering, using certain linguistic rules and codes for what can be said, how it can be said, and how it produces meaning. Language must select (reduce the possibilities of) what it articulates in order to ensure that what is said, or written or thought, sounds sensible (follows rules of meaning-making).

Meaning is made by differentiating the 'sign' being produced from all others in the signifying system. The signifier 'woman' for example gains its meaning by being differentiated from all those that pre-exist it. This denaturalised view of language makes it inherently social, therefore open to contestation, and with ongoing political effects.

Poststructuralism seeks to avoid the generalisations in Saussure's theory of an abstract system of language. It wants to look closely into the *contexts of specific moments and locations* in which historically specific discourses provide the basis for language formation and use. Specifically, Saussure's theory does not account for the plurality of meaning or for changes in meaning. In that sense it is too 'fixed' for a poststructuralist, who turns to 'discourse' to explain *both* the plurality and fixity of meaning. 'Discourse' refers to relatively well-bounded areas of social knowledge that both constrain and enable what can be written, spoken or thought within specific historical limits.

Poststructuralist organisation studies takes on this twofold task – to explain the plurality and fixity of meaning – by seeing discursive positioning (one's location within discourse) as an effect of particular organisation. They seek to characterise the intricate network of discourses, in the sites where these are articulated, including the institutionally legitimised forms of knowledge from which justification is sought. For example, the intervention into child sexual abuse in outback Aboriginal communities (referred to in Chapter 5) sought its justification by signalling the need for police and troops to organise the intervention process. This signified the intervention as a national 'emergency' of war-like proportions, requiring both military intervention and the coterminous curtailing of Aboriginal people's citizenry freedoms to normalise 'the situation', to bring it to order. The longstanding institutionalised racism since colonisation, informing legal, justice and welfare systems, and through which such Aboriginal communities are administered, was neglected in this signifying move. This 'reduction' of available meanings allowed the military movement against Aboriginal people to be implicitly justified as 'necessary' – even 'normal'.

Importantly, the meaning effects of this discursive positioning were by no means monolithic. Human rights groups, certain Aboriginal communities, and various political and media actions offered alternative frameworks to tell the story. Included here are the speaking positions about longstanding abuse, and the violence the intervention created for particular Aboriginal women in the communities, whose voices were, for a short time at least, broadcast for national consumption. We have here an example of discourse as an 'asset', 'by nature, the object of a struggle, a political struggle' (Foucault 1972: 120; see Introduction to book).

Poststructural organisation studies are variously interested in such issues of power, resistance and subjectivity, seeing them as relational aspects of discursive positioning. For these organisation theorists, organisation is viewed as a verb rather than as a noun (Chia 1996); organisation is an action rather than a fixed entity.

Such thinking feeds into the 'fluidity' or ontological 'becoming' framework that informs this chapter and the book. In this vein, in previous chapters, we talk about 'gender*ing*' (a gerund or form of verb), or about 'doing' gender, rather than about gender (a noun) as a characteristic of people, to remind us of the 'fixing', or reifying, capacities of language. When we (and others) talk about 'doing' gender we are using a repositioning designed to recall, or in some cases to demonstrate, the point just made about the productive elements of discourse – how discourse produces 'truths' like 'the intervention'. In that repositioning we also aim to show that the term 'gendering' is itself not a completely closed system of meaning. In suggesting that lack of closure about what gender 'is', we aim to intimate that gendering remains unfinished business in what it conveys and enables.

For public policy this shift from 'fixity' to 'becoming' draws attention to the actions, the 'doings', that install (or 'fix') certain meanings. Such an emphasis on meaning-making in policy formulation encourages a more questioning, or sceptical, stance towards commonly accepted meanings ascribed to 'things'. The example above that puts in question the way in which 'the intervention' was 'fixed' as a necessary (normal) 'response' to (what was described as) a 'national emergency', is an example of this scepticism at work.

Relations of power, knowledge and resistance

'The intervention' allows us to see the power involved in producing particular meanings of events and things. This understanding of power as productive is linked with Michel Foucault, but can also be found in Spinoza and Deleuze (Chapter 3). A 'productive' understanding sees power as producing, 'not so much repressions, as regularities' (Massumi in Zournazi 2002). Foucault's method does not start from a general theory of meaning and power, but looks to the local centres of power/knowledge, and their effects within discourse. As he (1977: 27) argues, 'there is no power relation without the correlative constitution of a field of knowledge, nor any knowledge that does not presuppose and constitute at the same time power relations'.

A key element in this productive notion of power is how social agents are subject to it. Foucault writes (1981: 86): 'power is tolerable only on condition that it mask a substantial part of itself. Its success is proportional to its ability to hide its own mechanisms.' A particularly effective method of hiding power's own mechanisms, for Foucault, occurs at the level of the 'most mundane and routine experience'. Here 'the normalising effects of power are most insidiously employed' (McNay 1994: 148) to make a particular action appear obvious and inevitable. Again, the example of 'the intervention' as necessary and normal illustrates how power, in this understanding, works.

When discussing 'power' in poststructuralist terms it is important to make some author disclaimers. Firstly, as the reader will have noticed, our account does not give a description of what power *is*. If the reader is looking for a dualistic theory of power that understands some people or groups as *having* it, or more of it, and using it selectively, while some others may resist it only in particular instances, with more or less success, s/he is going to be disappointed. Nor do we hold that some are powerful and others are powerless, a notion which conceptualises resistance as always opposite from and outside power (Knights and Vurdabakis 1994: 168).

In poststructuralist thought power is not like money one accumulates (and perhaps banks for a rainy day) but is immanent (occurs internally) to actions. As Massumi (in Zournazi 2002) says, 'It's always a power to', as opposed to 'power over':

> The true power of the law [and of policy] is the power to form us. It puts
> the paths in us ... So in a way it's as potentialising as what we call freedom
> ... only what it potentialises is limited to a number of predictable paths.

Power networks are 'always already there', argues Foucault (1980: 141), but so are their points of resistance (Weedon 1987: 125). Individuals are 'always in the position of simultaneously undergoing and exercising this power' (Foucault 1980: 98). It is this simultaneous action of both being subject to but exercising power that underpins the Foucauldian notion of 'power relations'.

Power and resistance, therefore, are an indispensable *relation* in each other's actions. Both are exercised *through a set of practices*, through taking *a particular action*. Resistance is not some people's particular reaction to more power being used by others, but is itself an exercise of power. It is immanent to power relations, an aspect of them, whose possibility must be present before there is an exercise of power (Knights and Vurdabakis 1994: 192). Without the possibility of resistance there would be no exercise of power. But this does not mean that power simply represses resistance, because a key feature of power is that it is productive – the exercising of power 'is a source of pleasure for both its agents and its subjects' (Weedon 1987: 121).

A productive view of power does not conclude that power and resistance are necessarily equal in their effects, however. Such a conclusion would deny the hierarchies by which the organisation of discourse takes effect. The practices that ensure gender analysis is contested in policymaking contexts, for example, are unlikely to make a gender analysis a concern when developing a policy on Australian relations with China or the United States, unless a gender analysis has been approved before or after it. The first policy approach, applying gender analysis, presupposes a challenge to the usual ways of doing policy; the second, proceeding to follow conventional policy practices, takes for granted that a gender analysis is not relevant (Chapter 12). The latter stance ranks higher in the hierarchy of policy discourse.

How can such a broad understanding of power be useful for policy? How should we understand the powerfulness of institutions, such as 'the state', the organisation of work, policing and military discourses, education discourses and the family – and their effects?

Let us start with the day-to-day 'organising' practices of education, the family and work, and examine their gendering effects. Each of these institutions employs particular taken-for-granted organising practices, such as: techniques and tools for learning; emphasis placed on sporting equipment; the organising of work and leisure spaces; the organising of work and domestic spaces; and the impact of media and consumption on toys and clothing. These practices constitute differences in skills and strengths between girls and boys, 'endowing individuals with specific perceptions of their identity and potential, which appear natural to the subjected individual, rather than as the product of diffuse forms of power' (Weedon 1987: 121).

For a critical theorist such as Foucault, power relations are evident through their capacity to 'produce' the truths we live by. Growing girls and boys are embedded in such truths from the day they are born; these operate through the family, their schooling and so on into the work they do, the pastimes they engage in and beyond. All of these institutions operate within relatively well-bounded areas of social knowledge, or discourses.

There is no all-powerful or central control for 'the state' in this understanding of discourse. Because power operates through diffuse and contrary forms, captured in Foucault's (1991) concept of 'governmentality', 'the state' instead operates as one important organising force among others. What gives these discourses their powerfulness, usually based on their institutionalised mechanisms, is their capacity to fix meaning alongside or against these other organising forces.

Gender mainstreaming – a policy initiative putatively designed to ensure that all policies are gender-sensitive and gender-inclusive – for example, is one form of policy intervention which is both enabled and constrained by the governance of 'the state'. Developing a policy approach titled 'gender mainstreaming' exercises power, but its social power and authority over how control is exercised is less profound in most gender mainstreaming contexts than is, say, education or foreign policy. Yet as an exercise in power it is more productive – or proliferative ('potentialising') – than repressive. For a start, it activates various forms of resistance, among feminists as well as among other policy workers, as many policy personnel in the field would attest. In naming a set of policy practices 'gender mainstreaming', policy workers are giving them meaning, defining gender mainstreaming as different from all signifiers that have been given a prior meaning (such as 'equal opportunity'). The taken-for-granted meaning of 'gender mainstreaming' cannot be thought about, or communicated to others, without giving it meaning through language.

However, this is not to claim that, because of the fixing capacities of language, the meaning of gender mainstreaming is inevitably fixed in discourse. Indeed, we want to claim just the opposite. Located as it is within policy discourses, gender mainstreaming enables the power of multiple possible meanings, as we have seen in preceding chapters. Indeed, gender mainstreaming gains its power as something that has stable social force through its degree of incorporation by discourses *in a particular context*. These include but are not limited to policy discourses such as the practices of the European Union and United Nations, legal discourse such as the practices of law in international or national sex and race discrimination, educational discourse such as the practices of universities, etc. But the power effects of these

146

discourses are neither totalising nor equal. While the linguistic meaning of 'gender mainstreaming', for example, seeks to differentiate it from 'equal opportunity', discursive power in particular contexts (or, in other words, discursive positioning) can make such interventions appear very similar, or derivative, or unnecessary. For example, as we saw in Chapter 5, gender mainstreaming in Ireland closely replicates the principles behind equal opportunity policy.

What makes some discourses more powerful than others in designing policy? Some of the everyday practices (such as issues people see as important in doing policy), that become part of a 'gender mainstreaming' approach, may well have been utilised under techniques that had been given another meaning. Some examples could be the notion that people *have* a 'gender' in 'equal opportunity' practices, or the practice of determinedly leaving talk of 'gender' out of policy documents in the belief that 'speaking it' undermines the delicate balance achieved in 'gender neutral' organisations (Chapter 12). These are just two examples of 'discursive effects' (that is, possible practices within policy discourses), but the potentialities are multiple.

Such multiplicity of available meanings makes the 'discursive positioning' of gender mainstreaming unstable, fragmentary, incomplete, and unpredictable, rather than 'fixed'. Contrary to its linguistic fixing as 'different' from all other signifiers, the discursive positioning of 'gender mainstreaming' is historically situated, contingent and provisional. Hence in previous chapters we have referred to the *contested concept* of gender mainstreaming, and what this contestation means with regard to the proliferating ways of 'doing' a mainstreaming program in different national, organisational and policy contexts. If the meaning of gender mainstreaming is, as argued, contested and provisional, policy workers need to be alert to the proliferation of meanings available and how some promise more in terms of social transformation than others. The particular scheme found wanting, of course, may be one they themselves have helped to develop.

It follows that the act of naming a set of practices 'gender mainstreaming', and having that meaning accepted in a particular discursive field (policymaking), is hardly the end of the matter. What fixes 'gender mainstreaming' as a relatively stable policy activity, in which policy people attempt to find the 'best way' to do it, is a network of power relations embedded in a hierarchy of discursive positioning. A fixed universal meaning of 'gender mainstreaming' cannot be abstracted from the history of usage through which that meaning (or various meanings) is produced.

Those meanings take the forms defined for them by historically specific discourses, which have competed in a contested space for making meaning.

This non-dualistic conception of power and resistance has important ramifications for any kind of intervention in governance practices, including government policy. Illustrating the importance of practices, government policy comes into effect because of how people do it and use it (see Chapter 12). Power relations, operating through policies, cannot occur without the actions of agents and subjects. To what extent does this claim make policy actors responsible for the effects of policy? This is where we turn to the idea of subjectivity, examining it as both a liberal humanist concept and in its poststructuralist version. It is important to reflect on these issues to clarify that a focus on policy practice and those who 'do it' does not imply that sovereign individuals 'practice policy'. Rather, how subjects are constituted *within* discourse forms a crucial part of this understanding, as the following section elaborates.

Subjectivity and change

Weedon (1987: 77) argues that common sense is 'the medium through which already fixed "truths" about the world, society, and individuals are expressed'. Common sense assumes that language is a transparent medium reflecting already existing facts, including changes which occur prior to language. A poststructuralist would argue that language does indeed give meaning to events retrospectively, but it gives a *version of meaning* rather than reflecting a meaning which is already fixed.

The appeal to 'experience' as a guarantee of truth is a key feature of commonsense knowledge. Commonsense knowledge about how to develop a policy proposal, for example, may rely on the collective professional experience of other public servants, trainers and consultants, or on the personal experience of oneself and close colleagues. In both cases, it is assumed that experience, like the knowledge it produces, 'is fixed, true and a guide to action' (Weedon 1987: 78).

Commonsense knowledge therefore relies on two key assumptions: a) the transparency of language; b) the evidential truth of experience. Both assumptions depend upon *a particular understanding of the individual and of subjectivity*. Such an understanding comes from a long history of humanist discourse in Western Europe, where the dominant assumption concludes that we come to know the world through experience; indeed experience gives access to truth. This offers a degree of certainty about our place in the world and who we are. If meaning is reflected in language and mediated by experience, our knowledge of the world is true knowledge. For the humanist, subject security comes from the assumption that one's individuality, including one's gender, are fixed qualities which constitute one's nature. A person's apparently coherent, knowing consciousness guarantees this belief, leading to assumptions about what she can achieve. But this commonsense belief that what we know stands outside its discursive construction can easily serve to justify and guarantee existing social inequities.

Take, for example, domestic violence. How a woman perceives domestic violence via her access to various understandings of 'the problem', including those produced through public policies (Bacchi 1999: 164-180), will affect her 'experience' of it, and how she responds. If she sees herself as provoking the violence or sees men as naturally violent, she is unlikely to perceive it as intolerable behaviour or illegitimate power. In effect, she is unlikely to call it 'domestic violence', unless she already begins to see it as an illegitimate practice. Particular cultural understandings play a role here (see Chapter 9). Note, this position does not imply that somehow it is more important to deal with competing understandings of domestic violence than with the material reality of that experience. Rather, the point is to recognise that competing meanings of 'problems', how 'problems' are discursively produced, have *material or lived effects*. In the case just discussed particular representations of domestic violence may impel some women to tolerate intolerable behaviour. That is, discourses have to be recognised as practices – with no suggestion of intentional deployment – that make things happen, challenging any supposed dichotomy between 'representation' and 'the real' (see Chapter 5).

Political struggle over the meaning of experience involves personal, psychic and emotional investment on the part of the individual. It is the most crucial of struggles because it plays such a key part in determining the individual's role as social agent. For a poststructuralist it is not the concept of 'experience' itself that needs questioning but an understanding of it as having a fixed truth pre-existing language and discourse.

Poststructuralist thinking sees subjectivity as open to continuous redefinition, a consciousness which is constantly slipping. An example of this view of subjectivity (in relation to people involved in policy work) is explored in Chapter 12. That chapter shows how the subjectivities of policy personnel (their understanding of what they are doing and the problem of gender irrelevance they are addressing) are constituted temporarily within the discourses available to them. It reflects on how those who engaged in the hands-on practices of conducting a gender analysis (in a context in which they were obliged to examine how gender relates to policy) began to understand why such an analysis was needed. They developed that understanding among specific conditions, including the practice of speech actions, yet allowed it to remain obscure in other events where the context of power relations was not conducive to expression.

Policy workers are not passive dupes of a bureaucratic and hierarchical organisation. Nonetheless poststructuralist theory would say that they, along with everyone else, are governed by the specific discourses in which they perform their work. The most powerful discourses have firm institutional bases – in the public sector these can come from law, medicine, education or welfare provision, to name just a few. An individual cannot become a social agent without being subject to such discourses. Hence, we require a different conception of 'agency' than the humanist conception of a coherent, knowing consciousness. In contrast the 'agents' in the understanding of policy practice discussed here need to be understood as constituted *through the work they do* and through the myriad day-to-day practices in which they engage (Chapter 12). As an example, policy actors follow systematic procedures and lines of command that produce them as 'rational actors', blocking sensitivity to entrenched ways of thinking (conceptual premises) that leave their stamp on policy 'outcomes' (Gill 2006; Chapter 5).

Still, as mentioned earlier, discourses both constrain and enable. While they regulate meaning, there are only finite numbers of discourses in circulation at any given time; hence they are competing for meaning. It is this competition for meaning among discourses 'which creates the possibility of new ways of thinking and new forms of subjectivity' (Weedon 1987: 139).

A hypothetical project on public rental housing for example might draw on a government policy on sustainable transport and cities. The government minister for infrastructure has come to office in a government elected to provide, among other things, greener policies. The minister recruits an expert, world-renowned for his designing of sustainable cities, who recruits in turn his local students to gather the materials needed for the policy. The students, employed on fixed contracts, work alongside career public servants for six months, under the tutelage of the expert, whose sustainable projects highlight public transport, high-density living and mixed communities (differing demographic characteristics of class and ethnic background). The knowledge the students, public servants and expert gather for the policy comes from environmental science, ethics, medicine, law, demography, transport, planning, community housing, political science and local governance. Feminist critiques of these expert knowledges are at best accorded a marginal positioning and in most cases are not in evidence. In each case these expert knowledges constitute the subject of the discourse (the possible people it will affect), but also subject them to its effects. Yet the subjugation of the subject is by no means total.

For example, the legalities that provide the meanings for socially and environmentally sustainable housing may contradict or play down those given in environmental science, local governance or community health, implying struggles between discourses of expert interests. Yet the nominated expert and those who work under him are employed to deliver a coherent policy, so they deal with this problem of conflicting meanings by selecting the meanings that best fit the coherent and useful message they plan to convey.

A week before the completed policy is due for release by the eager minister it lands on the desk of the director of the tiny policy unit for women, which has the task of assessing all policies before they are released, in order to check their gender analysis credentials. The director points out that the policy does not mention gender and that she should have been involved at an earlier stage – the policy needs to show an awareness of the issues affecting women's access to public transport, shopping and medical facilities, schools and child care (low or non-existent steps and provision for transporting baby trolleys, the greater use of public transport by women of all ages and abilities, provision for long hours child care, easy access to a variety of schools, shopping and medical facilities). The expert responds that more than half of his students are women as is the minister and that the policy has been written in an open way to make it gender-neutral. Nonetheless the principle of using ramps rather than steps in public transport, housing and buildings, which also coincides with the needs of people with disabilities, becomes a premise in the policy.

The relevant government agency purchases a tract of land for the public rental housing project. It has a rail station on one side and regular bus services on the other, plus nearby facilities to accommodate shopping, medical, child care and school requirements. Moreover, it is in an area that has desirable housing developments surrounding it, and is very close to recreational facilities such as a well-used beach. The only problem is that this is land that was used by a chemical firm for over fifty years and the soil is polluted by lead and other toxic chemicals. Its recognised toxicity has prevented redevelopment of this valuable land for fifteen years.

After the government buys the land much of the toxicity is removed by a long and costly process under the direction of a further range of experts, replacing many thousands of tonnes of toxic soil with non-toxic land fill. Campaigns run by residents and green groups to make this toxic removal safer have some beneficial effect in the safety measures used, particularly when blood tests show that children in the area have toxic levels of lead. But the recreation areas are to be paved to protect the populace from the remaining toxins, no one is allowed to grow a vegetable patch or keep fowls and a law against any digging in the ground is passed by the local government. This also means the rainwater storage tanks to be located underground are now to be located in the walls of the buildings, making bedrooms and internal living spaces small for residents.

However, the lack of discursive unity and uniformity on the meanings of the project provide a discursive resource, or 'asset' (Foucault 1972: 120), for prospective welfare tenants to resist at least part of their subjection to the housing policy. Through intensive campaigns and negotiations with government, council, surrounding residents and divergent experts informing all those groups, it is agreed that rooms will remain a good size in each unit. It is also agreed that an extra storey will be built onto the development to accommodate the original number of housing units. In this context of fluid relations of power and resistance, the policy actor that assumes a single true meaning to 'sustainable public housing development' must now provide a meaning for these diffuse exercises of power.

Like the residents in the rental accommodation and surrounding areas the subjectivity of the policy workers, students and experts involved in producing the sustainable housing policy have themselves been constituted and subjected by these diverse and divergent discursive constructs and their effects. For policy actors (as well as for us authors) a large part of their subjection comes from their actions of speaking about, and writing, the policy statement. Weedon (1987: 119) argues that: 'To speak is to assume a subject position within discourse and to become subjected to the power and regulation of the discourse'.

As mentioned above, because only finite numbers of discourses circulate at any one time, the competition for meaning through discourse is finite. However, the *possibility* of meaning itself is infinite. For a poststructuralist critic, meaning can never be finally fixed, giving meaning infinite possibility. For such critics all meanings have implications for existing social relations, whether the meanings contest or reaffirm those relations. Yet 'every act of reading is a new production of meaning' (Weedon 1987: 139) because the positions from which we read and the discourses through which we read are, in principle, constantly changing. So are our subjectivities, in contrast to the liberal humanist view, which seeks to portray people as unified and coherent subjects with the capacity to achieve our rational goals. For the feminist poststructuralist, therefore, modes of subjectivity, 'like theories of society or versions of history, are temporary fixings in the ongoing process in which any absolute meaning or truth is constantly deferred' (Weedon 1987: 173).

This is where feminist poststructuralist revisions often turn to Deleuze and Guattari (1987) for an ontology of becoming, or what they call the 'rhizomatic'. The rhizomatic in the view of Deleuze and Guattari is a working-out of organising processes. It has neither beginning nor end but grows and overspills from the middle. Think of a simple rhizome such as a bamboo shoot – you can believe you've found it, prune it into a plant, or cut it off, but each time this will be the result of a negative operation – but it will have, maybe unseen to you, its multiple branching roots and shoots, 'with no central axis, no unified point of origin, and no given direction of growth – a proliferating, somewhat chaotic and diversified system of growths' (Grosz 1994: 199). Each time we grapple with one of these growths, whether it be 'gender mainstreaming' or a public housing complex, we will be extracting from the possibilities – the 'endless becomings' (Puar 2007: 213) – we are probably walking across. Another way of speaking about this is referred to by Michael Booth (1988) as the discrete and wholistic, with, when elaborating meaning, one embedded within the other.

Along with Foucault's (1991) account of governmentality, these ideas can tell us that as people we are not simply what our subject positions would circumscribe, because of the multiplicity of ways in which individuals exceed discursive constraints (see Eveline 2005). A feminist rhizomatics requires expending (giving, proliferating, dispersing) not accumulating (taking, increasing incrementally, collecting). In line with this thinking Massumi (2002: 9) describes 'fields of emergence' where:

> In every situation there are any number of levels of organization and
> tendencies in play, in cooperation with each other or at cross-purposes
> … This uncertainty can actually be empowering – once you realize that
> it gives you a margin of manoeuvrability … You may not reach the end
> of the trail but at least there's a next step. (Massumi in Zournazi 2002)

In each case, however, we cannot quite 'speak' the next step without gender
(and all those other categories) becoming arrested and inscribed. This means
being interested not only in what we might 'change', but also in recognising the
times and places where we have imposed fixed meanings in order to try to make
an improvement in people's lives and thinking through the implications of these
'fixings'. For this reason the 'next steps' for gender analysis, we suggest, involve policy
workers adopting forms of *reflexive* practice, as explained below.

Reflexive practice

A key premise of a poststructuralist critique is that we are inside the processes we
are examining. There is no outside to discourse because discursive positioning
determines authoritative utterances. But if there is no outside, because for example
the organising of policy accounts is paradigmatically circumscribed, then it is wise
to apply this principle *reflexively* to any account, whether it is a policy statement or
an academic paper.

The 'reflexive turn' in academic theorising resulted from the increasing
realisation that the researcher/theorist plays an active role in constructing the very
reality s/he is attempting to investigate. In this schema theories and statements are
economising modes of abstraction inspired in part by a 'will to organise'. When we
write about ordering (or organisation), 'we participate in ordering too' (Law 1994:
2). Critics and researchers need to recognise that a symmetrical relationship exists
between the presumptive statements we critique in others and our own statements:

> There is no reason to suppose we are different from those we study. We
> too are products. If we make pools of sense or order, then these too are
> local and recursive effects … our own ordering is a verb. It reminds us
> that (sense-making) is precarious … incomplete … that much escapes us.
> (Law 1994: 17)

Speaking of himself, Foucault declared: 'It would not behove me, of all people, to claim that my discourse is independent of conditions and rules of which I am very largely unaware' (Foucault 1973 in Simons 1995: 90).

The problem of reflexivity arises because, through 'cognitive erasure', we come to believe that the things we consider to be concrete attributes pre-exist our knowledge formations. We turn such phenomena into the status of objects through an attributive process. 'In this abstractive manner, we selectively reduce and make more comprehensively manageable our lived experiences in the very act of recounting them' (Chia 1996: 39).

In this vein, the WPR approach constructs a particular version of knowledge. While it is not meant to be applied as a formula (Bacchi 2009: 101), it is carefully crafted for a specific purpose and, as an organisational theorist would say, in a highly organised or ordered way (as the list of six questions intimates). The crafting and ordering of the questions is designed to ensure that the integrity of the approach – its reliability and what it means – remains under the control (power) of the knowledge it produces. Hence it is a creative and productive process and, in the Foucauldian sense of power as productive, it exercises power through knowledge. Those who read it and use it can gain new ways of thinking about the possible effects of the unexamined logics and assumptions informing implicit representations of meaning in policy 'problems'.

The knowledge this approach produces for such readers and doers has a pleasurable effect in relation to their efforts. It is not a power which makes them feel powerless – there is no fixed opposition here between ruler and ruled. Yet it is the pleasure gained from producing and creating their knowledge which not only subjects them to the power of the creative product (WPR) but simultaneously hides power's own mechanisms. As Weedon (1987: 173) states: 'power is invested in and exercised through her who speaks'. The more the method of WPR is able to persuade its readers to invest their time and effort in its practices, the more successful and powerful its knowledge – and the less it appears to be an exercise of power.

By the same token, there is no suggestion here that those readers and doers are simply passive and unresistant subjects and therefore not empowered themselves. The Foucault (1980: 98) argument that individuals are 'always in the position of simultaneously undergoing and exercising this power' means that such readers and doers are exercising power and being subject to it *at one and the same time.*

To understand power as a sequence, where either power or powerlessness is being accomplished at a given time, is to fall back into an understanding of power as repressive and dualistic. The WPR approach makes no such claim about negative power, and in fact it sees power as productive and so as potentially empowering.

Still, WPR does not detail its own mechanisms as implicated in power relations; instead it concentrates on the crucial point about the need for policymakers to recognise how policies produce specific understandings of 'problems' through a power-knowledge nexus. In Foucault's thought, 'knowledge means not only technical know-how but more importantly the social, historical and political conditions under which statements come to be seen as true or false' (McHoul and Grace 1993: 29). WPR, along with multiple other examples of knowledgeable methods of analysis, exercises power through the authority of its knowledge construction. Its effectiveness, as a product within discourse, is related to how well it tells a particular 'truth'. As McHoul and Grace (1993: 83) suggest:

> It is not enough to hope that a 'better' truth is on its way. But neither can we be content simply to abandon belief in these truths, for they concern our very material existence: our experience of pleasure, illness, pain, suffering, joy and so on. We are in a sense compelled to take a position, to 'speak' our minds or voice our opinions. But this imperative is also what ensures the continued exercise of power through subjects.

In this sense, the WPR methodology must itself be recognised as a kind of intervention with power effects. It does not resile from this characterisation but recognises it as inevitable.

What we have just said about WPR can also be said of this chapter, as indeed a reader may well be thinking. Writing this chapter requires the writers to occupy the position of the writing subject in order to craft a carefully ordered proposal for how to assess relations of power, knowledge and subjectivity. The writing subject tends to neglect many elements which seem extraneous to the argument, while including those that seem pertinent. As Chia (1996: 49) argues, the reader's 'attention is thus directed away from the authorial role towards the substantive claims being made, thereby obscuring the active role of the author in constituting the problematic'. So, as with any text, this chapter is a partisan discursive construct offering particular meanings and modes of understanding of the particular 'truth' it tells. To the extent that it convinces the reader by the use of its authoritative mechanisms, it is exercising power.

Yet meaning is always political; for a poststructuralist, meaning can be fixed only temporarily. For this reason Chia (1996: 49) appropriately insists that 'our own theoretical products must be self-deconstructing'. In this spirit the WPR approach signals a commitment to the non-fixity of meaning in its directive at the bottom of the six questions – to apply the approach to *one's own* policy proposals. This directive offers a methodology through which policy analysts and researchers can interrogate *their own* problem representations *reflexively* for unexamined assumptions and the possible deleterious effects of such assumptions. Bacchi's earlier book (1999) performs this form of analysis for a wide array of 'women's' policies. For example, drawing upon Razack (1995: 59), it shows how gender persecution policies in Canada tend to portray the 'problem' as a man-woman 'problem', making it difficult to 'discuss the ravages of colonialism and neo-colonialism on the economies of the South'.

If we wish to hold on to the notion of policy as a set of practices *productive* of social conditions, social subjects and social relations, reflexivity of this kind must become a primary principle – to be built into any project such as gender mainstreaming. This reflexive practice must also acknowledge that the meanings we attach to the concepts and categories we decide to use are inevitably provisional (Chapters 4, 9, 10 and 13). Yet for us that does not mean that we agree with what Chia (1996: 49) asserts, that 'throw-away explanations are the essence of reflexive practices'.

A problem for Chia is that he writes his article on reflexivity without a sufficient analysis of power. In suggesting a need for 'throwaway explanations', Chia assumes that all explanations are equally dispensable – that there is a free play of meaning which is not already located in an hierarchical network of discursive relations. Chia thus reaffirms social power by denying it and rendering it invisible. A feminist poststructuralist reading, as we develop it here, is not prepared to ignore such institutionalised hierarchies.

In contrast to Chia, we do not suggest that exercises of power through the fixing of meaning are equal in their effects. Indeed an hierarchical organising of discursive relations precludes such equality of meaning in any given context. For example, the discursive capacities, and their effects, of calling an interventionist approach 'gender mainstreaming', 'diversity mainstreaming', 'indigenous mainstreaming' or 'disability mainstreaming' will be circumscribed by the availability and force of discourses in a particular context. But discourses with strong institutional mechanisms of power (such as medical discourses) are likely to carry more force than those with fewer such mechanisms (such as the home birth movement).

Subjecting explanations to critical scrutiny about their sources and power effects, as in a WPR approach, is a way of examining how positioning, with its power and politics, temporarily fixes the meaning of 'problems'. Rather than seeing a method such as WPR as a 'throwaway explanation', therefore, we see it as offering 'temporary' or 'provisional explanation', which signals an openness to, and recognition of, the pitfalls of discursive positioning. We are not suggesting here that completing the list of six WPR questions will ensure that policies can be protected from the effects of language, which inevitably builds categories to fix one meaning or another. For example, it can show us clearly how specific policies have a gender*ing* effect, as well as the relevance of these insights to policymakers. However, it cannot tell us how to avoid *ultimately* such effects, given the full array of institutions, governance practices and 'expert' knowledges to which any statement is subject. We also recognise, as Chia does, that we cannot determine in advance how the categories we deploy as a result of what we propose will be used once that proposal has been fixed in discourse – discursive competition for meaning does not allow such control over the effects of what we state. Nor can we assume that we have necessarily included all the sets of possibilities before we speak. But to conclude that the non-fixity of meaning makes all explanations equally dispensable is to deny the hierarchic organisation of discursive relations in the exercise of social power. Hence, we reject this proposition and defend temporary 'fixing' as necessary to a 'politics of movement' (see Conclusion to the book).

Conclusion

This chapter sees policy as a discursive practice. It is not reflected by language but developed within language. Policy is located within multifarious and contestational discourses, drawn from and asserting socially organised bodies of knowledge claims. We have argued here that this discursive organising means that policy exercises power through meaning which subjects people to its effects, and enables resistance. Such subjectivising effects are not merely confined to a particular population 'out there' but also subject and enable those who produce and those who analyse such policy.

The proposition we emphasise in this chapter is the discursive situatedness of not only the policy actor but also the supposedly 'outside' researcher.

There are important considerations of power and resistance here for analysing and 'doing' policy. Of necessity the speaking subject must fix the meaning of her statements to make them recognisable in a particular language; yet fixing such meaning involves an exercise of power which links to producing its meaning as the one real truth. To reduce this effect of discourse we suggest using a practice which permits a 'temporary explanation' of meaning in policies and in our analyses of those policies. Deploying the set of questions in the WPR approach, for the task of examining the effects of policy statements and theories, demonstrates how to begin this practice. However, we also need to couple our 'temporary explanations' with a reflexive practice that allows the challenging of our temporary meanings and the considered incorporation of new ones, often from quarters not previously considered pertinent. It is for this reason that a WPR approach includes the injunction to apply the set of six questions to one's own proposals.

None of this is designed to locate us as secure subjects of knowledge, with a fixed essence of identity experience. As you will read in the following chapters, we are not a complete success in keeping to our theories, or illustrating our points. Hence we need to practise scepticism about the truths we critique and produce. This is not new. A questioning scepticism has long provided grist for the mill of feminist concerns and granules for elaborating a feminist politics.

Note

1.   The authors would like to thank Joanne Martin for her helpful comments on this chapter.

References

(Websites valid as of publication date)

Bacchi, C. 1999. *Women, policy and politics: The construction of policy problems.* London: Sage.

Bacchi, C. 2009. *Analysing policy: What's the problem represented to be?* French's Forest, NSW: Pearson Education.

Booth, M.A. 1988. 'Elaboration and social science'. PhD thesis, Murdoch University, Murdoch, Western Australia.

Chia, R. 1996. 'The problem of reflexivity in organisational research', *Organization* 3 (1): 31-59.

Dean M. 1999. *Governmentality: Power and rule in modern society.* London: Sage.

Deleuze, G. and Guattari, F. 1987. *A thousand plateaus: Capitalism and schizophrenia.* Minneapolis: Minnesota Press.

Eveline, J. 2005. 'Woman in the ivory tower: Gendering feminised and masculinised identities', *Journal of Organizational Change Management*, 18 (6) December: 641-658.

Foucault, M. 1972. *The archaeology of knowledge.* Trans. A. Sheridan. New York: Pantheon.

Foucault, M. 1973. *The order of things: An archaeology of the human sciences.* New York: Vintage.

Foucault, M. 1979. *Discipline and punish: The birth of the prison.* Trans. A. Sheridan. Harmondsworth: Penguin.

Foucault, M. 1980. *Power/knowledge: Selected interviews and other writings, 1972-77*, Gordon, C. (ed.). Brighton, Sussex: Harvester Press.

Foucault, M. 1981. *The history of sexuality, volume one: An introduction.* Harmondsworth: Pelican.

Foucault, M. 1991. 'Governmentality', in Burchell, G., Gordon, C. & Miller, P. (eds) *The Foucault effect: Studies in governmentality.* Chicago: University of Chicago Press.

Gill, Z. 2006. 'Discourse, subjectivity and the policy realm: Reconceptualising policy workers as located subjects'. Ph.D thesis, Discipline of Politics, School of History and Politics, University of Adelaide.

Grosz, E. 1994. 'A thousand tiny sexes: Feminism and rhizomatics', in Boundas, C. and Olkowski, D. (eds) *Gilles Deleuze and the theatre of philosophy.* New York: Routledge.

Honkanen, K. 2008. 'Equality politics out of the subaltern', in Magnusson, E., Rönnblom, M. and Silius, H. (eds) *Critical studies of gender equalities: Nordic dislocations, dilemmas and contradictions.* Göteborg: Makadam Publishers.

Knights, D. and Vurdabakis, T. 1994. 'Foucault, power, resistance and all that', in Jermier, J., Knights, D., and Nord, W. (eds) *Resistance and power in organizations.* London and New York: Routledge

Law, J. 1994. *Organizing modernity.* Oxford: Blackwell.

McHoul, A. and Grace, W. 1993. *A Foucault primer: Discourse, power and the subject.* Melbourne: Melbourne University Press.

McNay, L. 1994. *Foucault: A critical introduction.* Cambridge: Polity Press.

Massumi, B. 2002. *From parables to the virtual: Movement, affect, sensation.* Durham: Duke University Press.

Puar, J. B. 2007. *Terrorist assemblages: Homonationalism in queer times.* Durham and London: Duke University Press.

Razack, S. 1995. 'Domestic violence as gender persecution: Policing the borders of nation, race, and gender', *Canadian Journal of Women and the Law* 8: 45-88.

Saussure, F. de. 1974. *Course in general linguistics.* London: Fontana (fr 1916).

Simons, J. 1995. *Foucault and the political.* New York: Routledge.

Weedon, C. 1987. *Feminist practice and poststructuralist theory.* Oxford: Basil Blackwell.

Zournazi, M. 2002. 'Navigating movements: An interview with Brian Massumi', in Zournazi, M. (ed.) *Hope: New philosophies for change.* Annadale, NSW: Pluto Press.

7

Gender mainstreaming:
The answer to the gender pay gap?

JOAN EVELINE AND PATRICIA TODD

Introduction: Joan Eveline and Carol Bacchi

The cross-fertilisation of ideas that is evident in earlier chapters, particularly in Chapters 3 and 4, is also clear in this study, which took place before the Gender Analysis Project actually commenced. We include the chapter here because it explores the question of gender mainstreaming in ways which dovetail with questions we raise in the earlier chapters, including whether gender mainstreaming can 'transform' policies and policy development organisations.

In 2004 Patricia Todd and Joan Eveline undertook a public inquiry into the gender pay gap in Western Australia, commissioned by the incumbent Labor Government. This chapter is from that study. It analyses Australian gender pay gap inquiries conducted over the past decade to identify those components with transformative potential in the context of Australian industrial relations regulations and conditions. It provides examples of when and how policymakers have deployed such components, and when they have not.

Interestingly, gender mainstreaming was the policy technique being mooted in only one of those inquiries, a suggestion that indeed has not since been initiated by the government involved. Rather than offering a study of how to close the gender pay gap through gender mainstreaming, therefore, this chapter asks what components we would wish to include if gender mainstreaming were used. Our earlier Chapters 2 and 3 introduced readers to the notion that gender mainstreaming is deeply contested as concept and practice – that it means different things in different locales – and this includes whether and when policymakers use it, how they use it and how they represent 'the problem' they hope to deal with (Chapter 5). Given such contestation, we can expect no standard gender mainstreaming tool kit for tackling the gender pay inequities that we find throughout post-industrial economies. Indeed, no gender mainstreaming approach can reduce the gender pay gap without thoroughly considering specific industrial and social conditions and developments, as well as how to ensure that key players see the relevance of gender pay inequities to their agendas.

The chapter gives the example of the New South Wales and Queensland inquiries, which were conducted to ensure that industrial parties, commissioners, employers, trade unions and government agencies would work together over extended periods of time. This lengthy process of bringing the parties together increased awareness of how gender inequity was continually produced by the concepts and regulatory practices they had always used. In short, the stakeholders' capacity to 'see' pay practices that were gender-inequitable grew as they were forced to work out what meanings they could make from the concept of 'historical undervaluation', the new principle which they now had to apply.

In applying the premises of gender mainstreaming to the Australian gender pay equity inquiries, this chapter reinforces the propositions put forward in Chapters 3 and 4: a) gender equity remains 'unfinished business'; b) any gender analysis needs to go hand-in-glove with generating awareness of the ongoing procedures that produce gender inequity through policy. As readers saw in Chapter 5, a key element in generating this awareness is for policy personnel to pay particular attention to the ways policy problems are represented and disseminated. And as this current chapter argues, such awareness is best generated in a context wherein legislation forces stakeholders to find common ground for their deliberations through on-the-ground discussion and reflection.

Abstract

This article examines the argument that gender mainstreaming offers the way forward for closing the gender pay gap. It juxtaposes research on the process of gender mainstreaming with our account of the processes involved in Australian state government inquiries into the gender pay gap since the late 1990s. We indicate that the continuous process of analysis and response that gender mainstreaming can offer demands political will, intensive links between research and action, and adequate resources – which means that gender mainstreaming is seldom delivered in practice. We use our account of the Australian inquiries to argue that, provided adequate political and financial resources are in place, the gender pay gap can be narrowed through the institutional mechanisms of an industrial relations system, but that the regulatory approach is limited by its vulnerability to changes in industrial relations policy. The article concludes that, whatever strategy is used to narrow the gender pay gap, it must be able to show those who use and observe it that gender itself is a continuous, effortful and political process.

Introduction

In March 2004 Australian Prime Minister John Howard announced a proposal to change the *Australian Sex Discrimination (1984) Act*, so that Catholic Education, the governing body for Roman Catholic primary and secondary schools in Australia, could offer men-only teaching scholarships. The problem for Catholic Education was that the *Sex Discrimination Act*, enacted during an earlier and more progressive era of government, disallowed such proposals for unequal remuneration based solely on gender. However, for both John Howard and Catholic Education, it made simple 'common sense' to remedy the lack of male teachers in their system by offering scholarships to men only.

The proposal to offer men-only scholarships lends considerable weight to the research that shows that, across all occupational groups, gender wage inequality is an integral feature of a system that values the work of men more than that of women (Pocock and Alexander 1999). Indeed, such a 'common sense' idea reminds us that a politics of advantage favouring masculine bodies and ideals (Eveline 1994) often underpins government policy from the highest levels down. Moreover, it demonstrates the everyday ease with which special treatment for men is labelled as a necessary advance for society, rather than as a form of affirmative action (Bacchi

2005).[1] In sum, Howard's statement is 'doing gender' (Gunnarsson et al. 2003; West and Zimmerman 2003) as a routinely acceptable relation of inequality. The ease with which Howard makes his male-biased proposal should remind us that a narrow focus on wage determination systems is going to be insufficient for dealing with the social, political, cultural and historical factors that reproduce sex-segregated occupations, the gender pay gap and gender inequality itself.

Increasing numbers of analysts are alert to the need to take account of such complexities, and in response recommend a multidimensional or multifaceted approach to challenging the gender pay gap (International Labour Organization 2003; Pillinger 2005; Rubery et al. 2005). As Armstrong (2005) argues, a systemic solution is needed for a systemic problem. The systemic approach said by several researchers to have transformative potential is gender mainstreaming (Pillinger 2005; Rubery et al. 2005; Walby 2005). Gender mainstreaming is the public sector policy tool that has become important not only in developing countries, where it first took hold in the early 1990s, but also in Canada, Europe (particularly in the EU member states) and New Zealand. Formulated initially by feminist practitioners in development fields, the principles of gender mainstreaming gained considerable ground as a policy tool for developed countries at the 1995 UN Decade for Women Conference in Beijing. In the EU it has been used quite widely with regard to aspects of gender inequality at work (Walby 2005), and more recently has been suggested as a way of dealing with the gender pay gap. In their analysis of the gender pay gap in EU member countries, for example, Rubery et al. (2005: 1) suggest that governments 'gender mainstream' pay and employment policy. Gender mainstreaming of the gender pay gap, they argue,

> shifts the focus from deficits or deficiencies in female characteristics,
> behaviour and preferences to the investigation and rooting out of gender
> pay discrimination as embedded in institutional arrangements, social
> norms, market systems and pay policies. (Rubery et al. 2005: 1)

The question examined in this article is whether, with regard to the gender pay gap, such faith in gender mainstreaming is warranted. As a form of policy intervention gender mainstreaming relies particularly on its use in the public sector and, given the monopsonistic nature of public sector employment, there is considerable potential for contestation if the aim is to narrow the gender pay gap by paying women relatively more.

Methodology

As Bacchi and Eveline (2003) argue, the meanings and efficacy of gender mainstreaming are highly contested. Thus the way forward, those writers suggest, is to assess in which contexts this policy tool can prove useful for advancing a change agenda, as opposed to those in which it might undermine gender equity.

This article addresses that question by examining a public sector in which gender mainstreaming has not caught on as a policy tool for addressing the gender pay gap – the Australian context. In particular, we examine high-level government reviews of the gender pay gap, which have included executive support from Australian public sector agencies with a responsibility for promoting gender equity in employment. Our aim is to assess what benefits a gender mainstreaming approach could have provided.

Since 1997 all six Australian state governments (with the exception of South Australia) have commissioned and completed at least one high-level review of the gender pay gap, covering occupational groups across both public and private sectors. In addition, the government in Victoria has undertaken a further inquiry focused solely on the public sector. This strategy of conducting high-profile state-funded inquiries was intended to produce new research as to why the gender pay gap is so persistent, and to provide institutional, legal and legislative remedies on which governments can act. In some cases (for example, New South Wales and Queensland) the process of the reviews was also designed to produce better understanding (among the three sectors of government, unions and business) of how and why employment practices, including their own, contribute to the gender pay gap.

In this article our methodology is to interrogate how gender mainstreaming may or may not benefit efforts to narrow the gender pay gap through three phases of discussion. Firstly, with specific reference to the Australian context, we review research which seeks to explain the gender pay gap, including research suggesting the need for a gender mainstreaming approach. We next consider the public sector and feminist challenge and the potentials for (and critiques of) gender mainstreaming. Thirdly, in light of the core premises of gender mainstreaming, we discuss and assess recent government-sponsored reviews of the gender pay gap in Australia that are invariably based on linking research to action plans. We then provide some preliminary observations as to how the insights and practices from both strategies might be of value.

Explaining and challenging the gender pay gap

As Preston and Crockett (1999: Table 1: 566) showed in their succinct summary of an array of econometric studies into the gender pay gap in Australia, most Australian studies have found that less than one-quarter of that wage gap is due to differences in the human capital characteristics (as, for example, educational levels and years of employment) of men and women. A recent British study shows a similar lack of support for human capital explanations, suggesting there are 'features of the life cycle (as well as the labour market)' that they cannot explain (Joshi et al. 2007: 52). Using comparative European data Rubery et al. (2005) concur with this critique of human capital theory, arguing that it is essential therefore to look beyond standard economic models for the causal components of the gender pay gap.

How the institution of the family is treated in capitalist societies is an overarching factor found to contribute to the gender pay gap. Having children has a positive impact on men's wages but a negative one on women's (Pocock and Alexander 1999). Assessments of the provision of family-friendly arrangements in Australian workplaces conclude that good practice initiatives are confined to a minority of employees. For example, up to 65 per cent of managers and 54 per cent of professional women have access to paid maternity leave, yet only 18 per cent of the much more numerous clerical, sales and service workers and 0.4 per cent of casual workers are entitled to it (Watts and Mitchell 2004: 179).

The institutions of an industrial relations (IR) system invariably impact on the gender pay gap. In Australia, for example, the wage determination system has played a key role. Some specific features of Australia's IR system have been the award system and legislative provisions for arbitration by industrial tribunals for setting wages and conditions and resolving industrial disputes. It is notable that until the 1990s Australia's gender pay gap was less than that in many other OECD countries. This is primarily due to the 1972 Equal Pay Case in Australia and its implementation through a system of centralised bargaining. This Case officially demolished the formal discrimination that had operated since the 1907 Harvester decision, which established the concept of wages being determined on a gendered needs basis, with a woman to be paid only 54 per cent of a man's wage. In most cases, however, the implementation of the 1972 Equal Pay Case has involved little or no evaluation of the work women performed, while most award variations were transfers to the lowest classifications on the male wage scale, and were made by consent rather than through a test case (Short 1986). Nonetheless, particularly for professional women, gains were made through two federal wage-fixing mechanisms: the 'anomalies and inequities' principle and the 'structural efficiency' principle (Rafferty 1989). Later still, the 'minimum rates adjustment' principle allowed some leeway for establishing comparable minimum rates of pay against the comparator of a metal industry tradesperson (Australian Industrial Relations Commission 1989).

However, Australian attempts to close the gender pay gap through wage determination decisions have been limited in two ways: (a) they have no way of addressing pay rates above the award minimums and (b) they fail to challenge the undervaluation of female-dominated occupations (Whelan 2005b: 1), apart from the few, albeit important, cases that have been resolved under the Equal Remuneration Principles introduced in recent years in New South Wales and Queensland.

In addition, the introduction of enterprise bargaining in Australia since the 1990s (and the consequent fragmented bargaining system) has exacerbated gender pay inequities. The distribution of female employment between wage determination streams and the inequalities within the streams is contributing to the overall gender pay gap. Recent studies using Australian Bureau of Statistics data show that women are strongly over-represented in the lowly paid award-only stream (Whitehouse and Frino 2003), which can operate at industry, sector, enterprise or occupation level. However, in the contemporary IR system, the pay of most workers is not set by awards alone but by registered and unregistered individual and collective agreements. Australian Bureau of Statistics data reveal that the gender pay gap is substantially greater for those on individual agreements than on collective agreements, a bargaining trend being encouraged by the Australian Government (Todd and Eveline 2006).

A number of studies have pointed to the sex-segregated labour market as a key factor in the gender pay gap (Heiler et al. 1999; Pocock and Alexander 1999). Pocock and Alexander (1999: 88), for example, concluded that 'between 58 and 81 per cent of the gender pay gap is associated with being in feminised work (whether occupation, industry, workplace or job-cell)'. Consequently, many argue that the paid work of women has been undervalued and that attempts to describe it have received little recognition (Acker 1989).

In late 2005 the federal government introduced changes to Australia's IR system that brought predictions from the states, the Human Rights Commission and IR academics of an even greater negative impact on women's wage and salary relativities (Group of One Hundred and Fifty One Australian Industrial Relations Academics 2005; Human Rights and Equal Opportunity Commission of Australia 2005; Joint States 2005). According to the Joint States (2005: 55) submission, 'as a package, the Work Choices Bill will render women even more isolated and precariously placed than before'. The new legislation provides for a new mechanism for setting the minimum wage, with most analysts predicting a reduction in the minimum wage relative to average earnings. It gives priority to individual over collective bargaining, in which agreements are able to satisfy lower minimum employment standards, and accepts a diminished role for the Industrial Relations Commission. It places greater restrictions on union activity and removes unfair dismissal provisions for employees in workplaces with fewer than 100 employees. In addition, the Work Choices Bill will deny approximately 85 per cent of the workforce access to state IR legislation which, in turn, will prevent most women workers from pursuing comparable worth cases through the state-based Equal Remuneration Principles introduced in 1998.

The public sector and feminist challenges

In Australia, as in the UK (Joshi et al. 2007), gender pay equity is somewhat better in the public than the private sector. Yet, as research elsewhere shows, the public sector has its own ways of maintaining that wage gap. The first of these is that the public sector, as a monopsonistic employer, uses its power to keep wages down in specific areas such as health and education (Rubery et al. 2005: 207). Secondly, there is the current influence of economic rationalist thinking that encourages restraint on public sector expenditure (Lonti and May 2004). Thirdly, the restructuring of the public sector, involving downsizing, privatisation and subcontracting, poses inherent risks to overall wage levels and decreases employment prospects in the public sector (Briar and Ang 2004). In Australia, moreover, a key factor in this continuing gap is the level at which women are appointed to public sector positions. For example, Probert et al. (2002: ii), in their review of gender pay equity in the Victorian public service, found that average starting salaries favoured men significantly because women continued to be appointed at lower levels.[2]

Yet while the persistence of the gender pay gap has serious economic and social consequences, the substantial benefits that the public sector reaps from undervaluing women's labour leave little room for optimism that governments themselves will do much to intervene.

It is clear that there is no one cause of the longstanding inequity of the gender pay gap. It is equally clear that the factors involved do not remain fixed but are reshaped in line with changing economic and political forces, as well as changes over the life cycle (Joshi et al. 2007). As Philippa Hall (2004: 4) notes:

> We need an intelligent and flexible appreciation of how ongoing social, political and economic change affects equal remuneration issues and solutions ... *One of the reasons is that the mix of contexts and drivers of remuneration is constantly changing* [emphasis added].

Those who suggest gender mainstreaming as a way of narrowing the gender pay gap want to predict and prevent the negative effects of those ever-changing contexts and drivers. Rubery et al. (2005: 209) in their argument for gender mainstreaming, suggest that:

> the gender dimension of specific policies should be anticipated, and amendments made on this basis. There must also be monitoring of the policy and subsequent amendments where the outcomes are unanticipated or even perverse.

But, in order to examine further the claims for gender mainstreaming made by Rubery et al. (2005) we must consider in more detail what that policy strategy entails.

The potential and critiques of gender mainstreaming

According to Walby (2005: 463) gender mainstreaming 'is a new and essentially contested form of feminist politics and policy, existing in the tension between the mainstream and interventions to secure gender equality'. Although its origins are in feminist activism, the proliferation of gender mainstreaming in public sector agencies has seen it become most visible as a practice of governance. Whether in public policy or in feminist activism, however, gender mainstreaming uses a form of gender analysis as its principal tool. Gender analysis begins from the premise that policy routinely (re)produces gender as a relation of inequality (Eveline and Bacchi 2005). To intervene in those routine policy practices, gender mainstreaming suggests the need for sex-disaggregated statistics (Pillinger 2005), and a well-developed understanding of gender as a product of social and political processes (March et al. 1999).

Those crucial features of gender mainstreaming have generated keen support among numbers of feminist researchers, including some working on gender wage inequality. Rubery et al. (2005) agree with Magnusson et al. (2003), who describe the potential of gender mainstreaming as 'transformative'. Rubery et al. (2005) offer three instances of how public sector organisations might use gender mainstreaming to counter the gender pay gap. In their view, and as noted above, the crucial advantage of gender mainstreaming is that it shifts attention from comparing characteristics of women and men onto gendered institutions, norms and policies, as the problem that must be addressed. This in itself is an important insight for those working on the gender pay gap. It brings research on the gender pay gap into the more recent conceptual frames used in feminist theories of organisation, and developed from Joan Acker (1989) to Martin and Collinson (2006). In effect, the promise of gender mainstreaming, for Rubery et al., lies in its activist roots. They write (2005: 44): 'Gender mainstreaming pay policies means questioning the gender effects of these developments and not just seeking gender equality' among specific groups of women and men.

It is crucial to note here that gender mainstreaming is a strategic intervention designed largely for public sector deployment. Jane Pillinger (2005) is one who emphasises its potential for political activism. Pillinger's study is on the public sector, where she analyses the Pay Equity Now! campaign, organised by an international alliance of public sector unions. This example of gender mainstreaming, she argues, was:

> aimed at tackling the low value of women's work, living minimum wages, privatization and liberalization, in parallel with enhancing the role and participation of women in trade union decision-making and activism. (Pillinger 2005: 598)

This capacity in gender mainstreaming for empowering women to make gender discrimination visible also moves Rubery et al. (2005) to suggest its use for pay equity, including in the public sector.

Rubery et al. admit that good examples of gender mainstreaming pay policy are scarce. Nonetheless, they offer three cases of a wider and more systematic approach consistent with gender mainstreaming (2005); one in France, another in Sweden and the third in the UK. The basis of the argument of Rubery et al. is that the three most crucial elements for recent pay policy have been and are represented with little or no reference to their gender effects. These elements are 'trend decline in the minimum wages, moves towards more decentralisation and individualisation, and the restructuring of the public sector' (Rubery et al. 2005: 208). The principles of mainstreaming, they note, require policymakers to 'examine the system of wage formation for evidence of gendered processes'. As they suggest (2005: 207), a projected outcome of gender mainstreaming is the prevention of policy errors which prove costly to rectify. Based on a preliminary analysis of the gendered processes, they claim that policymakers can consider likely future trends in these sectors and their implications for the gender pay gap.

In most forms of gender mainstreaming the goal of producing cost-efficient outcomes goes hand-in-glove with the goal of preventing gender inequities. However, in the cost-cutting climate of the contemporary public sector, that dual agenda can weigh too heavily on the side of cost efficiency. One result is the justifiable criticism that gender equity strategies are undermined by neoliberal premises (Bacchi and Eveline 2003).

Clearly, Pillinger (2005) and Rubery et al. (2005) see that a particular attraction of gender mainstreaming is that it enables a shift from merely explaining the components of the gender pay gap towards a responsible plan of action anchored to a complex interweaving of research findings and gender analysis. As Rubery et al. (2005: 208) remark, 'Gender mainstreaming offers a continuous process of analysis and response'. And in Pillinger's words (2005: 591):

> the practical realisation of this (gender mainstreaming) in the *Pay Equity Now!* campaign has been through transfer of capacity building, participatory research at the workplace level, donor funding and union networking.

Despite such glowing accounts of its potential, the use of gender mainstreaming is also strongly criticised by researchers across the world. Criticisms range from its ineffectiveness against 'institutional and legislative obstacles, as well as attitudinal, ideological, structural and political barriers' that sustain gender inequality (Pillinger 2005: 598) to a lack of clarity as to how it should be done, coupled with a lack of interest or resources for monitoring and evaluating its effectiveness (Moser

2005: 585). The crucial premise of the strategy is that because supposedly gender-neutral policy reproduces gender inequalities, gender mainstreaming requires an ongoing process rather than a sense of completion. As Eveline and Bacchi (2005: 502-503) note: 'the process of gender analysis of policy has no foreseeable end point – it must necessarily be sustained for as long as policymaking endures'. Yet according to Sandler (1997) the strategy is too often treated as a finite goal rather than an ongoing process. A more recent criticism is that most forms of gender mainstreaming pay insufficient attention to the way in which their premises and their advocates understand and portray 'gender', an oversight which severely limits their chances of success (Eveline and Bacchi 2005).

In attempting to assess further how gender mainstreaming might benefit research and action on the gender pay gap, we turn now to the Australian context, where the public sector has been devoid of any formal recognition of gender mainstreaming until very recently. In fact, women's policy units in South Australia and Western Australia were the first to begin gender analysis pilot projects in late 2004 (Eveline and Bacchi 2005), and the Australian Sex Discrimination Commissioner, Pru Goward, also announced gender mainstreaming as the preferred gender equity strategy of the federal Coalition Government only in late 2004 (Goward 2004). The state government inquiries into the gender pay gap that we outline below echo that transition in the wider policy domain, with little sign of gender mainstreaming terminology appearing in gender pay gap inquiries until the Western Australian Government review in 2004.[3]

Australian reviews of the gender pay gap

The audit society (Power 1997) ensures that we measure, identify and legitimate the elements that make us who we say we are and how we should perform, from the ingredients listed on soup cans to the surveillance techniques of call centres. That 'explosion of audit' has gone hand in glove with the trend to new public management that suffuses the public sector and the new accountabilities demanded of all employees, from university staff to police officers and government auditors themselves (to name just a few).

Reviews of the gender pay gap are just one of the many forms of formal auditing processes activated through public sector agencies such as equal opportunity units or industrial commissions. The UK for example has introduced not only occasional reviews but compulsory annual audits for the public sector and voluntary compliance for business and industry (Kingsmill 2001), monitored by public sector agencies. Indeed, reforms such as equal employment opportunity and, more recently, gender mainstreaming, rely upon such public sector accountability, performance measures and auditing techniques for their effectiveness. As with the critiques of gender mainstreaming noted above, feminist researchers remain divided as to what those ever-increasing performance measurements can achieve in addressing gender inequalities in employment, pay and organisational contexts, with their main critiques being the minimalist way in which such strategies and policies are applied (Bacchi and Eveline 2003; Walby 2005). With regard to Australian reviews of the gender pay gap, however, there is some evidence that the review process itself can become a means of raising awareness of how the gendering of wages and salaries has occurred over time.

The strategy of mounting reviews of the gender pay gap in Australia was in part a result of running out of other options for addressing wage inequality. Although the early comparable worth cases in North America resulted in some gains for women in certain occupations (Hallock 1999), in Australia comparable worth cases on the whole failed miserably. The Australian Industrial Relations Commission, for example, rejected comparable worth using points factor job evaluation as being incompatible with Australia's wage-fixing principles (Short 1986: 329).

Federally, the *Industrial Relations Act 1988* was amended in 1993 to include equal remuneration provisions and these were subsequently included in the *Workplace Relations Act 1996*, but the Australian Industrial Relations Commission has never made an equal remuneration order. The option of pursuing cases under these provisions in the federal legislation subsequently provided the opportunity for two test cases that amounted to exercises in comparable worth. However, as both these cases achieved negotiated settlements, the opportunity to set a pay equity precedent was lost (Reed 2002: 13-14). Accessing the provisions under the federal system is difficult because of a lack of clarity about how they can be applied, uncertainty as to whether they can adequately address undervaluation and the reliance on discrimination as a threshold test (Whelan 2005a: 5).

At an organisational level, job evaluation techniques have been utilised as seemingly objective tools to analyse jobs. These techniques, however, have been criticised for their inept undervaluation of some aspects of traditional female duties and skills (Probert et al. 2002: 6), for example, the more subtle skills involving human services compared with the visible and appreciated skills associated with using technology (Probert et al. 2002: 6). With the federal climate becoming increasingly conservative and deregulated since 1996, and with IR tribunals discouraging gender pay equity cases (Jamieson 2004: 10), the need to address undervaluation shifted to the states, and found some response in periods when Labor governments held power.

New South Wales set the scene for other states to follow. The New South Wales 1997 Pay Equity taskforce, comprising representatives of employer organisations, unions, government agencies, women's organisations and academic experts, generated case studies of six occupational groups and recommended a subsequent pay equity inquiry. Conducted by Justice Glynn in 1998, the central focus of the pay equity inquiry was how work can be evaluated and remunerated without those practices being affected by the gender of the workers. The inquiry used the case studies of the earlier New South Wales task force to investigate the history of wage fixing in the occupations studied and to identify the extent to which institutional arrangements influenced remuneration in ways that favoured one occupation over another.

The Glynn Inquiry identified undervaluation of female-dominated work in all the areas in which detailed case studies were considered, thus finding that gender-related undervaluation was routine and persistent. The report listed the following characteristics of occupations that signal historical undervaluation of the work: female dominated; female characterisation of work; little or no work value exercises by the Commission; inadequate equal pay application; a weak union, few union members; awards and agreements by consent rather than as test cases; inadequate recognition of qualifications, including the misalignment of qualifications; little access to training or career paths; a large component of casuals; small workplaces; a new industry or occupation; a service industry; home-based occupations (Hall 2004: 27-28).

In her report Justice Glynn endorsed the concept of historical undervaluation. She found that gender-related undervaluation is systemic and so should be made central to equal remuneration provisions. The Glynn Report recommended that, when historical undervaluation is evident, comparators are not necessary for establishing the value of work; and no specific proportion of an occupation, industry or enterprise work force should be required to be women as a condition for access to equal remuneration provisions (Hall 1999: 43).

In line with the Glynn Report the New South Wales Industrial Relations Commission established a new equal remuneration principle in 2000 (IRC of New South Wales File No. ARC 1841 of 1999). The New South Wales equal remuneration principle can be used by workers' unions to mount a case under the tribunal system. In mounting such cases it is no longer necessary to prove discrimination by employers or industries, provided the occupation shows evidence of the characteristics of historical undervaluation outlined in the Glynn Report. Mounting a case under the equal remuneration principle:

- allows for fresh assessments of the value of work and the rates of pay in an award where the current rate is undervalued on a gender basis

- ensures that the reassessment of the value of work is gender-neutral

- allows comparisons to be made across dissimilar work, industries and industry sectors and employers, and across enterprises

- is limited to awards, although account can be taken of actual rates paid (including over-award payments and payments under enterprise agreements and contracts) where they reflect the value of work

- provides a range of measures to remedy gender-related undervaluation

- includes a range of economic safeguards (Hall 2004: 29)

- excludes the need for a male (or any) comparator

- excludes the need for a specific gender proportion in the occupation or group making the claim

- requires no particular method of evaluating work (including job evaluations and independent experts)

- requires no proof that discrimination was/is the cause of a gender-related pay disparity

- forgoes the need to make a case within a particular enterprise, occupation, industry, or single employer (Hall 2004: 30).

It has been a disappointment to some observers that there has been only one arbitrated decision (for librarians and information workers) under the New South Wales equal remuneration principle, although that case resulted in significant gains for the low-paid groups of library workers. Moreover, the promise of the equal remuneration principle has been short-lived in the Australian IR system. As mentioned earlier, the new federal government Work Choices legislation explicitly excludes most Australian employees from accessing these provisions within the state IR regulatory frameworks, although the unused and largely unclear equal remuneration provision in the federal system is not affected. So what does this mean for the usefulness of the concept of undervaluation for the states that have applied it? According to Hall (2004), the costly process of mounting a pay equity claim through the New South Wales arbitration system is not the only way that the concept of historical undervaluation can prove effective. Hall (2004: 8) reports that pay equity issues have been considered in non-arbitrated cases, including nurses, psychologists and preschool teachers, and she suggests that this demonstrates that an increased awareness of undervaluation is spreading in the New South Wales industrial system.

The impetus the New South Wales Inquiry gave to other states has also been important. State jurisdictions in Tasmania and Queensland had by 2001 followed the lead of New South Wales in convening an inquiry and then endorsing the insertion of an equal remuneration principle based on historical undervaluation into their wage-fixing mechanisms, and by 2005 Western Australia and Victoria had also completed high-level reviews.

The Tasmanian Pay Equity Taskforce, established in 1999, accepted the findings of the New South Wales Pay Equity Inquiry and recommended the adoption of an equal remuneration principle as the most effective 'mechanism in this State for working women to find adequate remedy for the undervaluation of their work' (Tasmanian Industrial Commission 1999). On 6 July 2000 the Tasmanian Industrial Commission (2000) adopted a pay equity principle as part of its wage-fixing principles.

In contrast to the short Tasmanian inquiry (Tasmanian Industrial Commission 1999), the Queensland jurisdiction replicated and extended the New South Wales series of reviews. Justice Fisher decided that the scope and detail of the six case studies conducted for the New South Wales Inquiry should be replicated in Queensland to ascertain whether similar conclusions applied. The subsequent research, conducted by Griffith University, confirmed that the profile of undervaluation indicators developed in New South Wales were relevant to Queensland (Fisher 2001: 4). Consequently, the Queensland report found the findings of historical undervaluation in the New South Wales Inquiry to be directly relevant to Queensland and supported and adopted them.

Furthermore, in order to demonstrate to employer groups, unions and government jurisdictions how undervaluation occurs through the influence of wage-fixing systems in female-characterised occupations, the Queensland Inquiry completed an additional case study of dental assistants. Conducted by members of the inquiry team themselves, the case study of dental assistants revealed sets of skills and responsibilities that had not previously been taken into account in their remuneration (Fisher 2001: 5). The Queensland reform included legislative change. Unlike the New South Wales Principle, which is confined to dealing only with awards, orders made under the Queensland Principle can be applied also to 'employees whose wages and conditions are not governed by an industrial instrument' (Fisher 2001: 54).

In 2005, before the introduction of Work Choices, the Liquor, Hospitality and Miscellaneous Workers Union initiated and won a case on behalf of dental assistants under the new equal remuneration principle set by the Queensland Commission, building on the findings of the case study on dental assistants undertaken by the Pay Equity Inquiry (Whitehouse and Rooney 2006). Another claim was mounted for child care workers, leading Hall (2004: 29) to note, rather too hopefully, that Queensland unions will be focusing on pay equity cases until at least 2010.[4] The Queensland system makes funding (to a total value of $50,000) available to industrial parties in equal remuneration cases, subject to an agreed case plan. Unions in the first two cases to be taken under the new principle, the dental assistants and child care cases, subsequently gained approved funding (Hall 2004: 8). The scope of the Queensland legislation may mean that some sectors of the Queensland workforce can still access the equal remuneration principle, but an increasingly conservative industrial environment also undermines the impetus for future cases.

The Western Australian Gender Pay Gap Review, conducted by independent consultants to government in 2004, can be seen as actively responding to the increasingly neoliberal environment by recommending a gender mainstreaming approach to deal with Western Australia's unenviable position as the state with the widest gender pay gap in Australia. Rather than emphasising legislative and institutional remedies in this climate of federal government neo-conservatism the reviewers shifted attention to the multiple factors maintaining the gender pay gap. Although the workforce participation rate of Western Australian women is consistently higher than the Australian average, the gender pay gap has also been consistently wider (since 1993). In February, 2004, when the Western Australian Government's review was commissioned, the gender pay gap in Western Australia, based on full-time total adult earnings, was 26 per cent, as opposed to the national average of 19 per cent. The gap in full-time adult ordinary time earnings was 23 per cent and 15 per cent respectively. To combat this bleak comparison, the Western Australian Government commissioned a compact review. This was not meant to replicate earlier inquiries in other states, but to bring together insights from those and other prior Western Australia studies, from the national and international literature and through submissions and expertise from parties concerned with the Western Australia IR system. The terms of reference were recent research dealing with the gender pay gap, the capacity of the state wage-fixing principles to close the gap, the efficacy of voluntary strategies, the role of the state's *Minimum Conditions of Employment Act 1993* (Western Australian Government 1993) and strategies for training (Todd and Eveline 2004: 3).

In identifying a multiplicity of factors contributing to the gender pay gap, the Western Australian report concluded that a multidimensional approach is necessary to address not only historical undervaluation through wage-fixing mechanisms but also, and more widely, the current contexts of gender inequality in work and family arrangements. As noted above the holistic approach it advocated was gender mainstreaming to be implemented through the formation of a pay equity unit and under the auspices of a high level steering committee. Completed in the climate of uncertainty of radical changes occurring in IR legislation at both the federal and Western Australia state levels, the Western Australia review's raft of remedial measures recognise the vulnerability of relying upon regulatory measures to increase pay equity. Nonetheless, the report recommends that the 'IR Act be amended to establish an Equal Remuneration Part that can be applied with a high degree of certainty in assessing undervaluation on a gender basis' (Todd and Eveline 2004: 4), and amendments relating to the objects, award modernisation and aspects of enterprise bargaining to make them more receptive to pay equity claims (Todd and Eveline 2004: 4, 60-79).

Importantly, however, the report pays particular attention to the role of government as a large employer, recommending that 'the government apply gender analysis to all policies and practices in relation to the public sector so as to identify gendered employment and pay outcomes' (Todd and Eveline 2004: 10). With regard to voluntary strategies, it recommends the development of pay equity audits, mandatory within the public sector and voluntary in the private sector, along the lines of the UK strategy. The report views such audits, along with various recommended training strategies, as effective ways by which all groups and industry parties can gain an understanding of what the gender pay gap means and thereby build their capacity to implement equal remuneration. As of October 2006 the Western Australian Government had endorsed the report and recommendations and employed a director and staff for the recently established pay equity unit, which was in the process of designing and implementing gender pay equity audits for the public sector. With the funding so far only on a limited contract basis, the pressure will be on the Unit to implement the rest of the recommendations, as a way of securing a more permanent presence in the public sector.

The 2004-05 inquiry on behalf of the Victorian Government, chaired by Commissioner Whelan, followed the Western Australian example in deciding not to replicate the earlier reviews, but to draw instead on their findings, insights and recommendations. Alone among the states, Victoria's legacy of a 1990s conservative government at the state level is that it no longer has a state-based IR system. Instead, Victoria operates solely within the federal system of IR. Under the Australian Constitution Victoria's unique situation precludes its government from legislating on equal remuneration, therefore, the Whelan Report (2005a: 13) recommends that the Victorian Government undertake a review of the equal remuneration provisions in the federal Act, with the goal of clarifying and amending those provisions where needed.

In accord with the Western Australian recommendations, the Victorian pay equity working party recommended that a pay equity unit be established to implement a plan of action for the other recommendations (Whelan 2005a: 9, 19). Like the Queensland Inquiry, it also recommended the establishment of a pay equity fund (Whelan 2005a: 9, 20). Further key recommendations included, as in Western Australia, a long-running educational campaign to improve jurisdictional and community understanding of the gender pay gap issues; a series of case studies similar to those conducted in New South Wales and Queensland; a standardised system of data collection to provide more accurate data for equal pay cases and the introduction of pay equity audits along the lines proposed in the Western Australia review. In a similar vein to the Western Australian report, the inquiry recognised the undervaluation of women's work as requiring a multi-dimensional interventionist approach. Unlike the Western Australian report there is no specific recommendation for gender mainstreaming. Nonetheless, recommendation 15 calls for a similarly holistic strategy. It suggests that the pay equity unit 'should also review Canadian and European policy analysis and development that is assessing widening the scope of gender pay equity audits to include employment equity' (Whelan 2005a: 15).

In an earlier era the central bargaining mechanisms of the Australian system delivered Australian women better pay equity than countries without central arbitration, but in 2007 the promise of the equal remuneration principles of New South Wales, Queensland and Tasmania has been overtaken by the neoliberalism of federal Australian Government policy. The state reviews that occurred since 2001 were more actively responding to the growing awareness that relying on institutional mechanisms to reduce pay inequity was fraught with pitfalls. In that climate of change the promise of gender mainstreaming begins to look attractive and has prompted at least one of those review reports to recommend it. To what extent, then, might we expect gender mainstreaming to be more effective in the long term?

In our summary above we noted the two key facets of gender mainstreaming that attracted Pillinger (2005) and Rubery et al. (2005). These were that gender mainstreaming offers a plan of action based on research (in short, it links explanation to action) and a continuous process of analysis and response. In the final section below we read the process and outcomes of the Australian Government inquiries in the light of these features of gender mainstreaming and make some preliminary observations about their strategic value.

Is gender mainstreaming the way forward?

The Australian state government reviews on the gender pay gap outlined above have no problem meeting the criterion of a plan of action based on research – their terms of reference demanded exactly that. Through empirical case studies and a sensitivity to the norms and regulations of the Australian IR system the New South Wales series of reviews generated the concept of 'historical undervaluation' and developed a plan of action whereby the general agreement around that term could be exploited to narrow the gap through test cases and consensual bargaining. The later inquiries followed suit. They built their research findings (whether using primary data or based on earlier literature) around that concept and followed up with a plan of action. The effectiveness or otherwise of those reviews therefore was not the result of whether or not they linked a plan of action with their explanations of the gender pay gap. Rather, it was whether their plans of action offered and enabled what gender mainstreaming is supposed to offer – a continuous process of analysis and response that can overcome the lack of interest, concern and political will that 'invisibilises' (Moser 2005: 584) the gender pay gap.

Certainly, for two at least of the inquiries (New South Wales and Queensland) the process of the reviewing itself was lengthy and continuous. According to Hall (2004: 5, 26) the New South Wales Pay Equity Inquiry owes its success to two elements. The first was the way in which Justice Glynn used the concept of 'historical undervaluation' to inhibit the negative backlash and series of obstacles that had arisen through the earlier use of the concept of discrimination, which had been rarely applied or recognised in a systemic sense. The second was the extended period of grappling with pay equity issues, as engaged in by IR commissioners, employers, unions and government agencies. That process:

> has led us to rethink what is really required to secure pay equity, especially to refresh our focus on ways of valuing work free of effects of the sex of the workers who do it rather than focusing on requiring proofs of past discrimination. There has been a real increase in industrial parties' and tribunals' familiarity with, and understanding of, pay equity, why it is an important issue, and why some of the existing mechanisms need updating. (Hall 2004: 5)

For the new concept of historical undervaluation to be effective, therefore, a long and interactive process was required in order for the parties – employers, unions and public servants – to learn, understand, negotiate and accommodate gender pay equity issues. In working through how the new conditions could be applied (a lengthy period of negotiation and compromise) the parties had to develop a new mind-set in which they could grasp the concept of historical undervaluation. In the words of Hall (2004: 5), 'We broke through some seemingly unresolvable problems. We changed hearts and minds'.

The question for us here is just what it was that those 'hearts and minds' were changing towards. Hall is vague on this point and the reader can only surmise that she is saying how the concept of historical undervaluation overcame the problem of being forced to argue, as the quantitative human capital models do, that any unexplained gap must be attributed to discrimination. What might gender mainstreaming have added to this process?

A gender mainstreaming approach would have been designed to give the players in the New South Wales Inquiry an awareness that the devaluing of women's work is a major force in maintaining the gender pay gap. We would hope that it would have generated research on the outcomes of that devaluing process, with numbers and percentages taking centre stage, and research concentrating on which bit of the gap can be explained by which piece of the overall puzzle of causal factors. What a gender mainstreaming approach should also have provided is an awareness that, besides attending to the outcomes, it is equally important to attend to the ways in which that outcome is reproduced in the 'institutional arrangements, social norms, market systems and pay policies' noted by Rubery et al. (2005). In other words, if the gender mainstreaming strategy was working well there would have been continuous attention to the unexamined ways in which the gendering of the pay gap occurs, without losing sight of what outcomes that gendering produces.

On that score to date, the Queensland Inquiry should rate highest among the Australian reviews. Although its report makes no mention of gender mainstreaming, the Queensland Inquiry replicated the lengthy process of the New South Wales case studies, which developed some interest and awareness in the industrial parties and in women across six key occupational groups, and it also provided the fighting funds and the legal and legislative clarity to mount and win pay equity cases. These cases promised, before the federal work choices legislation at least, to continue for the best part of the decade that followed.

Ironically, as noted above, the only review to suggest gender mainstreaming as the way forward was that of Western Australia, yet that state shows little sign to date of the successful outcomes derived from the New South Wales and Queensland inquiries. Todd and Eveline (2004), in fact, used Rubery et al. (2005) to provide a rationale for the gender mainstreaming approach. Their report suggested that a multidimensional, holistic form of intervention was needed; one that could demonstrate and counter the widespread practices in policy, employment, IR systems and family arrangements through which the undervaluation of women's labour was routinely occurring. Although the Western Australian Minister for Consumer and Employment Protection instituted the recommendation of the review to implement a Pay Equity unit, that unit has limited resources and as yet little legislative backing for its cause. Instead the unit is forced to rely on a politics of persuasion so that more than three years after that review the state public sector charged with implementing that plan has little more resources than careful persuasion with which to deliver its goals. Thus, almost three years after that review it is too soon to predict to what extent that multi-dimensional approach will apply and succeed.

Concluding thoughts

What a gender mainstreaming approach can demonstrate is that dealing with the gender pay gap through a purely technical process of legislation, auditing, reviewing, monitoring and accountability measures will never be enough. This is not to deny the worth of those strategies but to recognise, with Pat Armstrong (2005: 22), that:

> all strategies have limitations and no single strategy can do it all ... Instead we need multiple strategies that are thought together, integrated through theory as well as legislation and enforcement.

Through both Rubery et al. (2005), who promote the use of gender mainstreaming, and Hall (2004) and Armstrong (2005), who do not, we are reminded that the factors producing the gender pay gap in the public sector as well as more generally do not remain fixed but are reshaped in line with shifting economic, social and political relations. It is important to note again that these inquiries occurred in the public sector itself, under state-based Labor governments, often reacting to an era of conservative federal politics. John Howard's proposal, outlined in our introduction, demonstrates not only his leadership of those conservative, anti-labour politics at the overarching federal level, but also how gender is shaped through political and economic relations. A compromise to Howard's proposal to facilitate men-only scholarships was reached: the Human Rights and Equal Opportunity Commission allowed Catholic Education to offer equal numbers of scholarships to men and women. However, only half of those offered to men were taken up, and although all the women's scholarships were filled, the scholarships not taken up by men were not subsequently offered to other women, who still comprise most of Australia's trainee teachers. The chief executive officer of Catholic Education is on record as saying that teacher salaries and career opportunities are significant factors in keeping men out of teaching (Catholic News 2006), but so far Catholic Education shows no sign of significantly increasing salaries. The doing of gender as a relation of inequality is what gender mainstreaming needs to be able to show and challenge. In short, we might raise much needed awareness of the problem of the gender pay gap if researchers and policymakers developed ways of highlighting that gap as an outcome of the process of gendering itself.

Our strategy for highlighting the process of gendering, following the argument of Eveline and Bacchi (2005), would be to treat gender as a verb, in order to make it clear to all observers that gender was something people do rather than something they have. Gender mainstreaming is meant to foster a continuous and never-ending process of analysis and revision, in line with good policymaking. In highlighting mainstreaming as an always unfinished process, it is important to show that gender, too, is never fixed and complete, but is continually worked at through effortful and routine practices. Acknowledging that incompleteness should lead us to watch for, and talk of, gendering rather than gender. To what extent we could make sense to public sector policymakers by referring to the gendering pay gap we leave to be explored elsewhere.

Notes

1. Bacchi (2005) uses this story and other quotes from Howard to build an argument about affirmative action. We use it here for a different purpose.

2. Reports for the New Zealand task force on pay and employment equity in the public sector also found 'broad and persistent patterns of occupational segregation and that women are generally still lower paid and lower in the relevant hierarchies than men' (Jones and Torrie 2004: 3). Nonetheless, there was considerable variation in the gender pay gap between areas of health services, education services and the rest of the public service. Although in this article our methodology is to concentrate on the Australian cases, from a comparative viewpoint it is worth noting that New Zealand has had gender mainstreaming in place since the mid-1990s.

3. In the late 1970s and into the 1980s the Australian women's budget statements, in which most government treasuries were required to report on the possible effects of budgets on women, were an early form of gender mainstreaming, although they were not named as such.

4. The introduction of the Work Choices Bill will now remove some of these groups of workers from the state's jurisdiction, preventing their cases from being heard.

References

(Websites valid as of publication date)

Acker, J. 1989. *Doing comparable worth: Gender, class and pay equity.* Philadelphia, PA: Temple University Press.

Acker, J. 1990. 'Hierarchies, jobs, bodies: a theory of gendered organizations', *Gender & Society* 4: 139-58.

Armstrong, P. 2005. 'Back to basics: Pay equity for women today'. Paper presented at *The gender pay gap: Assessing possible futures in the post-inquiries era.* International conference, University of Western Australia, Nedlands, Western Australia, 28-29 April 2005.

Australian Industrial Relations Commission. 1989. *National Wage Case.* Print, H9100. <http://www.airc.gov.au/safetynet_review/decisions/H9100.htm> accessed 24 October 2009.

Bacchi, C. 2005. '"Affirmative action for men": A test of common sense', *Just Policy* 36: 5-12.

Bacchi, C. and Eveline, J. 2003. 'Mainstreaming and neoliberalism: A contested relationship', *Policy and Society* 22 (2): 98-118.

Briar, C. and Ang, E.K. 2004. 'Women "returners" and the gender pay gap'. Paper presented at the New Zealand Conference on Pay and Employment Equity, National Advisory Council on the Employment of Women. Wellington, 28-29 June. <nacew.govt.nz/about/history/conference2004/papers.html> accessed 24 October 2009.

Catholic News. 2006. <cathnews.com/news/503/89.html> accessed 24 October 2009.

Eveline, J. 1994. 'The politics of advantage', *Australian Feminist Studies* 19: 129-54.

Eveline, J. and Bacchi, C. 2005. 'What are we mainstreaming when we mainstream gender?' *International Feminist Journal of Politics* 7 (4): 496-512.

Fisher, G.K. 2001. 'Worth valuing: Report of the Pay Equity Inquiry'. Queensland Industrial Relations Commission. Case No. B1568 of 2000. <deir.qld.gov.au/pdf/ir/worthvaluinga.pdf> accessed 1 November 2009.

Goward, P. 2004. 'Now we can all focus on women', *The Age,* 30 October: 9.

Group of One Hundred and Fifty One Australian Industrial Relations, Labour Market and Legal Academics. 2005. 'Research evidence about the effects of the "Work Choices Bill"'. A submission to the Inquiry into the Workplace Relations Amendment (Work Choices) Bill 2005. <nteu.org.au/campaigns/archive/ir/submissions/150academics> accessed 1 November 2009.

Gunnarsson, E., Andersson, S., Rosell, A. and Salminen-Karlsson, M. (eds) 2003. *Where have all the structures gone? Doing gender in organisations.* Stockholm: Centre for Women's Studies, Stockholm University.

Hall, P. 1999. 'The New South Wales Pay Equity Inquiry: A new approach for the new century', *Labour and Industry* 10 (2): 33-51.

Hall, P. 2004. 'Pay equity issues and prospects'. Keynote address, New Zealand Conference on Pay and Employment Equity, National Advisory Council on the Employment of Women. Wellington 28-29 June.

Hallock, M. 1999. 'Pay equity: The promise and the practice in North America', *Labour and Industry* 10 (2): 53-73.

Heiler, K., Arsovska, B. and Hall, R. 1999. 'Good and bad bargaining for women: Do unions make a difference?' *Labour and Industry* 10 (2): 101-127.

Howard, J. 2004. *News room*, David Speers Interview, Sky News, 10 March.

Human Rights and Equal Opportunity Commission. 2005. Submission to Senate Employment, Workplace Relations and Education Legislation Committee Inquiry into the Workplace Relations Amendment (Work Choices) Bill 2005. <aph.gov.au/Senate/committee/eet_ctte/wr_workchoices05/submissions/sublist.htm> accessed 20 November 2007.

International Labour Organization 2003. *Time for equality at work*. Global report, follow-up to the ILO Declaration of Fundamental Principles and Rights at Work. Geneva: ILO.

Jamieson, S. 2004. 'Australian working women and equal pay: The role of a contradictory style'. Paper presented to the International Industrial Relations Association, Asian Division Conference, Seoul 24-26 June.

Joint States. 2005. Submission to the Senate Inquiry into the Workplace Relations Amendment (Work Choices) Bill 2005. <deir.qld.gov.au/industrial/rights/system/submission/index.htm> accessed 24 October 2009.

Jones, D. and Torrie, R. 2004. 'What works, what doesn't: Employment equity in the public sector'. Paper presented at the New Zealand Conference on Pay and Employment Equity, National Advisory Council on the Employment of Women. Wellington, 28-29 June.

Joshi, H., Makepeace, G. and Dolton, P. 2007. 'More or less equal? Evidence on the pay of men and women from the British Birth Cohort Studies', *Gender, Work and Organization* 14 (1): 37-55.

Kingsmill, D. 2001. *Review of women's employment and pay*. London: Department of Trade and Industry, Women and Equality Unit.

Lonti, Z. and May, R. 2004. 'The impact of pay fixing mechanisms on the gender pay gap'. Paper presented at the New Zealand Conference on Pay and Employment Equity, National Advisory Council on the Employment of Women, Wellington, 28-29 June.

Magnusson, L., Mosesdottir, L and Serrano Pascual, A. 2003. *Equal pay and gender mainstreaming in the European employment strategy*. Brussels: European Trade Union Institute. <etui.org/research/activities/Employment-and-social-policies/Books/Equal-pay-and-gender-mainstreaming-in-the-European-Employment-Strategy> accessed 24 October 2009.

March, C., Smyth I. and Mukhodpadhyay, M. 1999. *A guide to gender analysis frameworks*. Oxford: Oxfam.

Martin, P.Y. and Collinson, D.L. 2006. 'What do we mean by communication? Responding to Mumby and Ashcraft', *Gender, Work and Organization* 13 (1): 91-95.

Moser, C. 2005. 'Has gender mainstreaming failed?', *International Feminist Journal of Politics* 7 (4): 575-590.

Pillinger, J. 2005. 'Pay equity now! Gender mainstreaming and gender pay equity in the public services', *International Feminist Journal of Politics* 7 (4): 591-599.

Pocock, B. and Alexander, M. 1999. 'The price of feminised jobs: New evidence on the gender pay gap in Australia', *Labour and Industry* 10 (2): 75-100.

Power, M. 1997. *The audit society: The rituals of verification*. Oxford: Oxford University Press.

Preston, A.C. and Crockett, G.V. 1999. 'Equal pay: Is the pendulum swinging back?', *Journal of Industrial Relations* 41 (4): 561-574.

Probert, B., Smith, M., Charlesworth, S. and Leong, K. 2002. *Victorian Public Service: Gender Pay Equity Review*. A report for the Gender Pay Equity Project Management Steering Group, Royal Melbourne Institute of Technology, Melbourne.

Rafferty, F. 1989. 'Equal pay – past experience, future directions: A practitioner's perspective', *Journal of Industrial Relations* 31 (4): 526-537.

Reed, R. 2002. 'A future for pay equity? From comparable worth to equal remuneration principle'. Paper presented at the XV World Congress of Sociology: *The social world in the 21ˢᵗ century: Ambivalent legacies and rising challenges*, Brisbane, 7-13 July.

Rubery, J., Grimshaw, D. and Figueiredo, H. 2005. 'How to close the gender pay gap in Europe: Towards the gender mainstreaming of pay policy', *Industrial Relations Journal* 36 (3): 184-213.

Sandler, J. 1997. *UNIFEM's experiences in mainstreaming for gender equality*. New York: UNIFEM.

Short, C. 1986. 'Equal pay: what happened?' *Journal of Industrial Relations* 28 (3): 315-335.

Tasmanian Industrial Commission 1999. Review of Wage Fixing Principles T8413 of 1999 and T8483 of 1999. <tic.tas.gov.au/decisions_issued/state_wage_case_decisions/t8413_and_t8483_7_april_2000> accessed 1 November 2009.

Tasmanian Industrial Commission 2000. State Wage Case Decisions and Review of Wage Fixing Principles. Hobart, Tasmania. <tic.tas.gov.au/decisions_issued/state_wage_case_decisions/t8413,_t8483__and__t8624> accessed 1 November 2009.

Todd, P. and Eveline, J. 2004. *Report on the Review of the Gender Pay Gap in Western Australia*. Ministry of Consumer and Employment Protection, Western Australia Government, Perth. <commerce.wa.gov.au/labourrelations/PDF/Publications/Gender_Pay_Final_Rep.pdf> accessed 24 October 2009.

Todd, P. and Eveline, J. 2006. 'Gender pay equity: It's time (or is it?)', in Davis E.M. and Pratt, V. (eds) *Making the link, no. 17, affirmative action and employment relations*. Sydney, NSW: Sydney Commercial Clearing House.

Walby, S. 2005. 'Introduction: Comparative gender mainstreaming in a global era', *International Feminist Journal of Politics* 7 (4): 453-471.

Watts, M. and Mitchell, W. 2004. 'Wages and wage determination in 2003', *Journal of Industrial Relations* 46 (2): 160-183.

West, C. and Zimmerman, D. 2003. 'Doing gender', in Ely, R., Foldy, E. and Scully, M. (eds) *Reader in gender, work and organization*. Malden, MA: Blackwell.

Western Australian Government. 1993. *Minimum Conditions of Employment Act*. <slp.wa.gov.au/statutes/swans.nsf/5d62daee56e9e4b348256ebd0012c422/03efe6e83099b29e482565d5002085ff/$FILE/Minimum%20Conditions%20of%20Employment%20Act%201993.PDF> accessed 1 November 2009.

Whelan, D. 2005a. *Advancing pay equity: Their future depends upon it*. Report by the Victorian Pay Equity Working Party to the Minister for Industrial Relations, Melbourne, Victoria: Victorian Minister for Industrial Relations. <business.vic.gov.au/busvicwr/_assets/main/lib60047/85_pay-equity-final-4-3-2005.pdf> accessed 1 November 2009.

Whelan, D. 2005b. 'The Victorian experience'. Paper presented at *the Gender pay gap: Assessing possible futures in the post-inquiries era.* International conference, University of Western Australia, Nedlands, Western Australia, 28-29 April 2005.

Whitehouse, G. and Frino. B. 2003. 'Women, wages and industrial agreements', *Australian Journal of Labour Economics* 6 (4): 579-596.

Whitehouse, G. and Rooney, T. 2006. 'The Queensland Dental Assistants' Equal Remuneration Case: An illustration of the pay equity implications of eroding the state system', in Pocock, B., Provis, C. and Willis, E. (eds) *21st century work: High road or low road*. Proceedings of the 20th Conference of the Association of Industrial Relations Academics of Australia and New Zealand, volume 2. South Australia: University of South Australia.

8

Gender analysis and community participation:
The role of women's policy units

KATY OSBORNE, CAROL BACCHI AND CATHERINE MACKENZIE

Introduction: Carol Bacchi and Joan Eveline

In Chapter 5 we identify the 'project trap' – subservience to wider policy objectives – as a major constraint on potentially transformative gender analysis processes. There we show, for example, how privatisation of health care (Armstrong 2002) increases the caring work that those marked as 'women' will have to do, reinforcing the conventional domestic division of labour. It follows that, in order to be transformative, a gender analysis must be able to scrutinise underlying premises in policy proposals, showing how they can be gender*ing* practices that *produce* gendered beings and gendered relationships.

A major factor deterring critical analysis of this type is the insider status of those performing gender analysis, since policy workers are obliged to an extent to perform assessment tasks as laid out by the government holding office (Chapter 11). To loosen the ties of this limiting 'insider' status and hence to enable policy workers to become more critical of government policies, some theorists emphasise the importance of forms of community involvement as a policy practice (see Chapter 1, p.30). The argument here is that members of the lay public may provide contesting views to perspectives shaped largely by business interests and senior management. As mentioned elsewhere (Chapter 3), one of the chief purposes of Linkage Grant projects is theory testing. Hence, the project organisers in South Australia constructed a qualitative research exercise to consider the extent to which community consultation might encourage the development of more transformative gender analysis processes. The results of this exercise form the basis of this chapter.

The issue of community consultation and its effectiveness, we discovered, is itself contested. Some theorists see community consultation as a token exercise and as limited in its democratic potential, in part due to reliance on existing and recognised identity groups (see Squires 2005). At the same time, other theorists place a good deal of faith in the democratic promise of community participation. Nott (2000), for example, distinguishes between a less democratic top-down, expert-led bureaucratic model of gender mainstreaming and a more democratic bottom-up, community-led model.

The research conducted for this chapter puts in question the tendency to contrast too sharply expert-bureaucratic and participative-democratic models of gender mainstreaming. The relationship we discover is more dialectical than this dichotomous distinction implies. Specifically, we found that 'insiders' (bureaucratic 'experts') play crucial roles in ensuring that consultation processes are more than a token exercise. Because of their on-the-ground dealings and deliberations with diverse groupings of women, many of whom face violence and discrimination in their daily lives, members of women's policy units are more likely to recognise the caring obligations many women have and the specific requirements of women with disabilities. Moreover, useful consultations require realistic parameters, appropriate representation and clear feedback, and women's policy units are ideally placed to coordinate these practices. For them to fill this role, of course, adequate resources – which can never be assumed – are a prerequisite.

This research on community consultation suggests that feminists need to be wary of the categories they create (Chapter 13) since, in this instance, setting democratic practices *against* bureaucratic expertise, as Nott does, with an implied critique of the latter, could well provide grounds for dismantling or reducing the standing of the very women's equality units that promise to make consultation processes more effective. It also highlights another important theme in the book, that reflections on the potential usefulness of reform initiatives like gender analysis need to be sensitive to the complexities and ambiguity of on-the-ground organisational priorities and the practices these involve (Chapters 9 and 11).

Reference

(Website valid as of publication date)

Armstrong, P. 2002. 'Speaking notes', Public consultations of the Commission on the Future of Health Care, 30 May, Toronto, Ontario. <cewh-cesf.ca/PDF/health_reform/speaking-notes.pdf> accessed 1 November 2009.

Abstract

Community consultation has become a widely accepted part of policy development in Australia. In this article, we consider how, in an Australian context, consultation can be incorporated within gender analysis processes. Gender analysis refers to systematic procedures to detect and correct gender bias in the full range of government programs, projects and policies. We draw upon insights from a qualitative case study to argue that policy workers located within women's policy units could play a key role in designing and coordinating meaningful and inclusive consultation. We conclude that well-resourced women's policy offices within Australian governments are essential to ensuring that effective, equitable consultation exercises are included within gender analysis processes.

Gender analysis refers to an innovative approach to enshrining gender equality in public policy. It offers systematic procedures, often in the form of a guide (for example, SWC 1998), to detect and correct gender bias in the full range of government programs, projects and policies. The question addressed in this article is how best to design and incorporate procedures for community consultation in gender analysis processes.

Since gender analysis represents an expressed commitment to examine policies across the board in every government department, it is often described as a method for 'mainstreaming' gender (Council of Europe 1998: 21-23). Mainstreaming, however, has become a hotly contested policy innovation. While some authors (True and Mintrom 2001) view the adoption of mainstreaming frameworks across different international contexts as a victory of the global feminist movement, others (Bacchi and Eveline 2003) see certain disturbing continuities between dominant mainstreaming approaches and neoliberalism, specifically in the commitment to the virtues of market liberalism and individual responsibility. There is particular concern that the trend within new public sector management (an institutional reform associated with neoliberalism) to disperse accountability for gender equality across government departments can provide the justification to downgrade or disband specialised women's policy units within government bureaucracies. Within Australia, for example, mainstreaming is widely considered to have provided the 'rationale for abolishing or downgrading women's units, services and policies at various government levels, by different administrations, at different times' (Mackay and Bilton 2000: 62). Given this history it is important to critically examine mainstreaming initiatives.

Using original research we demonstrate the key role played by specialist women's policy units in designing and coordinating effective consultation processes. The article emphasises the importance of retaining and indeed strengthening such units when gender analysis is introduced, expressly challenging moves to disband or downgrade these units. This argument, that specialist units are crucial to facilitating effective consultation, also suggests the need to rethink the commonly constructed dichotomy between 'expert-bureaucratic' and 'participative-democratic' models of gender mainstreaming, as explained in the next section.

Gender mainstreaming and community consultation

Community engagement and participation in policy decision-making has become a widely accepted and important part of policy development both in Australia and internationally (Reddel and Woolcock 2004). Approaches to gender 'mainstreaming' are commonly categorised according to the extent to which they incorporate strategies for community participation. In this vein Nott (2000; see also Donaghy 2004) argues that two models of mainstreaming can be identified: expert-bureaucratic and participative-democratic.

According to Nott (2000), in an expert-bureaucratic approach, policies are submitted to an 'impact assessment' by gender experts located within and/or outside bureaucratic institutions. Gender analysis is conducted in a centralised, top-down fashion. By contrast, the participative-democratic model specifies the need to incorporate widespread consultation and participation with a range of individuals, community, civic and interest groups. The central feature of the latter approach is the inclusion and representation of a wide range of community groups within the gender mainstreaming process (Nott 2000). As such, the participative-democratic model is described as less 'top-down' than the expert-bureaucratic model. While these two models are not necessarily mutually exclusive, Nott maintains that governments have generally chosen one approach, rather than try to combine aspects of both.

Since feminist approaches to policy development in Australia have been driven from within governments by specialist women's policy units (Sawer 1990) the model for gender equality that has developed in Australia is commonly described as expert-bureaucratic. Indeed Australia is well known for coining the term 'femocrat' to identify Australian bureaucrats who have argued from within government for gender equitable policies (Rankin and Vickers 2001; Sawer 1996). Here it is useful to remember that many femocrats came from within the women's movement, complicating a too simple distinction between 'expert-bureaucratic' and 'participative-democratic' models.[1] The goal of women's policy units has been to focus on the auditing, monitoring and coordination of policies to promote increased gender equality (Sawer 1996).

Australia's Women's Budget Program (1984-1996) is often identified as a precursor to gender analysis (Sharp and Broomhill 2003). Gender budgets refer to an exercise to assess government budgets to identify whether their commitment to gender equity is supported by financial resources. As they 'forge a strong link between resource allocation and policies across all government activities' (Sharp and Broomhill 2003: 26), they can be described as forms of mainstreaming (Donaghy 2002: 2), though the language was not used at the time.[2] A weakness of gender budgeting exercises was the lack of inclusion and consultation from women within the wider community (Sharp and Broomhill 2003), supporting the general characterisation of Australian gender equality approaches as 'expert-bureaucratic'.

The participative-democratic approach to mainstreaming has been developed most extensively in Northern Ireland where, historically, different groups have been excluded from government processes and decision-making on religious and ethnic bases (Donaghy 2004). A statutory duty was developed in Northern Ireland to underpin mainstreaming initiatives. This statutory duty applies to all public authorities and requires them to consider promoting equality in policy development across a number of categories, including religious belief, racial group, sexual orientation and disability. Thus, in Northern Ireland, the focus of mainstreaming has been expanded to incorporate more than gender (Donaghy 2004). A participative-democratic approach, as the description implies, explicitly specifies the need for consultation with diverse groups as part of the process of assessing policies to promote and increase gender equity.

In our view, while distinguishing between 'expert bureaucratic' and 'participative democratic' models of gender 'mainstreaming' provides a useful way to mark general trends in approaches to equity policy, the distinction fails to take into account the complexities and ambiguities of the consultation exercise (and perhaps other processes as well). As we discuss in the following section, consultation is not necessarily unequivocally positive; it all depends on how consultation processes are organised. Our research, described later in the article, highlights the key role played by 'insider' experts in ensuring sensitive and well-planned consultation exercises, challenging a simple 'expert' versus 'participation' characterisation of 'mainstreaming' initiatives and gender analysis. There are circumstances, our research shows, where 'expertise' facilitates, rather than blocks, consultation and participation.

The pros and cons of consultation

Consultation processes are seen as a crucial part of gender analysis frameworks for several reasons. Clearly, they are useful strategically. In general, policy initiatives are more likely to succeed if the bureaucrats that are responsible for developing them can demonstrate accountability by engaging with the diverse opinions and contributions of community members (Kane and Bishop 2002). In addition, Sawer (1996) highlights that the location of women's policy units within government departments means that they have to conform to rigid institutional practices and structures. Opening gender analysis processes up to consultation may allow feminist policy workers to escape the bureaucratic restrictions of their inside-government location and hence to consider policies in more critical ways (Staudt 2003). Finally, there is an ethical justification for incorporating consultation in gender analysis processes. Governments represent communities, and it is important that government departments not lose touch with public opinion (Kane and Bishop 2002). Notably, a participative-democratic approach to gender has the potential to include those who have previously been marginalised or under-represented in policy decision-making (Donaghy 2004). Consultation has been justified as a redistributive mechanism which has the potential to empower disadvantaged groups and promote greater social justice (Pickin et al. 2002; Putland, Baum and MacDougall 1997). Recognition on the part of government bureaucracies that the 'lay' knowledge of community members is valuable, as opposed to the privileging of 'expert' knowledge, is an important aspect of consultative strategies (Putland, Baum and MacDougall 1997; Popay and Williams 1996). These are important insights when considering the potential contribution of consultation in gender mainstreaming and gender analysis, as the ultimate goal of these processes is to promote social change.

On the other side, while community consultation has been viewed as redistributive and as a potentially empowering approach to policy decision-making, some scholars are sceptical about its effectiveness as a democratic exercise (Bishop and Davis 2002). For example, Squires (2005) and Arnstein (1969) present frameworks which view the inclusion of community participation in stages, moving from a least preferred position of bureaucratic power towards stages characterised by higher levels of citizen control.

Arnstein (1969) has conceptualised community participation in policy development in a linear, hierarchical fashion, as a 'ladder'. In Arnstein's framework, consultation is placed on a middle rung and is viewed as tokenistic. Ultimately, Arnstein views moves towards direct democracy, where community members have a more direct role in policy decision-making, as more empowering forms of participation than consultation. Similarly, Pateman (1970) argues that participation will only be meaningful where there is a significant transfer of power from government bureaucrats to citizens, and is doubtful about the effectiveness of government attempts to engage in consultation exercises.

Squires (2005) is also sceptical about consultation processes. She views gender mainstreaming approaches in a series of stages, from 'integrationist', which she identifies as a 'top-down' expert-bureaucratic approach; 'agenda setting', which involves consultation with organised interest and community groups; and 'transformative'. Squires argues that the 'transformative' model would utilise deliberative democracy methods, including widespread and diverse forms of community engagement. In her view this approach is preferable to conventional approaches to consultation as it avoids the essentialising of group identities, which she argues is a limitation of the 'agenda-setting' approach.

Squires (2005) argues that deliberative methods, such as citizens' forums, deliberative opinion polls, and referenda are potentially useful for gender mainstreaming. However, Bishop and Davis (2002) question the idea that deliberative methods that emphasise increased citizen control are necessarily useful for policy development. They highlight some examples of issues which may be subject to citizen-initiated referenda under deliberative approaches:

> Participation as control raises important questions about the quality of
> the decision-making. Citizen-initiated referenda can force politicians to
> confront difficult and divisive issues. This assumes it is in the interest of
> the polity to regularly debate abortion or gun-control, with the losing side
> forever able to renew the contest ... participation as control risks decisions

that are not grounded in appreciation of implications or consequences.
(Bishop and Davis 2002: 25-26)

It is possible that attempts to design redistributive policies to promote greater gender equity will encounter ideological resistance. Both the examples that Bishop and Davis (2002) highlight, abortion and gun-control, are hotly contested political issues that have a significant impact on the lives of both women and men. There is a danger that attempts to incorporate direct democratic approaches in gender analysis, such as the deliberative methods that Squires (2005) describes, could lead to unhelpful ideological struggle over the underlying goal of promoting gender equity, particularly over certain issues, for example, abortion and women's reproductive rights. It is also possible that community engagement may be used by governments as a strategy to undermine 'femocrat' insiders who are trying to work on behalf of women and promote feminist approaches to policy development.[3] The potentially divisive nature of the policy problems being considered in gender analysis, therefore, do not necessarily lend themselves to deliberative mechanisms which involve increased citizen control.

In each and every case therefore consultation and deliberation need to be recognised as, by their nature, political exercises, subject to contestation. Ultimately, then, in regards to gender analysis processes, it is important that policy workers, who are well informed about and sympathetic to the diversity of women's needs, and committed to gender equity, maintain some level of authority in the coordination of consultation exercises and policy decision-making.

On these grounds we argue that it is unhelpful to set expert-bureaucratic against participative-democratic approaches to mainstreaming. Rather we suggest that theoretical models need to be developed to combine these approaches. The case study to follow illustrates that, while gender analysis processes ought to include widespread consultation with interested individuals and community groups about how to develop gender equitable policies, some level of bureaucratic authority in the process should be preserved. Our research identifies crucial areas where policy workers who have a level of gender expertise are needed to guide the process of consultation. Rather than contrasting 'top-down' and 'bottom-up' models of policy development, our case study illustrates that more attention needs to be paid to what transpires on the ground and in the middle of policy development, including consultation processes.

Background and research method

This research was conducted as part of a wider Australian Research Council (ARC) Linkage project being conducted in South Australia and Western Australia. The project is designed to develop gender analysis methods specifically for an Australian context, and is being undertaken by researchers at the University of Adelaide and the University of Western Australia. The research on community consultation was conducted by the South Australian team. In South Australia, the Office for Women (SA) is the industry partner and three additional participating government agencies are involved in the research: the Department of Health, the Department of Correctional Services, and the Department of Further Education, Employment, Science and Technology (DFEEST). A reference group comprising university researchers and policy officers from each of the four government agencies guides the research in South Australia. The design and goals of the project are described in detail by Bacchi et al. (2005).

For the community consultation study, in-depth qualitative interviews were undertaken with ten community representatives who have been involved in consultation with government departments. The aim of these interviews was to explore existing community consultation strategies in South Australia, in order to identify potentially useful insights into how consultation could be included within gender analysis in a meaningful fashion.

Participants for this research were recruited using a snowball sampling technique: reference group members who work within the four government agencies involved were asked to refer the researchers to community representatives who had been involved in consultation with their departments. Community members were invited to contact the researchers if they were interested in participating in the research. Participants were interviewed from a range of community and interest groups including disability advocacy groups, a trade union, a women's health interest group, offenders' advocacy group and an older persons' advocacy organisation. Some of these participants had experiences both in being consulted and in organising and facilitating consultation processes for the groups they represent. Participants were asked to describe their experiences of consultation, and to discuss their perceptions of positive and negative consultations. The interviews also involved discussing how gender equity issues emerged and were managed in consultation.

This qualitative research gained ethics approval from the University of Adelaide Human Research Ethics Committee. Interviews were recorded and subsequently transcribed verbatim. Pseudonyms have been used to ensure participants' anonymity. Analysis of the qualitative data was conducted using grounded theory, whereby several readings of the transcripts led to the identification of key themes, and these were coded using Nvivo software. In the following sections, we will discuss some critical themes that emerged from the analysis of the qualitative data. In particular, we will highlight themes that relate to how consultations can be designed and undertaken in effective, positive and inclusive ways, in order to gain some insights into how consultation strategies can be incorporated into gender analysis. Importantly, the research confirms that, instead of setting 'expert-bureaucratic' against 'participative-democratic' models of gender analysis, it is more relevant to identify the ways in which 'expert' policy workers play crucial roles in enabling successful consultation to take place.

Research findings

Enabling meaningful contributions

Participants identified ways in which they felt that their contributions to consultation were not heard or valued. They spoke of consultations where the outcomes were pre-determined, and the process was undertaken as a cosmetic exercise. This type of consultation was viewed very negatively, as this comment from one participant illustrates:

> I have had a couple of issues with my local council area where you get the feeling that well they're asking you as a matter of course but 'we've already made our mind up' and that's very bad, I think. It does create a bad feeling for people being asked then. They wonder why people don't come up and put their opinions forward but if they've had an experience like that, why would they bother? (Virginia, representative of older person's organisation)

This frustration with tokenistic consultations was also reflected in participants' accounts of being 'over consulted'. They described their disillusionment at repeatedly contributing time and energy into a process where, ultimately, nothing was achieved. One participant described this experience:

> So, I think, another real frustration is … you come out of a consultation process and you might actually think we've set the agenda, okay, now, they're actually going to go there … they're going to do something about that, they're going to follow that up, but then you get asked basically the same set of questions, you know, in the next round of consultations and nothing changes.
> (Lesley, representative of disability advocacy organisation)

These accounts are revealing because they illustrate that those involved within consultations can feel that they are not being heard, that their contributions are not valued and will not make an impact or be used by government agencies. As a strategy for avoiding these negative experiences, participants discussed the importance of setting clear limits on what particular consultations can achieve. Some described feeling overwhelmed by involvement in wide-ranging consultations where the topic was too broad and the expectation for meaningful input was unrealistic. Clear communication about the aims, limits, and influence of the consultation, and how the contributions will be used towards these goals, was seen as essential by many of the participants. This comment from one participant illustrates what many viewed as a central element of successful consultations:

> I really like parameters about what I'm being consulted about. Don't consult me about something that I really haven't got any say or I can't influence. I find if someone says to me, 'Here's the parameters. Within this, what do you reckon?', I'm much happier with that than if someone says, 'What do you think?' in a global sense, because the reality is there will always be parameters and I'd rather know it up front.
> (Maxine, manager of women's health organisation)

Setting clear limits upon the aims of consultation, and communicating these to those involved, is essential because it is more likely that community members will feel that their contribution will have some kind of meaningful impact if they have a realistic idea of the scope of consultation. In relation to gender analysis, this involves clearly explaining the nature of the exercise – that the consultation is about increasing gender sensitivity and equity in a policy or policies being developed, and outlining the aims and limitations of particular consultations. Women's policy workers/units (the 'experts') therefore have a clear role to play at the level of organisation on community consultation.

In addition, many participants identified the importance of receiving clear feedback on the outcomes of the consultation. Again, this action acknowledges that the participants' contribution to consultation was valued and had some kind of impact on the process. One participant identified the advantage of using the feedback to be able to go and report to her interest group:

> It's really good to get that feedback after, particularly your session, to get some feedback on it, on what sort of stuff they gleaned out of that. It's really nice to get ... a bit of feedback with all the dot points of things they took out of the sessions, so that gives you the option to add things that you think of later ... which gives you an opportunity then to go back to your interest groups and say, 'Well, this is what happened. Is there anything that you wanted me to add to the points that were brought up?' (Rose, representative of women's health interest group)

These issues indicate that designing successful consultation is a process that requires considerable knowledge and skill, in order to ensure effective organisation which, in turn, enables the participants to feel that their contribution is of value. The role of 'experts' in delivering meaningful consultation processes is thus affirmed. While it is important to recognise that consultations, including those conducted as part of gender analysis processes, will not always be able to produce the outcomes that everyone involved would like, or that they may be limited in the extent to which they can use the information generated in the consultation, it is nevertheless critical that community members feel their contribution will have some value in the process.

Equitable access to consultation

Participants discussed the challenges associated with attending and participating in consultation, and talked of a number of ways in which consultations can become exclusionary through poor design. The importance of providing resources to enable people to attend consultation was viewed as important by participants. One participant talked of her experiences and the personal resources necessary to maintain her role, as someone frequently involved in various consultative processes through an older persons' organisation:

It's all voluntary really ... it is a case of having support and you do spend quite a bit in, if you work it out over the year you spend quite a bit in travelling. If I go to retirement villages to talk to them sometimes they will reimburse me for my travelling time, if I've had to go by car, but they don't always do that ... So there is a certain amount of support that you put in yourself and the time, of course. I mean I've devoted my second bedroom in my unit to become an office. Which was okay, but yeah ... you have to take those things into account. With any sort of voluntary work that you do ... it can become a burden on some people and this is another reason why I think the volunteer sector is finding it hard to attract people. (Virginia, representative of older persons' organisation)

Virginia's account highlights that volunteering to be involved in consultation processes can demand extensive personal resources. It is important to note that barriers to being involved in consultation may be gendered, as some of the women discussed their difficulties managing family commitments and child care requirements in order to participate in consultation. Rose highlights these issues by describing some of the difficulties she has faced to manage being involved in consultation:

I've had to juggle child care and things just to be able to get there for a meeting and inconvenience a lot of people around me, because I don't work, and you know I don't have child care facilities, so you know, yeah, time's valuable ... I think that is a real barrier to community consultation, is child care. (Rose, representative of women's health interest group)

If consultation is to be designed to be equitable and to gain a wide range of contributions, it is important to provide resources, such as reimbursement for time and costs associated with travel and child care, which will enable participants to overcome structural barriers to consultation exercises. Otherwise, consultation will attract only those who already have the means available to be involved. This point was reinforced by another participant who had experience in liaising with government departments to assist in the organisation of consultation exercises:

I think it's important to ask them what are the benefits for the community and also are you going to actually reimburse them for their travel? You know those things and are you going to have child care ... you're only going to get a certain stream of people if you don't provide all these sorts of things. (Elizabeth, chairperson of regional/remote health organisation)

Women with disabilities also stressed the importance of equitable access to consultation. One participant provided an example of a poorly designed consultation being run by a South Australian non-governmental organisation (NGO):

What happens with consultations is that people arrange them in inaccessible premises and at inaccessible times. In fact [NGO] have got one, it's a real beauty. It's about training requirements for our support workers, and employment for people with disabilities. Full day consultation with people with disabilities and unpaid carers of families. They're starting it at nine o'clock in the morning at [Suburban location]. Now in the nondisabled world, that's a reasonable thing ... this is for people with disabilities. Now for me to get there at nine o'clock in an access cab is impossible because the [name] Department book all the access cabs up for the school runs. So to get a cab at school times is you'll always be late, guaranteed ... And it's at [suburb] which isn't sort of like a central place that people can get to in public transport very easily.
(Nancy, representative of disability advocacy group)

This account is important because it illustrates how institutions can reinforce unequal power relations simply through poor organisation. Participants with disabilities repeatedly spoke about the ways in which issues such as transport and accessible locations are not considered by consultation organisers because they take their capabilities for granted and fail to consider the realities of life for people with disabilities. In particular, participants identified that these sorts of barriers to consultation may disproportionately affect women with disabilities, as in addition to their disability, these women face the challenge of everyday tasks involved with their gender roles. This meant that it was particularly difficult to engage women with disabilities in consultation, as Nancy describes:

If women get left off the list of people that should be consulted generally in the community, then I sure as hell aren't going to find out about it because I'm even further down the list as a woman with a disability, and women with disabilities are more disempowered than men with disabilities ... I'm generalising here, but men get looked after in society.

I mean if they don't do the dishes, their bloody wife'll do it, or she'll do the washing or she'll make sure the house is … whereas a woman with a disability, purely because she's a woman, she's supposed to look after herself … one of the minister's advisors … came up to me the other day and said 'you know, where are the other women leaders in the disability area?… getting women to come along and be activists, or even involved, is quite hard. (Nancy, representative of a disability advocacy group)

Consultations that are conducted as part of a gender analysis process would need to be organised to include consideration of practical issues such as time of day, transport and location, in order to involve people, and particularly women, with disabilities. It is important that such consultations are organised by those who have a clear understanding of the multiple barriers that impact upon women with disabilities.

While consultation can be designed in exclusionary ways, many participants expressed the belief that consultation was a useful and valuable exercise to undertake. One participant spoke of how consultation was a central aspect of democracy, and expressed the view that democratic processes require continual struggle in order to be maintained:

I think people do have the right to be informed, to take part, to be involved in decision-making at whatever level … I guess I would maintain that if consultation loses its place then … we have a dictatorship … I think that a process like consultation is something that occurs in a democracy but a democracy actually doesn't maintain itself, a democracy still has to be fought for, and I suppose what I'm also saying is so does consultation, so does good, inclusive, consultation. (Lesley, representative of disability advocacy group)

This participant is arguing that well-designed, accessible consultations do not merely happen; they occur as a result of hard-fought battles. Hence, it can be argued that those with a clear understanding of the many kinds of limitations that restrict diverse groups of women and men from involvement in consultation need to have a key role in arguing for well-designed equitable consultation practices.

It is particularly crucial for those who manage consultation to be aware of the gendered nature of barriers to consultation, and the specific requirements of particular cultural groups, and to design consultations in ways that are mindful of these factors. This requires that those who design and coordinate consultations are able to reflect critically upon their own practices and are aware of the potential for consultation to become exclusionary and oppressive through poor design and inadequate resources. It is also necessary that policy workers advocate within government for the allocation of resources for the consultation process. This highlights the importance of having policy workers within government committed to designing inclusive and meaningful consultation.

Relationships between government bureaucrats and community representatives

Participants reported how positive relationships with government workers can be a key element in successful consultation. This indicates the significance of communication between government and community members and that meaningful consultation will involve good relationships between these parties, suggesting limitations in analyses that set democratic-participative models of gender mainstreaming against expert-bureaucratic models. For one participant, the value of consultation was the opportunity to build social connections with bureaucrats and politicians located in state government departments. In her view ongoing relationships of this kind allowed her to keep the issues relevant to her group on the government's agenda and were more important than the success of any single consultation exercise:

> With regard to the work that we do, there is consensus and commitment, I think, from all areas, the ministers, Correctional Services, Justice, Health, they all know what we know and there's no disagreement, but it comes down to the bottom line about funding to provide a service ... We don't often find ourself in an adversary position with government ... You need to have a reality check on that stuff and just keep on keeping on and building a case, and hopefully when there is some money in the coffers you keep that on the agenda, keep it in the front of their minds and if there's money available you'll get a chunk of that pie. (Ann, representative of offenders' advocacy organisation)

This example is significant as it illustrates the value of building relationships with those within government. It is critical that consultation undertaken as part of gender analysis enables community members and policy workers within government to sustain ongoing, continuous relationships. Furthermore, it is important to recognise from this example that developing these relationships minimises the risk of political contest occurring over individual consultation exercises, where the community representative's preferred outcome may not have been achieved. It is therefore necessary to have policy officers located within government who can focus on maintaining relationships with community representatives.

Participants also emphasised the importance of organising consultations in ways sensitive to the requirements of particular community groups. In addition to providing resources to enable attendance, it was seen as necessary to invest time in developing relationships with members of particular cultural groups, in order to demonstrate sensitivity and to support their involvement in consultation. This was viewed as particularly important if these groups had been marginalised by governments in the past.

One participant had experience in organising and facilitating consultations for her health advocacy group, and inviting other community members from rural and regional settings to take part, in addition to being consulted herself. She discussed the process of approaching Aboriginal women to be involved in consultations about health issues:

> It's quite interesting that when you're setting up a committee and everyone goes 'thou shalt have a non English speaking background and an Indigenous and a something or other' ... it just doesn't work like that ... usually the only way to get Aboriginal women is to have two, so that they support one another and they feel better about things ... like in Murray Bridge you go to the [name] Club where they gather ... there are aunts and cousins ... So you go to aunty and you say 'Can we come at morning tea time?' and now we can go in, they're very welcoming to us, but you tread very carefully. (Elizabeth, chairperson of regional/rural health organisation)

These comments were echoed by other participants who discussed the importance of taking time to develop trust when inviting particular groups to take part in consultation. One participant spoke of her experiences, witnessing how women could be restricted by men from taking part in consultations that involved discussion of domestic violence. In such instances, she identified the importance of caution around communicating the topic of the consultation, and the necessity of excluding any mention of domestic violence initially to get these women involved. Clearly, organising such consultations involves sensitivity and awareness of issues of gender violence, suggesting a key role for policy officers with the appropriate background on gender equity issues. Both these cases also put in question Squires' (2005) concerns about essentialising targeted group identities. Rather, they point to the importance of acknowledging the specificity of group experiences in order to facilitate meaningful consultation.

The importance of political context also surfaced in the interviews. One participant explained that the success of consultation depended ultimately on whether those within government were committed to it:

> Here the national stuff is sort of slowing down a bit, with the change in health ministers and departmental people. Some of them now say, well they give the impression anyway 'we'll do this ourselves'. Which can be very frustrating ... because why did we waste our time, now it's all sitting on a shelf somewhere gathering dust and the patient is not able to benefit from it. (Elizabeth, chairperson of regional/rural health organisation)

A hostile political context can limit the achievements of consultation, as governments can manipulate and undermine consultation processes according to their own political agendas (Sawer 2002). However, while politicians ultimately influence the outcomes of consultation, public servants and departmental cultures can also have a role in shaping the results. One participant described how she felt that there was a very positive and supportive network of feminists working within the South Australian Government, and how she felt this was crucial in enabling useful consultation around issues of gender equity. At the same time she expressed her concern that, in the wider political context, the influence of this network was limited and tenuous:

> I guess I think it's wonderful that we have the [government office] ... but I just wonder how much influence they've really got or if it's not tokenistic. And that's no reflection on the work that they do, but in the gamut of all the issues the government has to deal with, how powerful really is that group? How much influence do they really have with the government to force women's issues? ... So I just often wonder really how much influence that office has in the state. It's a minority in parliament. It's a minority in policy, isn't it, still? So we've still got a long way to go

and just be careful they don't start chipping away at what's already there.
(Ann, representative of offenders' advocacy group)

Another participant supported the claim that governments in the main do not prioritise gender equity issues. She described her participation in a planning exercise conducted by senior bureaucrats who consulted employees across the South Australian state government and her repeated attempts to raise gender equity issues during the course of this consultation:

> It was quite clear they didn't listen. They're not interested in women ... every plenary it was very clear that they'd ignored it ... There's no movement, no willingness to even say, 'Yeah, we haven't thought about women', which they hadn't ... they just go, 'Oh could you girls shut up!', sort of thing. That's the attitude. (Maxine, manager of women's health organisation)

Crucially, in this environment participants stressed the importance of defending the existing, albeit fragile, women's policy machinery. It was viewed as critical to retain some kind of feminist representation inside government bureaucracies to ensure continued advocacy for gender equity issues. Policy officers within women's policy units were considered an important link between government and women in the community.

Conclusion: Combining 'participative-democratic' and 'expert-bureaucratic' models

The research therefore highlights that designing meaningful consultation is not simply a matter of developing a 'participative-democratic' community approach that somehow sits in opposition to the inclusion of bureaucrats with gender expertise. Indeed, and regrettably, constructing a dichotomy between 'expert-bureaucratic' and 'participative- democratic' processes could reinforce the tendency in many mainstreaming experiments to suggest that women's policy units are no longer useful, all in the name of 'community participation'. To the contrary the case study material presented here indicates that successful consultation, which minimises divisive political contest, can be contingent upon productive ongoing relationships between policy workers and community representatives. A primary goal of consultation, moving beyond the focus on specific single issues and policies, is in fostering 'developmental capacity' (Putland, Baum and MacDougall 1997) – the ability to cultivate ongoing relationships of respect, partnership and open communication between policy workers and community representatives. Policy officers that work within women's policy units need to be empowered therefore to develop and maintain such ongoing relationships with the communities they consult.

These findings point to the ways in which effective consultation is contingent upon the wider political context, and how the gender equity goals of women's policy units can be devalued within broader government agendas. In the European context, Verloo (2002) argues that strong gender equality units within governments are an essential asset for successful mainstreaming practices (Verloo 2002). We support this contention, and argue that policy officers with a level of gender expertise, located within women's policy units, are crucial for enabling meaningful consultation exercises.

Women's policy units generally display a level of knowledge of gender relations and intersecting equity issues, and are well positioned to design and coordinate inclusive and meaningful consultation processes. In addition, 'femocrat' policy officers can use their positions to advocate for resources to enable successful and effective consultation. Australian approaches to gender analysis therefore need to combine the 'participative-democratic' elements of inclusion of a wide range of community and interest groups with the 'expert-bureaucratic' element of 'femocrat' policy officers who coordinate and facilitate the consultation. Crucially, for this to occur, it is necessary to raise broad questions about the time and resource pressures facing the public sector (Bacchi et al. 2005) and the relative devaluing of women's policy units (Ramsay and Redden 2005; Teghtsoonian 2003). The challenge of developing gender-equitable policy is not a matter of experts versus community but of encouraging and supporting meaningful engagement between women's policy units and a wide range of community groups and representatives.

Notes

1. We would like to thank an anonymous reviewer for this and other useful comments.

2. While the language of mainstreaming appeared in some Australian universities in the 1990s (Bacchi 2001), the term was first used in reference to government gender equality policy in 2004 when the then federal Sex Discrimination Commissioner, Pru Goward (2004), described 'mainstreaming' as the Howard Liberal government's preferred approach to 'gender equity'. Given the use of the same term, 'mainstreaming', in Indigenous policy to dismantle ATSIC (Aboriginal and Torres Strait IslanderCommission), a national democratically elected body of Indigenous leaders, handing over funding programs to mainstream departments (Kemp 2005: 29), there is understandable disquiet in feminist ranks about the endorsement of gender 'mainstreaming'.

3. Again we would like to thank an anonymous reviewer for this comment.

References

(Websites valid at time of publication)

Arnstein, S. 1969. 'A ladder of citizen participation', *Journal of the American Institute of Planners* 35 (4): 216-224.

Bacchi, C. 2001. 'Managing equity: Mainstreaming and "diversity" in Australian universities', in Brooks, A. and Mackinnon, A. (eds) *Gender and the restructured university: Changing management and culture in higher education*. Buckingham: Open University Press.

Bacchi, C. and Eveline, J. 2003. 'Mainstreaming and neoliberalism: A contested relationship', *Policy and Society: Journal of Public, Foreign and Global Policy* 22 (2): 98-118.

Bacchi, C., Eveline, J., Binns, J., Mackenzie, C. and Harwood, S. 2005. 'Gender analysis and social change: Testing the water', *Policy and Society* 24 (4): 42-68.

Bishop, P. and Davis, G. 2002. 'Mapping public participation in policy choices', *Australian Journal of Public Administration* 61 (1): 14-29.

Council of Europe. 1998. *Conceptual framework, methodology and presentation of good practices: Final report of activities of the Group of Specialists on Mainstreaming* [EG-S-MS (98) 2]. Strasbourg: Council of Europe. <coe.int/t/e/human_rights/equality/02._gender_mainstreaming/100_EG-S-MS%281998%292rev.asp> accessed 24 October 2009.

Donaghy, T. 2002. 'Mainstreaming: Northern Ireland's participative-democratic approach'. Refereed paper presented at the Jubilee Conference of the Australian Political Studies Association, Canberra: Australian National University. <arts.anu.edu.au/sss/apsa/Papers/donaghy.pdf> accessed 24 October 2009.

Donaghy, T. 2004. 'Mainstreaming: Northern Ireland's participative-democratic approach,' *Policy and Politics* 32: 49-62.

Goward, P. 2004. 'Now everyone can focus on women', *The Age*, 30 October.

Kane, J. and Bishop, P. 2002. 'Consultation and contest: The danger of mixing modes', *Australian Journal of Public Administration* 61 (1): 87-94.

Kemp, M. 2005. 'Struggle for control of Aboriginal revolution', *The Advertiser*, 5 February.

Mackay, F. and Bilton, K. 2000. *Learning from experience: Lessons in mainstreaming equal opportunities.* Edinburgh: Governance of Scotland Forum, University of Edinburgh.

Nott, S. 2000. 'Accentuating the positive: Alternative strategies for promoting gender equality', in Beveridge, F., Nott, S. and Stephen, K. (eds) *Making women count: Integrating gender into law and policy-making.* Aldershot: Dartmouth.

Pateman, C. 1970. *Participation and democratic theory.* Cambridge: Cambridge University Press.

Pickin, C., Popay, J., Staley, K., Bruce, N., Jones, C. and Gowman, N. 2002. 'Developing a model to enhance the capacity of statutory organisations to engage with lay communities', *Journal of Health Services Research and Policy* 7: 34-42.

Popay, J. and Williams, G. 1996. 'Public health research and lay knowledge', *Social Science and Medicine* 42 (5): 759-768.

Putland, C., Baum, F. and MacDougall, C. 1997. 'How can health bureaucracies consult effectively about their policies and practices? Some lessons from an Australian study', *Health Promotion International* 12 (4): 299-309.

Ramsay, E. and Redden, M. 2005. *Women's Futures Reference Group report.* Adelaide: Office for the Status of Women.

Rankin, L.P. and Vickers, J. 2001. *Women's movements and state feminism: Integrating diversity into public policy.* Ottawa: Status of Women Canada. <rwmc.uoguelph.ca/cms/documents/88/Rankin_1-68.pdf> accessed 1 November 2009.

Reddel, T. and Woolcock, G. 2004. 'From consultation to participatory governance? A critical review of citizen engagement strategies in Queensland', *Australian Journal of Public Administration* 63 (3): 75-87.

Sawer, M. 1990. *Sisters in suits: Women and public policy in Australia.* Sydney: Allen and Unwin.

Sawer, M. 1996. *Femocrats and ecorats: Women's policy machinery in Australia, Canada and New Zealand.* Occasional paper no. 6. Geneva: United Nations Research Institute for Social Development. <unrisd.org/unrisd/website/document.nsf/462fc27bd1fce00880256b4a0060d2af/d1a254c22f 3e5cc580256b67005b6b56/$FILE/opb6.pdf> accessed 1 November 2009.

Sawer, M. 2002. 'Governing for the mainstream: Implications for community representation', *Australian Journal of Public Administration* 61 (1): 39-49.

Sharp, R. and Broomhill, R. 2003. 'Budgeting for equality: The Australian experience', *Feminist Economics* 8 (1): 25-47.

Squires, J. 2005. 'Is mainstreaming transformative? Theorising mainstreaming in the context of diversity and deliberation', *Social Politics: International Studies in Gender, State and Society* 12 (3): 366-388.

Staudt, K. 2003. 'Gender mainstreaming: Conceptual links to institutional machineries', in Rai, S.M. (ed.) *Mainstreaming gender, democratizing the state? Institutional mechanisms for the advancement of women.* Manchester: Manchester University Press.

SWC (Status of Women Canada). 1998. *Gender-based analysis: A guide for policy-making.* Ottawa: Status of Women Canada.

Teghtsoonian, K. 2003. 'W(h)ither women's equality? Neoliberalism, institutional change and public policy in British Columbia', *Policy, Organisation and Society* 22 (1): 26-47.

True, J. and Mintrom, M. 2001. 'Transnational networks and policy diffusion: The case of gender mainstreaming', *International Studies Quarterly* 45: 27-57.

Verloo, M. 2002. 'The development of gender mainstreaming as a political concept for Europe'. Paper presented at the Conference on Gender Learning, Leipzig, Germany, 6-8 September.

9

The invisibility of gendered power relations in domestic violence policy

KAREN VINCENT AND JOAN EVELINE

Introduction: Joan Eveline and Carol Bacchi

A fervent debate in mainstreaming policy surrounds the question of whether 'gender' or 'diversity' should provide the main focus. Lurking behind that debate is the discursive practice of 'commatisation', highlighted by Mary O'Brien (1984) as the definitive blind spot of equal opportunity policy. With commatisation, the policy emphasis goes onto the disadvantages of 'women (comma) blacks (comma) gays (comma) ...' etc. etc. and leaves the advantages available to the unspoken norm (white, male, straight etc.) hidden from view (Eveline 1994).

Although policymakers have tried replacing 'women' with 'gender' and the remainder of the commatised groups with 'diversity', the old dangers of commatisation remain. Most public servants who develop and implement policy still think 'gender' means 'women' (Chapters 3, 4 and 5), rather than an attributional process that maintains and obscures a masculinised ordering of privilege. And most of the groups who find themselves in the 'diversity' category see gender used invariably in white ethnocentric and heteronormative ways which obscure and sustain the cultural privileges that white heterosexual women take for granted in white racist homophobic societies.

Whether and how gender mainstreaming can adequately address this problem of commatisation was a key design question for our gender analysis project. As part of that design we initiated a PhD study dedicated to examining the interface between gender analysis and issues raised by Aboriginal communities in Western Australia. This chapter is an early outcome of that PhD project and the first in the book to focus primarily on the contested terrain of the gender *vs* diversity debate (see also Chapters 10, 12 and 13). The chapter examines two approaches to domestic violence policy in the Western Australian context. In the first, the attempt to make racism evident renders gendered power relations invisible; in the other, institutionalised racism and gendered power relations both disappear.

The chapter shows that developing and implementing policy never happens in a political vacuum. The political pressure most obvious to the voting public occurs when governments or their ministers change or change direction. The internal politics of public sector organisations are rarely as clear to the 'public', or indeed to many who work within the organisation in question, but they can be equally influential nonetheless. Bureaucracies normalise their practices through formal and informal rules about who makes decisions of particular kinds, and how and where these can be disseminated (Chapter 11). These normalised practices shroud or remove most signs that the outcomes of policy procedures have political effects, including any recognition that they are favouring a dominant voice, culture or group (Eveline 1994; Bacchi 1999).

White feminism provides the prevailing voice in highlighting and challenging ways of seeing and doing that favour male dominance. Yet as women of colour have argued since the 1970s, 'white' feminists must continually interrogate their own taken-for-granted assumptions (Chapters 5, 10 and 13). Politicising 'gender' as the problem in culturally insensitive ways has silenced the cultural and identity politics of non-dominant groups of women. Yet as this chapter shows, highlighting institutional racism rather than gendered power relations can carry its own dangers. Moreover, the anti-racist purpose is unthinkingly undermined when any analysis of both racism *and* gendered power relations are excluded from subsequent domestic violence policy.

References

Bacchi, C. 1999. *Women, policy and politics: The construction of policy problems.* London: Sage.

Eveline, J. 1994. 'The politics of advantage', *Australian Feminist Studies* 19: 129-154.

O'Brien, M. 1984. 'The commatisation of women: Patriarchal fetishism in the sociology of education', *Interchange* 15 (2): 43-60.

Abstract

This exploratory study seeks to illustrate how the policy context shapes the way policy actors engage with concepts of gender and practices of racism. The paper draws on two case studies in the context of family and domestic violence (FDV) policy and service development in an Australian State Government context. The first case study uses document analysis of a major public inquiry into government agency responses to FDV in Indigenous communities. The second uses a policy audit tool to examine a policy development process in a department responsible for coordinating human service agencies, services and funding of community-sector FDV projects. These case studies reveal that both Aboriginal women and non-Aboriginal women can disappear from the concerns that FDV policy purports to solve. To demonstrate our argument, we show how the policy terminology of both 'domestic violence' and that of 'family violence' can render gender and racism invisible.

> Every week in Western Australia police remove around 130 violent people from family homes during domestic violence call-outs, which equates to more than 18 every day. Children and young people live in up to 85% of these homes. Templeman 2006)

The above statement was made in a speech announcing a program titled 'No more violence: We're breaking the silence' by the Western Australian Government Minister with broad child and family welfare and community development portfolio responsibilities including the policy area of family and domestic violence (FDV). The speech was one of many over recent years by government about a subject once considered taboo: family and domestic violence in Aboriginal communities. The Western Australian Parliament has engaged in numerous debates and the government has responded to frequent media reports about the subject. Increasingly these have been about FDV experienced in Aboriginal communities. In contrast to a history of silence, the past five years has seen the policy context of FDV become highly politicised to the issue. Public sector agencies are under immense pressure, as the Australian public expresses 'moral outrage' (Cripps 2007) about endemic abuse against Aboriginal women and children.

Such outrage is overdue. Indigenous women are 45 times more likely to experience domestic violence than non-Indigenous women and ten times more likely to be killed as a result of domestic violence (Partnerships Against Domestic Violence

2001). In this context, the pressure is on departments most closely responsible for dealing with family violence against women and children – police, justice and community welfare – to counter and curtail the problem.

This paper examines the complexities and challenges of the public policy process in a fraught and challenging field at a time of turmoil and public visibility. We describe the research as exploratory since it draws on two case studies in one Australian state to examine the extent to which intersectionality is ignored in domestic violence policy. The paper suggests that, although the issue of family violence is now much more visible to public scrutiny and departments alike, the crucial issue of the gendered power relations that underpins this family violence remains as invisible as ever when it comes to policy development.

Our two case studies are drawn from the field of FDV in Western Australia. Our analysis of these case studies shows two different ways in which gendered power relations become invisible. The first case, commonly called the 'Gordon Inquiry', shows how gendered power relations can be omitted from family violence policy when the emphasis of the report is on institutionalised racism. The second shows how Indigenous women disappear in the departmental high-level policy for FDV, but so also does gendered power relations. Both of these public policy documents indicate a lost opportunity to explore intersectionality. Despite this similarity, the capacity of each to confront the white ethnocentrism of family violence policy is quite different.

Literature review

The historically and socially contingent nature of policy is particularly relevant in the field of Aboriginal affairs, where policies have been critically affected by recent media and public attention. At the same time, feminist studies point to the need for projected gender outcomes to be taken into account in all policy development processes. For some feminists the answer lies in what is now termed 'gender mainstreaming' (Walby 2005). However, as Eveline and Bacchi (2005) noted, that approach to policy is highly contested and subject to being infused with inadequate understandings of gender. As Bacchi (2005: 184) stated, 'the task is to examine how gendered concepts are *applied* in the lives of diverse groups of men and women'.

Domestic violence is a field of public policy in which one would expect that a gender analysis would be ubiquitous. Yet neither gender nor institutional racism is necessarily given priority in such policymaking. Once considered a taboo subject, domestic violence has become a subject for public and political attention, with the World Health Organization (WHO) estimating that between 15 per cent and 71 per cent of women have experienced physical or sexual assault from an intimate partner (World Health Organization 2005: xiii).

Despite gathering pace in the last decade, much domestic violence research has neglected or ignored Indigenous experience. There is significant under-reporting of FDV for all population groups, but particularly for Aboriginal women experiencing FDV. Nonetheless, statistical indicators reveal considerable over-representation of Indigenous women experiencing assault and death (Office for Women's Policy 2006). Aboriginal women are 10 times more likely to be murdered than non-Aboriginal women (Duff 1994: 38). In Western Australia, Aboriginal women 'make up only about 3 per cent of the adult female population [yet] they accounted for half of all the domestic violence incidents reported to the police in 1994 ... [they] are more than 45 times more likely than non-Aboriginal women to be a victim of domestic violence' (Ferrante et al. 1996). The Office for Women's Policy (2005: 57) has reported that 22.6 per cent of Indigenous women in Western Australia perceived family violence as a problem in their community. Despite their continued calls for improved safety and protection, Indigenous women have been described as 'the single most legally disadvantaged group in Australian society' (Australian Law Reform Commission 1994).

The full picture of FDV and its impacts on the social, emotional, physical and financial wellbeing of Indigenous women and communities is currently unmeasured and program evaluations report mixed success with efforts at prevention, intervention, punishment and treatment. The 2007 Social Justice Report (Aboriginal and Torres Strait Islander Social Justice Commissioner, Human Rights and Equal Opportunity Commission [HREOC] 2007) identified concerns with research and evaluation methods, including the privileging of statistical data by government that ultimately serves to reinforce negative stereotypes. 'One of the challenges that this demonstrates is to listen to communities and ensure that evaluation is conducted in a situational and culturally appropriate way' (Aboriginal and Torres Strait Islander Social Justice Commissioner, HREOC 2007: 22). Understanding the components for 'best practice' is still under-developed. However, common elements at community level include the importance of Aboriginal leadership and Aboriginal women project self-management. It has been of critical importance for the sustainability of Aboriginal communities to resist racist assumptions that problematise Aboriginal peoples by portraying Aboriginality as the source of FDV problems and presenting a chronic or recalcitrant 'Aboriginal problem' (Blagg 2008; Cripps 2004).

Aboriginal women and men continue to be affected by the traumatic legacy of historical institutional racism, expressed and reinforced by individual acts of racism by agents of the state. Conventional wisdom surrounding racial categories perpetuates discrimination and prejudice. Mainstream agencies continue to relate to Aboriginal women and men on the basis of racist stereotypes that are so familiar they are rarely challenged.

Institutional racism infuses domestic violence policy. Perpetrator treatments and crisis management systems have been based on western interventions and imposed by social institutions in ways described by Indigenous writers as epistemic and post-colonial (Duran et al. 1998). Western (white) theories of domestic violence have been increasingly challenged by Indigenous critics as tools for social control. Simplistic conventional solutions that exacerbate the problem include programs that pathologise Indigenous men, focus on parallel factors such as alcohol and drug abuse and treat violence as symptomatic of a general community deficiency. Duran concluded that 'authors maintain a definition of the problem that masks the issues of domination and subjugation, issues which must be considered given the historical context of this problem' (Duran et al. 1998: 98).

The literature shows that Indigenous women dealing with agencies experience racism as an everyday occurrence (Baldry, Green and Thorpe 2006; St. Jean and Feagin 1998). 'One in five Indigenous women experienced discrimination and/or racism in 2002' (Office for Women's Policy 2005: 58). In 2004, an inquiry into housing for Aboriginal people examined institutional racism and reported that 'Aboriginal women and children escaping domestic and/or family violence experience a higher degree of disadvantage than non-Aboriginal applicants' (Equal Opportunity Commission 2004: 179).

In an attempt to place Indigenous issues on policy agendas, activists have promoted and supported a politics of Indigenous identity. Pat O'Shane (1976), for example, showed how and why the primary concern for Aboriginal women was racism, not gender. Jackie Huggins (Huggins cited in Jones 2005) explained that 'there are some issues where Indigenous women can form alliances with non-Indigenous women, but that the form of feminism that is available to Indigenous women is not the model they prefer. Instead, they have their own brand of feminism that's all-encompassing'. In short, Aboriginal women's writings have stressed as their primary struggle the survival of their people, the recognition of their cultural identity and what those needs dictate for government policy.

In this context gender discrimination becomes secondary to cultural identity. The extent to which this much-needed emphasis on institutional racism can sustain a gender analysis has been strongly debated. Stubbs (2004: 4), for example, abhorred the backlash against gender policy and argued that 'denouncing domestic violence as a crime has been an important gain of feminist activism after a history of neglect and should not be undermined'. Others have argued that neither gender nor race should be the primary focus, but rather how the two intersect in different situations. Led by Black feminists in the United States, Crenshaw (1991) and Collins (1998), this concern for intersectionality has had very limited attention in Australian policy. It is that concern, coupled with the need to recognise the racism that underpins Aboriginal women's struggles, that provides the analytical starting point for this paper.

Research methodology

Qualitative methodology was considered most appropriate to gather new information and a deeper understanding about gender and racism, contested fields of study. Exploratory in its design, the research sought to gain an understanding of how particular policy objectives are conceptualised as well as operationalised.

We used a case study approach and the techniques of literature review, policy audits, document analysis and interviews with a number of key players. Case study is valuable for gaining a greater depth of understanding of the topic (Yin 1989). The two case studies in this research were designed to provide triangulation for the research question of when and how gender and racism are rendered invisible. We used issues and themes arising from document analysis of the two case studies to develop the interview questions and analyse the transcripts. Both case studies analysed Western Australian policy documents and reports.

The first case study examined in-depth a major inquiry report to government (Gordon, Hallahan and Henry 2002). The inquiry that developed the report was instituted by the Western Australian Government in 2001 as a response to media accounts of widespread sexual abuse and violence within the Aboriginal community. We selected the inquiry for its significance as a major policy 'driver' for what it calls 'family violence' services specific to Aboriginal communities. We complemented content analysis of the 'Gordon Report' and other inquiry publications by examining other relevant government documents. These included parliamentary debates, media statements, departmental policies and procedures concerning implementation plans and activities, operational guidelines for staff dealing with child protection and family violence, program outlines, implementation and evaluation reports.

Our second case study used a policy audit method. Techniques involved an initial meeting with senior policy staff, analysis of relevant policy documents, interviews with the staff who worked on drafting the policy, and a further meeting with this group to discuss and revise our policy audit draft report. Phone conversations and email communications were also sources of information.

The policy audit was undertaken during a review of the existing government 'mainstream' FDV Policy in order to appreciate experiences and perspectives of policy actors during the development process. Commencing the policy audit process during policy review was an opportunity to learn about the early stages of the 'policy cycle' rather than following policy adoption and implementation. The policy audit was conducted as part of a larger Gender Analysis of Policy research project, the stated goal of which was to refine existing models and develop gender analysis processes appropriate for application in the Australian public sector context (Bacchi et al. 2005).

Insights gained from semi-structured interviews as part of the policy audit contributed to a picture of the strategic thinking and motivations involved in policy development within that politicised environment. Interview questions were drawn from Status of Women Canada (2001) material to describe the policy context, question the extent to which the policy expresses intention to be gender-inclusive and culturally-inclusive, and the extent the FDV policy achieved gender equitable and culturally-equitable outcomes.

Case study one: 'Gordon Inquiry'

The inquiry that we examine in our first case study is known colloquially as the 'Gordon Inquiry' because it was chaired by prominent Aboriginal magistrate Sue Gordon. The inquiry was triggered by several incidents of sexual and physical abuse of Aboriginal children, which received significant media attention and resulted in a public outcry. The findings of a coronial inquest questioned government services and professional practices and prompted government action. Previous reports, parliamentary debates and media profiles revealed a highly political policy context within which public servants were delivering services to vulnerable, disadvantaged Aboriginal communities. Prior to the inquiry, independent research and government reports had criticised a range of structural, organisational, administrative and human resource factors impeding progress in responding to the needs and problems experienced by Aboriginal people.

The Gordon Inquiry worked within established terms of reference, with restricted time and resources, and in a climate of political and public pressure. The Committee of three heading the inquiry received submissions, heard personal evidence, travelled throughout the State for consultations, drew on a comprehensive contracted literature review, and engaged in dialogue with key human service agencies. Their report (Gordon et al. 2002) made over 190 recommendations for change to support successful local initiatives by government at community level and to address perceived problems at agency level and across inter-agency structures.

The approach taken by the inquiry reflected Aboriginal views that sustainability for Aboriginal peoples was dependent on finding ways to counter substantial intergenerational trauma, disadvantage and disempowerment in the face of white mainstream systems and practices that were destructive at their worst and negligent at their most benign. Dealing with substantial disadvantages was the challenge and theme throughout the report. The inquiry had a mandate to examine public services that Aboriginal people identified as problematic, identify how the extensive disadvantages experienced by Aboriginal communities could be dealt with by mainstream agencies, and areas for reform of FDV services was the task (Gordon et al. 2002: xx-xxi). The experiences of actual or potential Aboriginal FDV service users provided the material that informed recommendations for agency change. Public policy was viewed as having responsibility for Aboriginal disadvantage either directly or indirectly, immediately or historically; Aboriginal disadvantage was portrayed as being a causative factor which was intensified by FDV.

Institutional racism

The inquiry reported that racism was one of multiple contributing factors to the endemic violence against Indigenous women and children. A composite account of institutional racism was provided by the inquiry's examination of policy outcomes experienced by Indigenous clients. Intergenerational trauma was described as a legacy of colonisation, genocide, dispossession, forced removal of children, loss of land, destruction of culture, and persistent racism. Indigenous communities were reported to have become increasingly vulnerable to symptomatic family violence and white government interventions, potentially more destructive than beneficial. Within the picture of violence in Aboriginal communities presented by the inquiry, violence against women and children was perpetrated by potentially multiple abusers connected by extended family relationships located within the community. The inquiry concluded that future policy and service developments required a coordinated and well-resourced, culturally sensitive system that would be increasingly under the direction, if not controlled, by Aboriginal peoples themselves (Gordon et al. 2002; Kovacs 2002).

The government strongly endorsed the major thrust of the Gordon Inquiry's report (Government of Western Australia 2002). Subsequently, over a period of four years, Treasury injected major funding to the key agencies to implement recommendations for program initiatives, infrastructure development, and departmental projects to strengthen service delivery (Gallop 2002). Interim evaluations have been critical of implementation progress and monitoring, and comprehensive evaluations are underway (Auditor General for Western Australia 2005).

Gender dimensions of FDV in Indigenous communities

In making its recommendations, the committee encouraged human service agencies to ensure cross-cultural sensitivity and develop inclusive practices, such as promoting the language of 'family and community' instead of 'violence against women'. The report noted that for Aboriginal women and men, white mainstream agencies delivered FDV policy that effectively denied the history of oppression, genocide and systemic abuse of Aboriginal people. It also acknowledged that ethnocentric definitions, understandings and approaches created difficulties for intervening in family violence in Aboriginal communities.

There were two elements of FDV policy that the inquiry did not examine: (a) the structural arrangements whereby public sector institutions operate as systems of social control to protect and perpetuate inequalities, and (b) the intersections of gender and racism in family violence policy and what they might mean for that policy's capacity to protect Aboriginal women.

The inquiry's conclusions drew on a growing body of literature by Indigenous authors, especially Aboriginal women, which reveals the history of sexualised racist abuse by Anglo-Australians since white settlement and rebukes the role of the state and its agents for white ethnocentrism. In turn, several Aboriginal women who spoke to the inquiry rejected mainstream approaches that individualised social problems, arguing that these further victimised the whole Aboriginal community, criminalised Aboriginal men and indirectly blamed Aboriginal women for the violence they suffered.

In the light of such discussions, those leading the Gordon Inquiry decided to adopt the terminology of 'family violence' in place of the usual 'domestic violence'. However, this shift in terminology did not altogether resolve the definitional problems, and indeed raised voices of concern from Aboriginal women. These were subsequently reported in the community consultations: 'I would prefer to see family/domestic violence called "Violence against Women". "Family Violence" makes it sound nice!' (Gordon et al. 2002: 29).

In dealing with this debate among Aboriginal women the report of the inquiry added an appendix showing how definitions differed across Australia, and in the FDV sector, organisations and sections within agencies. The report advised that in light of these wide variations in terminology and categories used there was a call for a term which could capture the need to respect Indigenous calls for a focus on the broader experience of violence within extended Indigenous families (Gordon et al. 2002: 29). 'For many Indigenous people the term family violence is preferred as it encompasses all forms of violence in intimate, family and other relationships of mutual obligation and support' (Gordon et al. 2002: 26). The report also argued for a singular, shared definition for the purpose of ensuring 'collaborative and coordinated responses' (Gordon et al. 2002: 27).

Case study two: Western Australian Family and Domestic Violence Policy

The FDV Policy was intended to provide a framework for the guidance of department staff and the development of responses to individuals, families and communities affected by family and domestic violence. From the framework would follow documentation for policy implementation, including departmental operational guidelines and training manuals. The department involved carries responsibility for policy coordination across human services agencies. Unlike the Gordon Inquiry analysed above, the FDV Policy is not meant to provide a vehicle for the department to influence the broader FDV field (including inter-governmental, inter-departmental and the community services sector). Rather, it establishes the principles for how a department internally works with family and domestic violence. To establish what was needed for this task, the policy group drew on documents that had been available in the field for some years to outline principles for 'best practice' in service delivery across government and non-government organisations.

The policy development process was conducted according to a schedule of regular policy reviews across government departments. The review and development process updates and amends policies to reflect best practice developments, provide for changes such as organisational and structural requirements, meet new service needs and take account of expectations for policy responsivity and accountability. The FDV was initially developed in 1996. A relatively limited review was undertaken in 2000, so a substantial revision of the Policy was involved in 2005-06. The goal was to meet the requirements of recent legislative reform and to be forward thinking with holistic policy that was informed by the latest statistical data and research. Injecting more evidence and information into policy and practice has become more important in response to an increasingly 'audit culture' (Power 1999), where measurement and accountability identifies particular outcomes.

The political environment within which policy development took place was of primary importance to the review. The department's strategic plan reflected the breadth of focus and challenge of new directions experienced by the department from government planning, new legislation, implementation of new policies and a new Indigenous 'vision'. The department's structure reflected the wide range of functions and a number of policy units informed and supported the work of core regional and local fieldwork.

In tune with a government sensitive to media coverage of child abuse, most intense visibility was directed at children's welfare. Accountability for the agency against a primary objective of child protection was producing considerable pressure on department staff across functional areas. The department's service delivery based on community development approaches was being challenged by calls for a 'law and order' response that required increased crisis intervention with casework. The 'best practice' model for programs for victims of domestic violence had been criticised for its 'colour blindness', and policy development that considered Aboriginal perspectives was called for by the FDV field (HREOC 2002). And many departments were facing the challenge of allocating FDV funds to meet increasing demands for perpetrator education and violence prevention programs on the one hand and the needs of ongoing and new refuge and victim services for women on the other. The intensity of political sensitivity and media scrutiny created a degree of vulnerability and anxiety that affected the policy development. Subsequent to the case study period, the department experienced considerable instability with repeated restructuring and staff changes at the senior levels.

Some years earlier, observers viewed the forerunner of this department as dealing with 'women's issues' as a major part of its agenda. In the current climate, government departments had adopted a strategic approach and terminology of 'gender neutrality'. Consequently, the gender focus of policies across the department has in most cases been implicit rather than explicit. Policy actors expressed awareness of the need to be strategic in promoting particular concepts and approaches to specific audiences and participants in the policy process. A number of gender-based insights drive the department's operations, and it was explained that the high-level policies need to be deliberately broad in order to allow for gender as well as other kinds of diversity to be taken into account at the point of implementation.

Within this context, FDV Policy was presented as 'even-handed' to achieve a 'political balance' in policy statements. The approach was designed for public reassurance using policy language that was carefully pitched to sustain a gender-neutral tone. Policymakers explained during interviews that 'more ambiguous or neutral terms ... would enable current trends and findings to shape the services'. References are made in policy documents to 'individuals', 'families', 'communities' and 'young people'. The department's charter was presented in a way that was deemed acceptable to the broader community, that is, as inclusive (of men) rather than being concerned exclusively or predominantly with women's issues and needs.

A focus on domestic violence which had come to signify violence against women was shifted over time to a broader focus *onto family* and domestic violence. The policy document states that FDV 'impacts on all sections of the community, cutting across race, gender, age and social status'. The shift was explained as the department's responsiveness to feedback from Aboriginal women (Hovane 2006; Nancarrow 2006) and advice from government Aboriginal policy experts.

Despite this apparent concern for culturally sensitive policy, the Gordon Inquiry did not feature in the FDV Policy review. Nor was the inquiry and its recommendations raised as a policy driver by the policy actors in discussions, interviews or documentation. The fact that such a major inquiry, which was being implemented during the period of the audit, did not feature prominently during the review could be seen as indicative of functional separation. Here was a major inquiry into FDV in Aboriginal communities, but it did not immediately provide a backdrop for policy actors reviewing existing policy statements. Rather, political and agency imperatives shaped the framework for policy review. Yet the lack of integration within and across agencies, policy and services was a central conclusion reached by the Gordon Inquiry, and one that its implementation was meant to challenge. We might conclude that the policy process seen within the department during the FDV Policy audit could be considered an example of that compartmentalisation.

Given the gender-neutrality of high-level policy, these policy actors saw their task was to effectively translate abstract policy statements into the tacit understandings of gender and diversity dynamics so that implementation is sufficiently equipped for FDV service delivery. What may be understood implicitly by experienced senior policy drafters needs to be effectively communicated to operational staff.

However, the fact that the department identifies itself first and foremost as a child protection system, has particular implications for that capacity to translate gender-neutrality into effective FDV implementation. To the extent that gender relations are considered, paramount attention is to the care and safety of the children in situations of FDV. Here the primary focus on women and men is not as battered and batterers in domestic violence situations, but as ungendered and potentially dangerous parents and ineffective carers as part of risk aversion priorities in child protection work. Thus the capacity of frontline staff to meet service expectations and deliver policy goals may be weakened by policy concepts and language that render gendered power relations invisible and cultural sensitivity an empty promise.

Discussion

Our study shows that the field of FDV is politically sensitive. In such an environment the high profile and sharp criticism accorded government intervention means policy actors adopt ways and means to do their work that will bring them as little public attention as possible. The case studies show how power dimensions in gendered relationships as well as those in institutional racism, can be rendered invisible through the daily reality of work in public policy development. In trying to highlight how white racism produced the bedrock of FDV in Aboriginal communities, the Gordon Inquiry submerges the gendered power relations underpinning contemporary violence against women and children. In trying to meet the need for an overriding child protection agenda, the FDV Policy makes gender and gendered power relations at best implicit and at worst irrelevant and outdated. That policy also shows that when the emphasis is not on institutionalised racism, then the discussion of racism as an aspect of policy also goes missing.

In the Gordon Inquiry the unintended consequence of defining the violence against women in 'inclusive' ways represented a lost opportunity to investigate gendered power relations involved in processes and interactions (for example, between women and men at interpersonal points of connection) within the wider community and in relation to state interventions. The inquiry did not look at the dynamics, complexities and impacts of gendered power relations on community leadership as affected by FDV, or at how those relations might affect patterns of family responsibilities and obligations for caring, law and education practices and a host of cultural traditions and ceremonies.

By not focusing on gendered power relations involved in the violence between women and men, the Gordon Report effectively represented all the different forms of violence being experienced in Aboriginal communities as indistinguishable. The inference was that all forms of violence operated on the same plane in terms of occurrence, severity and consequences. Some Aboriginal women warned the inquiry that opting for a single definition of 'family violence' risked losing sight of the damage being done to women. By failing to show how 'family violence' could incorporate an understanding of the ways in which racism intersects with gender, the Gordon Report deflected attention from the power differentials based on gendered notions of masculinity and femininity, roles and responsibilities.

Blagg (2007) argued that reaching agreement on a single definition is inappropriate and homogenising of Aboriginal peoples:

> Let us dispense with the notion that there is, or can be, a unitary definition of family violence and explore the construct in its diversity. There is no settled, one-fits-all definition and the meanings associated with the term shift from region to region in the light of local history, circumstances and concerns. They can also shift over time as new issues emerge. (Blagg 2007: 10)

Taking account of gender, Pease and Camilleri (2001) argued that a 'one size fits all' definition that captures a range of forms and relationships within families and communities hides the reality that overwhelmingly women are the victims of male violence. Domestic violence is the most common form of violence perpetrated against women (United Nations Population Fund 2005: 66). Statistical evidence confirms what Bolger (1991) and other writers have revealed for years that the most common form of violence taking place in Aboriginal communities is violence against women who are most at risk from their husband/spouse/partner.

The department which instituted the revised FDV Policy also missed an opportunity to get to the heart of the problem. This department is well placed with its leadership role within the larger policy framework of whole-of-government responses to FDV to influence wider public policy. By opting for a gender-neutral approach, the department's high level FDV Policy falls silent on the issue of women's greater vulnerability. Rhonda Sharp and Ray Broomhill (1988) argued that most claims to be gender-neutral are indeed gender-blind. A gender-neutral policy approach that assumes that women and men are affected by policies in the same way is inadequate for FDV where the consequences of not explicitly analysing gender relations can be a life and death matter. The stance taken could inadvertently weaken or undermine the capacity of the department to deliver gender sensitive field services. Connell (2006: 449) has noted that the principal goal of a gender-neutral public sector workplace limits the state's steering capacity in regard to societal gender relations.

Although experienced feminist policymakers may fully intend to rectify this façade of gender neutrality by ensuring that the operational guidelines are sufficiently gender specific, that solution must be unreliable in terms of dealing with a vast majority of cases, inevitably short-term in an ageing labour market, and destined to dissolve without structural backup and leadership direction. Moreover, if the department presents its policies as gender neutral, it could be assumed that the department operates internally as gender blind.

The potential dangers of poorly informed public policy and broad definitions that disguise vulnerability predictably fall upon Aboriginal women and their children. Interventions that can be equally directed to elder abuse will fail to address the gendered nature of FDV, described by David Indermaur (2006) as 'domestic terrorism'. Donaghy (2003) criticised the lack of informed decision-making when gender-disaggregated statistics are available but largely under-utilised in policy development, and the United Nations reported that data collection on this topic remains largely ad hoc and has not been incorporated into the regular statistical work programs of national statistical offices (Grown 2007: 205). Kurz (1993) criticised definitions of violence that fail to show how the context of domestic violence is the inequality and power differences between women and men.

Intersectionality (Crenshaw 1991) would offer a more inclusive approach to policy development by enabling the multiplicity of connections to be addressed simultaneously. The moral and political imperatives prompting and guiding intersectionality theory also lead us to conclude that the two policy developments we describe here are quite different in terms of their capacity to put institutionalised racism under the spotlight in domestic violence discussions. The Gordon Inquiry confronts head-on the contemporary race relations that render past and present racism invisible in domestic violence policy, and it draws on those with expertise in critical race theory and practice in order to do so. There is no sign of such theory, practice or indeed intervention by Indigenous women into past policy inadequacies evident in the Western Australian Government's FDV Policy Framework. Indeed, since the interviews with policy actors in this study indicated, they experienced a degree of anxiety about the concepts of gender and racism (and their relevance in terms of agency and government priorities). It would seem that much more needs to be done to bring the processes and insights of the Gordon Inquiry into everyday policy development.

The present study intimates that policy domains that are traditionally reactive, subject to backlash from political and community directions, and imbued with unrecognised institutional racism will provide at best limited support for the gender and racialised dimensions of FDV to be adequately seen and challenged. The promise initiated with the Gordon Inquiry shows that this fear and neglect does not have to remain the case. There is already evidence in the Western Australian context that, in other policy fields, interventionist efforts by Indigenous women have produced a collaborative approach to challenging and reshaping the particular context of culture and community in which they need to operate. It is through such collaborations, designed to make the best of local experience and knowledge, that Aboriginal women can begin to realise their political, economic and community goals (Eveline, Bacchi and Binns 2009). For future research in domestic violence policy what these case studies suggest is that more attention be paid to how mainstream policy actors can support the lead taken by discrete and experienced Indigenous women's groups in their endeavours to combat domestic violence.

Acknowledgements

The authors wish to acknowledge the Australian Research Council (ARC) for providing the funds for this study, and the government departments and policy actors who collaborated in this research. We thank also the anonymous reviewers who engaged with this paper and gave helpful suggestions for revision.

References

(Websites valid as of publication date)

Aboriginal & Torres Strait Islander Social Justice Commissioner. Human Rights and Equal Opportunities Commission (HREOC). 2007. *2007 social justice report*. Canberra ACT: HREOC.

Auditor General for Western Australia. 2005. *Progress with implementing the response to the Gordon Inquiry*, Report 11, November 2005. Perth, Western Australia: Government of Western Australia.

Australian Law Reform Commission (ALRC). 1994. *Equality before the law: Justice for women*, vol. 69, part 1. Canberra, ACT: ALRC.

Bacchi, C. L. 2005. 'Policy', in Essed, P., Goldberg, D. T. and Kobayashi, A. (eds) *A companion to gender studies*. Malden, MA: Blackwell Publishing.

Bacchi, C., Eveline, J., Binns, J., Mackenzie, C. and Harwood, S. 2005. 'Gender analysis and social change: Testing the water', *Policy and Politics* 24 (4): 45-67.

Baldry, E., Green, S. and Thorpe, K. 2006. 'Urban Australian Aboriginal peoples' experience of human services', *International Social Work* 49 (3): 364-375.

Blagg, H. 2007. 'Zero tolerance or community justice? The role of the Aboriginal domain in reducing family violence'. Paper: Queensland Centre for Domestic and Family Violence Research Conference: *Breaking the chains – reclaiming our future*, 2-3 May, Mackay, Queensland.

Blagg, H. 2008. *Crime, Aboriginality and the decolonisation of justice*. Sydney, NSW: Hawkins.

Bolger, A. 1991. *Aboriginal women and violence: A report for the Criminology Research Council and the Northern Territory Commissioner of Police*. Darwin, Northern Territory: Australian National University North Australia Research Unit.

Collins, P. H. 1998. 'It's all in the family: Intersections of gender, race, and nation', *Hypatia* 13 (3): 62-82.

Connell, R. 2006. 'The experience of gender change in public sector organizations', *Gender, Work and Organization* 13 (5): 435-452.

Crenshaw, K. 1991. 'Mapping the margins: Intersectionality, identity politics, and violence against women of color', *Stanford Law Review* 43 (6): 1241-1299.

Cripps, K. 2004. 'Enough family fighting: Indigenous community responses to addressing family violence in Australia and the United States'. Unpublished doctoral thesis, Monash University, Victoria.

Cripps, K. 2007, 18 March. Indigenous violence. Interview with Karen Dorante on *Speaking out* program, ABC Radio Message Stick. <abc.net.au/speakingout/stories/s1874310.htm> accessed 5 November 2009.

Donaghy, T.B. 2003. 'Gender and public policy making in Australia: The Howard Government's big fat lie'. Paper: Australasian Political Studies Association Conference, 29 September - 1 October, University of Tasmania, Hobart.

Duff, C. 1994. 'Racism, sexism and white feminism', *Polemic* 5 (1): 56-40.

Duran, E., Duran, B., Woodis, W. and Woodis, P. 1998. 'A postcolonial perspective on domestic violence in Indian country', in Carrillo R. and Tello J. (eds) *Family violence and men of color: Healing the wounded male spirit*. New York: Springer.

Equal Opportunity Commission. 2004. *An inquiry into the existence of discriminatory practices in relation to the provision of public housing and related services to Aboriginal People in Western Australia*. Perth: Government of Western Australia.

Eveline, J. and Bacchi, C. 2005. 'What are we mainstreaming when we mainstream gender?' *International Feminist Journal of Politics* 7 (4): 496-512.

Eveline, J., Bacchi, C. and Binns, J. 2009. 'Gender mainstreaming versus diversity mainstreaming: Methodology as emancipatory politics', *Gender, Work and Organization* 16 (2): 198-216.

Ferrante, A., Morgan, F., Indermaur, D. and Harding, R. 1996. *Measuring the extent of domestic violence*. Perth, Western Australia: Hawkins Press.

Gallop, G. 2002. 'Government commits $75 million to combat child abuse and family violence in Aboriginal communities'. Media statement by the Premier, 3 December 2002, Government of Western Australia, Perth.

Gordon, S., Hallahan, K. and Henry, D. July 2002. *Putting the picture together: Inquiry into response by government agencies to complaints of family violence and child abuse in Aboriginal Communities*. Perth, Western Australia: Government of Western Australia.

Government of Western Australia. 2002, November. *Putting people first: The Western Australian State Government's action plan for addressing family violence and child abuse in Aboriginal communities*. Perth, Western Australia: Government of Western Australia.

Grown, C.A. 2007. Review essay: 'Gender equality: Striving for justice in an unequal world/progress of the world's women 2005: Women, work, and poverty/The world's women 2005: Progress in statistics', *Feminist Economics* 13 (2): 203-207.

HREOC (Human Rights and Equal Opportunity Commission) 2002. *Social justice report*. <hreoc. gov.au/social_justice/sj_report/sjreport02/chapter5.html> accessed 5 January 2010.

Hovane, V. 2006. 'White privilege and the fiction of colour blindness: Implications for best practice standards for Aboriginal victims of family violence', *Australian Domestic and Family Violence Clearinghouse* 27: 8-12.

Indermaur, D. 2006. 'Domestic terrorism'. Paper: Family and Domestic Violence Unit Breakfast event at the Perth Town Hall for White Ribbon Day, 25 November, Perth, Western Australia.

Jones, R. 2005. 'What is the status of Indigenous women and Indigenous feminism in Australia?', AWID (Association for Women's Rights in Development), 2 December 2008. <awid.org/ eng/Issues-and-Analysis/Library/What-is-the-status-of-indigenous-women-and-indigenous-feminism- in- Australia/(language)/eng-GB> accessed 5 November 2009.

Kovacs, K. 2002. 'Overview of the Gordon Report', *National Child Protection Clearinghouse Newsletter* 10 (2). Melbourne, Victoria: Australian Institute of Family Studies (AIFS).

Kurz, D. 1993. 'Social science perspectives on wife abuse: Current debates and future directions', in Bart, P.B. and Moran, E.G. (eds) *Violence against women: The bloody footprints*. Newbury Park, CA: Sage.

Nancarrow, H. 2006. 'In search of justice for domestic and family violence: Indigenous and non-Indigenous Australian women's perspectives', *Theoretical Criminology* 10 (1): 87-106.

Office for Women's Policy. 2005. *Indigenous Women's report card 2005: Supplement to the women's report card.* Perth, Western Australia: Department for Community Development.

Office for Women's Policy. 2006. *Indigenous women's report card: Summary 2006.* Perth, Western Australia: Department for Community Development.

O'Shane, P. 1976. 'Is there any relevance in the women's movement for Aboriginal women?' *Refractory Girl* 12: 31-34.

Partnerships Against Domestic Violence. 2001. Rekindling family relationships: A national forum on Indigenous family violence, 9-11 April 2001. Canberra: Commonwealth of Australia.

Pease, B. and Camilleri, P. (eds) 2001. *Working with men in the human services.* Crows Nest, NSW: Allen & Unwin.

Power, M. 1999. *The audit society: Rituals of verification.* Oxford/NewYork: Oxford University Press.

Sharp, R. and Broomhill, R. 1988. *Short-changed: Women and economic policies.* Sydney NSW: Allen & Unwin.

St. Jean, Y. and Feagin, J.R. 1998. *Double burden: Black women and everyday racism.* Armonk, NY/London: ME Sharpe.

Status of Women Canada. 2001. *Gender-based analysis (GBA) policy training: Participant handbook.* Ottawa: Government of Canada.

Stubbs, J. 2004. 'Restorative justice, domestic violence and family violence', *Australian Domestic and Family Violence Clearinghouse,* Issue paper 9. University of NSW, Sydney.

Templeman, D. 2006. 'No more violence – we're breaking the silence' program: Statement by Minister for Community Development. <parliament.wa.gov.au/web/newwebparl.nsf/iframewebpages/Hansard+Search> accessed 5 November 2009.

United Nations Population Fund (UNPF) 2005. *The state of the world's population.* New York: UNFPA.

Walby, S. 2005. 'Gender mainstreaming: Productive tensions in theory and practice', *Social Politics: International Studies in Gender, State and Society* 12 (3): 321-343.

World Health Organization (WHO). 2005. *WHO multi-country study on women's health and domestic violence against women: Initial results of prevalence, health outcomes and women's responses, summary report.* Geneva: WHO.

Yin, R. K. 1989. *Case study research: Design and methods.* Newbury Park, CA: Sage.

10

Gender mainstreaming versus diversity mainstreaming: Methodology as emancipatory politics

JOAN EVELINE, CAROL BACCHI AND JENNIFER BINNS

Introduction: Joan Eveline and Carol Bacchi

The gender analysis project gathered pace in its last few months. Developments that are noted briefly in earlier chapters, such as the topic of this chapter, the Indigenous Electoral Strategy (Chapter 3), and the inclusion of 'cultural analysis' in SAGA (South Australian Gender Analysis; Chapter 3) acquired their full significance as we began to reflect on the project as a whole and on what we had learned (on SAGA and 'cultural analysis', see Chapter 13). We also began to reflect critically on the relative 'success' of the project and more broadly on how change occurs, or fails to occur (Chapters 11 and 12). In tune with the perspective developed in this book, our contributions on these topics represent our current thinking about the complex interactions we have studied.

In analysing the Indigenous Electoral Strategy, the chapter discusses further the issue raised in Chapter 9, that any understanding of gender used in our policies incorporates a particular cultural base. Arguments for 'gender mainstreaming', for example, rest on the assumption that highlighting 'gender' as the primary category will have similar effects in differing cultures, a contentious claim, as we proceed to discuss.

The chapter examines a Western Australian project in which Aboriginal policymakers challenged this supposition of cultural neutrality. They argued that the understanding of gender used in western societies has privileged white women's interests over those of Aboriginal people. Consequently, they refused 'gender equity' as a term to use in their project of increasing Indigenous participation in local government.

Given this refusal of gender equity discourse, the project's results showed none of the negative outcomes that a gender mainstreaming perspective might predict, assuming that somehow if 'gender' were not mentioned, the place of women would not be addressed. Instead, there were considerable increases in Indigenous people's participation in the targeted local government elections, and in particular more first-term Aboriginal women elected to office than men.

The chapter analyses the methodology the Indigenous policymakers in Western Australia used to achieve their purpose, including how that methodology met gender equity goals without privileging the need for 'gender' awareness. Their approach was designed to ensure that the racist oppressions staining the lives of Aboriginal people are unable to overshadow their proposals for, and acts of, democratic participation. How the Indigenous Electoral Strategy developed on the ground at a specific time and place in Western Australian political life, where Indigenous policy workers could and did make a difference, highlights the kind of *time-and-place specificity* to developments in gender mainstreaming and gender analysis that this book sees as important. Chapter 13 revisits this topic with material from South Australia.

This particular case also made the authors confront the fact that feminist researchers are not immune from conceptualising a 'problem' in ways which reflect and sustain a dominant system of thought. This chapter marks a place in our gender analysis research and as the overall project proceeded, therefore, where the researchers themselves began to show increasing reflexivity about our own problem representations (Chapter 5).

Reflexivity is an essential tool in gender analysis research. The methodology of our project was based on the understanding that events can be understood adequately only if seen in relation to specific locales. We also wanted the inquiry to be fluid and flexible, rather than specifying in advance all that the research would involve. We aimed to learn from the data how, when and where to augment or change the research direction, emphasis, methods and design. Encountering the unexpected and the challenges that did not 'fit' the concepts neatly were the as-yet-unknown 'qualities' for which we were looking; these could prove to be touchstones for building a new theory.

Yet doing such 'open-ended' research does not save a researcher from needing to challenge her or his own taken-for-granted assumptions, or from needing to prise loose old rigidities that have protected a limited and privileged 'patch' of understandings. Clinging too fiercely to familiar ways of representing a 'problem' or to established, dominant investments in intervention can doom the study to providing merely a pallid copy of something that's been done already. For this very reason Bacchi's WPR methodology includes a directive for researchers to analyse reflexively their own proposals for deep-seated presuppositions and their possible deleterious effects (Chapters 5 and 6).

Reflexivity is the technique, the softening filter, that turns the harsh light of 'outside' scrutiny into a bonus for the committed researcher. It works through a dialogue with oneself, but is probably more immediate through dialogue with like-minded others who share common commitments and egalitarian political objectives. Parties to this dialogue may have goals that appear oppositional, as when the non-Aboriginal researchers on our gender analysis project sought to advance gender equity, while the Aboriginal policymakers sought to advance Indigenous democratic participation. However, as both this chapter and Chapter 13 show, the parties involved must nonetheless understand and care for both goals, which means they are able to include in any revised policy what is essential for that context and what cannot be compromised. The reflexivity that needs to accompany the constant learning involved in gender analysis is given further substance in Chapter 11, which recounts the insights gained when reflecting on the nature of research collaborations.

Abstract

This article examines the question of whether and how the intersectional oppression of sexism and racism can be challenged by government policy. It draws on a case study of an Indigenous policy strategy in Australia to argue that, in contrast to concerns expressed by feminist policymakers, gender equality is not inevitably neglected when the target for remedial action is institutional racism. Our study suggests that successful action on Indigenous emancipation necessarily mobilises a methodology for moving past one-dimensional category distinctions. Therefore, focusing on the task of translating declared policy goals into action can provide a way out of the impasse over whether 'diversity' or 'gender' is the better vehicle for mainstreaming equity policy. To develop its case, the article draws conclusions about the politics of methodology from gender mainstreaming debates, intersectionality theory and institutional ethnography, then uses our conclusions to analyse the political and methodological effectiveness of the Indigenous policy strategy.

Introduction

The policy approach called 'gender mainstreaming' (GM) has been the subject of much debate. A significant and unresolved question is the strategy's capacity to challenge intersectional oppressions, such as when sexist and racist practices intersect in Black women's lives (Crenshaw 1991). Arguments that GM should change its focus and terminology to 'diversity' (Hankivsky 2005; Squires 2005; Verloo 2005) form part of this debate. This article contributes to that discussion. It examines a case study in which Indigenous policymakers find they must exclude and revise westernised representations of racism and sexism if they are to achieve their emancipatory goals. The case study is part of an Australian project that maps the development of a GM initiative in the public sectors of two Australian states.

We argue that in order to challenge intersectional oppressions, GM needs to incorporate the process of translating declared goals into action. Our starting proposition is that the question, such as of 'race' versus gender versus class, is premised on a categorical view of advantage (and disadvantage) that 'denies the effortful "doing" of asymmetrical power relations' in the everyday world (Eveline and Bacchi 2005: 508; see also Bacchi 1996; Eveline 1994). Smith (1999: 42) highlights the category problem for policymakers by arguing that, 'in the everyday/everynight world, divisions between gender, "race" and class don't exist'. The problem is, however, that sexist, racist, ethnocentric and heterosexist practices divide the world into categories of haves and have-nots, creating the need for, but also obstacles to, effective equity policy outcomes (Crenshaw 1991).

The article develops through seven sections. The first starts with a brief description of GM and the complex and contested nature of international discussions over how it should be done. In the second section of the paper we outline debates over whether gender or diversity offers the better political category for mainstreaming equity policy, linking these debates to discussions over the analytical category of gender as well as to intersectionality theory. We discuss several suggestions for diversity policy and argue that they lack sufficient substance for translating declared policy goals into action. The third section of the paper turns to the practical but difficult task of moving policy goals past the obstacle of categorical distinctions. To this end we outline what in our view are the principles and benefits of the methodology of institutional ethnography (IE). The fourth and fifth sections detail the context, method and outcomes of our case study, a policy project designed to increase Indigenous people's engagement in the politics and management of local government councils. Since that project delivers both anti-racist and gender equity outcomes, the sixth section assesses whether IE or arguments for a diversity strategy can best explain how and why it does so. In the conclusion (seventh section) we coin the term 'textual (re)-mediation' to summarise how the Indigenous local government project challenged the usual forms of textual mediation through which racism and sexism are represented and incorporated in what Smith (1999) calls 'ruling relations'.

Gender mainstreaming (GM)

The policy approach called GM has been described as the most modern approach to equality policy compared with other notions (Daly 2005) and has grown in popularity since the early 1990s. With origins in the development field, this process for vetting policy for its gender impact has been introduced in key international organisations, including the World Bank, the UN and the ILO. Versions also appear in the national contexts of many western democracies, including Canada, New Zealand, Australia and much of Europe, where it is linked to the standardising of equality measures through the European Commission.

Broadly, GM seeks to guarantee that every part of an organisation or national policy machinery assumes responsibility for ensuring that policies impact evenly on women and men (Benschop and Verloo 2006). Gender analysis – the most common method offered for achieving GM – is a process for scrutinising policies to detect gender bias and ensure that they pay due heed to the differing experiences of women and men.

Feminist theorists and policy analysts remain divided as to the benefits of this purportedly system-wide approach to gender equity policy. For some writers GM has transformative potential (Rees 1998; Verloo 2005; Walby 2005). As Rees (1998: 41) notes, 'the transformation of institutions becomes the agenda, rather than the continuing attempt to improve women's access and performance within organisations and their hierarchies'. Other researchers (Bacchi and Eveline 2003; Daly 2005; Verloo 2001), while more or less agreeing that GM has potential to increase equitable outcomes, express concern that mainstreaming is unreliable in delivering on its promise.

As we illustrate below, most of these critiques point to flaws in the way GM is done, including the analytical categories it utilises and sustains. At the heart of these criticisms, we argue, are broad questions of methodological approach. We use the term 'methodology' here to signal the processes and techniques of translating declared policy goals into action, which we see as a requirement for an effective policy outcome. In short, our focus is on the relationship between better policy and the methodological approach used to achieve it. So we are not concerned solely with methods or techniques but with the broader questions of the philosophical underpinnings of the approach taken and the forms of knowledge and outcomes that those approaches and techniques produce. As we hope will become clear, our use of the term 'methodology' is not meant to claim a disinterested standpoint. Nor is it an appeal to objectivist science in which researchers can remain outside the politics and power relations of policy work.

A common criticism of GM is the lack of standardisation in goals, procedures and methods, underscored by the lack of an unambiguous definition of just what it is (Moser and Moser 2005: 585; Walby 2005: 455). Lack of standard procedures and conflicting understandings are due in part to increasing interest in the strategy, with versions proliferating in international programmes and across both national administrations and public sector organisations. The question of methodology, of how GM gets done, is central here.

Claims of inadequate economic, political and bureaucratic support underpin a key set of methodological concerns. Benschop and Verloo (2006), for example, argue that the transformative potential of GM is seriously hindered when economic and business interests conflict with feminist goals. A further problem, which again is not unique to gender equality projects, is cited as the highly contested nature of the strategy, since it both reflects and challenges neoliberal agendas (Bacchi and Eveline 2003). An ever-present barrier is the lack of commitment and time of the policymakers who are tasked with implementing the strategy. This can lead to what Daly (2005: 436) calls the 'à la carte' approach: adopting a particular tool kit or technique, often in the absence of an overall theoretical framework or the research and analysis needed for a full gender-based assessment. Eveline and Bacchi (2005) suggest that a minimalist or technocratic solution is frequently coupled with the view that GM can be done as a one-off project, rather than recognising that the process 'must necessarily be sustained for as long as policymaking endures' (Eveline and Bacchi 2005: 503).

Within these wider concerns about methodology there is increasing attention as to how the analytical category of gender is understood and utilised. The first of these critiques highlights a lack of attention to the process of gendering, while the second turns to the question of intersectionality theory and asks what role it should play in GM methodologies.

What should be mainstreamed: Gender or diversity?

Eveline and Bacchi (2005) use poststructuralist theory to highlight a tendency in GM to portray gender as fixed oppositional categories of 'men' and 'women', a theoretical stance that they see as denying the complex ways in which power and privilege circulate in specific social contexts. They suggest that policymakers and organisational strategists can counter this tendency to categoricalism by treating gender as a verb rather than as a noun, arguing for a focus on 'gendering as an incomplete and partial process in which bodies and politics are always becoming meaningful' (Eveline and Bacchi 2005: 502). The question, then, is how policymakers can work with such a concept, and it is here that a methodology focused on processes is needed.

The second concern about analytical categories is the claim that GM ignores feminist theories of intersectionality. The origins of intersectionality theory lie in the critiques of feminism by women of colour from the early 1980s. Theorists and researchers such as Davis (1981), hooks (1984) and Spelman (1988) argued that white feminism essentialises the category 'woman' around a gender binary based on white women's lives. Moreover, the ethnocentrism of white feminism compounds the problem that the issues for women of colour are absent in feminist theory and activism, while also denying them a voice (Collins 1998, 1999; Sandoval 1991). Crenshaw (1989, 1991) is credited with being the first of these critics to highlight the term 'intersectionality'. Located at the junctures of sexism and racism, she argues, women of colour are marginalised or excluded from both feminist and antiracist considerations and politics.

Crenshaw's methodology delineates three 'categories' (her term) for demonstrating the ways in which women of colour sustain 'intersectional injuries'. She names these as structural, political and representational intersectionality. Injuries wrought by structural intersectionality include a greater risk of rape and battery for women of colour. Her focus on the political includes intra-group identity politics, for example, the way in which the notion of Black solidarity obscures and reproduces gender hierarchies. And in the representational field she includes the double privileging of white man relative to Black woman (Crenshaw 1989), resulting in less access to social goods such as education, careers, employment, healthcare and political representation.

Like the women of colour in the USA, whose work she develops, Crenshaw (1991: 1245) adopts the language of subordination, oppression and exploitation to convey 'the multi-layered and routinised forms of domination' to which women of colour are subjected. In line with her focus on the complex yet unacknowledged details of intra-group exclusions and marginalisation, Crenshaw opts for qualitative methods to analyse case studies of feminist and anti-racist politics and strategies, using policy documents, news media material, research literature and available statistics.

In terms of insights and methods of analysis, intersectionality theory has much to offer GM. Unfortunately, some who use it to argue for diversity mainstreaming have a tendency to lose its critical insights about power and exclusion. This is largely because they pay insufficient attention to how diversity discourses can so easily become a management tool, for example, as has happened with managing diversity frameworks. Diversity management echoes the dominant discourse of the westernised business world: that managing diversity offers a way for businesses to reap positive dividends in labour supply and profits. Yet as research has shown, managing diversity practices prioritise business interests over employee equity (Bacchi 1999; Eveline and Todd 2002). Moreover, it rests on the insecure ground of voluntary business-case-driven initiatives with no recourse to regulatory devices (Dickens, 1999).

With regard to GM, Hankivsky (2005) provides an example of how intersectionality can be too closely aligned with diversity discourses. Hankivsky (2005: 996) uses intersectionality theory to highlight the 'impasse' that she sees in policy development around the Canadian experience of GM. Suggesting that 'the conceptualisation of gender that GM relies upon is clearly outdated' because it 'always prioritises gender as *the* axis of oppression', Hankivsky (p. 978) proposes a shift to diversity mainstreaming – a strategy which, in her view 'is able to consistently and systematically reflect a deeper understanding of intersectionalities'. Unfortunately, Hankivsky's argument for a category shift to 'diversity' lacks a critical analysis of the individualising and apolitical tendencies evident in previous experiments with the concept of diversity (Bacchi 1999; Eveline and Todd 2002). Consequently, Hankivsky offers no practical procedures that would enable diversity mainstreaming to overcome the politics of interpretation and manipulation that beset GM (Verloo 2001). In sum, her approach inhibits the transformative potential of GM since it fails to encourage policymakers to see and rectify the ways in which policy itself can produce inequalities (Verloo 2001, 2005; Bacchi and Eveline 2003).

Squires (2005), by contrast, shows that she is well aware of the need for caution in characterising 'diversity' as the answer. Her critique of diversity management and how its focus on business rewards might undermine GM policy is outlined fully. For Squires (2005: 378-80) it is not so much diversity mainstreaming that is needed but democratic 'diversity politics' based on displacing the essentialising category of 'gender'.

Squires attends directly to methodological questions – how mainstreaming should be done to result in better policy. Her focus is on how GM conceptualises its goals with regard to the policymakers who implement it. Policy effectiveness, argues Squires (2005: 380), will come from a process of 'inclusive deliberation' designed to enable 'excluded groups to unsettle institutionally accepted conceptions of equality' through deliberative democracy.

In our view, Squires' focus on deliberative democracy lacks viable application to the process of GM because she envisages her methodology for better policy occurring in separated spaces of policy machinery and community implementation. Yet, since GM has gained its foothold in policy development as a strategy for modernising bureaucratic procedures, the key task must centre on developing a methodology that can transcend the usual public sector silos of 'policy-making' and 'implementation'. In order to achieve such a goal, the citizens' forums and referenda suggested by Squires, which operate beyond the purview of policymakers and so for them have little relevance, are unlikely to prove sufficient for the task of translating affirmed goals into action.

The process of social elaboration (Booth 1988) that is needed for the complex and highly fraught task of making better policy must be able to map the institutional processes through which inequalities are produced and reproduced. Secondly, this mapping process needs, as Squires (2005: 379) notes, to be capable of showing policymakers how their own work is itself involved in the production of inequalities without alienating them from the project of GM. Thirdly, it must be able to avoid the 'rhetorical entrapment' (Verloo 2001: 10) that can come when attempts to seduce policy actors into using GM soften the critical edge of that strategy and lapse into endorsing a purely business case perspective.

To summarise our argument so far: making better equity policy entails the need to understand and challenge the ways in which inequality is regularly reproduced. An approach that we believe shows much promise for that task is Dorothy Smith's IE. In the sense that IE's key focus is on the ruling relations through which institutions reproduce inequalities, it satisfies the criterion of emancipatory politics needed for a transformative practice of GM, as outlined by Squires (2005) and others (Bacchi and Eveline 2003; Daly 2005; Verloo 2001). Since the methodology of IE shifts attention from individual responsibility to how those responsibilities are coordinated through institutional practices, remedies lie in reshaping those practices rather than trying to change policymakers' attitudes or values. The stated goal of GM is to rectify policy omissions and flaws while keeping policymakers committed to supporting future programmes (Verloo 2001). For such a task, IE theory and principles look promising.

Institutional ethnography (IE)

Smith's practice of IE highlights what she calls the 'work-text-work nexus' (Smith 2005a). In tune with many other feminist thinkers, Smith's notion of work is a generous one. Rather than being confined to paid employment, it includes all effortful endeavours. Work is:

> what people do that takes some time and effort, that they mean to do, that relies on definite resources, and is organized to coordinate in some way with the work of others similarly defined. (Smith 2002: 46)

It also means the interwoven acts of thinking, reading and interpreting that activate those work efforts. Texts, in Smith's framework, provide the key mechanisms for coordinating all forms of work. Thus institutional practices are textually mediated, as exemplified in parking or bus tickets as well as the 'boss texts' of organisational mission statements, laws and statutory regulations (Smith 2006). Indeed, our modern form of social organisation depends upon texts to locate us 'in the objectified modes of the ruling relations' (Smith 1999: 54).

Smith (1999: 49) defines ruling relations as 'that internally co-ordinated complex of administrative, managerial, professional, and discursive organisation that regulates, organises, governs, and otherwise controls our societies'. Textual mediation is essential to ruling relations, which 'couldn't operate without texts, whether written, printed, televised or computerised' (Smith 1999: 49). Texts are physical things capable of being reproduced. They operate to join, coordinate and regulate people's everyday/everynight endeavours (that is, work). Institutional texts, such as education and employment regulations, bus tickets and TV programs, are actively produced by people's particular work.

Institutional ethnography adopts a particular standpoint from which to explore ruling relations. Smith's view of a 'standpoint' is not the social positioning of the subject of knowledge as it is in Harding (1986), but a methodology that 'starts from the local actualities of lives ... to explicate the social relations organising everyday worlds across multiple local sites' (Smith 2005b: 205). Importantly, although the methodology starts from where the subject is located, it is not the subjective experiences of the people who do the work that interests the IE researcher. Rather, the focus is on how institutionalised ruling relations are maintained and coordinated via mediating texts connecting the work people do. For Smith, the textual mediation of western industrialised societies began in earnest with the rise of large, bureaucratised, faceless organisations and the burgeoning print industry in the late 19th and early 20th centuries, but is now organised just as much through cyberspace. Although texts provide the key means of ensuring current social organisation, Smith (2005b: 108) wants us to remember that it is 'a reader who activates the text'.

Although activated by human activity, Smith's mediating text (whether in written, televised or computerised form) is unresponsive to the locally situated individual. Take as examples: (a) an application form for a job; (b) a tool kit or training package for GM; (c) an online quantitative survey instrument; (d) a train timetable. Workers and users in different sites are regulated by the same text. While people are intimately acquainted with the actualities of their own everyday/ everynight doings, their specific standpoint does not allow them to see how 'the local settings of their work are organised into the relations that rule them' (Smith 2002: 21). From within their unique local settings people can rarely perceive the ways in which their particular work, when textually coordinated with the work of others, produces institutional forms, reports and practices that are indifferent to and objectify individuals, linked back through economic and political imperatives that may seem distant and extraneous. The task of IE, therefore, is to map these hidden links and work practices so that they become visible to locally situated individuals.

The key influences on Smith's work are ethnomethodology and Marxism, both of which she critiques and revisions through her development of feminist theory. Although much of her early writing on IE preceded the development of poststructuralist thought as we know it today, her views of knowledge, power and discourse share some ground with Foucault. Smith (2005b: 17) notes that an important element of her framework of ruling relations 'is that identified by Michel Foucault (1970) in his concept of discourse'. Foucault describes discourse as 'regulating how people's subjectivities are coordinated, what can be uttered, what must be excluded, what is simply not made present' (Smith, 2005b: 17-18). Smith's development of feminist theory wants us to take this understanding of discourse back into the body so that we reject the Cartesian split on which our modern organised societies are built. Situating discourse as embodied helps us to remember that, although Foucault's concept of discourse locates knowledge and knowledge-making as being independent of particular individuals, the 'phenomena of mind and discourse ... [can be] recognised as themselves the doings of actual people situated in particular local sites at particular times' (Smith, 2005b: 25). Therefore, her focus on the everyday work that goes into textual mediation aims to show how the work we do in and around texts is coordinated through the social relations that regulate our lives.

For the institutional ethnographer the goals of research are emancipatory. The ability to resist the generalising and objectifying mechanisms of textual mediation is grounded in fostering a critical awareness of how such mechanisms feature in shaping ruling relations (or regulatory power). In the words of Smith (2002: 40):

> the ways in which power is brought into view as a mobilization of people's coordinated activities also points to ways in which change can be inserted into organization from within.

We do not claim here to show how to do IE. Explicating how to undertake that complex and nuanced approach would take more space than is available. Instead, we deploy some key elements and principles of IE to help analyse how and why a group of Indigenous policymakers are able to make better policy by navigating the obstacle of categorical distinctions. We begin with some background to the GM project, including a section on the methods used and a brief history of relations between white and Indigenous populations in Australia.

Context and methodological approach

The literature suggests that the conditions for successful GM include political and bureaucratic will, resources (time and money), sex-specific statistics, techniques and consistent monitoring, and an emancipatory organisational agenda (Benschop and Verloo 2006: 23; Council of Europe 1998). In designing our GM study we added to this list the need for disaggregated statistics (such as age, social background and ethnicity), to help counter the category politics (Bacchi 1996) that suffuse gender and diversity policy. A crucial goal of our three-year Australian study, funded by the Australian Research Council, was to identify if and how a policy strategy designed to incorporate such factors can become part of a deep-seated change process for organisations, institutions and a diversity of individuals and groups.

Piloted in two Australian states, our project focused on a small number of policy areas. In the state from which our case study is drawn (Western Australia), 27 public sector departments have jurisdiction over 124 agencies. Therefore, the policy personnel involved in our project, which in WA comprises eight agencies overseen by five departments, represent only a tiny proportion of their peers. Nonetheless, these small numbers allowed for a close engagement with policymakers in participating agencies over the period of the project. The aim was to find out what works or fails for these specially selected policy groups, and on the basis of an iterative learning process to produce a GM framework that can subsequently be applied in further Australian policy contexts. The project developed through nine interrelated tasks, including audits of existing policies, plus the design, delivery, monitoring and assessment of training and consultation processes. A goal common to all nine tasks is to assess the capacity of GM to accommodate women's diverse needs and interests.

The methodology used is best described as participatory action research, and it has been used in other national contexts to undertake GM initiatives (Benschop and Verloo 2006). It uses statistical and qualitative data gathered about a variety of policy projects by participating agency teams, with methodological, developmental and analytical support from the university research teams in two states. The techniques and tools used, which involve serial trials and monitoring in each agency, are developed through this collaborative, spiral process. There are also regular inter-agency meetings where progress and concerns are further discussed and decisions made as to how to utilise, report on and disseminate the kinds of knowledge, skills and tool kits gained. The case we focus on in this article, titled the 'Indigenous election strategy' (IES), was a late addition to a trial project developed in the WA Department of Local Government and Regional Development (DLGRD). We chose to explicate this case because it raises important questions about whether and how policy can circumvent the problem of categorical distinctions. The section below provides further background details and a description of methods utilised.

The Indigenous Election Strategy (IES)

The 2005 local government election strategy was chosen by DLGRD's chief executive officer to pilot one of our GM projects. As one of only two female CEOs heading public sector departments in Western Australia (out of 27), this CEO was viewed as determined to create a culture of egalitarian practice within it.

Historically, local government elections rarely highlight the party politics that drive federal and state elections. They are of little interest to news media, which generally means they are of little interest to WA electors. Indeed, most potential voters have little understanding or exposure to the decisions made in local government and, under Australia's three-tier system of governance (federal, state and local), voters pay most heed to state government politics. Moreover, in contrast to the compulsory voting at the federal and state levels, local government voting is voluntary in WA. Consequently, few local government elections enjoy more than a 20 per cent voter turnout.

The 2005 local government election strategy, like its predecessor two years before, was primarily designed to encourage more eligible voters to enrol, vote and stand for local government. The strategy comprised a set of focused texts, including a planning document incorporating core principles and values, plus several supporting documents which provide information and training for, and advertising to, potential voters and councillors. The DLGRD's gender mainstreaming team of researchers and policymakers had the task of ensuring that the strategy (this series of documents, supporting meetings and training sessions) was made gender-sensitive in time for the 2005 local government elections. After those elections, the success of the strategy was evaluated using statistical and interview data. The results also underwent a GM analysis and were then used to inform a revised 2007 election strategy.

The IES was an addition to the 2005 election strategy and was developed quite late in the lead up to the 2005 elections. This was the first time that an election strategy focused specifically on Indigenous people had been developed in WA for any tier of government. Several imperatives operating at the three tiers of government, local, state and federal, fostered the conclusion that such a strategy was now needed to improve Indigenous representation in local government. The representation of Indigenous women was particularly poor. With regard to employment, for example, in 2005 Indigenous women comprised only 0.88 per cent of local government employees, and 1.94 per cent of all public sector employees, although they represented 2.75 per cent of the overall population (Office for Women's Policy 2005). Similar under-representation applied to Indigenous women as elected members of all tiers of government, and on governing boards and committees.

The state of Western Australia has a larger than average percentage of its population who register as Indigenous (4 per cent as compared to 2.1 per cent Australia-wide) yet its history of Indigenous governance is dismal. From white colonisation in the 1820s until the federal government took over most responsibility for Indigenous people in the 1960s, WA government regimes show a consistent history of harsh political repression, economic exploitation, health and welfare neglect, and cultural decimation of Aboriginal people. For example the 'stolen generation', when

Aboriginal children over a period of some 40 years were forcibly removed from their parents to be raised thousands of miles away in 'training' hostels, has contributed not only to fractured Indigenous family systems but also to high levels of substance abuse, health problems, and excessive levels of domestic violence and child abuse (Human Rights and Equal Opportunity Commission 1997; Read 1999). Life expectancy for Indigenous people is 20 years lower than for the non-Indigenous (Human Rights and Equal Opportunity Commission 2007). A particularly tragic case of child sexual abuse in 2001 prompted not only huge media coverage but also a WA government inquiry led by a well-known Indigenous legal figure. The outcome was a report (Gordon *et al.*, 2002) recommending a total shake-up of governance strategies and an injection of funds into state government departments to achieve the recommended goals.

These state-based tensions coincided with changes at the federal level of politics. A decision in 2004 by the conservative federal government to abolish the Aboriginal and Torres Strait Islander Commission (ATSIC) and 'mainstream' Aboriginal services was not viewed kindly by the state governments with the largest Indigenous populations (WA and Queensland). ATSIC was a self-governing body of Indigenous representatives that distributed federal funds to state-based and territory-based groups. Thus its removal put pressure on those states to take more responsibility for Indigenous welfare. Indigenous women were considerably under-represented at all levels in ATSIC. In the policy considerations following its disbandment, a recommendation at state level was to increase their political representation across the three tiers of government (Office for Women's Policy 2005: 14).

In this political climate government ministers and departmental CEOs saw benefits in WA government departments mainstreaming Indigenous issues, ideally with guidance and participation from Indigenous people. This was particularly the case for a department whose jurisdiction had formal oversight of the regional and remote areas where most Indigenous people live. Thus, a project designed to ensure that Indigenous capacity-building gained leverage became an additional component of the 2005 local government election strategy.

The three Indigenous communities officers who designed what became known as the IES were based in the community capacity-building agency of DLGRD. This meant they were not part of the GM team. The GM team was based in another division that had responsibility for designing, mounting and evaluating the overall 2005 election strategy. The Indigenous communities officers were therefore not included in any of the GM team training or discussions, nor were they expected to undertake a gender analysis of their strategy. For this reason the CEO of DLGRD offered the IES as a policy case on which the GM team could do a gender audit. In our research design one of the nine tasks outlined was to conduct audits on policies in which no specific emphasis had been given to gender, in order to provide points of comparison with those developed within our GM project.

What distinguished this audit from the seven others we conducted in WA was the large amount of documentary material that the Indigenous communities officers had compiled, reviewed and produced. This included the history of Road Board legislation (a precursor to current local government laws), showing the ordinances that had excluded and outlawed Indigenous people from white communities.

The Indigenous communities officers indicated they were well aware of the scrutiny that they and their project were under. Their methodology shows them attempting to steer a sensitive and bipartisan path between using the procedures and resources of governance and locating Indigenous capacity-building within the hands, needs and values of Indigenous communities. In compiling the recommendations for their strategy, the Indigenous communities officers demonstrated the historical antecedents that had determined and justified the exclusion of Indigenous people, not only from local government participation but also from most jobs and forms of non-welfare independence, from the everyday provisions and services that comprised those governing practices, and indeed in many cases from town sites and nearby farmlands, rivers and parklands. The Indigenous communities officers used the continuing ramifications of those earlier government practices in designing their information and marketing publication (described more fully below), as well as the methodology through which they translated those texts into successful policy outcomes.

Moreover, the female team leader of the Indigenous communities officers produced further documents in preparation for our policy audit itself. These included a memorandum providing an account of the historical context, with analysis and justification from an Indigenous viewpoint of the approach taken in developing the strategy.

In that memo (Elliott 2005), and in the interviews conducted by the GM team, the Indigenous communities officers highlighted four outcomes of their six-month strategy: (a) a significant rise in elected Indigenous councillors, almost half of whom were women; (b) the evaluators decided the information publication developed for Indigenous communities was more user-friendly than the original 'high English' version designed for general use; (c) the Indigenous publication has become a template for all subsequent 'marketing' documents in this department and (d) the department has resolved to mainstream Indigenous issues in all future policy developments.

The Elliott memorandum points out that the 2005 local government election strategy includes only four paragraphs on Indigenous electors. Awareness of institutional racism, therefore, had to be developed not only among government agents (policymakers, administrators, managers and politicians) but also in Indigenous communities themselves. Yet in marketing the strategy to Indigenous communities, portraying such institutional racism was not the goal. Instead, the aim was to present and achieve a vision of Indigenous democracy.

In developing that vision, the Indigenous communities officers saw as a primary task the redesign of the original 'high English' document that was part of the overall 2005 election strategy, and was being used by local government authorities to provide information and generate community interest. In order to achieve their dual purpose (of challenging both the structural dominance of white men and women and the representational stereotyping of Indigenous and non-Indigenous leadership), the Indigenous communities officers needed to provide a portrait of how democratic Indigenous community is 'done'. At the same time, they wanted to move away from a wordy document using distancing language to a text based on pictorial imagery. To develop such imagery the team of officers engaged an Indigenous artist and provided him with the following brief:

- In the cover picture, no one person should have more status than another – therefore no one is positioned in the centre of the picture.

- The depiction of a gathering on the cover must visually underline this neutrality and the absence of any one dominating person.

- There must be equal numbers of men and women in the picture and women must not be positioned alone with children.

- Aboriginality should be visible.

- There should be some visual uncertainty about the 'race' of some people.

- The environment must be shown to be family friendly (University of Western Australia and DLGRD, 2006: 4-5).

The resulting image highlights the Aboriginal flag colours of red, gold and black. It shows a group of people, of all ages and skin colours, and both sexes, in an outdoor meeting circle held under shady gum trees. Men and women are depicted as equally sharing in participation in the meeting and family care roles. The image featured on the front cover of the subsequent information booklet and posters. Similar but smaller pictures are used throughout the strategy documents. When it came to turning the strategy recommendations into action by taking the information out to Indigenous communities, the Indigenous communities officers insisted that there be one female and one male Indigenous officer at all meetings, that no meetings would be held unless women were present, and that both male and female translators would be used in overcoming language barriers.

The question of the role played by GM in the process and outcomes was addressed directly by the development officers in the same memorandum (Elliott 2005), and revisited in audit interviews. The memo reported that, in preparing the IES, a key goal was to avoid restricting Indigenous women within the westernised 'sociological confines of gender' and instead to 'position and perceive them as a vehicle of influence in the local Aboriginal community'. Rather than 'referring to gender in this policy and publication', the goal was to highlight 'the leadership roles available to the Indigenous Community'. In addition: 'policy was shaped by an awareness of Indigenous subjugation, not gender, because gender as it is assigned remains a western construction' (Elliott 2005: 3).

With the position they take on gender, the Indigenous communities officers seek to unsettle westernised portrayals of gender inequality. In most established GM framing strategies, for example, gender is represented as a relation of inequality and the declared concern is that such inequality is unrecognised or ignored. Gender is emphasised in words in order to show that the GM goal is to rectify inequality between women and men. In the texts produced for the IES the word 'gender' is almost absent. Yet in the visual dimensions of those texts gender issues are central. And, rather than depicting gender equality as being absent, this vision of Indigenous participation portrays egalitarian relations between women, men and children as a taken-for-granted aspect of a democratic community. Also in this portrayal is the common Indigenous practice of holding meetings under gum trees rather than in a westernised building. In effect, the IES illustrates an emancipatory strategy – to declare (when writing about its process) a serious questioning of the westernised concept of gender, while making gender and Indigenous issues equally paramount in the visual dimensions of the texts it produced for turning the strategy into action.

Discussion

As this article has argued, an important question for those wanting to implement GM is whether current and proposed GM methodologies can produce better policy by avoiding the impediment of categorical distinctions. Although we make no claim to have covered the spectrum of methodologies suggested in GM, we reviewed (in the section of the paper entitled: What should be mainstreamed?) two recent theorists who argue for a diversity framework as the way forward. Below we compare these approaches with IE to ask how helpful they may prove in understanding why the IES achieved a better policy outcome.

The methodologies suggested by Hankivsky (2005) and Squires (2005) fail to provide viable techniques for translating declared policy goals into effective actions. With regard to Hankivsky's call for a shift of name to diversity mainstreaming it is questionable whether Indigenous people would have responded to the call for participation in local government had they simply received a mailed document entitled 'Diversity Election Strategy'. In relation to Squires' claims about deliberative democracy, her tools for making that happen as a form of GM are wide of the mark because they leave in place the unhelpful division between policy development and implementation.

The success of the IES did not come from citizens' forums or referenda (as in Squires' 2005 methodology). Rather, the strategy involved bridging and framing techniques (Verloo 2001) activated by the policy officers to connect the public sector and Indigenous communities in the process of taking effective action to achieve their carefully researched and argued policy goals. As a change-agency strategy, this methodology makes the most of political expedience, emancipatory politics and the insightful capacity-building that can grow from intimate knowledge and experience of a particular culture. As a strategy for better policy, it forges a carefully maintained bridge between policymaking regimes and the community engagement practices of local government, and it recognises that the process of interconnecting policy and community achieves more than the sum of their parts.

Institutional ethnography, with its focus on identifying the work-text-work nexus that mediates and sustains 'ruling relations', can help explain how and why the IES methodology works. Smith (1999: 49) writes that IE begins 'from where the subject is actually located'. From this standpoint, rather than positioning gender, 'race' and class as the ground of separate oppressions, the methodology aims to show that, for example, 'to be black, a woman and working class are not three different and distinctive experiences' (Smith 1999: 42, citing Bannerji).

In conducting the IES the Indigenous policy officers use a similar technique to Smith's version of standpoint. They started from the local actualities of Indigenous lives and set out to explicate how those lives are coordinated or, to use the words of the Indigenous communities officers, 'subjugated' through the everyday work of Roads Board and local government officers as well as through decisions made by policy officers in state government departments. They find in texts and policy practices evidence of racist language and laws, and ethnocentric policy techniques that objectify, belittle or erase the circumstances and experiences of Indigenous people. Through those investigations they find what Smith would call textual mediation producing institutional racism. They find similar textual mediation at play in the documents they are meant to use as touchstones for their own strategy, such as the 'boss text' of the 2005 local government election strategy. The methodology used by these officers was to redesign existing policies and procedures (texts) to remedy those earlier objectifying and racist mechanisms. This, then, was a strategic intervention in the textual mediation of their policy work in order to produce better outcomes for Indigenous women and men.

The texts produced by the Indigenous communities officers do not use the terms 'sexism' and 'racism' (the word 'racism', they said, was too confrontational for their departmental milieu). Nonetheless, their methodology signals an awareness of dominant gendering and racialising processes, and a desire to counter them. It does so by insisting that equal numbers of men and women be shown in the cover picture of the IES documents and that both men and women were shown in democratic interaction with children. For the Indigenous policymakers, these pictorial design features were not proposed as a remedy for gender inequality as a single form of oppression. Rather, gender equality was integral to the emancipatory goals of Indigenous community.

Conclusion

We suggest that the methodology for turning strategy into action employed in the IES provides a creative solution to the category politics that prompts unresolved debate in GM circles. The emphasis on Indigenous participation did not stop the strategy from also being gender-sensitive. The evidence for this lies in the guidelines for the overall project, in the brief given to the Indigenous artist, in the gender-disaggregated data displayed in reports on the election outcomes of the strategy, and in the carefully choreographed use of equal numbers of women and men to take the strategy into Indigenous communities.

As intersectionality theory shows, the meanings attached to gender, 'race' and other analytical categories organise, coordinate and become part of embodied experience. As IE indicates, the usual ways of connecting work efforts uses objectifying texts to entrench the institutionalised norms, definitions and practices that produce inequality. Rather than a theory of multiple inequalities, our case study shows the need for a methodology that pays attention to the way in which gender, 'race' and other categories are not only conceptualised in the policy process, but also coordinated into existence within ruling relations of advantage and disadvantage (Eveline 1994: 2005). As Smith insists, it is the coordinated work efforts of everyday life, rather than static categories or social locations that must be the starting point for understanding the extra-local mechanisms that reproduce injustice and inequality.

The IES provides an important lesson for GM on two counts. Firstly, a methodology that simply informs or develops a policy to unsettle those extra-local mechanisms is not going to suffice when the agenda is emancipatory. The Indigenous policy officers who designed and implemented the IES mapped the textual mediation of Indigenous subjugation then utilised that map to develop a textual (re)mediation which could guide, encourage and then achieve Indigenous participation. A key facet of their textual (re)mediation was to set what they termed 'a non-western agenda' in the politics of representation and to use that framing to create a bridge between the governance strategies of policy development and the communities it sought to encourage. The strategy foregrounded a vision of Indigenous democracy rather than iterating again, for a people who know it only too well, a tragic history of oppression.

The test for any form of GM of policy is its methodology for overcoming the tendency to be assimilationist in its attempts to incorporate differences in culture, gender, ethnicity, identity and power. Perhaps the greatest challenge for both diversity mainstreaming and GM is not so much to choose which is better, but to ensure, through its methodology for better policy, that one of those strategies does not erase the other. Achieving that goal, we have argued, entails moving beyond a one size fits all methodology to one that can start with an ethnographic principle – 'from the local actualities of lives' (Smith 2005b: 205).

Note

The author bell hooks specifically requests that her name not be spelt with capitals.

Acknowledgement

The authors wish to acknowledge and thank research associate Susan Harwood, who helped to implement the participatory action research techniques in this GM project, and gathered and reviewed some of the data and literature.

References

(Websites valid as of publication date)

Bacchi, C. 1996. *The politics of affirmative action: 'Women', equality and category politics.* London: Sage.

Bacchi, C. 1999. *Women, policy and politics: The construction of policy problems.* London: Sage.

Bacchi, C. and Eveline, J. 2003. 'Mainstreaming and neoliberalism: A contested relationship', *Policy and Society: Journal of Public, Foreign and Global Policy* 22 (2): 98-118.

Benschop, Y. and Verloo, M. 2006. 'Sisyphus' sisters: Can gender mainstreaming escape the genderedness of organizations?' *Journal of Gender Studies* 15 (1): 19-33.

Booth, M. 1988. 'Elaboration and social science'. Unpublished PhD thesis. Perth, Western Australia: Murdoch University.

Collins, P.H. 1998. 'It's all in the family: Intersections of gender, race, and nation', *Hypatia* 13 (3): 62-82.

Collins, P.H. 1999. 'Moving beyond gender: Intersectionality and scientific knowledge', in Ferree, M.M., Lorber, J. and Hess. B.B. (eds) *Revisioning gender.* Thousand Oaks, CA: Sage.

Council of Europe. 1998. *Gender mainstreaming. Conceptual framework, methodology and presentation of good practices.* Strasbourg: Council of Europe.

Crenshaw, K. 1989. 'Demarginalizing the intersection of race and sex: A Black feminist critique of antidiscrimination doctrine, feminist theory and anti-racist politics', *University of Chicago Legal Forum* 139: 139-167.

Crenshaw, K. 1991. 'Mapping the margins: Intersectionality, identity politics, and violence', *Stanford Law Review* 43 (6): 1241-1299.

Daly, M. 2005. 'Gender mainstreaming in theory and practice', *Social Politics: International Studies in Gender, State and Society* 12 (3): 433-450.

Davis, A. 1981. *Women, race and class.* New York: Random House.

Dickens, L. 1999. 'Beyond the business case: A three-pronged approach to equality action', *Human Resource Management Journal* 9 (1): 9-20.

Elliott, V. 2005. 'Internal memorandum: Indigenous participation in local government elections'. Unpublished. Perth: Department of Local Government and Regional Development, Western Australia.

Eveline, J. 1994. 'The politics of advantage', *Australian Feminist Studies* 19: 129-154.

Eveline, J. 2005. 'Woman in the ivory tower: Gendering feminised and masculinised identities', *Journal of Organizational Change Management* 8 (6): 641-658.

Eveline, J. and Bacchi, C. 2005. 'What are we mainstreaming when we mainstream gender?', *International Feminist Journal of Politics* 7 (4): 496-512.

Eveline, J. and Todd, P. 2002. 'Teaching managing diversity', *International Journal of Inclusive Education* 6 (1): 33-46.

Gordon, S., Hallahan, K. and Henry, D. 2002. *Putting the picture together: Inquiry into response by government agencies to complaints of family violence and child abuse in Aboriginal communities.* Perth: Department of Premier and Cabinet, Western Australia.

Hankivsky, O. 2005. 'Gender vs diversity mainstreaming: A preliminary examination of the role and transformative potential of feminist theory', *Canadian Journal of Political Science* 38 (4): 977-1001.

Harding, S. 1986. *The science question in feminism.* Ithaca, NY: Cornell University Press.

hooks, b. 1984. *Feminist theory: From margin to center.* Cambridge, MA: South End Press.

Human Rights and Equal Opportunity Commission. 1997. *Bringing them home: Report of the National Inquiry into the Separation of Aboriginal and Torres Strait Islander Children from their Families.* Sydney: Commonwealth of Australia.

Human Rights and Equal Opportunity Commission. 2007. *Face the facts — Some questions and answers about refugees, migrants and Indigenous people.* <humanrights.gov.au/racial_discrimination/face_facts/index.html> accessed 5 November 2009.

Moser, C. and Moser, A. 2005. 'Gender mainstreaming since Beijing: A review of successes and limitations in international institutions', *Gender and Development* 13 (2): 11-22.

Office for Women's Policy. 2005. *Indigenous women's report card.* Perth, Western Australia: Office for Women's Policy, Department of Community Development.

Read, P. 1999. *A rape of the soul so profound: The return of the Stolen Generations*. St Leonards, New South Wales: Allen & Unwin.

Rees, T. 1998. *Mainstreaming equality in the European Union: Education, training and labour market policies*. London: Routledge.

Sandoval, C. 1991. 'U.S. Third World feminism: The theory and method of oppositional consciousness in the postmodern world', *Genders* 10: 1-24.

Smith, D.E. 1999. *Writing the social: Critique, theory, and investigations*. Toronto: University of Toronto Press.

Smith, D.E. 2002. 'Institutional ethnography', in May, T. (ed.) *Qualitative research in action*. Sage: London.

Smith, D.E. 2005a. 'Institutional ethnography'. Keynote address, Gender Work and Organization Conference, Keele University, June 24.

Smith, D.E. 2005b. *Institutional ethnography: A sociology for people*. New York, London, Oxford: AltaMira Press.

Smith, D.E. 2006. Institutional ethnography workshop, Department for Community Development, Perth, Western Australia, April 28.

Spelman, E. 1988. *Inessential woman: Problems of exclusion in feminist thought*. Boston, MA: Beacon.

Squires, J. 2005. 'Is mainstreaming transformative? Theorising mainstreaming in the context of diversity and deliberation', *Social Politics: International Studies in Gender, State and Society* 12 (3): 366-388.

University of Western Australia and Department of Local Government and Regional Development. 2006. 'Gender analysis of policy project, policy audit report: Indigenous election strategy'. Unpublished. Perth, Western Australia.

Verloo, M. 2001. 'Another velvet revolution? Gender mainstreaming and the politics of implementation', *IWM working paper no. 5/2001*. Vienna: IWM Publications.

Verloo, M. 2005. 'Displacement and empowerment: Reflections on the concept and practice of the Council of Europe approach to gender mainstreaming and gender equity', *Social Politics: International Studies in Gender, State and Society* 12 (3): 344-365.

Walby, S. 2005. 'Introduction: Comparative gender mainstreaming in a global era', *International Feminist Journal of Politics* 7 (4): 453-471.

11

University-public sector research collaboration: Mine the space, never mind the gap

CATHERINE MACKENZIE AND CAROL BACCHI

Introduction: Carol Bacchi and Joan Eveline

This chapter offers additional reflections on the 'learnings' that emerged from the Gender Analysis Project. With a particular focus on the South Australian experience, it outlines how the shared practice of collaborative discussion within the project's reference group (which consisted of the university research team; representatives of the industry partner, Office for Women; and representatives of the three participating agencies) encouraged reflexivity among participants. Reflexivity here refers to an ability and willingness to examine one's own presuppositions and to take on board novel perspectives. Becoming reflexive, we argue throughout, is a subjectivising effect of the practices in which we engage. Practices that focus on shared, interpersonal exchange and discussion promote the production of reflexive modes of being and thinking. That is, practices that foster a heuristic approach (learning by doing) in tough interactions with similarly committed but questioning colleagues, *can promote* reflexivity.

The Gender Analysis Project in South Australia brought together feminist researchers and policymakers, mainly women, who shared a commitment to redressing gender inequality, although not everyone would have agreed about what exactly this entailed. The concept of 'mining the space' in the title refers to the determination of group members to work through differing perspectives and to overcome blockages within an institutionally sanctioned space.

The chapter describes how the regular meetings of the reference group set up to oversee the project created the space and time required to examine and debate the contested meanings of gender and gender relations. As described in Chapter 3 (p.78) collaborative exchange of this form encourages the testing of ideas and some, albeit unpredictable, shifting of positions. At the same time specific bureaucratic conventions, such as confidentiality rules, ministerial discretion and the timing of elections, created the conditions in which it became necessary for the university researchers to allow the policy workers on the team to set the pace of change for the project. A shared political purpose required a willingness to ensure that the project fitted within the ambit of their mandate so that it did not undermine their always-vulnerable status.

On the one hand the space and time created by the collaboration allowed and encouraged reflexive speculation on both concepts and goals. On the other hand immersion in the exigencies of either a marketised research culture at the university or the time- and resource-poor public sector produced researchers and policymakers as strategic, 'rational' planners (Gill 2006). That is, bureaucratic conventions are not simply impediments to change; they themselves have subjectivising effects. This complex assemblage of factors shapes a terrain in which change is uneven, and never finally secure, occurring 'somewhere in the middle' of institutional constraints, 'effortful' interventions and subjectivising effects. This chapter pursues these issues within the broad context of the research-policy nexus of organised 'spaces' – the interface between 'outsider' researchers and 'insider' public servants – and within debates about the 'know-do' gap (Bacchi 2008)

The Gender Analysis Project's initial objective was to bridge the chasm that currently exists between policy development at the government level and implementation in specific organisational contexts. We hypothesised that to bridge this chasm required ways be found to generate a sense of 'ownership' in staff charged with implementation of the framework. Antecedent to 'ownership', we discovered, is the need to encourage reflexivity through creating the circumstances in which participants reflect upon the operations of gendering practices. This theme, and the attendant relationship between a *requirement* (obligation) to practise gender analysis and a *commitment* to gender equity, is the focus in the next chapter.

The research-policy nexus

Collaborations between university researchers and government policy workers, while not new, have received a great deal of attention in recent years. Most of this attention, in Australia and internationally, relates to the best ways to achieve research transfer into policy (Lavis et al. 2003; South Australian Health Department 2008; European Commission 2007). While some attention has been directed at the ways in which collaborative research is contextually mediated, referring to ways in which different and potentially competing agendas affect research aims and policy outcomes, very little attention has been directed at the space in which researcher-policy worker project decisions are made. When we refer to 'space', we mean the iterative space (and time) that is provided by the research project in which university researchers and policy workers share ideas, critique policy practices and generate understandings that potentially lead to policy change. In addition, within the context of an Australian Research Council Linkage Grant project, such as the one considered here, the collaborative space is authorised, and so the time and space is set aside for exactly this purpose.

This chapter takes as its starting point literature on the contextual environments of universities and governments, where both universities and governments are *required* increasingly to collaborate. We then reflect critically on the experience gained from involvement in the Gender Analysis Project. In particular, this chapter reflects on the dynamics and activities of the South Australian reference group, which was set up to provide a collaborative space for the university project team and members of participating South Australian Government agencies. It adds to the literature on the nature of university-public sector agency partnerships that are created with the purpose of guiding innovative policy development processes (Lomas 2000; Putland et al. 1997; Williams et al. 2005; Williams, Holden et al. 2008; Birnbaum 2000). We argue that in cases where researchers and government workers share common goals such as advancing the status of women, researchers' sensitivity to the internal politics affecting research partners is crucial. The emphasis is not so much on a knowledge gap or a 'know-do gap', referring to the low impact of university research on public policy, but rather on ways in which participants could 'mine' the collaborative space provided by the reference group to develop and test their understandings of key issues and to enable the shaping of outcomes through on-the-ground political moves.

International and Australian policy and research context

While the idea of using social research to influence public policy is not new, over the last decade a significant amount of literature has debated a so-called 'policy-research divide' or 'know-do gap'. Commonly, this 'gap' is addressed as a problem associated with either a lack of communication or collaboration between researchers and policy workers from the early stages of research, or with researchers not producing 'evidence' that is useful or useable for policy workers (Lomas 2007; Lavis et al. 2003; Nutley 2003; Lomas 2000; Thomas 1982; Parsons 2004; Williams, Holden et al. 2008; Bacchi 2008; Adams 2004). More recently, policy-research literature focuses on ways in which the personal and professional networks that people establish and maintain affect the likelihood of university research influencing policy (Lewis 2006). The argument here is that, if researchers know where decisions are made and are able to access those decision-making points, then this also may affect the degree to which research is incorporated into policy (Lewis 2005). Our specific interest is not the 'uptake' of research into policy, but the creation of an iterative space where new understandings emerge.

Over the past thirty years, the management and role of government in western Anglo-Saxon nations has changed dramatically (Chapter 2). While thirty years ago there existed a relatively distinct (although interconnected) line between the private 'free enterprise' sector and the public 'government' sector, in the 2000s the line is blurred. In the mid-1970s major changes were made to the public sector, when reformers declared an interest in improvements in efficiency and accountability in public administration (Considine and Lewis 2003). In the 1980s further changes were made when governments moved toward corporatisation, requiring government agencies to develop and follow specific corporate plans in line with an overall guiding state and/or national plan. In the 1990s, 'market bureaucracy' or a combination of market and 'corporate bureaucracy' emerged (Considine and Lewis 2003). More recently, Considine and Lewis (1999, 2003) have identified 'networking governance' as gaining prevalence in Australia. Networking governance is associated with a global blurring of the boundaries between private and public sectors, including fostering partnerships and collaborative projects between the government and university sectors.

Added to the complex mix of private and public networks, western bureaucracies are regularly restructured in an expressed drive for improved performance and efficiency. Individual public sector agencies are small dynamic cogs within the government machine and are subject to change beyond their control. Such agencies may be moved between major departments, renamed or dissolved, depending upon the political context in which they operate (van Eyk and Baum 2003; Hurley et al. 2004).

Over this same period of time Australian universities have also undergone extensive changes that in many ways parallel the restructuring of the role of government, reflecting a push toward marketisation. Consequently, the ways in which some parts of the academy go about the business of research have altered greatly. A feature of the new 'enterprise universities' is that they are increasingly encouraged to form research partnerships (with the public and private sectors) in order to receive funding for research (Marginson and Considine 2000; Bacchi 2008). While research partnerships can be fruitful, the extent to which they bring about change (through government policy-making) leading to reduced inequity among individuals and among social groups, and under what conditions, is contested (Thomas 1982; Lewis 2005; Bacchi 2008). The argument for collaborative research is that (at least in theory) it is helpful in ensuring that research is 'useful' or 'relevant' (Thomas 1982; Bacchi 2008). This emphasis on the need for 'relevance' in current university research is a development that warrants critical scrutiny (see Chapter 10 in Bacchi 2009). What constitutes 'useful' research should be seen as both context- and value-dependent.

In Chapter 8 we considered how meaningful collaboration with communities can provide a lever for innovative and community-sensitive policy developments. A specific example here is the successful integration of community collaboration into health and social services management, where a feature of the collaboration is shared decision-making (Baum 2002).

In the research and policy fields it is becoming common knowledge that the extent to which well-thought-out, robust collaborative research influences policy is dependent on many more factors than on the research results alone (Bacchi 2008). One extremely public example where political ideology has overridden research results is work on heroin trials in Australia (Bammer 1997; Ritter et al. 2007). In 1991 the ACT Legislative Assembly Select Committee on HIV, Illegal Drugs and Prostitution invited the National Centre for Epidemiology and Population Health to run a feasibility study into a trial of heroin on prescription. A multidisciplinary team, with input from key interest groups, including heroin users, police, people involved in the treatment or support of heroin users, the general public, opinion leaders and policymakers, developed a robust feasibility study which included investigation into a comprehensive range of related issues (for a full description, see Bammer 1997). Despite strong evidence supporting the feasibility of a full-scale heroin trial, the heroin trial did not go ahead. On the positive side, the study did lead to further collaborative activity between the researchers and practitioners and may yet lead to policy change (Brown et al. 2003; McDonald et al. 2005). Nevertheless, such experiences put trepidation into the hearts and minds of researchers seeking to create university-public sector research partnerships, particularly when the research relates to a politically contested subject – in our case, gender inequality.

The Gender Analysis Project

As described elsewhere (Chapter 3) the key goal of the Gender Analysis Project was to develop procedures for use in Australian government policy and program development processes. Gender analysis can be defined as: 'an innovative process that enables policy makers to analyse whether proposed and existing policies/programs/projects produce equally beneficial outcomes for diverse groups of women and men' (Government of South Australia 2008: 4). The main task of the project was to test two existing models of gender analysis from Canada and the Netherlands. The Canadian model of gender analysis is based on a 'policy cycle' approach, while the latter is based on an impact assessment methodology similar to that used in environmental impact assessment. Through an iterative process of adaptation and modification, it was proposed that gender analysis processes would be developed to suit the specific contexts of Western Australia and South Australia. From the outset the project was underpinned by a commitment to engage closely with state policy officers from the participating agencies to produce a form of gender analysis that they found meaningful so that the gender analysis processes produced by the project would generate greater understanding of gendering practices.

In addition to the goal of developing appropriate gender analysis processes for each of the two states, the project included several discrete tasks (see Chart at end of the Introduction to the book). As part of the project's responsiveness to each state's particular policy context, the project teams in the two states developed different methods by which project tasks would be achieved. This chapter reflects on the experience of the South Australian part of the project, including the implementation of the following tasks:

- A benchmarking process for which the participating agencies selected policies from the previous five years to test (i) the extent to which they were intended to be gender-inclusive; (ii) the extent to which they are perceived to have fulfilled that goal; and (iii) how gender analysis would have affected the development and implementation of these policies (Chapter 3). The methods applied to the benchmarking process included interviews with key people involved in the development and/or implementation of the policies or programs analysed, and document analyses of the policies or programs and associated background documents.

- Introduction of two international gender analysis frameworks (based on Canadian and Netherlands models) to participating agencies. Booklets based on each model were produced for agency use, and these booklets included some local examples and content from Aboriginal communities. The project team worked with participating agencies to assess the usefulness or limitations of these frameworks when applied to new policy developments or reviews of existing policies (Chapter 3).

- A smaller research project to explore how best to include community consultation within gender analysis processes. This qualitative study involved in-depth interviews with government agency staff who consult community groups and with community representatives who have been consulted by government agencies (Chapter 8).

- Global comparisons of gender analysis processes, including those used by 'developed' countries: the Netherlands, New Zealand, Canada, the Republic of Ireland and Northern Ireland, and those used by 'developing' countries: South Africa, Indonesia, Papua New Guinea and India, with an additional section on the Commonwealth Secretariat. This task was shared between the South Australian and Western Australian teams (Gordon et al. 2008).

To facilitate an iterative process, the South Australian project team established a reference group in May 2005, with the inaugural meeting in June of that year. The purposes of the reference group were to provide strategic advice to the project, to provide a link between the project team and the participating agencies, to ensure close engagement over the period of the project, and to facilitate the identification of policies or programs with which to test the two gender analysis models. The group comprised the university team, including the Chief Investigator (Bacchi) and Research Associates (including Mackenzie), representatives from the industry partner (Office for Women) and from participating agencies; the group met roughly two-monthly, with the final meeting being held in June 2008.

The reference group contributed a great deal to the South Australian part of the Gender Analysis Project. The group i) provided extensive feedback for drafts of SAGA (South Australian Gender Analysis), the South Australian version of a gender analysis guide; ii) sought and gained feedback from the networks of group members on drafts of SAGA; iii) produced the interview design and conducted recruitment of interviewees for the community consultation task; and iv) provided a space for general discussions about strategies to promote the project.

Critical reflection on a university-public sector research collaboration

From the outset, the research team had an agenda to establish an opportunity for critical reflection on the collaborative space provided by the reference group. An objective here was to provide guidance on how future university-public sector research collaborations may best proceed, particularly in cases where collaborations are established with the purpose of introducing across-government innovative policy development processes that may be contested both between and within agencies. To facilitate this analysis, all reference group meetings were digitally recorded and transcribed verbatim by professional transcribers. The first author (Mackenzie) read and coded the transcripts of the first ten meetings using NVivo 7 and identified several emergent themes. In consultation with the reference group, the themes were discussed in terms of the question: 'what are the most important "learnings" for future collaborative research projects?' The remainder of this chapter discusses the key themes identified: *conceptual engagement, uncertainty* and *internal scrutiny-external conformity*.

Conceptual engagement

In Chapter 4 we provide an overview of the contested nature of the concept of gender within feminist theory. Given this situation, it should come as no surprise that understandings of gender vary widely in the public sector. At times the term is used as a synonym for 'women'; at other times, as a shortcut for 'men and women'.

Agency representatives reported back on their experiences with either the Canadian or Netherlands gender analysis models (see Tasks 4 and 5 on the Chart provided in the book Introduction). The Canadian model, which is based on a 'differences' (between women and men) argument (Bacchi 1990; Chapters 3 and 5), fitted more easily the commonsense understanding of gender as an attribute of a person. The model was described as more in tune with 'counting' mechanisms (statistics) that are understood and deemed acceptable to government policy workers. By contrast, the Netherlands model, with its theoretical conceptions of gender relations, seemed, to some, to be too complex to apply, and to be fraught with dangers of alienation.

Nonetheless, as reported in Chapter 3, regardless of the framework used, through discussion and group work a conception of gender as a principle of social organisation, created and perpetuated in relations between people, emerged. The definition that was finally agreed by the group to be included in SAGA states that the concept of 'gender':

> is culture-specific and therefore varies according to history and country. It shifts the focus from the individual to the interactions between people and groups. It is not a simple property of an individual, but rather a principle of social organization. (Government of South Australia 2008: 20)

Important input from Aboriginal public sector employees provided elaboration to ensure that this definition acknowledged the specific situation of Aboriginal and Torres Strait Islander people. In SAGA the concept of gender is mediated by 'race and cultural analysis', explained in these terms:

> Race and cultural analysis broadens the 'gender based' framework to include and reflect the multidimensional experiences of Aboriginal and Torres Strait Islander women, and of women from culturally and linguistically diverse backgrounds. All discussions about equality, equity

or disadvantage must be inclusive of discussions about diversity and human rights. (Government of South Australia 2008: 6; Chapter 13)

The reference group also provided a space in which to discuss a variety of methods by which data on gender/gender relations may be collected. In an attempt to move away from the tendency simply to count 'women' and 'men', and to try to capture the relational aspects of gendered interactions, the group agreed upon a distinction between 'sex-disaggregated data' and 'gender-disaggregated data', with the following definitions appearing in SAGA:

> Sex-disaggregated data is data that has been broken down by sex, or where sex is one of the variables in a study. It is important to note that such data needs to recognise sub-groups of women and men. Such data can provide the starting place for analysis but needs to be accompanied by grounded empirical research (qualitative research).

> Gender-disaggregated data is data that considers culturally defined gender roles and responsibilities. Gender disaggregated data involves applying a gender lens to sex-disaggregated data, plus asking deeper gender-oriented and other equity questions, for example, about class and poverty. (Government of South Australia 2008: 20)

By using the language of 'data', the group negotiated ways in which to maintain politically acceptable methods, such as the collection of statistics, while simultaneously defending the need for forms of qualitative research that can more thoroughly explore gender relations.

The group constantly struggled with ways in which discussions about gender can be introduced to policy work and workers across government agencies. There was concern that definitions of concepts should be accessible to government workers, while retaining a determination to produce a document committed to reducing gender inequality and intersectional oppression (Crenshaw 1991; Chapters 9, 10 and 13). Discussions highlighted the importance of the project not being compartmentalised as 'women only' and that gender relations refer to women *and men*, and to the socially constructed power relations between and among them across all policy development (Chapter 12).

In the end, conceptual engagement contributed to the development of shared understandings of project goals. This outcome highlights the importance of creating space for debate and discussion of key concepts among policy workers as a step towards bridging the chasm between policy development and policy implementation. This point is central to the book: 'doing' gender analysis, which basically involves the kind of conceptual exchange discussed in this section, is crucial to recognising the need for gender analysis.

Using terms adopted in Chapter 12, *obligation* can produce *commitment* if adequate time and resources are provided to allow the task to be thought through and undertaken in a context of free exchange of views. While training is often described as a necessary component of gender analysis, 'training' suggests an expert-non-expert relationship that we find unhelpful. What appear to be more useful are 'experience modules' rather than 'training modules'. In addition, building on the argument that practices influence subjectivity (Chapter 10; see introduction above), the kind of conceptual exchange endorsed here might well produce policy workers and university researchers more sensitive to the complex and constitutive nature of public policy (see Gill 2006).

As mentioned elsewhere (Chapter 3), we are well aware that suggestions to create an iterative space for exchange of views face an uphill battle in the current climate, when members of the public sector face increasing time and resource constraints. This situation, however, does not delegitimise the urgent need for such developments.

Uncertainty

In western democracies, policy work is conducted in a context of three-to-four-year political terms. Timeframes in which policies may be developed outside political campaigning are short. Policy workers therefore are required to conduct their work in a context of organisational change, be it changing priorities or structures, directed by the government of the day (Chapters 8 and 12).

In the time period in which reference group meeting data were analysed for this chapter, there was a state government election in which the Rann Labor Government was re-elected, following which all of the participating agencies underwent at least some degree of high-level organised change, including new chief executives and new ministers, as well as agencies moving between departments.

It is understandable therefore that, despite high-level commitment at the outset of the project, reference group members did not always know exactly what they could commit to, or when they could commit. One of the main purposes of the reference group was to identify policies that could be developed or reviewed using one of the gender analysis models, enabling subsequent testing of the models (as explained above). Based on their understanding of the internal politics of their organisation, each agency member identified policies which would be used for the testing process; however, in most cases it became difficult to test thoroughly the gender analysis models because of the shifting policy context.

In addition, throughout 2006, all government agencies were required to fulfil their commitment to South Australia's Strategic Plan (SASP 2007). While this meant that reference group members' time became more restricted, SASP 2007 presented an opportunity for linking SAGA to a high-level document that would guide the work of government agencies for several years ahead.

The state of flux within agencies, including the state of flux about what is politically relevant at any given moment, poses challenges for those working in policy and therefore for those who wish to research policy process innovations. It is important that university researchers are aware of what may and what may not be achieved in the development of policy innovations. As mentioned above, it is essential that researchers understand that regular restructuring is a feature of western bureaucracies, and is therefore part of working life for most (if not all) government workers. Hence, projects need to be designed accordingly. Project designs need to be flexible enough to incorporate variable timeframes and commitments, and also changing research team membership, as government workers are seconded or promoted between positions and departments. So too, flexibility to take on opportunities as they arise, such as linking to SASP 2007, must also be built in to project design. There is no suggestion here that researchers ought to constrain or restrict research objectives to fit the world of 'real politics' but that greater awareness of contextual factors and organisational mechanisms of control can assist in realising those objectives.

Internal scrutiny-external conformity

An additional factor influencing the progress of research objectives is the extent to which public organisations are somewhat private. That is, all government workers conduct their work under a strict code of confidentiality that requires public sector workers to sign a contract stating they will not criticise the government. The political environment in which government agencies operate, including the gendered hierarchy in public sector organisations (Chapter 12), influences the degree to which particular policy processes and their content remain internal (private) or external (public) at particular times.

The main goal of the project was to bring about policy change to ensure that gendering practices are considered at all levels of policymaking and implementation. The most successful contributions to the project were achieved through work that was not considered as potentially causing disruption or difficulties for individual reference group members or their agencies. That is, tasks that were critical or involved scrutiny of government policies were kept 'internal'. For example, the benchmarking reports (see earlier) contained some critical comments on a number of policies and programs that were analysed for that task. In this case criticism was welcome, as long as the reports remained internal. It followed that reports were kept internal to the group, or were shared only with agency participants' immediate colleagues for discussion and feedback to the group. Critical reports were, therefore, not disseminated to participants' agencies more broadly, or to other agencies or policy areas.

Tasks that conformed to existing institutional structures and were uncritical of (current) government policies and processes could become public or 'external' without debate. Moreover, some 'internal' tasks could become 'external' if they were subject to specific institutional processes, for example, if they were signed off by the appropriate minister. One document that has made it to the public domain and includes gender analysis is the Women's Health Action Plan, which includes the key initiative:

> Key Initiative 2: Contribute to the research project being undertaken by the Office for Women to develop a gender impact assessment tool that can be used in the development and review of all major health policies and programs. (Government of South Australia 2006)

Wholly external tasks included the global comparisons task (Gordon et al. 2008). This task was viewed by the reference group as useful because it provided evidence of ways in which other countries conducted gender analysis. The task was viewed as unproblematic for the internal teams, despite being highly critical of some existing gender analysis processes, because the focus was external. This point about organisational 'distancing' strategies (Connell 2005) is developed further in Chapter 12.

Tasks that involved internal and external elements included 1) the small community consultation research project and 2) the provision of comments on the developing gender analysis guide that was to be used in South Australia. The report on the community consultation task included some criticism of past state government-commissioned community consultation processes; however, on the condition that participants could not be identified, it was endorsed by the group for external publication. A refereed paper has also been published on this task (Osborne et al. 2008; Chapter 8). Drafts of a gender analysis guide for use in South Australia (later to become SAGA) were disseminated for comment outside the reference group, although not strictly for 'public' viewing, as part of conforming to usual bureaucratic processes, whereby draft documents are kept within state government agencies – internal to government, although external to the group.

An example of a proposed task that was not followed through (it was raised by the reference group and not a formal predetermined project task) was the presentation of a seminar or forum to agencies external to the project on how to apply gender analysis; it was believed that that this would result in the process being applied more widely. The seminar was proposed in response to results from questionnaires received by the group with responsibility for the gender analysis models. Several of the responses suggested that it would be helpful if there were concrete, South Australian examples on how to 'do' gender analysis rather than merely being guided by a step-by-step model. The idea was to present case studies of the experiences of reference group members who had at least partially tested the gender analysis models on a policy or program development process. The notion of a seminar foundered since people were unable to talk about their uses of gender analysis prior to the public release of policies or programs to which the analysis had been applied.

Discussions about how to encourage wide promotion of the Gender Analysis Project, while at the same time conforming to institutionalised political processes, took place several times over the course of the project, but without resolution. Due to the challenges of timing mentioned earlier (for example, during a state government election campaign, or when new minister/s or chief executives had been appointed) and to the complexities of agency protocol, it became apparent that public sector workers in the reference group needed to take the lead on promoting the project when and wherever this became feasible.

Being clear about what must remain confidential and what may be made public is crucial when researchers form university-public sector research partnerships. From the outset, university and public sector workers need to negotiate public-private boundaries and revisit these throughout the course of the project. If being able to critique government policymaking processes publicly is important to researchers, they must build into their research projects clear distinctions between which aspects of their research are developed within partnerships and which aspects remain outside government. As Hurley et al. (2004) argue in relation to evaluation processes, there is a fine balance between 'insider knowledge' and 'outsider objectivity' because of the real danger of causing harm to research partners (for example, losing funding, being ostracised or being made a scapegoat).

Given the state of play in government bureaucracies and the tenuous position of women's policy units (see Chapter 8), there were times throughout the project when research results had the potential to cause problems at work for reference group members, or even for their entire agencies. The issue of 'internal scrutiny and external conformity' meant that public dissemination of findings presented a constant concern to agency members. This leads to the question: how can change occur without critique?

For this group, where it was possible to keep critique internal – as for the benchmarking process – it was theoretically possible to influence future policymaking processes without the need for external critique and potential disruption. Moreover, incremental theories of organisational change such as the benefits of 'small wins' (Weick 1984; Meyerson and Fletcher 2000) argue that the process of changing practices need not become a major disruptive event. The production of SAGA will be linked to South Australia's Strategic Plan, which means that the policy innovation will be successful as part of ongoing incremental change, without necessarily providing a strong external critique of government policymaking practices. We conclude that researchers who wish to form collaborative spaces with governments in order to produce innovative policy processes need to be able to negotiate between which aspects are acceptable for involving internal scrutiny and which can be more widely disseminated because they conform to existing bureaucratic processes.

Conclusion

The reference group was the key site for action for the Gender Analysis Project in South Australia, although actual action was different from that expected at the outset. The university team started out with particular expectations, including an expectation that at least several state government agencies would take on the testing of the two gender analysis models in the first year of the project, and in so doing would provide the project team with rich data exemplifying the ways in which agency staff had used the models. The research team expected to be able to examine the form of gender analysis that allowed participating agencies to make meaningful sense of the process. It was expected that, ultimately, a model of gender analysis would be produced that would be full of local examples showing how gender analysis could work most effectively.

While that is not how the model-testing progressed, a model has been produced, through a process of combining the parts of the two international models (Canadian and Netherlands) that agency representatives believed would best communicate the purposes of gender analysis. This model, as described above, has been developed using the collaborative space provided by the reference group. At the time of writing this article, the model was being piloted and it is expected that, after this process, there will be local examples included in the final 'SAGA'. The ability to 'mine the space' has been crucial to the development of SAGA, in particular:

- by ensuring that the key concept of gender is defined in such a way that it may be more easily communicated to the broad policy worker environment

- by developing a concept of gender mediated by 'race and cultural analysis', reflecting the situation of Aboriginal and Torres Strait Islander women and men

- by producing a document (SAGA) that facilitates keeping gender relations as a focus in government policy.

The experience in this project indicates that, particularly when research relates to a politically contested subject, 'mining the space' for collaboration produces significant learnings for participants and important changes in some associated policies. This kind of negotiated change takes place 'in the middle' of messy, partial and unpredictable exchanges (Chapter 3). Moreover, creating space for public servants and research partners to discuss and debate concepts and goals has the beneficial effect of producing reflexive political subjects (Chapters 10 and 13) and an institutional culture where it is deemed to be appropriate to reflect broadly on the nature and consequences of the policymaking enterprise.

Acknowledgements

The authors wish to thank Fiona Mort for reading and providing valuable comments on the manuscript. We thank the project's participating agencies for taking part in the reference group meetings which form the basis of this chapter.

References

Adams, D. 2004. 'Usable knowledge in public policy: Symposium on appropriate policy knowledge', *Australian Journal of Public Administration* 63 (1): 29-42.

Bacchi, C. 1990. *Same difference: Feminism and sexual difference*. Sydney: Allen and Unwin.

Bacchi, C. 2008. 'The politics of research management: Reflections on the gap between what we "know" [about SDH] and what we do', *Health Sociology Review* 17 (2): 165-176.

Bacchi, C. 2009. *Analysing policy: What's the problem represented to be?* French's Forest, NSW: Pearson Education.

Bammer, G. 1997. 'Multidisciplinary policy research: An Australian experience', *Prometheus (St Lucia, Qld)* 15 (1): 27-39.

Baum, F. 2002. *The new public health, 2nd edition*. Melbourne: Oxford University Press.

Birnbaum, R. 2000. 'Policy scholars are from Venus: Policy makers are from Mars', *The Review of Higher Education* 23 (2): 119-132.

Brown, D.L., Bammer, G., Batliwala, S. and Kunreuther, F. 2003. 'Framing practice-research engagement for democratizing knowledge', *Action Research* 1 (1): 81-102.

Connell, R. 2005. 'Advancing gender reform in large-scale organisations: A new approach for practitioners and researchers', *Policy and Society* 24 (4): 5-24.

Considine, M. and Lewis, J.M. 1999. 'Governance at ground level: The frontline bureaucrat in an age of markets and networks', *Public Administration Review* 59 (6): 467-480.

Considine, M. and Lewis, J.M. 2003. 'Bureaucracy, network, or enterprise? Comparing models of governance in Australia, Britain, the Netherlands, and New Zealand', *Public Administration Review* 63 (2): 131-140.

Crenshaw, K. 1991. 'Mapping the margins: Intersectionality, identity politics, and violence against women of color', *Stanford Law Review* 43 (6): 1241-1299.

European Commission. 2007. *Improving knowledge transfer between research institutions and industry across Europe*, Directorate-General for Research, EUR 22836EN. Luxembourg: European Communities.

Gill, Z. 2006. 'Discourse, subjectivity and the policy realm: Reconceptualising policy workers as located subjects'. PhD thesis, Politics Discipline, School of History and Politics, University of Adelaide.

Gordon, Z., Binns, J., Palmer, E., Bacchi, C. and Eveline, J. 2008. 'Gender analysis and social change. Task 1. Comprehensive comparisons'. Adelaide, unpublished manuscript.

Government of South Australia. 2006. *The South Australian Women's Health Action Plan: Initiatives for 2006/2007*. Adelaide: Department of Health.

Government of South Australia. 2008. 'South Australian gender analysis'. Adelaide: Office for Women. Unpublished draft.

Hurley, C., Baum, F. and van Eyk, H. 2004. '"Designing better health care in the South": A case study of unsuccessful transformational change in public sector health service reform', *Australian Journal of Public Administration* 63 (2): 31-41.

Lavis, J.N., Robertson, D., Woodside, J.M., McLeod, C.B. and Abelson, J. 2003. 'How can research organizations more effectively transfer research knowledge to decision makers?' *The Milbank Quarterly* 81 (2): 221-248.

Lewis, J. 2006. 'Being around and knowing the players: Networks of influence in health policy', *Social Science and Medicine* 62 (9): 2125-2136.

Lewis, J.M. 2005. *Health policy and politics: Networks, ideas and power*. East Hawthorn: IP Communications.

Lomas, J. 2000. 'Using "Linkage and exchange" to move research into policy at a Canadian foundation', *Health Affairs* 19 (3): 236-240.

Lomas, J. 2007. 'The in-between world of knowledge brokering', *BMJ* 334 (7585): 129-132.

Marginson, S. and Considine, M. 2000. *The enterprise university: Power, governance and reinvention in Australia*. Cambridge: Cambridge University Press.

McDonald, D., Bammer, G. and Breen, G. 2005. *Australian illicit drugs policy: Mapping structures and processes: Drug policy modelling project monograph 04*. Canberra: National Centre for Epidemiology and Population Health, Australian National University.

Meyerson, D and Fletcher, J. 2000. 'A modest manifesto for shattering the glass ceiling', *Harvard Business Review* January-February: 127-136.

Nutley, S. 2003. 'Bridging the policy-research divide: Reflections and lessons from the United Kingdom'. Edited version of a keynote address to the National Institute for Governance Conference, *Canberra Bulletin of Public Administration* 108: 19-28.

Osborne, K., Bacchi, C. and Mackenzie, C. 2008. 'Gender analysis and community consultation: The role of women's policy units', *Australian Journal of Public Administration* 67 (2): 149-160.

Parsons, W. 2004. 'Not just steering but weaving: Relevant knowledge and the craft of building policy capacity and coherence', *Australian Journal of Public Administration* 63 (1): 43-57.

Putland, C., Baum, F. and MacDougall, C. 1997. 'How can health bureaucracies consult effectively about their policies and practices? Some lessons from an Australian study', *Health Promotion International* 12 (4): 299-310.

Ritter, A., Bammer, G., Hamilton, M., Mazerolle, L. and Drug Policy Modelling Program Team. 2007. 'Effective drug policy: A new approach demonstrated in the Drug Policy Modelling Program', *Drug & Alcohol Review* 26 (3): 265-271.

South Australian Health Department 2008. *Research transfer discussion paper.* <health.sa.gov.au/Default.aspx?tabid=59> accessed 6 November 2009.

Thomas, P. 1982. 'Social research and government policy', *Futures* 2-10.

van Eyk, H. and Baum, F. 2003. 'Evaluating health system change – using focus groups and developing a discussion paper to compile the "Voices from the field"', *Qualitative Health Research* 13 (2): 281-286.

Weick, K. 1984. 'Small wins: Redefining the scale of social problems', *American Psychologist* 39: 40-49.

Williams, A., Labonte, R., Randall, J.E. and Muhajarine, N. 2005. 'Establishing and sustaining community-university partnerships: A case study of quality of life research', *Critical Public Health* 15 (3): 291-302.

Williams, A., Holden, B., Krebs, P., Muhajarine, N., Waygood, K., Randall, J. and Spence, C. 2008. 'Knowledge translation strategies in a community-university partnership: Examining local quality of life (QoL)', *Social Indicators Research* 85: 111-125.

12

Obeying organisational 'rules of relevance': Gender analysis of policy

JOAN EVELINE AND CAROL BACCHI

Introduction: Joan Eveline and Carol Bacchi

There is considerable research showing that organisations, including government agencies and the policies they produce, consider gender irrelevant to their core business. The gender mainstreaming of policy is designed to challenge such an assumption, using the argument that mainstreaming gender can 'transform' the ubiquity of gender-blind policies. Various countries, as this book (among others) shows, have developed particular methods and tool kits for transforming the outcomes of their policies, in order that those policies take seriously the relevance of gender.

This chapter underscores the question of gender (ir)relevance, and how it is produced by complex organisational practices. It turns to feminist organisational theory to analyse the institutionalised practices that construct and organise policy priorities (see Chapter 6). In agreement with Benschop and Verloo (2006), we argue that effective gender mainstreaming cannot be achieved without attention to the specific organisational sites in which policy is developed and implemented. The chapter draws on the 'turn to practice' in organisational studies, and feminist strategies of 'sudden seeing', to consider what our insights from the gender analysis study might offer future interventionist projects.

Western Australia furnishes most of the examples used in the chapter, although general descriptions of the project's aims and challenges apply also to South

Australia. The starting point for the chapter is our finding in Western Australia that it was only through *doing* the gender analysis in their organisational contexts that policy actors came to see the relevance of gender to policy. In other words, the 'doing' of gender analysis (the practice) in a context of collaborative research became the learning experience that showed why it needed to be done. The chapter links this finding with a further key result: the people who had the most institutional power to foster an interest in gender analysis – those in upper and line management in the collaborating agencies – were not the ones who undertook a gender analysis of policy. Instead, those who 'did', and who subsequently learnt to see the importance of such policy, were mid-level policy officer staff, mostly women. The chapter discusses what these findings may mean for those seeking to institutionalise a gender analysis of policy.

The question of learning by 'doing' provides a key focus not only for this chapter, but also for the overall development of our Gender Analysis Project. The cultural politics of such effortful 'doing' is discussed in Chapter 10 and taken up further in Chapter 13, while Chapter 11 looks in particular at the learning (reflexivity) that comes when both researchers and policy collaborators 'do' the negotiation work of developing shared meanings and goals for the project.

In this chapter the crucial and wider question of organisational practices and how they are institutionalised takes centre stage. One issue impacting on the institutionalising of gender mainstreaming is that of organisational commitment versus obligation (Benschop and Verloo 2006). The Western Australian study shows that, while obligation can turn to commitment for policymakers who undertake the gender analysis of policy in research teams, this does not necessarily translate to *organisational* commitment. Unlike those who emphasise the role of feminist 'experts' in gender mainstreaming (Verloo 2001), we suggest that collaborative studies offer the best hope for long-term learning and commitment.

The chapter shows that organised hierarchies of decision-making use dominant systems of thought which make established or 'normal' ways of seeing and doing seem the correct or 'only' way, therefore favouring entrenched groups. To pursue a transformative agenda, a gender analysis of policy needs to highlight and challenge these normalising practices that 'disappear' the inequitable gendering of people, organisations and policies. The chapter outlines what was required for 'sudden seeing' to take place 'in the middle' of such normalising constraints, and for that 'seeing' to be translated into new policy practices in the Western Australian pilot studies. However, an entrenched lack of interest in gender analysis as a core organisational concern continues to present in these collaborating agencies as unthinking gender-blindness. Such an outcome may well ensure that the institutionalising of gender mainstreaming remains unfinished business for future policymakers.

Abstract

There is considerable research showing that gender is deemed irrelevant to organisations and to policy. This paper examines the results of a research project that sought to reverse those 'rules of relevance'. The project required policy actors in several public sector organisations to undertake a gender analysis of their policies. We found that it was through the collaborative work of doing the gender analysis that policy actors came to see why such an analysis was needed. This necessarily meant seeing the relevance of gender to the policies they dealt with, which could also highlight gender bias in their organisations. Yet, a bureaucratic and gendered division of labour ensured that those who got to do the gender analysis were those in relatively powerless positions, predominantly women. We draw on the 'turn to practice' in organisational studies and feminist strategies of 'sudden seeing' to consider what our results might offer future projects of gender analysis and organisational intervention.

A three-decade dialogue between feminist theory and organisational theory has done little to encourage people who work in organisations to be able to see, much less highlight, the intricate organisational practices that 'do' gender (West and Zimmerman, 1987) as a path to inequality. Consequently, gender, in all its diversity, 'gets disappeared' as a key organisational concern (Fletcher 1999). In other words, gender obeys the 'rules of relevance' (Patai 1983) that situate it below the horizon of central organisational matters.

The shift towards 'diversity' has prompted a further rationale for dismissing gender as an appropriate organisational topic. Well-deserved critiques of gender theory by women of colour (Davis 1981; Spelman 1988) played a part. Particularly influential at the level of organisational human resource management is the argument that diversity should replace gender as the focus of attention in workplaces and government policy alike (Hankivsky 2005; Squires 2005). However, as other research has shown, managing diversity practices not only prioritises business interests over employee equity but also individualises the problems of group disadvantage, while resting on the insecure ground of voluntary business-case-driven initiatives (Bacchi 1999; Eveline and Todd 2002). Recent publications by Bacchi and Eveline (2009) and Eveline, Bacchi and Binns (2009) have used material from the Australian research project we outline below to examine the contested terrain of diversity vs gender in equity mainstreaming policy. Those papers outline the history of that debate in

Australia and elsewhere, and its relationship to the arguments about 'intersectionality' (Crenshaw 1991). They argue that policy practitioners and researchers need to treat context, particularly regarding identity politics, as of major concern when either 'diversity' or 'gender' is to be privileged. Although space precludes us covering that history and argument in this paper, it underpins our thinking about gender and organisations.

This paper analyses an attempt to counter the trend to see gender as irrelevant to organisational practices. The research employed a collaborative approach, between university researchers and several public sector organisations in two Australian states, designed to 'mainstream gender' in public policy.

First highlighted at the 1995 Beijing Decade for Women Conference, gender mainstreaming is used currently in a wide range of countries by policy developers and analysts. The aim is to undo the skewing of policy outcomes that occurs when a gender analysis is lacking (Eveline and Bacchi 2005). The idea of 'mainstreaming' gender analysis of policy is that the analysis is necessary for each and every policy to be successful. Unlike equal opportunity with its relatively finite goals, gender mainstreaming cannot be treated as a one-off exercise, but must continue as an aspect of all policy (Verloo 2001).

Australia had its own early version of gender mainstreaming, although it was not called that, in the 'women's budget' strategy implemented in many public sector organisations in the 1970s (Eveline and Todd 2009). Yet that strategy fell out of favour and indeed Australia has lagged behind countries such as New Zealand and Canada, which joined in the 1990s international trend nominating 'gender mainstreaming' as a strategy for making current policies more gender-sensitive (Bacchi et al. 2005).

Our project required policy actors in eight Australian public sector organisations to implement a gender analysis in their policies. A key problem for the project was that most policy actors are trained to be gender-blind in their policy development, yet in order to effect a useful gender analysis they needed to see and acknowledge gender relevance.

The starting point for this paper is our finding that it was only through doing the gender analysis that policy actors came to see the relevance of gender to policy. In short, the doing became the learning experience that showed why it needed to be done. In our paper we link this finding with our second key result: that the people who got to do a gender analysis of policy were not those at the upper levels of the organisations involved, who had the most power to organisationally extend the strategy. Instead, they were mid level policy officer staff, who were almost always women.

This paper uses a 'gender lens' (Rao, Stuart and Kelleher 1999) to analyse the intricate politics of doing, learning and knowing signalled by those two findings. We suggest that the results of our research project raise a number of strategic issues for both gender mainstreaming and for organisational analysis.

The first we deal with here relates to the question raised by Benschop and Verloo (2006: 30): is obligation enough to ensure that gender analysis of policy is done well, or is commitment the key to success? Benschop and Verloo (2006) argue for commitment to go hand-in-hand with obligation. We agree with them, but wish to take their argument further. On the basis of our findings we suggest that commitment to gender analysis can only be sustained if people can see the relevance of gender to the work they do, and that this acknowledgement of relevance must become an organisational rather than an individual issue. The lack of gender relevance, we suggest, is so familiarised in organisational life, that a key plank of any gender mainstreaming effort must be altering the practices through which the normalising of irrelevance occurs.

In developing our argument we begin with the literature that backgrounds the study. Firstly, we show that gender mainstreaming generally suffers from the want of an organisational analysis. Secondly, we examine arguments for a collaborative approach, between organisations and researchers, to the wider issues of gender equity. Thirdly, we outline the feminist turn-to-practice in organisational studies, to ask what it promises for raising awareness of gender inequalities. Fourthly, we propose the strategy of 'sudden seeing' as an essential step in countering the irrelevance of gender in organisations. We then describe the aims, setting and methodology of the action research project we draw on below. Our data analysis follows, which examines common but different struggles over the 'rules of relevance' within various public sector organisations involved in the study. We conclude with a summary of our findings.

Literature and background

The (ir)relevance of organisational theory to gender mainstreaming

The gender mainstreaming of policy is not new. Since the mid-1990s First World governments have increasingly followed the lead of development countries and introduced it as a tool of public policy, often in collaboration with feminist academics or 'gender experts' (Verloo 2001; Walby 2005). Either in conjunction with, or in place of, two earlier gender equality approaches (equal opportunity and 'special' [positive] measures for women), gender mainstreaming aims to promote equitable outcomes by integrating gender considerations into routine policy processes (Council of Europe 1998). This integration is achieved through what Bacchi and Eveline (2003) term the 'gender analysis of policy'.

Gender analysis begins from the premise that policy routinely (re)produces gender as a relation of inequality (Eveline and Bacchi 2005). To intervene in those customary policy practices, gender mainstreaming suggests that both statistical and qualitative data be used (Bacchi and Eveline 2003), alongside a well-developed understanding of gender as a product of social and political processes (Verloo 2001; Eveline and Bacchi 2005).

Research into gender mainstreaming has been largely dominated by feminist political theory, with particular reference to the sub-discipline of policy studies. This disciplinary background means that most research on gender mainstreaming pays little critical attention to the organisation itself. Among the exceptions is an article by Benschop and Verloo (2006), who argue that effective gender mainstreaming cannot be achieved without attention to the organisational contexts in which policy is developed and implemented. While such an argument may seem obvious to feminist organisational theorists (Acker 1990; Connell 2005), it is not so apparent in feminist policy studies, where the politics of gender is likely to be analysed using more macro-level theory. For example an explanation for gender-blindness of policy could include the subordination of women across public and private spheres, yet fail to analyse how this is reproduced through the organisational and management practices of policymakers themselves.

For Benschop and Verloo (2006: 31) the intricate ways in which everyday organisational practices produce gender-blindness is just as crucial to analyse when gender mainstreaming is introduced, because such policy and its implementation is conducted within organisations. They write:

> [G]ender blind and gender biased attitudes are important manifestations of the genderedness of organizations and ... any gender mainstreaming project has to deal with these attitudes and the accompanying escape tendencies.

There is little to suggest that either gender mainstreaming exponents or policy organisations hear or respond to the idea that an organisational change process is needed if gender analysis is to be done well. In a climate wherein gender-blindness is normalised there is little hope of getting across the idea that a gender analysis is crucial to effective policy unless managers develop an organisational plan through which policy actors can debate the relevance of 'gender' to across-the-board policy development (Verloo 2001; Eveline and Bacchi 2005; Benschop and Verloo 2006). But such debate is not sufficient. Policy actors must then go on to learn how to 'see' the ways in which a recognition of gender inequality is institutionally repressed. In our experience some people could learn to see that institutional repression through using the gender analysis tool. In this paper we outline what was required for that 'seeing', but also why such requirements are likely to remain unfinished business.

In outlining the result of their large project with the Belgian Government, Benschop and Verloo (2006: 30) challenge the idea pursued by some exponents of gender mainstreaming (for example Stark 1998) that policy actors need only obligation, rather than commitment, for the strategy to work. Benschop and Verloo (2006: 30) write:

> Gender mainstreaming cannot ignore existing attitudes, since organizing obligations to ensure equality implies the critique of attitudes and the questioning of existing routines.

The conflict that ensues when such critique and questioning occurs, however, leads Benschop and Verloo (2006: 31) to query the value of feminist researchers engaging in collaborative programs for gender mainstreaming with policy departments. They suggest (2006: 31) that, despite such participatory coalitions 'invoking an image of cooperation between equal parties pursuing a dual agenda of business needs and feminist goals', collaborative gender mainstreaming projects fail in their transformative potential because of crucial differences in power between the parties. A central plank of the model of gender mainstreaming developed by Verloo (2001), therefore, is that it be conducted by consultant gender experts alone. As we show in the next section, a number of feminist researchers on organisations, whose findings about the pitfalls facing gender reforms are similar to those of Benshop and Verloo, are less inclined than the latter to forgo the idea of collaboration as a form of organisational intervention.

Feminist organisational studies and the collaboration argument

The term 'dual agenda', to which Benschop and Verloo (2006) refer, is a model of intervention developed by organisational researchers affiliated with the Center for Gender and Organizations in Boston (see full explanations in Meyerson and Kolb 2000; Rao et al. 1999). Based mainly in the United States, these researchers have undertaken several collaborative research projects seeking to increase gender and racial equality in organisations and public policies. Their conclusions show many similarities with those of Benschop and Verloo. Through their action research projects they indicate that the power dynamics shaping the gendered organisation continually 'disappear' from organisational agendas much of the focus on gender inequalities that their projects try to establish. These 'dual agenda' theorists are courageously frank about their disappointments in a special issue of *Organization* (2000). However, this failing of the dual agenda model does not turn them away from the idea of collaboration. Instead, they argue that they need more emphasis on power-sharing in their collaborative organisational studies (Coleman and Rippin 2000).

The findings of a collaborative study of women's participation in the public realm in Australia (Schofield and Goodwin 2005) parallel those of the 'dual agenda' theorists, drawing precisely the same conclusions about the difficulties and necessity of collaborative work in gender equity studies. Mounted by Connell and Schofield in New South Wales, with collaborators from several public sector organisations, the study aimed to show why equal opportunity programs had such limited success and to seek more viable forms of organisational change (Connell 2005). They found a 'marked consensus that gender and gender equity were not relevant to the policies in which they were involved' (Schofield and Goodwin 2000: 31). Moreover, they found only one of the organisations studied had the necessary characteristics to successfully develop gender equity policy (Schofield and Goodwin 2000: 31).

Drawing on their study Connell (2005) outlines five ways in which gender relations operate so that people fail to see gender in organisational contexts. These include denying there is a problem, and 'distancing' by locating the problem outside the organisation. Despite such obstacles, Connell (2005: 21) situates collaborative research as one of the two key components of her strategy for producing 'the next generation of gender equity policy'. Collaborative research has most potential as a change agent, she argues (2005: 21), because it involves 'staff of the organisations being studied in the research process itself', allowing those with practical experience of the studied organisations the opportunity to see and redress the problems.

Joan Acker (2000), whose theory of the gendered organisation has been used extensively in feminist organisational studies, sounds a more cautionary note about the prospects for effective collaborations between researchers and organisations. The 'dual agenda' researchers mentioned above base their model of intervention on Acker's theory of the gendered organisation (Acker 1990). In responding to the dilemmas they disclose in their papers, Acker (2000: 626-629) clarifies six sets of contradictions and conflicts that hamper the prospects for power-sharing in such action research: i) top-down bureaucratic structures contradict goals for egalitarian collaboration; ii) support from those at the top is crucial yet gender equity sets out to challenge the authority of long established patterns; iii) gender equity goals often conflict with other organisational change goals so the 'dual agenda' (which attempts to couple these diverse goals) promises a flawed alliance; iv) those with relative power and rewards will usually oppose changes that challenge their advantage; v) gender is closely aligned with class structures of organisational control so challenging those structures is likely to fail; vi) organisations operate on short and fast time schedules which conflict and compete with the extensive time needed for changing gendered organisations.

We join in the argument for an organisational analysis of the policy context for gender equity strategies and policies. Yet we break with Benschop and Verloo's non-collaborative model by following the path to collaborative teamwork between researchers and researched. In designing the study we were mindful of Acker's cautions. We examined strategies for combating organisational gender-blindness, which foster ways to help participants see the relevance of gender analysis to their work. We describe these shortly, after discussing what the turn to practice in organisational studies promises for understanding change.

From structural to poststructural: The turn to practice

Most gender studies of organisation now recognise, as West and Zimmerman (1987) did years ago, that gender asymmetry is something we do, not something we have. West and Zimmerman's work is in the ethnomethodological tradition. Ethnomethodologists want to see how cultural groups are formed (or performed) through their practices and actions. Thus the focus is on members' practices, and what members of groups and societies do, in response to societal and/or group expectations of behaviour and self-presentation, and how the doing of those practices is a core element of what many call 'structures'.

Poststructural gender studies take those ideas of practice and the ongoing nature of social and institutional shaping further. Butler (1990, 1993), for example, moves beyond the idea that we retain an essential sexed self while social practices turn us into gendered subjects. Rather, she argues that both gender and sex are performative. It is not that we have an essential sex which is overlain by gender constructions. Rather, doing gender constitutes our selves as both sexed and gendered beings. In short the social practices of doing sex are indivisible from those of doing gender. Butler (1990: 33) stresses, moreover, that this activity is not 'a doing by a subject who might be said to pre-exist the deed'. Rather, subjectivity is 'performatively constituted by the very "expressions" that are said to be its results' (Butler 1990: 33). Doing sex/gender, therefore, 'is an activity which creates what it describes' (Poggio 2006: 226). We don't simply perform a pre-existing script, as an actor does. Instead our gender performance is so integral to the theatre of social scripting that it brings our very identities into being as subjects of discourse. Does this mean that there is no way of moving beyond that social scripting?

Butler's doing of gender is informed by both Foucauldian and Deleuzian thought. Foucauldians are concerned with the nexus of power and knowledge and with how the disciplinary practices of organisations and institutions shape and reflect what can be done and said in any knowledge regime to produce people as subjects of discourse. Feminists influenced by Deleuzian thought are keen to point out the always incompleteness of all practices, a way of thinking which (as with Foucault) moves beyond fixed categories (Eveline 2005). In addition, however, Deleuzian accounts of doing as becoming uses the notion of the rhizomatic to depict the unpredictability of always incomplete practices, a conceptual schema which creates space for imagining new kinds of practices for doing gender and sexuality (Butler 1993), or gender and 'race' (Gatens 1996).

This 'practice' turn in studies of gender is increasingly evident in organisational studies (see as examples Cockburn 1991; Fletcher 1999; Poggio 2006). Such research recognises to some degree that a focus on practice is needed if we are to see that we can change what was thought of as unchangeable. In this paper we utilise that 'practice turn' so we can emphasise the organisational practices involved in policy development. In particular, we are concerned with how policy practices are affected when the goal is to raise awareness that both a gender analysis and a critical whiteness analysis are relevant. In order to raise such awareness, however, policy actors need to be persuaded that they can, and want to, learn a new way of seeing themselves and what they do.

Gherardi (2003: 1) puts such a quest for new knowledge-building in very positive terms. Her paper explores how 'desire for knowledge may operate in organizing'. Gherardi's work is in the poststructural organisational studies paradigm which for her grows out of the practice-based canon of organisational symbolism. For Gherardi, desire plays a major part in the production of knowledge. She considers 'desire as a social force leading to discovery and mastery as collective achievements' (Gherardi 2003: 7). The urge to gain new knowledge comes from a 'compulsive need to understand', a 'desire to master' unknowing (Gherardi 2003: 7).

The problem with Gherardi's account of becoming a knowing subject, however, is that she fails to see how her uses of organisational symbolism 'do' gender, class and 'race' inequality. In effect she reiterates rather than critiques organisational assumptions that learning practices have neutral effects in terms of social differentiation. Her turn to Ulysses and his followers as an example of how 'actors seduce (and select) new participants and meanings' is an unreflexive acceptance of the status quo of most organisational hierarchies, in which an heroic male is positioned as the seductive producer of knowledge (Fletcher 1999). If we were to utilise Gherardi's framework without seeing it through a gender lens, therefore, it is likely to perpetuate the unawareness of gendering practices we might wish to challenge.

Patai (1983) offers another way of understanding what is needed to transform outdated ways of seeing and knowing. Her work is more about the seduction of 'sudden seeing' than it is about the desire to know.

Seeing gender in organisations and research

Patai (1983) argued that because male supremacy in heteronormative contexts was socially familiar to the point of appearing inevitable, social subjects fail to see the ways in which 'rules of relevance' operate continually to produce men and their interests as relevant and women and their interests as irrelevant. To discursively counter this normalising of male and heteronormative supremacy, she suggests a strategy of defamilarisation, to 'startle' readers into seeing what they think of as 'natural' and inevitable in a new light of mutability (Patai 1983: 179).

Patai's strategies of reframing are designed to persuade or seduce the reader into seeing the relevance of gendered power relations to how the world becomes ordered. One of her ways to do this is to reverse the order of usual forms of speaking. In Patai's words (1983: 181) this involves 'startling the audience ... and thereby arousing [their] critical consciousness'. Patai (1983: 181) continues:

> This experience of *sudden seeing* is a kind of revelation, in which what one
> has known abstractly comes to life with special force and immediacy ...
> Such a revelation implies a transition from passive perception to active
> participation, from theory to practice [our emphasis].

To illustrate how this 'sudden seeing' works, Eveline (1994) used one of Patai's strategies (reversal) to show the terminological flaws of much equal opportunity policy in the 1980s and 1990s. By reversing the usual rules of relevance, Eveline sought to defamiliarise the normalisation of 'men's advantage'. Both quotes below are drawn from Eveline (1994: 149). The first quote, drawn from a decision about award restructuring in an industrial relations tribunal, shows the ways in which gender inequity is usually portrayed in equal opportunity language:

> And women could well be disadvantaged by their relative efficiency, as
> they usually work in areas where there has been little scope for developing
> the kind of rorts to be renounced in exchange for wage increases.

The second quote shows the opportunity for 'sudden seeing' when the emphasis on disadvantage is reversed:

> And men could well be advantaged by their relative inefficiency, as they
> usually work in areas where there has been much scope for developing the
> kind of rorts to be renounced in exchange for wage increases.

The first point we wish to make is that, as we show above, Patai's 'rules of relevance' are alive and well in organisational life after 25 years. Secondly we wish to make it clear that we are not suggesting here that perceptual change in organisational members is all that is needed to change organisational practices. Far from it. But we are suggesting it as a necessary element.

The concepts of 'men's advantage' and 'white privilege' (Moreton-Robinson 2000; Rothenberg 2000) prove useful because of their discursive power to produce the irony of seeing both advantage and disadvantage at the same time. This 'double vision' can defamiliarise men and women, whites and blacks to their usual ways of seeing what 'the problem' is. Defamiliarisation is a necessary but insufficient step to combating the taken-for-granted privileges that are woven through dominant institutional practices and habits of 'seeing' and 'doing'. However, both terms (privilege and advantage) can suffer from the problem of fixity, based on a discursive tendency to situate them as nouns rather than as verbs (Eveline and Bacchi 2005). The result is that privilege is conceived therefore in purely structural terms rather than as a continual and always incomplete process (Eveline and Bacchi 2005). It is more useful, we suggest, to understand the use of those terms (along with other terms such as 'equality', 'essentialism', 'gender' and 'diversity') as strategic aspects of the 'politics of doing' (Bacchi and Eveline 2009). The goal is to avoid the perceptual trap of seeing any of them as a fixed entity that can be adequately measured in quantitative terms. Such fixity means researchers cannot adequately show how or why for example one measure of privilege should be emphasised over another. As examples: how do we measure the advantages of ablement against those of masculinity/ies and/or whiteness? can we measure practises of racism, heteronormativity and sexism quantitatively in order to decide which deserves primary (or sole) remediation? Such questions point to the problems inherent in all category-building, well-meant or not (see also Connell 1987; Bacchi 1996).

Nor are we implying that for Patai, or for us, the strategy of reversal is the only way that 'sudden seeing' occurs. Indeed, we found in the research described here that case studies of doing gender analysis, particularly those which showed an unexpected result, were one of the most effective ways of making this sudden seeing relevant to policy actors.

Study design and methods

Our Gender Analysis Project, funded by an Australian Research Council Linkage Grant and industry partner contributions, commenced in late 2004 and finished in late 2008. Its goal was to develop gender analysis guidelines appropriate to the contexts of the South Australian and Western Australian state public sectors. Guides for gender analysis were produced in both states after research results. Our conviction that context matters a great deal meant we decided to involve two states, and sought government agencies that gave a spread of service and administrative organisations. We expected to find that specific circumstances and identities marked the different contexts, and that these would require different intervention approaches, and produce differing models of gender analysis. We proved correct in those assumptions.

For an action study of this kind, choosing and recruiting the various collaborators can be a lengthy and in many ways difficult and careful process. In both states the authors had prior good standing with the industry partners based on earlier projects. In Western Australia ministerial intervention played a role in recruiting the in-kind organisations, with a sponsoring minister approaching ministerial colleagues to ask for suitable prospects. The CEO of the industry partner subsequently presented the case for gender mainstreaming to CEOs of nominated organisations, gaining agreement from most of those approached. All CEOs who collaborated were reputed to be open to diversity concerns.

Linkage Grant projects intend to create conditions for testing theory in practical situations and hence for theory modification and development. Our project had two objectives: first, to trial existing overseas models of gender analysis that were based on sharply differentiated theoretical stances; second, to contribute to organisation theory on the importance of policy actors gaining a shared commitment to the strategy by collaboratively studying it. The two objectives merge in the investigation of how to create gender analysis processes responsive to the needs and wishes of diverse groups of women. All members of the university research teams (chief investigators and research associates) were women.

From the outset in the project the term 'gender', as in gender analysis, created a number of challenges. In particular there was expressed concern that the concept masked asymmetrical power relations based upon 'race'/ethnicity and sexual orientation. To move past this dilemma, we made three theoretical interventions, all intended to shift the focus from fixed categories of people to the social relationships among them: 1) we stressed the importance of understanding gender as a social principle rather than as a synonym for women, or as a shorthand for 'men and women'; 2) as in the study by Schofield and Connell mentioned above we made the idea of gender relations a central notion in the deliberations; we built on this notion by directing attention to the practices of gendering; 3) to highlight our focus on 'doing', which was an attempt to destablise fixed categories, we referred to gender as a verb rather than as a noun (Eveline and Bacchi 2005; also Gunnarsson et al. 2003). These strategies helped examine the impact of gendered assumptions on the maintenance of hierarchical social relations beyond those between men and women.

The project began by testing two different gender mainstreaming frameworks. We called these the 'Canadian model', which emphasises sex differences, and the 'Netherlands model', which calls attention to gender relations. Each model comprises a set of steps or stages to guide policy staff in implementing gender mainstreaming. Trialling these models and reflecting on their efficacy was designed to build awareness of the relevance of gender analysis, and a means towards developing a model specific to the needs of the two states.

Ten pilot projects were conducted in eight government agencies, across the two states. An additional government agency in each state operated as the coordinating agency for the involvement of the eight agency teams. This collaborative agreement about coordination had its benefits and disadvantages. The great benefit was that it provided an insider connection to the government agencies needed to carry out the study, provided a sense of how to manage the local and state government politics of a delicately balanced project, and the coordinating agency undertook the massive task of coordinating very different groups. The downside was that as the researchers, we were one step removed from the organising practices of securing and coordinating the groups to be involved in the project. Agency heads selected team members and the policy area to be used for the pilot projects, while the coordinating agency decided timelines for meetings and events along with the development of materials. Project teams comprised between two and eight policy staff in each of the participating agencies. This paper draws on our experience in the two states, although the data analysed comes mainly from Western Australia.

Training and its evaluation were built into the study's design from the start, as was wider community interaction. Learning events, comprising group workshops and lectures, training delivered by experts from both Canada and the Netherlands, as well as in-house discussion groups, coincided with key stages of the study. Unlike the earlier research by Schofield and Connell, ours was never designed as a comparative study of how organisations engaged with gender equity. Although a focus on organisational practices was an integral part of the design, the overriding aim was to provide research participants with a practical understanding of gender analysis and a model for practice which suited their contexts. We used interlinked learning methodologies including formal and informal training workshops, discussion of the organisation's existing policy practices (using policy 'audits' conducted by the researchers), ongoing liaison between the researchers and individual agency teams via meetings, email and phone, and inter-agency planning, information and feedback meetings.

In Western Australia the learning strategy was evaluated using both quantitative and qualitative methods. At the end of the first year, study participants completed a questionnaire which used a five-point rating scale for each element of the strategy and also included the opportunity to provide general comments. The other components of the evaluation methods occurred during the second and third years. They comprised semi-structured interviews, plus transcripts and notes from worksheets, meetings and 'learning journey' papers written by the project teams themselves. These 'journey' documents were revised several times and then agreed on by teams as accurate records, which were then subsequently signed off by their agency heads, as well as by the relevant industry partner. The analysis that follows draws on data collected from these sources and events. Ethics approval was secured by ensuring reports compiled from interviews and questionnaires were returned to the teams, who then made what revisions they required before achieving final agreement among team members, prior to presentation to their departmental heads. Publications from this data needed approval from the industry partners (the coordinating agencies for the project); the Western Australian industry partner [Office for Women's Policy], for example, approved for publication the final draft of this paper. All data was analysed through qualitative data procedures of 'goading and coding', techniques developed over a long period by qualitative researchers who then articulated and established them as part of the NVivo program of data analysis (Richards 2005).

Data analysis

Wrestling with the (ir)relevance of gender

The research team in Western Australia identified as crucial the strategies for developing 'sudden seeing' (Patai 1983) among the policy actors involved in the project. Before the ARC project began these strategies were used in the talks and lectures given by the coordinating agency in the early development of the research project's proposal, and helped to convince several government ministers and five CEOs to participate in the study. Initial events for senior managers used sex statistics in their policy fields,

299

coupled with case studies of policy examples in overseas jurisdictions. The 'seeing strategies' used in these case studies helped show the way in which organisational and policy norms operated to marginalise and exclude a gender analysis.

At the outset the study encountered a number of the contradictions Acker (2000) outlines with regard to interventionist research. While the CEOs involved were well-intentioned and able to speak convincingly in public on the need for this new strategy, they operated in hierarchical and time-poor organisations. Bureaucratic procedures meant that the decision to collaborate was passed on through top-down directives. Status differences between the coordinating agency and organisations contributing the in-kind contribution meant that the latter decided how each would proceed in this new learning project. In all cases CEOs delegated the carriage of the project to mid-level managers. Those mid-level staff had not been trained in the specialised gender analysis required for the project. This was to be expected, since at that time this new approach to gender mainstreaming was only just beginning to gain support in Australian policy development (see Goward 2004). In most cases middle-management staff had the responsibility to decide how much they would contribute in staff and resources. They in turn delegated downwards to the team they had chosen to be involved. Among this latter group the team supervisor, usually at senior policy officer status, decided for the most part how and when internal meetings should be held, what should be the topic of meetings, and what policy projects should become part of their gender analysis pilots.

The delegation of duties and siloing of responsibilities meant that, after they had made their initial decisions about team leaders and in two cases delineated the project focus, upper levels of management had little direct input into the study. Nonetheless, in order to make an early statement about the university/public sector partnership, two of the five CEOs presided over the initial launch of their gender analysis team's pilot studies. This lack of common interest about gender concerns meant that for those doing the gender analysis it was difficult to pass on the information they received and the experience they gained.

Indeed the passing on of information, even among those teams who showed most commitment to the study, was a major hurdle. In Western Australia, once task delegation and project launches had occurred, for example, there was considerable reluctance among most team leaders, and therefore among team participants, to involve their superordinates in the general progress of the team's work. Although for quite different reasons two of the CEOs asked for regular updates from team leaders, most teams were left to proceed without further senior input. Even where the CEOs expressed interest, there was a strong tendency to join in the general trend to distance the gender analysis procedures and teams from others in their organisations, which ensured that gender remained largely irrelevant to most policy and departmental business. The fear of being seen by their colleagues as 'gender champions' or 'gender leaders' was deeply embedded for many (see also Eveline and Booth 2004), and although most of this fear disappeared over time in the teams themselves, it usually held sway in interactions with colleagues outside the team. In most cases, therefore, the CEOs whose decisions to initiate the gender mainstreaming were crucial to the study happening at all, had little further knowledge of it until projects were completed. Yet display of upper managerial support has been shown to be crucial for the long-term life of gender interventions in organisations (Acker 2000; Eveline 2004).

The hierarchical division of labour also meant that those who had most opportunity to learn about gender analysis were policy actors at lower-mid levels. The majority of these were women. Men represented one-third of the people on the five Western Australian teams. In part because of status issues but also in some cases through inclination, men on the teams contributed less than one-tenth of the in-kind time delegated to the project.

Organisational context also played a role in the wide diversity of gender balance on the project teams themselves. In Western Australia several teams changed their membership during the study, which again affected gender balance. This sometimes meant that those who had completed initial training were replaced on teams by those who had not. Much of the teams' learning, therefore, occurred in the team meetings attended by researchers.

Organisational and ministerial context also meant considerable variations in labour and time resources allocated to teams and projects. In WA, teams from highly feminised agencies suffered more in this regard. The prevailing understanding that gender was about counting 'women', meant that the feminised departments were more likely to be seen as doing better on the gender front than the masculinised ones, therefore they needed less time and resources. For example, when reflecting in their journey papers on what they had learnt during the project, two WA teams noted the underlying premise of their agency was that women's disadvantage had been overcome, and that what was needed now was an equalising strategy that fostered equal benefits for men. Such local constraints made it difficult to ensure all participants had workloads that could accommodate the team meetings needed for their gender analysis tasks.

In early discussions with project teams in Western Australia, it became clear that most departments cultivated a consciously gender-neutral stance, using the language of 'inclusiveness' to deny the need for attention to gender. Some participants intimated that an earlier concern for gender had disappeared over the years with government changes and departmental and ministerial directives. This gender-neutral stance prompted some initial cautiousness in most people delegated to teams in the Gender Analysis Project.

One of the teams provides a good example of how gender-blind policies could affect both men and women detrimentally, but in different ways. The team used statistics and interviews to do a post-policy gender analysis of a new human resource directive in their department. The results showed that those most disadvantaged by the policy were not, as was expected, women with family responsibilities but men with those responsibilities. In the heavily male-dominated department, managers had no knowledge that a sizable proportion of its younger male employees had also taken on family responsibilities, and relocations caused them and their working wives and families hardships. The data was skewed towards men because males comprised over 80 per cent of employees. Some supervisors organising the transfers knew they had to worry about this 'problem' with female employees but not with men. Adding to the almost total lack of women who experienced family problems in this operational re-organisation was the fact that most of the women trained for core-function roles in that male-dominated department had no young children, since the organisation had an earlier history of discouraging women from taking pregnancy and family leave. The gender analysis results showed that some men and some women were disadvantaged by the organisation's gender 'rules of relevance', but in quite different ways.

Progressive outcomes of the projects, such as the one above, were discussed among the project teams undertaking the gender analysis. The Western Australian research team used some of these outcomes (such as the one above) as further evidence of how 'sudden seeing' could occur in the doing of gender analysis. Such feedback and discussion occurred mainly in the inter-agency meetings, but also at times in the Agency team meetings attended by researchers. Attendees at the inter-agency meetings included team policy officers, heads of teams, members of the coordinating agency (industry partner), and the researchers. Those who were best able to make sense of the intricacies of gender positioning in an example like the above were the policy officers who were learning how to do the gender analysis in the training sessions, and in their agency's pilot projects were putting into practice what they had learnt. Although as mentioned earlier there were some men in the project teams, in Western Australia it was women in mid ranks, accompanied by one junior male, who were delegated to attend the training sessions and gather the material for the gender analyses. The hierarchical ordering of their departments played a role in this outcome, but so did the organisational assumption of relevance, held by many public sector managers, that women (but not men) will be better attuned to gender issues because of some natural proclivity.

While some women initially seemed to accept this allocation of 'women's business' as appropriate, others sensed the unfairness of such normative expectations. As one example, a female manager involved in the study spoke of 'making sure that everything that has got the label "women" on it doesn't end up on my desk' (Meeting, 28/3/06). Despite such resolutions, the general rule was that women did the work of gender analysis and men did the leadership roles.

Power works through leadership decisions about the relevance of gender to policy. It circulates often through a no-talk 'rule' about gender itself. One way, as Connell (2005: 17) notes, is through distancing strategies.

Two scenarios from Western Australia help illustrate that point. The first is from one of the training workshops, the second from a team meeting some weeks later. In a project team of two male middle managers and three women in slightly more junior roles, only the women attended a two-day training workshop on how to use the Canadian model, although the men came to the shorter, prestigious public breakfast at which the gist of the approach was outlined. At the longer workshop the women involved experienced an epiphany of 'sudden seeing', related to discussing the material used, which gave them insights into the gendering of their own lives. Although they had shown only obligatory interest in the project earlier, they subsequently used the opportunity of a lunch break to voice their sense of unfairness about the unequal gender division of labour and power in their team, and how it meant they were the ones left to convince their male colleagues of why a gender analysis was important. Later, an hour after the workshop's conclusion, one of the chief investigators on the project found them still in the car park. They were conducting an intense brainstorming of the organisational obstacles to seeing the relevance of gender to policy development, finishing with a plan for how to convince the leaders of their project team (all men) that gender was more than just of statistical relevance to policy.

In a subsequent meeting between the whole team and the Western Australian research team, the woman (mid-level policy officer) whose task it was to compile and analyse the sex-disaggregated statistics for their project had this to say:

> I think the other thing ... was to do with assumptions ... Because when you get the statistics it's still – they're sex-disaggregated stats. They are 'males' and 'females', and part of the process with gender analysis is that we're not talking about 'males and females' – the physical differences between them, but the 'gender roles' that they play within society. So that required us then to talk about...what do we know about the roles that women generally assume in society? And what do we know about the roles that men generally assume? (Female policy officer at meeting of 2/6/05)

This policy officer was recounting how she and the other women on her team had used examples of gendered social roles to persuade their two male seniors to agree that more qualitative elements than statistics should be brought into the ways in which a gender analysis of policy could be done effectively. In the discussion that followed it was obvious the men on the team had been well persuaded, being keen to see a comprehensive gender analysis of the policy project completed. The younger man showed a good grasp of the language of gender analysis, while the more senior was ensuring the necessary resources of time and task allocation.

The women on the team revealed later that, in the meetings in which they had convinced their colleagues, the women had avoided any examples that 'personalised' the problem. By 'personal' they meant the 'internal' issues of hierarchy and promotion that had helped them in the training session to see why gender analysis was organisationally relevant. Instead, they had used 'safer' overseas case studies. This 'distancing' strategy, of placing gender 'out there' as simply a policy issue rather than 'in here' as an organisational issue is one way in which gender is made to vanish (Connell 2005: 17). Work organisations are built on and around such techniques of distancing and denial, which is the point we wish to make. The women evidently achieved their goal of convincing their colleagues. So does it matter that distancing normalises the gender rules of relevance that pervade organisational life?

The subsequent policy that the team developed addressed several previously unseen aspects of the diversity of gender inequality. In later meetings between the team and the researchers all team members spoke confidently of how they could see the benefits of gender analysis in policy work, and expressed a wish to persuade their organisational colleagues to follow suit. At the same time the team talked at length about the organisational difficulties they faced in undertaking such a task. They named a generalised lack of interest and lack of organisational time and resources as primary hindrances. Although the team went on to write a paper outlining how their agency as a whole could bring gender analysis into their policy work, that paper has not to date been presented to senior management. The reason given was that the organisational climate of ministerial and directional changes is such that the timing has not so far been 'right'. The question of what is deemed relevant to fund and allocate time for underpins such decisions.

Most other teams showed a similar reluctance to be in the vanguard of taking the gender analysis beyond their immediate teams (for exceptions see Eveline et al. 2009, and Bacchi and Eveline 2009). When questioned, team members gave two reasons for this reluctance. Both showed signs of the unimportance accorded gendering by established organisational practices.

The first was that they understood the charter they had been given by their organisational leaders was to come up with a cost-efficient way for others to do gender analysis. The model they said their departments required could not provide the time and labour resources they had enjoyed but one requiring no more than a two-hour session on how to implement a particular tool kit. One woman expressed the sentiments of many: 'it would be nice if everyone could have the time luxury that I've had to get that understanding, but there's no way we could argue for that.' Even when gender analysis was no longer organisationally irrelevant for those policymakers doing it, they felt unable to argue that it deserved more than minimal organisational time. One of the men involved clarified this point: 'we have to come up with something quick and easy or it will never be used'.

The second reason these participants gave for their reluctance to take their awareness 'out' to their agency colleagues was that they doubted their capacity to combat the common perception they encountered – that gender equity, and in this case gender analysis, favoured women at men's expense. To quote two participants on their colleagues:

> I think they felt like 'gender' had been done to death ... and they wanted something a bit more inclusive. (Interview with female manager 20/4/06)

> Even the word 'gender' is interpreted as meaning 'women'. And it's [seen as] a sneaky way for women to get in 'pretending' it's about 'gender' but really it's just about women! (Interview with female senior policy officer 16/1/06)

Despite the insights gained by some individual women, at the conclusion of the project in most WA agencies gender neutrality remained not so much an official position as a dominant viewpoint. The women who decided once they began their gender analysis that they wanted to change that perspective puzzled about the difficulties they faced with deeply held assumptions and language:

> The overall principle of ... doing an analysis of whatever problem you have before you in terms of gender; 'how does it impact differently?' ... is perfectly straightforward. But the methodology to do that, almost by definition, is going to be at this point in history sort of shaped by the same assumptions and prejudices about women. It's very hard to get a clear idea in my mind of the methodology for doing Gender Analysis that wouldn't, if you like, be sort of tainted by assumptions [about] men and women. (Interview with female senior policy officer 16/1/06)

In such organisational climates, inclusivity is coded to mean that gender, and by association gender analysis, has little or no relevance. As long as that assumption is galvanised through institutionalised practices, the efforts and learnings of a few relatively junior policy officers, most of them women, would appear to offer only slow progress towards substantive change.

Conclusion

This paper seeks to contribute to organisation theory by showing the need for those involved in reform initiatives to gain hands-on experience of what organisational mechanisms they will need to see, say and do before that initiative can succeed. We agree with Benschop and Verloo (2006) that organisational commitment is the way to effective results in gender mainstreaming of policy; unlike them we suggest such commitment does not come with the policy work being done by 'outside' experts, but through the careful 'doing' of reform initiatives by internal policy actors themselves.

Our data shows that commitment may follow from obligation, particularly if those doing the analysis are trained to use a gender lens and are able to practice their learning collaboratively. That collaborative learning is a two-way process. Researchers must learn to make gender analysis relevant to policymakers, which can mean relaxing old rigidities of thinking, and policymakers must learn to see the relevance of gender analysis to their work. Unlike Benschop and Verloo, therefore, we are unwilling in doing gender analysis to discard the need for collaboration between research teams and policy teams. As the learning journey papers from Western Australia show, it was through that collaborative learning and doing that policy actors came to see why gender analysis was needed.

We have used the contemporary organisational focus on 'practice' to show that those who did the gender analysis well were 'doing' what they became – experts in seeing the relevance of gender to organisation, and to bring that recognition into their policy analysis, if not into the wider organisational practices themselves. Yet bureaucratic, hierarchical organising of duties, roles and tasks meant that those who did the work of analysis were the ones who grasped the need to analyse and challenge the deeply gendered outcomes of their policy domain. These were predominantly women with little organisational power. Thus the research indicates that, if learning is about desire, then learning to see how organisational practices 'do' gender is usually shaped as feminised desire, a gendering of the desire to 'see' beyond taken-for-granted assumptions.

The theory of gender mainstreaming recognises that policy actors need highly visible and very long-term support from all levels of management to be able to utilise the ongoing gender analysis needed to change gender-blind practices (Verloo 2001). Along with Patai (1983) we have called these established practices 'rules of relevance'. In a neo-liberal climate of smaller budgets, fast 'products' and tightened labour supply (Bacchi and Eveline 2003; Connell 2006), it is seldom the managers who sponsor a gender mainstreaming project who go through the challenging process of learning to do it. Consequently, entrenched management practices ensure the agency is at best likely to provide policy actors with generic tool kits, guides and training materials, leaving it to individuals to work out how to utilise them effectively in their local contexts when and if they can fit such work into their schedules.

In summary, we suggest that under such management practices the gendering of organisational rules of relevance will remain in play for many years to come. As Eveline and Bacchi (2005) argue, gender analysis is always unfinished business. And therein lies the hope for perpetual learning, doing and becoming.

Acknowledgements

The authors wish to thank two anonymous reviewers for their insightful comments, which we enjoyed utilising in our revisions.

References

(Websites valid at time of publication)

Acker, J. 1990. 'Hierarchies, jobs and bodies: Towards a theory of gendered organizations', *Gender and Society* 4 (2): 139-158.

Acker, J. 2000. 'Gendered contradictions in organizational equity projects', *Organization: Beyond Armchair Feminism* 7 (4): 625-632.

Bacchi, C. 1996. *The politics of affirmative action: 'Women', equality and category politics*. London: Sage.

Bacchi, C. 1999. *Women, policy and politics: The construction of policy problems*. London: Sage.

Bacchi, C. and Eveline, J. 2003. 'Mainstreaming and neoliberalism: A contested relationship', *Policy and Society: Journal of Public, Foreign and Global Policy* 22 (2): 98-118.

Bacchi, C., Eveline, J., Binns, J., Mackenzie, C. and Harwood, S. 2005. 'Gender analysis and social change: Testing the water', *Policy and Society* 24 (4): 45-68.

Bacchi, C. and Eveline, J. 2009. 'Gender mainstreaming or diversity mainstreaming? The politics of "doing"', *NORA – Nordic Journal of Feminist and Gender Research* 17 (1): 3-18.

Benschop, Y. and Verloo, M. 2006. 'Sisyphus' sisters: Can gender mainstreaming escape the genderedness of organizations?' *Journal of Gender Studies* 15: 19-33.

Butler, J. 1990. *Gender trouble: Feminism and the subversion of identity*. London: Routledge.

Butler, J. 1993. *Bodies that matter*. New York: Routledge.

Cockburn, C. 1991. *In the way of women: Men's resistance to sex equality in organizations*. Ithaca, New York: ILR Press.

Coleman, G. and Rippin, A. 2000. 'Putting feminist theory to work: Collaboration as a means towards organizational change', *Organization: Beyond Armchair Feminism* 7 (4): 573-587.

Connell, R 1987. *Gender and power*. Cambridge: Polity Press.

Connell, R. 2005. 'Advancing gender reform in large-scale organizations: A new approach for practitioners and researchers', *Policy and Society* 24 (4): 5-24.

Connell, R. 2006. 'The experience of gender change in public sector organizations', *Gender, Work and Organization* 13 (5): 435-452.

Council of Europe. 1998. *Conceptual framework, methodology and presentation of good practices: Final report of activities of the group of specialists on mainstreaming* [EG-S-MS (98) 2]. Strasbourg: Council of Europe. <coe.int/T/E/Human_Rights/Equality/02._Gender_mainstreaming/100_EG-S-MS%281998%292rev.asp> accessed 22 October 2009.

Crenshaw, K. 1991. 'Mapping the margins: Intersectionality, identity politics, and violence', *Stanford Law Review* 43: 1241-1299.

Davis, A. 1981. *Women, race and class*. New York: Random House.

Eveline, J. 1994. 'The politics of advantage', *Australian Feminist Studies* 19: 129-154.

Eveline, J. 2004. *Ivory basement leadership: Power and invisibility in the changing university*. Nedlands, WA: University of Western Australia Press.

Eveline, J. 2005. 'Woman in the ivory tower: Gendering feminised and masculinised identities', *Journal of Organisational Change Management* 18 (6) December: 641-658.

Eveline, J. and Booth, M. 2004. 'Don't write about it: Writing "the other" for the ivory basement', *Journal of Organisational Change Management* 17 (3): 243-255.

Eveline, J. and Todd, P. 2002. 'Teaching managing diversity', *International Journal of Inclusive Education* 6 (1): 33-46.

Eveline, J. and Todd, P. 2009. 'Gender mainstreaming: The answer to the gender pay gap?' *Gender, Work and Organization* 16 (5): 536-558.

Eveline, J., Bacchi, C. and Binns, J. 2009. 'Gender mainstreaming versus diversity mainstreaming: Methodology as emancipatory politics', *Gender, Work and Organization* 16 (2): 198-216.

Fletcher, J. 1999. *Disappearing acts: Gender, power and relational practice at work*. Cambridge: MIT Press.

Gatens, M. 1996. *Imaginary bodies: Ethics, power and corporeality*. London: Routledge.

Gherardi, S. 2003. 'Knowing as desiring. Mythic knowledge and the knowledge journey in communities of practitioners', *Journal of Workplace Learning* 15 (7/8): 352-359.

Goward, P. 2004. 'Now everyone can focus on women', *The Age*, 30 October.

Gunnarsson, E., Andersson, S., Rosell, A. and Salminen-Karlsson, M. (eds) 2003. *Where have all the structures gone? Doing gender in organizations*. Stockholm: Stockholm University, Centre for Women's Studies.

Hankivsky, O. 2005. 'Gender vs. diversity mainstreaming: A preliminary examination of the role and transformative potential of feminist theory', *Canadian Journal of Political Science* 38 (4): 977-1001.

Meyerson, D. and Kolb, D. 2000. 'Moving out of the "Armchair": Developing a framework to bridge the gap between feminist theory and practice', *Organization: Beyond Armchair Feminism* 7 (4): 553-571.

Moreton-Robinson, Aileen. 2000. *Talkin' up to the white woman: Aboriginal women and feminism*. St Lucia, Qld: University of Queensland Press.

Patai, D. 1983. 'Beyond defensiveness: Feminist research strategies', *Women's Studies International Forum* 6 (2): 177-189.

Poggio, B. 2006. 'Editorial: Outline of a theory of gender practices', *Gender, Work and Organization* 13 (3): 225-233.

Rao, A., Stuart, R. and Kelleher, D. (eds) 1999. *Gender at work: Organizational change for equality*. West Hartford, CT: Kumarian Press.

Richards, L. 2005. *Handling qualitative data: A practical guide*. London, Thousand Oaks and New Delhi: Sage.

Rothenberg, P. (ed.) 2005. *White privilege*. New York: Worth Publishers.

Schofield, T. and Goodwin, S. 2005. 'Gender politics and public policy making: Prospects for advancing gender equality', *Policy and Society* 24 (4): 25-44.

Spelman, E. 1988. *Inessential woman: Problems of exclusion in feminist thought*. Boston: Beacon.

Squires, J. 2005. 'Is mainstreaming transformative? Theorizing mainstreaming in the context of diversity and deliberation', *Social Politics* 12 (3): 366-388.

Stark, A. 1998. 'Developments in mainstreaming sex equality in Europe', in Vieill, M. (ed.) *Sex equality in the public sector*. Report of a Joint Equal Opportunities Commission and European Commission Conference. Equal Opportunities Commission, London.

Verloo, M. 2001. 'Another velvet revolution? Gender mainstreaming and the politics of implementation', *IWM Working paper no. 5/2001*. Vienna: IWM Publications.

Verloo, M. 2006. 'Multiple inequalities, intersectionality and the European Union', *The European Journal of Women's Studies* 13 (3): 211-228.

Walby, S. 2005. 'Introduction: Comparative gender mainstreaming in a global era', *International Feminist Journal of Politics* 7 (4): 453-471.

West, C. and Zimmerman, D. 1987. 'Doing gender', *Gender & Society* 1 (2): 125-151.

13

Gender mainstreaming or diversity mainstreaming? The politics of 'doing'

CAROL BACCHI AND JOAN EVELINE

Introduction: Carol Bacchi and Joan Eveline

This chapter applies the concept of 'doing' to the practices of feminist researchers. Under scrutiny are the ways in which unexamined presumptions about the main business of gender mainstreaming as *gender* equality foreclose consideration of the lives and experiences of specific groups of women, here Aboriginal and Torres Strait Islander women. Following from Chapters 10, 11 and 12, the chapter emphasises the critical importance of collaborative spaces to the character and shape of egalitarian politics.

The chapter highlights the continuing dispute in feminist communities about whether or not the term 'diversity mainstreaming' better reflects current sensitivities to differences among women, commonly described as an 'intersectional' sensitivity. It shows how the South Australian research team in the Gender Analysis Project dealt with this issue, deciding to include 'race and cultural analysis' *within* a gender analysis guide (SAGA).

This decision, as we describe, was not, as might first appear, a *compromise* position. Rather, non-Aboriginal members of the group accepted that Aboriginal women were best placed to articulate a political vision of use to their communities – a vision based on the *identity* of those communities. This acceptance compelled those non-Aboriginal members to rethink assumptions about the obviousness of gender as an analytical priority. This rethinking is an outcome of what we describe in the book as the process of reflexivity – finding ways to reflect critically on one's own starting points for thinking (all the while recognising that there are no agentic subjects who can invariably avoid traps of discursive positioning).

A key issue for the GAP project became finding ways to 'trigger' reflexivity. In the particular case of SAGA, new positions on how best to articulate a relationship between 'gender' and 'race/culture' as analytic categories occurred as a result of the space and time created to listen 'deeply' (Gabb and McDermott 2007) to alternative perspectives on identity and politics. A shared commitment to egalitarian social relations, which we describe as a 'coalition of engagement', enabled a working-through for the moment of a way forward.

Our particular experience in this case reopened, in our minds, current theoretical debates about identity politics and democratic practice, raising questions about recent tendencies to criticise identity politics for 'fixing' the meaning of constructed identities. The resolution in SAGA to leave judgment about the uses of identity claims to those who live the pain of racism reflected a *political* decision about the necessary temporary 'fixing' of meaning in this particular situation (see Introduction to the book). The broader point, and one central to the book, is that analytic categories (for example, gender) and people categories (for example, Aboriginal and Torres Strait Islanders) are always political interventions and should be assessed in terms of their political usefulness in specific situations (Bacchi 1996). This assessment relies upon reflexive thinking conducted in collaborative time and space.

The decision of the South Australian research team to produce a gender analysis guide (SAGA) mediated by 'race and cultural analysis' is not, however, the end of the story. How that recommendation gets translated into a specific policy and how that policy is interpreted and implemented in specific organisational sites will reflect the indeterminacy and unpredictability of other political decisions, influenced by a wide range of factors, including gendered, heterosexual and racialised norms (Chapters 11 and 12). Regardless of what they are called (for example, gender mainstreaming, diversity mainstreaming, etc.), therefore, reform initiatives remain fields of contestation with indeterminate meanings and complex and ambiguous effects. Nonetheless and because this is the case, we believe that it is important to recognise the interplay and exchange within the collaborative spaces of the research groups – the actual 'doings' involved in producing SAGA – as key sites for political and social reflection and negotiation. It is here that minds and hearts were altered in ways that signal the possibility of less hierarchical and more egalitarian social relations.

References

Bacchi, C. 1996. *The politics of affirmative action: 'Women', equality and category politics.* London: Sage.

Abstract

Amongst recent debates about whether it is preferable to campaign for gender mainstreaming or diversity mainstreaming this paper makes the case that both proposals involve fields of contestation. Either reform, it argues, could be taken in anti-progressive directions. Hence, we redirect attention to the processes and practices that give an initiative content and shape, which we call the politics of 'doing'. The argument here is that the actual 'doings' involved in producing reform initiatives are key sites for social change. Hence, in order to produce reforms responsive to the needs and wishes of diverse groups of women, attention ought to be directed to ways of making those 'doings' inclusive and democratic. Specifically we highlight the importance of privileging the views of marginalised women in any such policy deliberations and respecting their perspectives on the usefulness of appeals to identity. We introduce the concepts of 'coalitions of engagement' and 'deep listening' to generate discussion around these contentious issues.

In this paper we engage in current theoretical discussions about whether it is preferable to talk about (and campaign for) *diversity* mainstreaming or *gender* mainstreaming. Several theorists (Hankivsky 2005; Squires 2005) argue that 'gender' is essentialist and predicated on a male-female binary. They suggest that a more plural understanding of social relationships is captured in the concept of diversity.

We develop the argument that it is impossible to 'script' reform initiatives or to predict how they will be deployed. In our view the concepts of gender and diversity, and even mainstreaming itself, are contested, meaning that they are all 'up for grabs'. Hence any reform initiative may be taken in directions not intended, or indeed in directions opposite to the goals of those who put them forward (Bacchi 1996: 1-2). Since this is the case, we recommend that more attention be directed to the practices, processes and procedures associated with *developing* those initiatives. Indeed, in our view these are the spaces where political change is most likely to take place. We capture this idea in the phrase 'the politics of "doing"'. Building on the language Ahmed (2007b) uses to describe her frustration at attempts to introduce a diversity initiative at her university, we suggest that 'doing the document' is a crucial part of 'doing' change.[1]

We use our experience in a research project aimed at developing gender analysis guidelines for the Western Australian and South Australian state public

314

sectors to reflect upon these issues. The authors are the Chief Investigators for the project. After a brief section introducing the project we highlight the contestation around both gender mainstreaming and the concept of diversity, leading to our contention that more attention be paid to practices and processes. On the question of what *appropriate* processes should look like, we identify an important disagreement among mainstreaming theorists about the place of appeals to identity and of identity groups in such processes. As ways forward we develop the concepts of 'coalitions of engagement' and 'deep listening', which build on the premise that, in order to reflect the diversity of women's experiences, marginalised groups of women ought to become leaders in deciding when and which identity categories matter.

The Gender Analysis Project

The Gender Analysis Project, funded by an Australian Research Council Linkage Grant and partner contributions, commenced in late 2004 and is at the time of writing in its final year.[2] Its goal has been to develop gender analysis guidelines appropriate to the contexts of the South Australian and Western Australian State public sectors. Gender analysis is a form of policy analysis associated with gender mainstreaming. Its intent is to scrutinise existing and proposed policies to ensure that they are gender-sensitive and gender-inclusive. Guides for gender analysis are currently in the final stages of production in both South Australia and Western Australia.

Linkage Grant projects have the intent of creating conditions for testing theory in practical situations and hence for theory modification and development. With this goal in mind, from the outset, the project had two objectives: first, to trial competing models of gender analysis that were based on sharply differentiated theoretical stances; and, second, to contribute to organisation theory on the importance of involving policy actors directly in the development of reform initiatives in order to create a sense of ownership. The two objectives merge in the investigation of how to create gender analysis processes responsive to the needs and wishes of diverse groups of women, the particular focus in this paper.

From the outset in the project the term 'gender', as in *gender* analysis, created a number of challenges. In particular there was expressed concern that the concept masked asymmetrical power relations based upon 'race'/ethnicity and sexual orientation. To move past this dilemma, we made three theoretical interventions, all intended to shift the focus from fixed categories of people to the social relationships among them: 1) we stressed the importance of understanding gender as a social principle rather than as a synonym for women, or as a shorthand for 'men and women'; 2) the idea of gender relations became a central notion in the deliberations, directing attention to the *practices* of gender*ing*; 3) to highlight our focus on 'doing' we referred to gender as a verb rather than as a noun (Eveline and Bacchi 2005; also Gunnarsson et al. 2003).

We argued that, since these theoretical interventions serve to destabilise categories of people commonly thought of as fixed, they offer the opportunity to examine the impact of gendered assumptions on the maintenance of hierarchical social relations *beyond those between men and women*. Our objective was to treat gender, not as a characteristic of people or as a cultural cloak to be removed, but as a 'constellation of ideas and social practices that are historically situated and that mutually construct multiple systems of oppression' (Hill Collins 1999: 263). Articulating this stance, the 'draft' guide in South Australia3 specifies that 'Thinking about gender in relational terms facilitates analysis of the ways in which other social relations intersect and influence gender relations and one another' (Government of South Australia 2008: 20).

However, in these interventions gender continues to be privileged as an analytical category, which caused concerns for Aboriginal and Torres Strait Islander women in both states. In Western Australia the members of an Indigenous Election strategy expressed strong reservations about the usefulness of the concept 'gender' to their work. As outlined in the Memorandum (Elliott 2005: 3): 'Policy was shaped by an awareness of Indigenous subjugation, not gender, because gender as it is assigned remains a western construction'. Similar qualms were expressed by the Aboriginal senior officers (all women) who provided feedback to assist the project team in South Australia. Gender in their view, in any of its grammatical incarnations, was understood to privilege male/female relations and hence was deemed to be problematic for their social analysis of racialisation.

In South Australia the challenge, therefore, became designing a guide that reflected the perspectives of Aboriginal women as articulated by those senior officers. In response to a series of meetings and exchanges of draft material the guide, called SAGA (South Australian Gender Analysis), offers a unique blending of theoretical perspectives. The introductory section specifies that gender analysis in South Australia is informed by 'race and cultural analysis', explained in the following terms:

> Race and cultural analysis broadens the 'gender based' framework to include and reflect the multidimensional experiences of Aboriginal and Torres Strait Islander women, and of women from culturally and linguistically diverse backgrounds. All discussions about equality, equity or disadvantage must be inclusive of discussions about diversity and human rights. (Government of South Australia 2008: 6)

Before proceeding to elaborate how on-the-ground deliberations over the content of SAGA provide examples of a 'coalition of engagement' and 'deep listening' it is necessary to substantiate the claim that both gender mainstreaming and diversity initiatives are fields of contestation. This is accomplished in the following two sections, followed by a third section in which we problematise prevailing critiques of identity politics, with particular attention to implications for inclusive, democratic practices.

Gender mainstreaming and gender analysis: A field of contestation

Gender mainstreaming is the most recent approach to equality policy for women. It has its genesis in development policy and can be seen as a reaction to the tendency to quarantine so-called 'women's issues' from mainstream policy. The shift from WID (Women in Development) to GAD (Gender and Development) was meant to highlight the need to cease creating 'women' as the problem, as the ones 'done to' (Chant and Gutmann 2000). There are links here to developments in feminist theory around the concept 'gender'. As described above the turn to 'gender' was meant to direct attention away from understandings of 'men' and 'women' as fixed categories to the relationships among women and men, broadening the reform agenda (see Eveline and Bacchi 2005).

As an equality policy gender mainstreaming is meant to complement rather than to replace existing approaches to gender equality. In the UK for example the 'gender perspective' sits alongside 'equal treatment approaches' and 'positive action or the women's perspective'. Gender equality is described as a '"three-legged stool" with each approach representing a support' (Mackay and Bilton 2003: 4).

At the same time a number of authors (True and Mintrom 2001) stress the innovative aspects of mainstreaming as an intervention. Rees (1998), for example, describes equal opportunity as 'tinkering', positive action as 'tailoring', and gender mainstreaming as 'transformative'. The argument here is that equality approaches such as equal opportunity and positive action aim to fit women to existing institutional arrangements while gender mainstreaming challenges those institutions because it insists that *all* policies are scrutinised to ensure that they are gender-sensitive and gender-inclusive. To quote Rees (1998: 27), mainstreaming moves beyond earlier equality initiatives by seeking 'to transform organisations and create a culture of diversity in which people of a much broader range of characteristics and backgrounds may contribute and flourish'.

Experiences with mainstreaming have been mixed, however, leading to considerable debate about whether it is a reform worth pursuing. In some places the introduction of mainstreaming has meant the curtailment of funding for dedicated (that is, specific) women's policy units. In other places it has meant an attack on women-specific interventions, including positive/affirmative action. There are some concerns then that the reform actually detracts attention from a range of issues considered central to women's equality. As a recent example, in Canada, one of the world leaders in introducing gender-based analysis, there has been a decision to excise the term 'equality' from the mandate of Status of Women Canada, the federal department dedicated to women's equality issues, in order 'to achieve equality in every government department' (*Feminist Daily News Wire* 2006). This disturbing development confirms, in our view, the position we develop elsewhere (Bacchi and Eveline 2003; see also Walby 2005: 321), that mainstreaming is a contested concept.

The specific politics surrounding the concept 'mainstreaming' in Australia have produced serious concerns about the implications of declaring support for gender mainstreaming. Under the previous Howard-led coalition government, mainstreaming was introduced into Aboriginal and Torres Strait Islander affairs to justify disbanding the democratically elected representative body ATSIC (Aboriginal and Torres Strait Islander Commission) (Pratt and Bennett 2004-05). For this reason those associated with our research project decided to refer to gender *analysis* rather than to gender *mainstreaming*.

This may appear to be a difficult move to make since, as mentioned earlier, gender analysis is commonly described as one of the major tools in a mainstreaming approach. The decision to stop using the language of mainstreaming is a political one. Moreover, we are not alone in this decision. In the UK it seems that 'In some cases there is reluctance to label integrated gender-based analysis as "mainstreaming" because of experiences of mainstreaming being used as an excuse to disband specialist structures' (Mackay and Bilton 2003: 3).

In Europe and elsewhere one of the major issues in current gender mainstreaming developments is the relationship of gender mainstreaming with other 'complex inequalities' (Walby 2005: 331). The imperative driving this concern is the expressed desire to address gender issues alongside a range of other inequalities, including 'race'/ethnicity, disability, and class, with occasional mention of gay/lesbian issues. This imperative is reflected in current proposals to replace gender mainstreaming with a diversity framework, as outlined in the following section.

Diversity management and diversity mainstreaming: Fields of contestation

There is a growing tendency in European national organisations and in important international organisations like the United Nations and the World Bank to embrace the language of diversity to describe equality initiatives. The term has become shorthand for describing the full list of groups commonly identified as excluded from the mainstream, including women, Blacks, the disabled and gays/lesbians. EU directives 'require member states to promote equality in relation to sexual orientation, age, and religion, in addition to race, gender, and disability' (Squires 2005: 367). A five-year, EU-wide campaign, entitled 'For Diversity – Against Discrimination', aims to 'promote the positive benefits of diversity for business and for society as a whole' (EC Green Paper 2004: 13 in Squires 2005: 377). In the United Kingdom, meanwhile, although the language used is '*equality* mainstreaming' rather than '*diversity* mainstreaming', the intent is similar to the EC documents just mentioned – to capture in a *Single Equality Act* all the groups commonly identified as 'disadvantaged' (Department of Trade and Industry 2004).

Some leading theorists in the gender mainstreaming field are concerned by the current trend to link together a long list of inequalities in single policy instruments. According to Mieke Verloo (2006: 211) 'there are tendencies at EU level to assume an unquestioned similarity of inequalities, to fail to address the structural level and to fuel the political competition between inequalities'. In her view the establishment of single equality bodies to deal 'with all the grounds of discrimination' seems 'too fast and overlook[s] political intersectionality'.[4] Commenting on the lessons learned from experience in the UK, Mackay and Bilton (2003: 9) warn that 'Dilution and blandness are the very real potential dangers of a generic approach.' The Canadian theorist, Katherine Teghtsoonian (1999), recommends that separate instruments be developed and elaborated for other groups, including Aboriginal women and lesbians, before there are attempts to blend the analyses.

In the United States, where diversity management appears to have had its genesis, there is considerable disagreement about how the approach should be understood, leading Bacchi (1999a) to describe 'diversity' as a contested concept. There are (at least) two quite different political agendas associated with the term 'diversity': an individual differences approach and a social justice approach. In the former there is an emphasis on the multitude of characteristics that mark each person as unique, supporting an individualistic approach to business practices and government policy. In this case diversity becomes a key term in human resource management. In the latter, social justice approach, there is an attempt to incorporate sensitivity to the experiences of diverse groups of underrepresented people. Equity groups are commonly targeted.

This background makes it easier to understand the qualms expressed by many feminist activists and theorists about diversity approaches to equality. Ahmed usefully summarises some of these concerns: that some models of cultural diversity tend to reify difference as 'something that exists "in" the bodies or culture of others', and that 'a managerial focus on diversity works to individuate difference and to conceal the continuation of systemic inequalities' (Ahmed 2007a: 235-236).

As with gender mainstreaming, therefore, it appears to be impossible to predict whether or not diversity mainstreaming will produce the kinds of change its proponents envisage. What then are the arguments that have led Hankivsky (2005) and Squires (2005) to make such a move?[5] The point of pursuing this question is not to suggest that it would be preferable to retain *gender* mainstreaming, which has itself been identified as contested, but to draw attention to the ways in which diversity proponents conceptualise group dynamics. Specifically, among those who endorse diversity mainstreaming, an underlying motivation is to question the democratic potential of identity group recognition. Our proposal, developed later in the paper, to respect the views of marginalised women on the possible need to make appeals based on identity, challenges this position.

Diversity, democracy and identity

To an extent, the turn to diversity mainstreaming is a response to the concerns of some feminist theorists that the concept gender is invariably tied to a male-female binary and hence is limited in its ability to reflect differences among women. From the 1970s Black feminists have drawn attention to the tendency in feminist theory to treat all women as white women (Spellman 1988). Butler (1990) meanwhile argued that those who used the concept of gender not only universalised 'women' but also essentialised 'sex'. Accepting this argument Toril Moi (1999) recommends that feminist and other queer theorists abandon the concept of gender in favour of an account of the 'lived body'.

This background helps to explain Hankivsky's claim (2005: 996) that 'there is a clear disjuncture between GM [gender mainstreaming] and contemporary feminist theory'. The argument here is that feminist theory has problematised the category 'gender' to a point beyond which it is no longer useful. Hence, in Hankivsky's (2005: 978; emphasis in original) view, 'GM is inherently limited and limiting because it prioritises gender as *the* axis of discrimination'. Hankivsky is particularly concerned to find a notion that is 'able to consistently and systematically reflect a deeper understanding of intersectionalities - the combination of various oppressions that together produce something unique and distinct from any one form of discrimination standing alone'. She believes the term 'diversity' best achieves this goal.[6]

As we saw above, given the competing political agendas associated with diversity, more information is needed about just what a diversity mainstreaming approach involves. In particular, it is important to clarify how equality is theorised. Hankivsky (and the EC documents quoted earlier) endorses an anti-discrimination model of political change, paying little heed to the many critiques of such a model among equality theorists. Duclos (1993: 26), for example, identifies the way in which the concept of discrimination 'conceives of difference as an inherent characteristic of the non-dominant group rather than a feature arising out of the relationship between groups'. Because of this, as Crenshaw (1989: 151; emphasis in original) states, 'the *privileging* of whiteness or maleness is implicit'. The tendency to examine continuously those inhabiting categories of 'disadvantage' has important political effects. The focus is kept firmly on those currently excluded from institutional power, creating those groups as the 'problem' (see Bacchi 1999b). Little to no attention is directed to those who maintain institutional power and the processes that allow this to continue (see Eveline 1994).

Squires (2005, 2007) directly addresses the need to create a more democratic politics around equality and mainstreaming policies. She delineates the distinction between expert-bureaucratic and participative-bureaucratic models of mainstreaming, with the first in the hands of technocratic experts and the latter favouring forms of consultation with equity groups. While wishing to challenge the technocratic model, she does not believe that the consultative form of mainstreaming adequately taps the views of diverse groups of citizens. Her primary concern here is the 'reductive logic of group identity' (Squires 2007: 138).

According to Squires (2005: 368) 'there are three analytically distinct ways of conceptualising mainstreaming, informed by three distinct theoretical frameworks', which she defines elsewhere (Squires 1999) as inclusion, reversal and displacement.[7] Inclusion focuses on equal opportunities; reversal stresses the importance of women's perspectives gained through 'consultation with women's organizations'; and displacement conceives of mainstreaming in terms of 'complex equality (which recognises diversity)', achievable 'via inclusive deliberation'. Each conception of mainstreaming, she suggests, has its weaknesses: inclusion 'is constrained by its individualism and its elitism', reversal 'is constrained by its essentialism and fragmentation', while displacement requires greater specificity, 'practical and conceptual' (Squires 2005: 375). For Squires deliberative democracy proponents answer this last need with their focus on 'deliberative mechanisms, such as citizens' forums' (Squires 2005: 384).

The portrayal of displacement as the transformative version of mainstreaming hinges upon a critique of identity group politics. Squires (2005: 384; emphasis added) argues that, in a reversal conceptualisation (based on women's perspectives), 'mainstreaming becomes delimited by an *identity politics* approach that pursues equality via the recognition of authentic voices, often at the expense of redistributive concerns'. Here Squires appears to accept Nancy Fraser's (1998) distinction between recognition and redistribution reform strategies, and to share Fraser's anxiety about the former:

> To conceive of diversity mainstreaming from a group rights perspective
> is to focus attention on cultural identity and to embrace a potentially
> essentialist affirmative politics of authenticity. (Squires 2005: 379)

While such an approach might, she admits, 'create new political opportunity structures that would empower the spokespersons of particular groups', 'its weakness would be that it reduces the incentive for people to speak across groups and thereby makes the pursuit of genuine diversity more difficult'. In her view, 'widespread consultation with a whole range of (frequently competing and conflicting) identity groups' inevitably produces perceived 'hierarchies of oppression' and fragmentation. As a way forward she (2005: 384) endorses a 'non-Habermasian dialogic ethics' based on 'dialogue with diverse social groups' and facilitated by such institutional reforms as mediation, citizens' forums, and citizen initiative and referendum (Squires 2005: 381-383).

The proposal here is for a form of 'transversal politics', an idea that originated with Italian feminists and that has been developed by both Yuval-Davis (1997) and Cockburn (1998). The model of feminist politics endorsed is one which takes account of 'forms of difference among women, without falling into the trap of identity politics' (Yuval-Davis 1997: 4). The aim is to challenge conceptions of groups constructed as homogeneous and with fixed boundaries and to encourage dialogue 'determined by common political emancipatory goals' (Yuval-Davis 2006: 206).

> In 'transversal politics', perceived unity and homogeneity are replaced by
> dialogues which give recognition to the specific positionings in them as
> well as to the 'unfinished knowledge' that each such situated positioning
> can offer ... The boundaries of a transversal dialogue are determined by
> the message rather than the messenger. (Yuval-Davis 1997: 130-131)

Significantly, Cockburn (1998: 10) states that she does not assume that 'identity processes are the source of all evil'. Rather she recommends theorising identity as 'social and relational, complex, always in process, taking shape in discourse' (Cockburn 1998: 11).

Despite their differences Hankivsky and Squires share a conviction that diversity mainstreaming is preferable to gender mainstreaming because it moves beyond identity categories and identity groups to embrace a wider conception of people's complex identities. They are in good company here. Identity politics has been 'on the nose' for some time in contemporary social and political theory (Butler 1990; Mouffe 1992). Few (see Bickford 1997) seem to have a kind word to say about it. According to Phoenix and Pattynama (2006: 187), all 'intersectionality' approaches 'critique identity politics for its additive, politically fragmentary and essentialising tendencies' (see Yuval-Davis 2006: 195).

However, there are contesting views that ought to be acknowledged. The place of groups in democratic practice continues to be hotly debated (see Flax 2005). bell hooks (1989: 109) insists that 'for many exploited and oppressed peoples the struggle to create an identity, to name one's reality is an act of resistance.' Crenshaw argues that 'to say that a category such as race or gender is socially constructed is not to say that the category has no significance in the world.' Rather she emphasises the importance of recognising 'the way power has clustered around certain categories and is exercised against others' (Crenshaw 1991: 1296-1297).

Martha Minow's (1990) work on relational theory supports these arguments. Minow challenges the location of something called 'difference' in a group or individual. That is, someone is 'different' only in relation to someone else. Someone either labels you as 'different', or you claim to be 'different'. The characteristics that become 'difference' emerge from the relationship. This insight shifts attention from those deemed to *be* 'different' to the *dynamics of the processes* of attributing or claiming 'difference/s'. Attributing 'difference' is almost invariably a process of 'othering' (Schwalbe 2000: 777); claiming 'difference' is often a form of resistance (see Bacchi 2001).

Crenshaw recognises both sides of 'differencing' practices ('race'-ing and gendering, for example). On the one side, since such practices often mark outgroups as 'other', the project becomes attempting 'to unveil the processes of subordination and the various ways those processes are experienced by people who are subordinated and people who are privileged by them' (Crenshaw 1991: 1297). On the other side Crenshaw notes that 'categorization is not a one-way street' and that 'identity continues to be a site of resistance for members of different subordinated groups' (Crenshaw 1991: 1297). In this understanding claims to identity are political rather than essentialist in character (see Bacchi 1996: xii). You simply have to recognise that politically there are times when it is more useful and appropriate to challenge constructed identities and that at other times it is necessary to challenge the practices of racialised oppression, which will involve working through and with the category 'race' and with other categories: 'Recognizing that identity politics takes place at the site where categories intersect thus seems more fruitful than challenging the possibility of talking about categories at all' (Crenshaw 1991: 1299). Members of marginalised groups, those who live the effects of 'differencing' practices, are ideally placed to know which strategy is appropriate politically in which situation. Hence, their views on this issue ought to be respected.[8]

On this topic mainstreaming theorists disagree about who to include as primary contributors to the development of the reform. Above we saw that Hankivsky and Squires both wish to bypass or 'displace' identity groups. By contrast Verloo (2005: 351) wants mainstreaming proposals to 'give voice to the feminist movement' and 'to those suffering from gender inequality'. According to Verloo (2005: 346) and using Squires' typology, displacement is not the only way to produce meaningful change: 'the strategy of reversal also implies a need for fundamental change', and hence can be described as potentially transformative. The emphasis, according to Verloo, needs to be placed, therefore, on creating the opportunities for 'women's voices' to steer the transformation: 'To be transformative, gender mainstreaming should then be not only a strategy of displacement but also a strategy of empowerment by organizing space for non-hegemonic actors to struggle about the (promotion of the) agenda of gender equality' (Verloo 2005: 348).

The key issue that surfaces in this debate is disagreement about which groups to consult or involve in developing mainstreaming (and by implication other) policy – should they be identity groups or some more amorphous collection of citizens? It is here that our experience in the Gender Analysis Project sheds some light and reopens some of these discussions in new ways.

Gender analysis in South Australia: The politics of 'doing'

Earlier we noted our suggestion that treating gender as a verb rather than as a noun has some useful effects. Specifically it challenges the fixity of categories and draws attention to the contingent and located practices that produce gender inequality. The idea of gender as an effortful and political process is not new (West and Zimmerman 2003). However, the focus on the politics of 'doing' expands this insight and adds to it. Basically the argument is that in each case (be it gender mainstreaming, diversity mainstreaming, or anything else you choose to call it) it is crucial to pay heed to how the policy is created and enacted, the practices that give it life. How you decide to 'do the document' matters.

In South Australia, as we have already seen, the question of gender proved central to deliberations about SAGA. Aboriginal and Torres Strait Islander spokeswomen expressed concerns that references to gender made it difficult to recognise the oppression of racialisation. Their views were elaborated in written comments on a working draft of the guide and at meetings organised specifically to listen to their qualms and recommendations. As mentioned at the outset, as a result of these deliberations, the notion of 'race and cultural analysis' is introduced as 'informing' gender analysis. In race and cultural analysis, the guide explains, the whole discussion of equality and equity needs to be rethought through the specific perspective of Aboriginal peoples:

> It is important to also acknowledge that Aboriginal women's concerns regarding 'equity' are most often driven not by the desire for equality with men [and in this context 'white men'], but by community based issues and fundamental human rights that include land and cultural rights, and the right to health, education and employment status equal to other Australians. ... In a cultural context 'gender' based initiatives are not just about increasing the status of Aboriginal women, but the whole community. (Government of South Australia 2008: 6)

In addition, the guide emphasises the diverse and pluralistic character of Aboriginal cultures:

> It is essential to recognize the complexity of identity and the diversity of all Aboriginal and Torres Strait Islander people including their relationship to land/country, colonial histories, rural/remote/urban experiences, cultural knowledge, life experiences, kinship, clan and language-groups. (Government of South Australia 2008: 6)

We have here a complex understanding of identity sitting alongside a culturally-informed political stance that puts in question white supremacy.[9] Importantly for this paper, this contribution is contained in a guide that introduces *gender* analysis and not *diversity* analysis.

We see the SAGA guide as an example of Crenshaw's (1991: 1299) model of coalition that focuses on the cooperation of those who choose to align politically around a particular commitment, which we call a coalition of engagement. The emphasis in a coalition model such as this one is on the intellectual, political and emotional work involved in coalition (Burack 2004: 159). That is, one cannot assume that people will align around a particular position because they are born a 'woman' or a member of a particular 'racial'/ethnic grouping, for example. Rather political positions have to be developed and defended in coalition. On one issue I may claim to be a woman; on another I will claim to be 'different' in some other way, depending upon the politics of the situation. As developed in Foucault (1982) and Butler (1989), 'political collectivities and movements rest not on extra-political justifications and foundations, but on action and practice' (Simons 1995: 110).

There are definite links here with the notion of 'transversal politics', discussed earlier. Yuval-Davis states clearly that, in transversal politics:

> The boundaries of the dialogue should be determined by common political
> emancipatory goals while the tactical and strategic priorities should be led
> by those whose needs are judged by the participants of the dialogue to be
> the most urgent. (Yuval-Davis 2006: 206; emphasis added.)

However, while Yuval-Davis wants to acknowledge the 'differential positionings and perspectives of the participants in a dialogue' *without* 'treating them as representatives of any fixed social grouping' (Yuval-Davis 2006: 205), we argue that 'those whose needs are judged by the participants of the dialogue to be the most urgent' need *to become the leaders in deciding strategically when identity categories matter*. As hooks (in Grünell and Saharso 1999: 214) explains, 'you cannot simply dismiss an identity politics because at a concrete level of struggle in everyday life people fall back on it again and again'.

Illustrative of these premises SAGA took a specific shape, one more or less recommended by the Aboriginal and Torres Strait Islander women involved in its development. If they had decided that the policy should have been called 'diversity analysis', this proposal should have been accepted. Instead of proposing the diversity option they chose to mediate the analytical force of gender by introducing race and cultural analysis.

With this understanding of coalition as work among those sharing a political goal the focus shifts to the obligation to create conditions that allow this work to be done in a meaningful and effective fashion. Squires' conviction that a deliberative model is preferable to forms of consultation/engagement with identity groups rests on her premise that institutional reforms such as mediation, citizens' forums, and citizen initiative and referenda 'would be sensitive to diverse citizen perspectives without reifying group identities' (Squires 2005: 383). Here she neglects the prospect, supported in the literature (Hill 2003: 9), that such reforms are susceptible to capture by the wealthy and the powerful.

A more promising way forward, we suggest, is the concept of 'deep listening' developed among transcultural mental health practitioners (Gabb and McDermott 2007; see also Bickford 1996). We are not talking here about consultation in any conventional sense. Deep listening is a way of engaging with people. By listening ('tuning in with the whole being') you are showing respect by what you are doing. Deep listening entails 'an obligation to contemplate, in real time, everything that you hear – to self-reflect as you listen, and then, tellingly, to *act* on what you've registered' (Gabb and McDermott 2007: 5; emphasis in original).

This perspective informs questions of method. In another article we (Eveline et al. 2009) suggest that Dorothy Smith's (2005) institutional ethnography offers a promising methodology for gender analysis since it starts with a person's location and allows them to take the lead in exploring the meaning of texts in their lives. The broader point is to create methods that facilitate exchange and indeed change in views.

We are not meaning here to reopen the old debate about quantitative versus qualitative research methods. Indeed it became clear in the gender analysis project that all sorts of data were needed and could be useful. The point here is that data do not describe reality; they create it. Hence the focus shifts from the 'facts' produced to the questions asked and who gets to ask them (Bacchi 2009). We return therefore to the need to 'listen deeply' to the kinds of questions women from a wide array of backgrounds want to ask. Since 'truth' is a political phenomenon, the key issue becomes the conditions and procedures, the 'doings', that generate 'truths', including 'truths' about methodology.

Conclusion

To be clear, there is no suggestion that what occurred in South Australia – introducing 'race and cultural analysis' within guidelines called *gender* analysis – is a model or blue-print for developments elsewhere. Indeed, the idea of a blue-print would go against the theoretical perspective outlined in this paper: the need to respond to on-the-ground political developments with arrangements that are worked out in coalitions of engagement. That is, different coalitions elsewhere might very well come up with different models.

To those who are concerned at our lack of attention to questions of implementation and the many obstacles that may mean that the impact of the SAGA guide is minimised, we wish to make the case that a good deal has already been accomplished politically in the production of the guide. In our view the coalition of engagement established between the research team and Aboriginal spokeswomen, the exchange of views and the growth in understanding that accompanied this exchange count as political success stories. However, this success cannot be considered some static and finished outcome. Rather 'coalitions of engagement' and 'deep listening' need to be practised over and over again, to become part of 'normal' policymaking.

In this understanding 'outcomes' become less important than processes, the actual 'doings' involved in producing a policy. More fundamentally, this perspective puts in question a distinction between process and outcomes. Recalling the earlier discussion about the many unpredictable and uncontrollable ways in which both gender mainstreaming and diversity initiatives can be deployed, we argue that the best protection against political capture, for example by a tick-a-box system of paper trails, is precisely this politics of 'doing' and the social change it generates.

This perspective gives rise to some guiding principles for political practice around mainstreaming and a range of other feminist projects. These include: a caution against blanket generalisations about how to label mainstreaming, that is, as either gender mainstreaming or diversity mainstreaming; a willingness to hold categories in abeyance until the views of those whose needs are most urgent are heard; creating the conditions for deep listening with participants from a wide variety of backgrounds; ensuring that those whose needs are judged to be most urgent get the opportunity to shape the policy in ways that they see as politically useful; respecting how these groups choose to represent their identity. These principles constitute a contribution to the theory of transversal politics. The goal of creating democratic spaces inclusive

329

of 'those whose needs are judged by the participants of the dialogue to be the most urgent' (Yuval-Davis 2006: 206) means respecting their possible decision to use and defend appeals based on group identity.

Acknowledgements

We wish to thank the members of participating agencies for their time and assistance with this project. We also wish to acknowledge the Australian Research Council, which funded the project.

Notes

1. While Ahmed (2007b: 592-593) directs attention to the importance of the procedures put in place to write up equity or diversity documents, her primary concern is how these documents are or are not taken up. By contrast we highlight the former, arguing that change is most likely to take place in the discussions and negotiations leading to policy initiatives such as the ones we are studying.

2. Further details on the project can be found in Bacchi et al. 2005.

3. The term 'draft' has been problematised because the South Australian Gender Analysis Guide is designed to incorporate an iterative process based on continuous feedback and amendment. In a sense, therefore, the Guide will always be in 'draft' form.

4. Political intersectionality, a concept borrowed from Crenshaw (1991), refers to the need to address 'sexism, racism, class exploitation or homophobia in policy-making processes and policies' (Verloo 2006: 222).

5. It should be noted that Squires (2005: 378-379), a proponent of diversity mainstreaming, is well aware of the unintended directions in which diversity proposals can be taken. Given its 'roots in corporate human resources management', she advises those keen to 'find a possible synergy between diversity management and gender mainstreaming' to 'proceed with caution'.

6. The possible usefulness (Davis 2008) or limitations of (Puar 2007) the language of intersectionality to describe differences among women is not addressed in this paper. For a discussion of intersectionality with regard to this research project see Eveline et al. (2009)

7. Squires identifies distinctions in approach within mainstreaming, distinctions that parallel Rees' (1998) analytic categories of 'tinkering', 'tailoring' and 'transformative'. Clearly, for Squires, not all mainstreaming is transformative.

8. Burack's (2004) exploration of the reparative dimension of Black feminist thought supports this conclusion.

9. bell hooks' idea of 'white supremacy' is described in Grünell and Saharso (1999: 214). bell hooks specifically requests that her name not be spelt with capitals.

References

(Websites valid at time of publication)

Ahmed, S. 2007a. 'The language of diversity', *Ethnic and Racial Studies* 30 (2): 235-256.

Ahmed, S. 2007b. '"You end up doing the document rather than doing the doing": Diversity, race equality and the politics of documentation', *Ethnic and Racial Studies* 30 (4): 590-609.

Bacchi, C. 1996. *The politics of affirmative action: 'Women', equality and category politics*. London: Sage.

Bacchi, C. 1999a. 'Managing diversity: A contested concept', *International Review of Women and Leadership* 5 (2): 1-8.

Bacchi, C. 1999b. *Women, policy and politics: The construction of policy problems*. London: Sage.

Bacchi, C. 2001. 'Dealing with "difference": Beyond "multiple subjectivities"', in Nursey-Bray, P. and Bacchi, C. (eds) *Left directions: Is there a third way?* Perth: University of Western Australia Press.

Bacchi, C. 2009. *Analysing policy: What's the problem represented to be?* Frenchs Forest, NSW: Pearson Education.

Bacchi, C. and Eveline, J. 2003. 'Mainstreaming and neoliberalism: A contested relationship', *Policy and Society: Journal of Public, Foreign and Global Policy* 22 (2): 98-118.

Bacchi, C., Eveline, J., Binns, J., Mackenzie, C. and Harwood, S. 2005. 'Gender analysis and social change: Testing the water', *Policy & Society: Journal of Public, Foreign and Global Policy* 24 (4): 45-68.

Bickford, S. 1996. *The dissonance of democracy: Listening, conflict and citizenship*. New York: Cornell University Press.

Bickford, S. 1997. 'Anti-anti-identity politics: Feminism, democracy and the complexities of citizenship', *Hypatia* 12 (4): 111-131.

Burack, C. 2004. *Healing identities: Black feminist thought and the politics of groups*. Ithaca: Cornell University Press.

Butler, J. 1989. 'Foucault and the paradox of bodily inscriptions', *Journal of Philosophy* 86 (11): 601-607.

Butler, J. 1990. *Gender trouble*. New York: Routledge.

Chant, S. and Gutmann, M. 2000. *Mainstreaming men into gender and development: Debates, reflections, and experiences*. Oxford: Oxfam.

Cockburn, C. 1998. *The space between us: Negotiating gender and national identities in conflict*. London: Zed Books.

Crenshaw, K. 1989. 'Demarginalizing the intersection of race and sex: A Black feminist critique of antidiscrimination doctrine, feminist theory and antiracist politics', *University of Chicago Legal Forum* 139: 140-167.

Crenshaw, K. 1991. 'Mapping the margins: Intersectionality, identity politics, and violence against women of color', *Stanford Law Review* 43 (6): 1241-1299.

Davis, K. 2008. 'Intersectionality as buzzword: A sociology of science perspective on what makes a feminist theory successful', *Feminist Theory* 9 (1): 67-85.

Department of Trade and Industry. 2004. *Fairness for all: A new commission for equality and human rights*. HMSO: Norwich. <equalrightstrust.org/ertdocumentbank/Fairness%20for%20all.pdf> accessed 8 November 2009.

Duclos, N. 1993. 'Disappearing women: Racial minority women in human rights cases', *Canadian Journal of Women and the Law* 6 (1): 25-51.

EC (European Commission). 2004. *Equality and non-discrimination in an enlarged European Union: Green paper*. Luxembourg: Office for Official Publications of the European Communities. <ec.europa.eu/social/search.jsp?langId=en&menuType=basic> accessed 29 October 2009.

Elliott, V. 2005. 'Internal memorandum: Indigenous participation in local government elections'. Department of Local Government and Regional Development, Western Australia. Unpublished.

Eveline, J. 1994. 'The politics of advantage', *Australian Feminist Studies*. Special issue: *Women and Citizenship* 19: 129-154.

Eveline, J. and Bacchi, C. 2005. 'What are we mainstreaming when we mainstream gender?' *International Feminist Journal of Politics* 7 (4): 496-512.

Eveline, J., Bacchi, C. and Binns, J. 2009. 'Gender mainstreaming versus diversity mainstreaming: Methodology as emancipatory politics', *Gender, Work and Organization* 16 (2): 198-216.

Feminist Daily News Wire. 2006. 'Canadian women's minister says her office hinders equality', December 14. <msmagazine.com/news/uswirestory.asp?id=10059> accessed 8 November 2009.

Flax, J. 2005. 'Review: Healing identities: Black feminist thought and the politics of groups by Cynthia Burack', *Perspectives on Policy* 3 (1): 150-151.

Foucault, M. 1982. 'The subject and power', in Dreyfus, H.L. and Rabinow, P. (eds) *Michel Foucault: Beyond structuralism and hermeneutics*. Brighton: Harvester Press.

Fraser, N. 1998. 'From redistribution to recognition? Dilemmas of justice in a "postsocialist" age', in Fraser, N. (ed.) *Justice interruptus: Critical reflections on the 'post-socialist' condition*. New York: Routledge.

Gabb, D. and McDermott, D. 2007. 'What do Indigenous experiences and perspectives mean for transcultural mental health? Towards a new model of transcultural teaching for health professionals'. Conference paper, *Psychology & Indigenous Australians: Teaching practice & theory*, Adelaide, South Australia.

Government of South Australia. 2008. 'South Australian gender analysis'. Unpublished.

Grünell, M. and Saharso, S. 1999. 'bell hooks and Nira Yuval-Davis on race, ethnicity, class and gender', *The European Journal of Women's Studies* 6 (2): 203-218.

Gunnarsson, E., Andersson, S., Rosell, A. and Salminen-Karlsson, M. (eds) 2003. *Where have all the structures gone? Doing gender in organisations*. Stockholm: Centre for Women's Studies, Stockholm University.

Hankivsky, O. 2005. 'Gender vs. diversity mainstreaming: A preliminary examination of the role and transformative potential of feminist theory', *Canadian Journal of Political Science* 38 (4): 977-1001.

Hill, L. 2003. 'Democratic deficit in the ACT: Is the citizen initiated referendum a solution?' *Australian Journal of Social Issues* 38 (4): 13-19.

Hill Collins, P. 1999. 'Moving beyond gender: Intersectionality and scientific knowledge', in Ferree, M.M., Lorber, J. and Hess, B.B. (eds) *Revisioning gender*. London: Sage.

hooks, b. 1989. *Talking back: Thinking feminist, thinking black*. Boston: South End Press.

Mackay, F. and Bilton, K. 2003. 'Learning from experience: Lessons in mainstreaming equal opportunities', Edinburgh: Scottish Executive Social Research. <scotland.gov.uk/Publications/2003/05/17105/21750> accessed 29 October 2009.

Minow, M. 1990. *Making all the difference: Inclusion, exclusion and American law*. Ithaca: Cornell University Press.

Moi, T. 1999. 'What is a woman?: Appropriating Bourdieu: Feminist theory and Pierre Bourdieu's sociology of culture', in Moi, T. (ed.) *What is a woman and other essays*. New York: Oxford University Press.

Mouffe, C. 1992 'Democratic citizenship and the political community', in Mouffe, C. (ed.) *Dimensions of radical democracy*. London: Verso.

Phoenix, A. and Pattynama, P. 2006. 'Editorial: Intersectionality', *European Journal of Women's Studies. Special Issue: Intersectionality* 13 (3): 187-192.

Pratt, A. and Bennett, S. 2004-2005. 'The end of ATSIC and the future administration of Indigenous affairs', *Current Issues Brief* 4. <aph.gov.au/library/pubs/CIB/2004-05/05cib04.htm> accessed 8 November 2009.

Puar, J.K. 2007. *Terrorist assemblages: Homonationalism in queer times*. Durham: Duke University Press.

Rees, T. 1998. *Mainstreaming equality in the European Union: Education, training and labour market policies*. London: Routledge.

Schwalbe, M. 2000. 'Charting futures for sociology: Inequality mechanisms, intersections, and global change: The elements of inequality', *Contemporary Sociology* 29 (6): 775-781.

Simons, J. 1995. *Foucault & the political*. New York: Routledge.

Smith, D. 2005. *Institutional ethnography: A sociology for people*. New York, London, Oxford: AltaMira Press.

Spelman, E. 1988. *Inessential woman: Problems of exclusion in feminist thought*. Boston: Beacon Press.

Squires, J. 1999. *Gender in political theory*. Cambridge: Polity Press.

Squires, J. 2005. 'Is mainstreaming transformative? Theorizing mainstreaming in the context of diversity and deliberation', *Social Politics: International Studies in Gender, State and Society* 12 (3): 366-388.

Squires, J. 2007. *The new politics of gender equality*. London: Palgrave Macmillan.

Teghtsoonian, K. 1999. 'Centring women's diverse interests in health policy and practice: A comparative discussion of gender analysis'. Paper prepared for *Made to measure: Accessing approaches to eliminate gender inequity*, hosted by the Maritime Centre of Excellence for Women's Health, Halifax, Nova Scotia. <acewh.dal.ca/eng/reports/teghtsoonian.pdf> accessed 8 November 2009.

True, J. and Mintrom, M. 2001. 'Transnational networks and policy diffusion: The politics of implementation', *International Studies Quarterly* 45: 27-57.

Verloo, M. 2005. 'Displacement and empowerment: reflections on the concept and practice of the Council of Europe: Approach to gender mainstreaming and gender equality', *Social Politics: International Studies in Gender, State and Society* 12 (3): 344-365.

Verloo, M. 2006. 'Multiple inequalities, intersectionality and the European Union', *The European Journal of Women's Studies* 13 (3): 211-228.

Walby, S. 2005. 'Gender mainstreaming: Productive tensions in theory and practice', *Social Politics* 21 (3): 321-343.

West, C. and Zimmerman, D. 2003. 'Doing gender', in Ely, R., Foldy, E., and Scully, M. (eds) *Reader in gender, work and organization*. Malden, MA: Blackwell Publishing.

Yuval-Davis, N. 1997. *Gender & nation*. London: Sage.

Yuval-Davis, N. 2006. 'Intersectionality and feminist politics', *European Journal of Women's Studies*. Special issue: *Intersectionality*. Phoenix, A. and Pattynama, P. (eds) 13 (3): 193-209.

Conclusion
A politics of movement

CAROL BACCHI AND JOAN EVELINE

This collection of essays establishes the claim that it is unwise to think about 'gender mainstreaming' or 'gender analysis' as sets of procedures that necessarily make useful changes when they are put into place as policies. Rather we direct attention to the on-the-ground political deliberations (at every level of social interaction) that affect what gets done and who gets to do it. It is the 'doings', the practices, that generate long-term learning and commitment, and that create the possibility that gender analysis can have some impact over time on the asymmetrical power relations between women and men (Chapters 7, 10 and 13).

The implications for policy development are significant. One overriding message is the need to create the time and space for public servants both to reflect upon the nature of 'gender analysis' and to participate actively in applying it. As Chapter 12 makes explicit, in the GAP project those who were personally engaged in the work of gender analysis were the ones most likely to come to see its relevance. As also noted in that chapter, those policy workers tended, in the main, to be women with lesser institutional authority. It follows, as argued there, that, if gender analysis is to become a meaningful and useful equality initiative, all policymakers, *especially* those in positions of institutional authority, need to 'do' gender analysis.

As part of this 'doing', there is need for reflection on the concepts and categories produced as part of the gender analysis exercise, for example, 'gender', 'equality', 'difference'. Developing policies that redress inequitable gender relations requires extended discussion and debate about the nature of the 'problem' of gender inequality, and in particular about how particular policy interventions 'create' it, or

335

represent it, as one sort of 'problem' rather than as some other sort. For example, the book spells out important political distinctions between a 'differences' approach, which can create the 'problem' of gender inequality as women's need to become more like men, and a 'gender relations' approach, which focuses on the asymmetrical power relations between women and men (Chapters 1 and 5).

We develop an alternative approach that treats policies as gender*ing* practices, which constitute (form or shape) 'women' and 'men', and 'gender relations' (Eveline 2005; Chapters 3 and 4). In this perspective, the starting point for analysis is recognising the role that policies, as discursive practices, play in *generating* gendered bodies and gendered lives. For example, the World Bank's (2002) 'Case for Mainstreaming Gender' and other free market policies that place a priority on 'productivity' neglect people's care needs, ensuring that women will continue in their role as primary carers (Chapter 5). If, as this instance suggests, policies are constitutive of 'problems', of social relations and of social beings, just talking about their *impact on* men and women, as if they exist separately from these processes, seems to be a sadly inadequate exercise. On the other hand, recognising that policies, such as the World Bank's gender mainstreaming policy, are gender*ing*, we suggest, increases the political potential to identify how policies can (re)produce gender as a relation of inequality (Chapter 2). Bacchi's 'what's the problem represented to be?' (WPR) approach to policy analysis encourages recognition of this constitutive dimension of public policies (Chapters 1, 2 and 5).

Part of the purpose of the GAP project and of the book is to find ways to communicate this constitutive understanding of policy to policy workers and to other researchers. To this end we recommend talking about gender as a verb or gerund (gender*ing*), to shift attention from the idea that gender is a fixed or essential characteristic of a person, to understanding gender*ing* as an attributional process. We also suggest that, for the same reason, it may be useful to talk about the heteronorming, classing, racialising and disabling effects of policy and other (for example, legal, medical) practices.

In this understanding, 'differences' are conceptualised as attributions assigned to or claimed by people through political meaning-making practices rather than as personal characteristics (Bacchi 2001: 117). It follows that, since 'differences' are attributions, attention shifts from those deemed *to be* 'different', and from the characteristics identified *as the basis* of 'difference', to the *dynamics* of the processes of declaring or claiming difference/s. Who is doing the designating of difference? What kinds of power do they exercise? What are the effects that accompany particular kinds of 'differencing' practice? Importantly, gender*ing* is understood as an ongoing and always-incomplete process, explaining why gender analysis will need to continue indefinitely. The phrase 'unfinished business' captures this sense that there can be no 'sunset clause' on gender analysis (Chapters 4 and 6).

In terms of the methodologies associated with gender analysis, we make two observations. Experience in the working groups for GAP showed that *any* methodology, including the most common method of collecting sex- or gender-disaggregated statistics, could produce useful political reflections and insights. It was not so much the *kind* of method (quantitative or qualitative) that proved most important to understanding the need for gender analysis as the *space* and *time* to reflect on the implications of the 'information' collected. As we say in Chapter 3, it all depended on the questions asked.

The book advances several suggestions for producing probing and inventive questions. The WPR approach (Chapter 5) has this objective as its major *raison d'être*. Institutional ethnography, developed by Dorothy Smith (2000), also promises to breathe new life into gender analysis procedures. It was this methodology that allowed the authors to better grasp the full implications of *gender* analysis for Aboriginal women and men (Chapter 9). To invigorate this question-generating exercise, as the book highlights (Chapters 8, 9 and 13), genuine efforts have to be made to broaden the traditional policymaking constituency.

Several times in the book the authors raise the question of the feasibility of altering work practices in the public sector in the ways recommended here. The introduction to Chapter 4 reads: 'The question we proceed to take up is whether or not gender analysis procedures can be designed to incorporate this understanding of gendering as an unfinished, embodied effect of discourse or whether they are likely to remain trapped by "categoricalism"'. In the Introduction to the book we mention our concern that procedural checklists would most likely come to replace the time-consuming reflection involved in 'doing' gender analysis as it took place through GAP – the 'doing' that in our view changed hearts and minds. As noted in Chapter 3, the public servants with whom we worked, well aware of the importance of personal engagement in generating commitment and understanding, displayed a keen desire to create work practices to facilitate interactions of this sort – although they were not optimistic about the prospect of this happening in the current climate. At the same time, however, both researchers and policy workers recognised the learning that took place *through* GAP, suggesting that *on its own* GAP can be considered a political success story, regardless of future developments.

For example, the exchange of views and indeed change of views that resulted in the incorporation of 'race and cultural analysis' in SAGA (South Australian Gender Analysis) stands as a record of political movement in the understanding of gender analysis among participants (Chapters 11 and 13). That is, the *practice* of collaboration among university researchers, agency staff and Aboriginal senior policy spokeswomen produced shifts in perspective more attuned to the racialising effects of mainstream policies. Chapter 10 relates a similar experience in Western Australia, where the GAP research team observed how Indigenous women created an Indigenous Electoral Strategy that *practised* gender equality, while refusing the designation of *gender* analysis.

This pattern of movement through engagement and interaction appears in other sites described in the book. For example, Chapter 7 notes that those who participated in on-the-ground deliberations about pay equity policy displayed greater understanding of the myriad factors generating unequal pay for women than those located at a distance from these negotiations. Along similar lines, we see in Chapter 8 that women's policy units, with staff attuned to the perspectives of specific women's groups, are best placed to facilitate meaningful consultation with those groups. That is, they are able, through the well-designed consultation practices they set up, to generate movement in the understandings of women's needs both for their unit and, through their unit, for the policy community. Chapter 3 explores how, through a similar dynamic of close collaboration and discussion, the GAP working groups in Western Australia generated support for gender analysis, while Chapter 11 identifies the South Australian reference group, set up to oversee the Gender Analysis Project there, as another space where close interaction and rigorous debate with like-minded colleagues promoted learning and reflexivity. In each case the practices – the 'doings' – generate movement in political perspectives and encourage the production of more reflexive political subjects.

As mentioned several times already, the authors dedicated increasing attention to the issue of reflexivity as the project progressed. As poststructuralist academics sensitive to the power effects of the 'knowledges' they produce, they felt it necessary to think through with some thoroughness their place within the project. The tendency in certain geopolitical sites to identify feminist academic researchers as 'experts' in the gender analysis field made them distinctly uncomfortable. Rather, they sought a space for movement around their status and role in the project, as described in these reflections on their experiences.

At one level the authors were seen as 'experts'. And, indeed, we often found ourselves offering bits of 'knowledge' from our years of reflecting on gender-related issues, and on organisational and policy theory. At the same time we made clear that we, along with our research teams, were there to learn – about the specific challenges of working within a women's policy unit, of working to near-impossible deadlines, and of working with a wide range of 'stakeholder' groups. The issue here was *not* that researchers needed simply to become attuned to what could be accomplished in 'real-world politics'. Rather, the relation of sharing and collaboration created a space in which political movement on a range of issues, including understandings of gender, took place. For this reason we invest more hope in the transformative potential of such collaborations and of on-the-ground gender analysis practices performed by policy workers than in the model of 'flying gender experts' (academics who study 'gender') promoted in some European countries (Mazey 2002: 234).

Part of this movement or shifting of views resulted from the researchers themselves closely scrutinising their models and frameworks. As discussed in Chapters 10 and 13, interactions with Aboriginal policy workers compelled the authors and their research teams to stand back from their proposals and to examine them critically. The authors were well aware of the years of dispute among feminist theorists about the place of 'race' and other cross-cutting social factors (for example, class, 'disability', sexuality) in thinking about gender relations, a topic pursued further below. However, the face-to-face encounter between researchers and Aboriginal spokeswomen provided a different form of experience, one which promoted a kind of 'sudden seeing' (Chapter 12). As with the revelation that 'doing' gender analysis led participants to understand why it was needed, the face-to-face practice of negotiating the meaning of 'gender' and its relationship to 'race' and 'culture' heightened awareness of the racialising effects of policy practices.

The significance of this development should not be under-estimated. A follow-up project that ought to be pursued, in our view, would identify additional ways to 'trigger' this form of reflexive sensibility, which we consider conducive to egalitarian politics. To this end, Bacchi (1999: 205) highlights the importance of 'broadening the feminist constituency, either directly or through affiliation' in order 'to prevent the unthinking imposition of frames which enshrine the exploitation' of Black and poor women. Our experience in GAP confirms that on-the-ground encounters with those designated 'other' can act as a spur to reflexivity. For this reason Chapter 13 reflects on the conditions necessary to promote such encounters on a basis of reciprocity (for example, 'deep listening'). Bacchi also encourages application of her WPR methodology to policy proposals advanced by avowed feminists, to assist in the process of identifying underlying presuppositions and lacunae (silences) that may reinforce asymmetrical power relations among women (Chapter 5).

Our work with Aboriginal spokeswomen prompted reflection on the contentious issue of identity politics. As feminist researchers we have read the plethora of studies that posit 'intersectionality' as a way forward in recognising and perhaps reconciling the divergent interests of different groups of women (Collins 2000; Crenshaw 1991; Davis 2008). We, with others (Puar 2007), feel some disappointment at the unworkability of the concept, wanting to make it meaningful at more than a purely abstract level with little purchase on how people live their lives 'across' the commonly listed categories, for example, gender, 'race', and sexuality. We are also sensitive to the fact that intersectionality theorists tend to position themselves as *critics* of identity politics (Phoenix and Pattynama 2006: 187).

While we share some of the obvious concerns about embracing 'fixed' identities, we also accept that in specific political situations identity claims are necessary. The question, as we pose it in the Introduction, is not *whether* to fix meaning (since it will inevitably be fixed) but *when* to fix (or unfix) it and *who* should be involved in this process. As Chapters 10 and 13 make clear, experience in GAP and reflections on our positioning as white academic researchers led us to conclude that we were not the ones who should judge when the 'fixing' of Aboriginal identity needed (or did not need) to take place. Rather, we concluded that the Aboriginal contributors to the project were better placed politically to make this determination. In our view the political exigencies of racialising practices in Australia meant recognising Aboriginal spokeswomen as the ones who should decide if a temporary fixing of identity through a claim to 'difference' was appropriate.

To shift the discussion away from the 'problem' of 'fixed' identities, we suggest turning attention to the politics involved in the gendering, heteronorming, classing, racialising and disabling practices raised above (see also Chapter 10). For example, gender analysis frameworks that assume and hence support a two-sex model of gender relations ought to be recognised as a heteronorming practice. So, too, as was experienced in both South Australia and Western Australia, for Aboriginal women a 'gender' framework may in some circumstances be considered racialising. With a focus on the practices that 'gender', 'race', 'class', 'heteronormalise' and '(dis)able' – all to be read as verbs – coalitions committed to egalitarian politics ('coalitions of engagement'; Chapter 13) can direct their efforts to altering those practices. To this end, members of such coalitions would scrutinise their own policy proposals to identify problem representations that might well have deleterious effects for certain groups (Chapter 5).

As mentioned in the Introduction we describe the perspective developed in the book as a *politics of movement*. That is, we believe that decisions about fixing and unfixing meanings – of identities as one example, of categories of analysis as another (Chapter 13) – need to be made in specific locales at particular times by the participants in collaboration, and based on reflexive judgment. All the while these 'fixings' are recognised as temporary and political, rather than essential, in nature (Bacchi 1996: 11). They therefore require further scrutiny and reconsideration when the circumstances change, in order to generate new meanings.

This perspective requires researchers to acknowledge their political investments in research practice. Clearly this acknowledgement is currently difficult to voice, given the dominant research paradigm of 'evidence-based policy', which argues that the task of researchers is to provide governments with objective knowledge to 'address' policy problems (Bacchi 2009: 252-253). Recognising, however, that 'knowledge' is inherently political and that policy 'problems' accrue meanings that could well be otherwise creates an impetus for *research as political practice*, an impetus that motivates this book.

One final theme that invites comment and that is undeveloped in the book, although it is raised briefly in Chapter 11, is consideration of the current work practices of university researchers. That is, on numerous occasions the book recommends changes to the work practices of policymakers, highlighting the tight scheduling and anti-intellectual climate which undermines the kind of collaborative, reflexive engagement the authors deem essential to progressive change. However, inadequate attention has been paid to the changing work practices facing university researchers. While it may seem counter-intuitive to suggest that the climate in universities is also anti-*intellectual*, there are indeed similarities in the circumstances facing both academics and policy workers – severe time constraints, under-funding and burgeoning administrative demands. If this is the case, serious questions need to be raised about the kinds of researcher subjectivities that are generated by these conditions (practices) and how to respond to this situation (Bacchi 2008; Davies 2005).

A politics of movement relies on the view that power relations remain partial and incomplete, and that dominance and resistance are both opposing effects of the same power relations (Chapter 6). With this understanding, gender mainstreaming is recognised not as some final goal for equality practitioners but as a field of contestation involving discursive struggle over the very meaning of 'gender equality'. In this view movement towards more egalitarian social visions and relationships is non-linear and unpredictable, taking place at particular times and under specific circumstances, such as those identified in the book – in close collaborative exchanges among policy workers, community representatives and researchers, and among similarly committed but questioning colleagues and co-workers. The demanding task therefore becomes the creation of the conditions for additional on-the-ground engagements of this sort.

More broadly, the book challenges feminists to see themselves as politically invested cultural beings who need to examine critically the analytic categories they adopt and to participate in collaborative spaces with diverse groups of women. It questions the view of research as 'informing' policy, recognising that politics is always involved in research practice. And, finally, it provides insights into the complex processes of theory generation, indicating how authors with related but far from identical theoretical positions can work together and influence each other's perspectives, moving each other along.

References

(Website valid at time of publication)

Bacchi, C. 1996. *The politics of affirmative action: 'Women', equality and category politics.* London: Sage.

Bacchi, C. 1999. *Women, policy and politics: The construction of policy problems.* London: Sage.

Bacchi, C. 2001. 'Dealing with "difference": Beyond "multiple subjectivities" ', in Nursey-Bray, P. and Bacchi, C. (eds) *Left directions: Is there a third way?* Perth: University of Western Australia Press.

Bacchi, C. 2008. 'The politics of research management: Reflections on the gap between what we "know" [about sdh] and what we do', *Health Sociology Review* 17 (2): 165-176.

Bacchi, C. 2009. *Analysing policy: What's the problem represented to be?* Frenchs Forest, NSW: Pearson Education.

Collins, P. H. 2000. 'It's all in the family: Intersections of gender, race and nation' in Narayan, U. and Harding, S. (eds) *Decentering the center: Philosophy for a multicultural, post-colonial, and feminist world.* Bloomington: Indiana University Press.

Crenshaw, K. 1991. 'Mapping the margins: Intersectionality, identity politics, and violence against women of color', Stanford law Review 43 (6): 1241-1299.

Davies, B. 2005. 'The (im)possibility of intellectual work in neoliberal regimes', *Discourse: Studies in the cultural politics of education* 26 (1): 1-14.

Davis, K. 2008. 'Intersectionality as buzzword: A sociology of science perspective on what makes a feminist theory successful', *Feminist Theory* 9 (1): 67-85.

Eveline, J. 2005. 'Women in the ivory tower: Gendering feminised and masculinised identities', *Journal of Organizational Change Management* 18 (6): 641-658.

Mazey, S. 2002. 'Gender mainstreaming strategies in the EU: Delivering on an agenda?' *Feminist Legal Studies* 10: 227-240.

Phoenix, A. and Pattynama, P. 2006. 'Editorial: Intersectionality', *European Journal of Women's Studies.* Special issue, *Intersectionality* 13 (3): 187-192.

Puar, J.B. 2007. *Terrorist assemblages: Homonationalism in queer times.* Durham: Duke University Press.

Smith, D.E. 2005. *Institutional ethnography: A sociology for people.* New York: AltaMira Press.

World Bank. 2002. *Integrating gender into the World Bank's work: A strategy for action.* <siteresources. worldbank.org/INTGENDER/Resources/strategypaper.pdf> accessed 21 October 2009.

Author index

Electronic Index

This book is available from the University of Adelaide Press website as a down-loadable PDF with fully searchable text. Please use the electronic version to complement the index.

General index

Electronic Index

This book is available from the University of Adelaide Press website as a down-loadable PDF with fully searchable text. Please use the electronic version to complement the index. It may be necessary to remove quotation marks from some terms to locate them in the text, depending on your software.

inventive thinking, 115

Ireland, 6, 121, 122, 125, 128-130, 147; *see also* Republic of Ireland

Irish gender proofing handbook, 121, 126

Italian feminists, 323

iterative learning process, 250

iterative space, 265, 266, 273

job evaluation, 175, 176

Joint States, 170

Justice Fisher, 178

Justice Glynn, 176, 183

key concepts, 5, 30, 53, 75, 121, 273

'know-do' gap, 264-266

knowledge construction, 156

knowledge economy, 46

knowledge formations, 155

knowledge of gender relations, 22, 54, 211

knowledge production, 139

knowledges, 5, 6, 9, 117-119, 141, 338

labour force participation, 76, 130

language-groups, 326

language of 'diversity', 319

language of 'family and community', 22

language of 'gender relations', 74

language of 'impact assessment', 130

language of 'inclusiveness', 302

language of 'intersectionality', 330 n6; *see also* intersectionality

language of 'mainstreaming', 319

'law and order', 114, 228

'lay' knowledge, 197

leadership training programs, 114

learning by 'doing', 263

learning experience, 284, 287

learning journey papers, 299, 307

learning outcome, 61

'learnings', ix, 263, 270, 278, 306

legal discourse, 146, 319

lesbian, 93

lesbians, 27, 319, 320

library workers, 178

life expectancy for Indigenous people, 252

Liquor, Hospitality and Miscellaneous Workers Union, 179

'lived body', 94-95, 321

'living body', 95

'living bodies', 97, 119

local experience and knowledge, 233

local government elections, 238, 250, 251

Local Government Electoral Strategy, 77

located social subjects, 113

'logic of intersectionality', 77, 129; *see also* intersectionality, intersectionality theory, language of 'intersectionality'

lone mothers, 29, 53, 130; *see also* single mothers, sole supporting mothers, sole parents

loss of land, 225

low-waged service economy, 101

macro-economic, 29, 39, 33 n3

mainstreaming Indigenous issues, 252

mainstreaming models, 49, 51, 90

mainstreaming strategy, 90, 184

mainstreaming theorists, 315, 325

male model, 92

male norm, 25, 92, 103

male-female binary, 314, 321

managerialism, 79

managing diversity frameworks, 244

Maori women, 27, 77

marginalised groups, 2, 315, 325

marginalised women, 314, 321

'market bureaucracy', 266

market liberalism, 39, 194

marketing tool, 125

www.ingramcontent.com/pod-product-compliance
Lightning Source LLC
Chambersburg PA
CBHW080243030426
42334CB00023BA/2684